Resolutions and Decisions

adopted by the General Assembly during its seventy-eighth session

Volume III

23 December 2023 – 10 September 2024

General Assembly

Official Records • Seventy-eighth session
Supplement No. 49

United Nations • New York, 2024

NOTE

The resolutions and decisions of the General Assembly are identified as follows:

Regular sessions

Until the thirtieth regular session, the resolutions of the General Assembly were identified by an arabic numeral followed by a roman numeral in parentheses indicating the session (for example: resolution 3363 (XXX)). When several resolutions were adopted under the same number, each of them was identified by a capital letter placed between the two numerals (for example: resolution 3367 A (XXX), resolutions 3411 A and B (XXX), resolutions 3419 A to D (XXX)). The decisions were not numbered.

Since the thirty-first session, as part of the new system adopted for symbols of General Assembly documents, resolutions and decisions have been identified by an arabic numeral, indicating the session, followed by an oblique stroke and another arabic numeral (for example: resolution 31/1, decision 31/301). When several resolutions or decisions were adopted under the same number, each of them has been identified by a capital letter placed after the two numerals (for example: resolution 31/16 A, resolutions 31/6 A and B, decisions 31/406 A to E).

Special sessions

Until the seventh special session, the resolutions of the General Assembly were identified by an arabic numeral followed, in parentheses, by the letter "S" and a roman numeral indicating the session (for example: resolution 3362 (S-VII)). The decisions were not numbered.

Since the eighth special session, resolutions and decisions have been identified by the letter "S" and an arabic numeral indicating the session, followed by an oblique stroke and another arabic numeral (for example: resolution S-8/1, decision S-8/11).

Emergency special sessions

Until the fifth emergency special session, the resolutions of the General Assembly were identified by an arabic numeral followed, in parentheses, by the letters "ES" and a roman numeral indicating the session (for example: resolution 2252 (ES-V)). The decisions were not numbered.

Since the sixth emergency special session, resolutions and decisions have been identified by the letters "ES" and an arabic numeral indicating the session, followed by an oblique stroke and another arabic numeral (for example: resolution ES-6/1, decision ES-6/11).

In each of the series described above, the numbering follows the order of adoption.

*

*   *

The present volume contains the resolutions and decisions adopted by the General Assembly from 23 December 2023 to 10 September 2024. Resolutions adopted by the Assembly from 5 September to 22 December 2023 appear in volume I. Volume II contains the decisions adopted by the Assembly during that period.

ISSN 0252-7014

Print ISBN: 978-92-1-003332-9

eISBN : 978-92-1-106904-4

Contents

Annexes

I. Resolutions adopted without reference to a Main Committee

Contents

RESOLUTION 78/259

Adopted at the 52nd plenary meeting, on 9 January 2024, without a vote, on the basis of draft resolution A/78/L.34, sponsored by Cuba (on behalf of the States Members of the United Nations that are members of the Group of 77 and China)

78/259. International Day of Science, Technology and Innovation for the South

The General Assembly,

Recalling its resolution 78/160 of 19 December 2023 on science, technology and innovation for sustainable development and its previous resolutions on the issue,[1]

Reaffirming its resolutions 53/199 of 15 December 1998 and 61/185 of 20 December 2006 on the proclamation of international years, and Economic and Social Council resolution 1980/67 of 25 July 1980 on international years and anniversaries,

Recognizing the importance of creating synergies, developing expertise and boosting resources in various regions and institutions, and in this regard taking note of the Summit on Science, Technology and Innovation of the Group of 77 and China, held in Havana on 15 and 16 September 2023, and the Havana Declaration on Current Development Challenges: the Role of Science, Technology and Innovation,[2] as an effort to boost cooperation in this field,

Stressing the important role of science, technology and innovation to support economic growth and sustainable development and to accelerate the full implementation of the 2030 Agenda for Sustainable Development[3] and the Addis Ababa Action Agenda of the Third International Conference on Financing for Development,[4] as well as the political declaration of the 2023 Sustainable Development Goals Summit,[5]

Noting with deep concern the existing disparities between developed and developing countries in terms of conditions, possibilities and capacities to produce new scientific and technological knowledge,

Recognizing that science, technology and innovation cooperation and collaboration with, as well as foreign direct investment in and trade with and among, developing countries, as well as international support, are fundamental to enhancing developing countries' ability to benefit from technological advances and to produce, nurture, access, comprehend, select, adapt and use science, technology and innovation knowledge,

Emphasizing the need to encourage the promotion of North-South cooperation projects and programmes to improve developing countries' access to more and better resources for the implementation of technical and scientific initiatives and to continue working on the development of science and technology in developing countries by strengthening South-South and triangular cooperation, while recalling that South-South cooperation is not a substitute for, but rather a complement to, North-South cooperation,

Welcoming the operationalization of the Technology Bank for the Least Developed Countries, and inviting Member States and other stakeholders to provide voluntary funding to the trust fund of the Technology Bank so that it can pursue its objectives in the area of science, technology and innovation for the least developed countries,

Calling upon the international community to foster an open, fair, inclusive and non-discriminatory environment for scientific and technological development and to support the efforts of the countries of the South to develop and strengthen their national science, technology and innovation systems,

1. *Decides* to proclaim 16 September as the International Day of Science, Technology and Innovation for the South, to be observed annually;

---

[1] Resolutions 58/200, 59/220, 60/205, 61/207, 62/201, 64/212, 66/211, 68/220, 70/213, 72/228, 74/229 and 76/213.

[2] A/78/393, annex.

[3] Resolution 70/1.

[4] Resolution 69/313, annex.

[5] Political declaration of the high-level political forum on sustainable development convened under the auspices of the General Assembly (resolution 78/1, annex).

2. *Invites* all States Members of the United Nations, members of the specialized agencies and observers of the General Assembly, as well as organizations of the United Nations system, other international and regional organizations, academia, civil society, the private sector and other relevant stakeholders, to observe the International Day of Science, Technology and Innovation for the South, in an appropriate manner, by presenting initiatives, including cooperation projects in the areas of science, technology and innovation that contribute to the development of developing countries in those fields;

3. *Stresses* that the cost of all activities that may arise from the implementation of the present resolution should be met from voluntary contributions, including from the private sector;

4. *Requests* the Secretary-General to bring the present resolution to the attention of all States Members of the United Nations, members of the specialized agencies and observers of the General Assembly, as well as the organizations of the United Nations system, academia, civil society, the private sector and other relevant stakeholders, for appropriate observance.

RESOLUTION 78/260

Adopted at the 57th plenary meeting, on 26 February 2024, without a vote, on the basis of draft resolution A/78/L.42, sponsored by: Algeria, Andorra, Antigua and Barbuda, Armenia, Austria, Azerbaijan, Bahrain, Barbados, Belarus, Bhutan, Bolivia (Plurinational State of), Bosnia and Herzegovina, Botswana, Cabo Verde, Cambodia, Cameroon, China, Colombia, Costa Rica, Croatia, Cyprus, Dominican Republic, El Salvador, Equatorial Guinea, Georgia, Germany, Ghana, Greece, Guinea-Bissau, Honduras, Hungary, Indonesia, Ireland, Italy, Jamaica, Jordan, Kazakhstan, Kiribati, Kyrgyzstan, Latvia, Lesotho, Luxembourg, Madagascar, Malawi, Malaysia, Maldives, Mali, Malta, Monaco, Montenegro, Morocco, Mozambique, Namibia, Nepal, Netherlands (Kingdom of the), New Zealand, Nicaragua, North Macedonia, Norway, Pakistan, Paraguay, Peru, Philippines, Portugal, Qatar, Republic of Korea, Republic of Moldova, Rwanda, Samoa, San Marino, Saudi Arabia, Senegal, Singapore, Sri Lanka, Suriname, Tajikistan, Thailand, Togo, Türkiye, Turkmenistan, Tuvalu, Ukraine, United States of America, Uzbekistan, Viet Nam, Zambia

78/260. International Year of Sustainable and Resilient Tourism, 2027

The General Assembly,

Guided by the purposes and principles of the Charter of the United Nations,

Reaffirming its resolutions 53/199 of 15 December 1998 and 61/185 of 20 December 2006 on the proclamation of international years, and Economic and Social Council resolution 1980/67 of 25 July 1980 on international years and anniversaries, in particular paragraphs 1 to 10 of the annex thereto on the agreed criteria for the proclamation of international years, as well as paragraphs 13 and 14, in which it is stated that an international year should not be proclaimed before the basic arrangements necessary for its organization and financing have been made,

Recalling its relevant resolutions, in particular resolutions 70/193 of 22 December 2015 on the proclamation of 2017 as the International Year of Sustainable Tourism for Development, 74/214 of 19 December 2019 on sustainable tourism and sustainable development in Central Asia, 75/223 of 21 December 2020 on the Global Code of Ethics for Tourism, 77/178 of 14 December 2022 on the promotion of sustainable and resilient tourism, including ecotourism, for poverty eradication and environmental protection, 78/145 of 19 December 2023 on sustainable and resilient tourism and sustainable development in Central America and the Dominican Republic, and other related resolutions,

Reaffirming its resolution 70/1 of 25 September 2015, entitled "Transforming our world: the 2030 Agenda for Sustainable Development", in which it adopted a comprehensive, far-reaching and people-centred set of universal and transformative Sustainable Development Goals and targets, and its commitment to working tirelessly for the full implementation of the Agenda by 2030,

Recognizing that sustainable tourism, including ecotourism, is a cross-cutting activity that can contribute to the three dimensions of sustainable development and the achievement of the Sustainable Development Goals, including by fostering economic growth, alleviating poverty, creating full and productive employment and decent work for all, accelerating the change to more sustainable consumption and production patterns and promoting the sustainable use of oceans, seas and marine resources, promoting local culture, improving the quality of life and the economic empowerment of women and young people, Indigenous Peoples and local communities and promoting rural development and better living conditions for rural populations, including smallholder and family farmers,

Emphasizing that sustainable and resilient tourism can contribute directly to the conservation of environmentally vulnerable natural areas and habitats through a variety of activities and by raising awareness of the importance of biodiversity, and stressing the urgent need to address the unprecedented global decline in biodiversity,

Welcoming the efforts of those United Nations system entities that promote ecotourism and sustainable tourism worldwide,

Recognizing the importance of international tourism, and particularly of the designation of an international year of sustainable and resilient tourism, in fostering better understanding among peoples everywhere, leading to a greater awareness of the rich heritage of various civilizations and bringing about a better appreciation of the inherent values of different cultures, thereby contributing to the strengthening of peace in the world,

Recognizing also that sustainable consumption and production in tourism is aimed at increasing net welfare gains from economic activities by improving resource use and reducing ecosystem degradation and pollution along the entire tourism value chain, and that a systemic approach and cooperation among actors operating along the value chain, from tourism service providers, to adjacent communities, to tourists, can ensure the sustainability of the sector,

1. *Decides* to proclaim 2027 the International Year of Sustainable and Resilient Tourism;

2. *Invites* the World Tourism Organization, mindful of the provisions contained in the annex to Economic and Social Council resolution 1980/67, to facilitate the organization and implementation of the International Year, in collaboration with Governments, relevant organizations of the United Nations system, international and regional organizations and other relevant stakeholders;

3. *Stresses* that the costs of all activities that may arise from the implementation of the present resolution should be met from voluntary contributions;

4. *Encourages* Member States, the United Nations system and all other actors to take effective measures, in the context of sustainable and resilient tourism, including ecotourism initiatives, to promote the equal participation of women and the balanced participation of youth, older persons, persons with disabilities, Indigenous Peoples and local communities, at all levels and in decision-making processes in all areas, and to promote effective economic empowerment, mainly through decent job and income creation;

5. *Encourages* all States, the United Nations system and all other actors to take advantage of the International Year to promote actions at all levels, including through international cooperation, and to support sustainable and resilient tourism as a means of promoting and accelerating sustainable development;

6. *Invites* the World Tourism Organization, mindful of the provisions of paragraphs 23 to 27 of the annex to Economic and Social Council resolution 1980/67, to inform the General Assembly at its eighty-third session on the implementation of the present resolution, elaborating on the evaluation of the International Year.

RESOLUTION 78/261

Adopted at the 57th plenary meeting, on 26 February 2024, without a vote, on the basis of draft resolution A/78/L.39, sponsored by: Andorra, Austria, Belgium, Bosnia and Herzegovina, Botswana, Bulgaria, Cabo Verde, Cambodia, Chile, China, Croatia, Cyprus, Czechia, Denmark, Dominican Republic, Equatorial Guinea, Eswatini, Finland, France, Georgia, Germany, Greece, Iceland, Ireland, Italy, Kazakhstan, Kyrgyzstan, Latvia, Lesotho, Luxembourg, Malawi, Maldives, Malta, Monaco, Montenegro, Morocco, Mozambique, Netherlands (Kingdom of the), North Macedonia, Poland, Portugal, Republic of Moldova, San Marino, Singapore, Slovakia, Slovenia, South Africa, Spain, Sri Lanka, Sweden, Switzerland, Tajikistan, Togo, Türkiye, Turkmenistan, Uzbekistan, Viet Nam, Zambia

78/261. "World Social Summit" under the title "Second World Summit for Social Development"

The General Assembly,

Recalling the World Summit for Social Development, held in Copenhagen from 6 to 12 March 1995, and the twenty-fourth special session of the General Assembly, entitled "World Summit for Social Development and beyond: achieving social development for all in a globalizing world", held in Geneva from 26 June to 1 July 2000,

Reaffirming that the Copenhagen Declaration on Social Development and the Programme of Action of the World Summit for Social Development[6] and the further initiatives for social development adopted by the General Assembly at its twenty-fourth special session,[7] as well as a continued global dialogue on social development issues, constitute the basic framework for the promotion of social development for all at the national and international levels,

Reaffirming also all previous resolutions on the implementation of the outcome of the World Summit for Social Development and of the twenty-fourth special session of the General Assembly, including resolution 78/174 of 19 December 2023,

Welcoming the progress made towards the full implementation of the Copenhagen Declaration and the Programme of Action through concerted action at the national, regional and international levels, and expressing its deep concern that more than 25 years after the convening of the World Summit for Social Development, progress has been slow and uneven, and major gaps remain, and recognizing the three core themes of social development, namely, poverty eradication, full and productive employment and decent work for all and social integration, are interrelated and mutually reinforcing, and that an enabling environment therefore needs to be created so that all three objectives can be pursued simultaneously,

Recalling General Assembly resolution 70/1 of 25 September 2015, entitled "Transforming our world: the 2030 Agenda for Sustainable Development", in which the Assembly adopted a comprehensive, far-reaching and people-centred set of universal and transformative Sustainable Development Goals and targets and affirmed its commitment to working tirelessly for the full implementation of the Agenda by 2030 with a view to leaving no one behind and reaching the furthest behind first, and its recognition that eradicating poverty in all its forms and dimensions, including extreme poverty, is the greatest global challenge and an indispensable requirement for sustainable development,

Recalling also its resolution 76/6 of 15 November 2021, entitled "Follow-up to the report of the Secretary-General entitled 'Our Common Agenda'"[8] and noting the proposal contained in that report to convene a world social summit in 2025, to be discussed and agreed upon by Member States, including its modalities, title, objectives, scope and possible outcomes, and emphasizing that the possible summit's outcome should have a social development approach including the need to place people at the centre of development and the pledge to make poverty eradication, full employment and social integration the overriding development objectives, and give momentum towards the implementation of the 2030 Agenda,

Recalling further the Political Declaration adopted at the High-Level Political Forum on Sustainable Development convened under the auspices of the General Assembly[9] last September, where Heads of State and Government agreed to look forward to the proposed World Social Summit in 2025, subject to discussion and agreement by the General Assembly on its modalities, and emphasized that the possible summit outcome should have a social development approach and give momentum towards the implementation of the 2030 Agenda,

1. *Decides* to convene the "World Social Summit" in 2025, under the title "the Second World Summit for Social Development", to address the gaps and recommit to the Copenhagen Declaration on Social Development and the Programme of Action and its implementation and give momentum towards the implementation of the 2030 Agenda;

2. *Requests* that the President of the General Assembly, consistent with the rules of the General Assembly, appoint two co-facilitators, one from a developing country and one from a developed country, to facilitate the intergovernmental preparatory process leading up to the Summit consisting of its modalities and outcome, which should be a short and concise political declaration adopted by consensus, and should have a social development approach and give momentum towards the implementation of the 2030 Agenda;

3. *Also requests* the Secretary-General to provide adequate support within existing resources to the intergovernmental preparatory process of the Summit.

---

[6] *Report of the World Summit for Social Development, Copenhagen, 6–12 March 1995* (United Nations publication, Sales No. E.96.IV.8), chap. I, resolution 1, annexes I and II.

[7] Resolution S-24/2, annex.

[8] A/75/982.

[9] Resolution 78/1, annex.

RESOLUTION 78/262

Adopted at the 57th plenary meeting, on 26 February 2024, without a vote, on the basis of draft resolution A/78/L.38, sponsored by Cuba (on behalf of the States Members of the United Nations that are members of the Group of 77 and China)

78/262. New Partnership for Africa's Development: progress in implementation and international support

The General Assembly,

Recalling its resolution 57/2 of 16 September 2002 on the United Nations Declaration on the New Partnership for Africa's Development,

Recalling also its resolution 57/7 of 4 November 2002 on the final review and appraisal of the United Nations New Agenda for the Development of Africa in the 1990s and support for the New Partnership for Africa's Development and all its subsequent resolutions, including resolution 77/270 of 20 February 2023, entitled "New Partnership for Africa's Development: progress in implementation and international support", and Economic and Social Council resolution 2023/13 of 7 June 2023 on the social dimensions of the New Partnership for Africa's Development,

Reaffirming its resolution 70/1 of 25 September 2015, entitled "Transforming our world: the 2030 Agenda for Sustainable Development", in which it adopted a comprehensive, far-reaching and people-centred set of universal and transformative Sustainable Development Goals and targets, its commitment to working tirelessly for the full implementation of the Agenda by 2030, its recognition that eradicating poverty in all its forms and dimensions, including extreme poverty, is the greatest global challenge and an indispensable requirement for sustainable development, its commitment to achieving sustainable development in its three dimensions – economic, social and environmental – in a balanced and integrated manner, and to building upon the achievements of the Millennium Development Goals and seeking to address their unfinished business,

Reaffirming also its resolution 69/313 of 27 July 2015 on the Addis Ababa Action Agenda of the Third International Conference on Financing for Development, which is an integral part of the 2030 Agenda for Sustainable Development, supports and complements it, helps to contextualize its means of implementation targets with concrete policies and actions, and reaffirms the strong political commitment to address the challenge of financing and creating an enabling environment at all levels for sustainable development in the spirit of global partnership and solidarity,

Recalling that the 2030 Agenda for Sustainable Development underscores the special challenges facing the most vulnerable countries, including African countries, and recalling also that significant challenges remain in achieving sustainable development in Africa and the importance of fulfilling all commitments to advance action in areas critical to Africa's sustainable development,

Recognizing the adoption of Agenda 2063 by the Assembly of Heads of State and Government of the African Union at its twenty-fourth ordinary session, held in Addis Ababa on 30 and 31 January 2015, as the African Union long-term political strategy for Africa's development and its first 10-year implementation plan (2014–2023), which outlines key flagship projects and programmes to be fast-tracked during the decade, and recognizing the commitment to the full implementation of the political declaration on Africa's development needs, adopted on 22 September 2008,[10]

Reaffirming the Paris Agreement[11] and encouraging all its parties to fully implement the Agreement, and parties to the United Nations Framework Convention on Climate Change[12] that have not yet done so to deposit their instruments of ratification, acceptance, approval or accession, where appropriate, as soon as possible,

Urging parties that have not yet communicated new or updated nationally determined contributions to do so as soon as possible in advance of the sixth session of the Conference of the Parties serving as the Meeting of the Parties to the Paris Agreement,

---

[10] Resolution 63/1.

[11] See FCCC/CP/2015/10/Add.1, decision 1/CP.21, annex.

[12] United Nations, *Treaty Series*, vol. 1771, No. 30822.

Noting with concern the growing gap between the needs of developing country parties, in particular those due to the increasing impacts of climate change and their increased indebtedness, and the support provided and mobilized for their efforts to implement their nationally determined contributions, highlighting that such needs are currently estimated at between 5.8 trillion and 5.9 trillion United States dollars for the pre-2030 period,

Taking note of the Moroni Declaration for Ocean and Climate Action in Africa,[13] and underlining the common goal of African countries to harness the potential of their oceanic resources and strengthen capacity for the sustainable management of these resources for sustainable development and climate resilience,

Recalling the fifteenth session of the Conference of the Parties to the United Nations Convention to Combat Desertification in Those Countries Experiencing Serious Drought and/or Desertification, Particularly in Africa, held in Abidjan, Côte d'Ivoire, from 9 to 20 May 2022, and the offer made by the Government of Saudi Arabia and the Government of Mongolia to host the sixteenth and seventeenth sessions of the Conference of the Parties, in 2024 and 2026, respectively,

Welcoming the Doha Political Declaration,[14] and reaffirming the Doha Programme of Action for the Least Developed Countries,[15] which represents a new generation of renewed and strengthened commitments between the least developed countries and their development partners, including Governments, the private sector, and civil society, cognizant that many least developed countries are in Africa,

Highlighting the synergies between the implementation of the 2030 Agenda for Sustainable Development, the Addis Ababa Action Agenda, and the Paris Agreement, the New Urban Agenda,[16] the Sendai Framework for Disaster Risk Reduction 2015–2030,[17] and other relevant major intergovernmental outcomes of United Nations conferences and summits in the economic, social and environmental fields,

Welcoming the Political Declaration adopted by the High-Level Political Forum on Sustainable Development convened under the auspices of the General Assembly (Sustainable Development Goals Summit), held in New York on 18 and 19 September 2023,[18] and urging timely action to ensure its full implementation,

Noting with great concern the continuing multidimensional repercussions of the coronavirus disease (COVID-19) pandemic on African countries, including significant impacts on poverty, food security, unemployment, trade, disrupted supply chains, tourism and financial flows, as well as its social impacts, including violence against women and girls, causing more challenges for African countries to achieve the 2030 Agenda and Agenda 2063, and recognizing the great efforts made by African countries in combating the COVID-19 pandemic to save lives and achieve sustainable, inclusive and resilient recovery,

Recalling its resolution 78/140 of 19 December 2023 on the promotion of international cooperation to combat illicit financial flows and strengthen good practices on assets return to foster sustainable development,

Underlining the need to promote peaceful and inclusive societies for achieving sustainable development and to build effective, transparent, accountable and inclusive institutions at all levels, and reaffirming that good governance, the rule of law, human rights, fundamental freedoms, equal access to fair justice systems and global collaboration and mutual accountability measures to combat corruption and curb illicit financial flows will be integral to our efforts,

Recalling its resolution 71/254 of 23 December 2016 on the Framework for a Renewed United Nations-African Union Partnership on Africa's Integration and Development Agenda 2017–2027, and its resolution 66/293 of 17 September 2012, by which it established a United Nations monitoring mechanism to review commitments made towards Africa's development, and looking forward to the sixth biennial report of the Secretary-General on the review

---

[13] Available at www.uneca.org/eca-events/sites/default/files/resources/documents/sro-ea/blue-future-conference-2023/Declaration%20English.pdf.

[14] *Report of the Fifth United Nations Conference on the Least Developed Countries, New York, 17 March 2022, and Doha, 5–9 March 2023* (A/CONF.219/2023/3), chap. I, resolution 2.

[15] Resolution 76/258, annex.

[16] Resolution 71/256, annex.

[17] Resolution 69/283, annex II.

[18] Resolution 78/1, annex.

of the implementation of the commitments made towards Africa's development, to be submitted to the General Assembly at its seventy-ninth session,

Welcoming the high-level events organized by the Office of the Special Adviser on Africa during the 2023 Africa Dialogue Series on the theme "Market and scale: unlocking industrialization through intra-African trade", in close partnership with the African Union Commission and other United Nations system and African organizations,

Emphasizing economic development, including inclusive industrial development, and policies which seek to enhance productive capacities in Africa, bearing in mind that African countries have primary responsibility for their own economic, social and environmental development and that the role of national policies and development strategies cannot be overemphasized, and recalling the African Union Strategy on Small and Medium Enterprise/Industries and its Delivery Framework, adopted in 2019,

Welcoming the ongoing support of the United Nations Industrial Development Organization to Agenda 2063, the African Accelerated Agribusiness and Agro-industries Development Initiative, the Pharmaceutical Manufacturing Plan for Africa and other programmes of the African Union aimed at further strengthening the industrialization process in Africa,

Noting that the impact of the COVID-19 pandemic exacerbates the inequalities caused by digital divides, especially in African countries, since the poorest and the most vulnerable, who are the hardest hit, are also those who lag behind the most in access to information and communications technologies,

Noting with great concern the severe negative impact on human health, safety and well-being caused by the coronavirus disease (COVID-19) pandemic, as well as the severe disruption to societies and economies and the devastating impact on lives and livelihoods, and that the poorest and most vulnerable are the hardest hit by the pandemic, reaffirming the ambition to get back on track to achieve the Sustainable Development Goals by designing and implementing sustainable and inclusive recovery strategies to accelerate progress towards the full implementation of the 2030 Agenda for Sustainable Development and to help to reduce the risk of and build resilience to future shocks, crises and pandemics, including by strengthening health systems and achieving universal health coverage, and recognizing that equitable and timely access for all to safe, quality, effective and affordable COVID-19 vaccines, therapeutics and diagnostics are an essential part of a global response based on unity, solidarity, renewed multilateral cooperation and the principle of leaving no one behind,

Reaffirming the convening of the intergovernmental conference held on 10 and 11 December 2018 in Marrakech, Morocco, and recalling the adoption of the Global Compact for Safe, Orderly and Regular Migration, also known as the Marrakech Compact on Migration,[19]

Reaffirming also the outcome of the second High-level United Nations Conference on South-South Cooperation, held in Buenos Aires from 20 to 22 March 2019,[20]

Welcoming the convening of the Third South Summit, hosted by the Government of Uganda in Kampala on 21 and 22 January 2024, and taking note of its outcomes,

Taking note with appreciation of the transformation of the New Partnership Planning and Coordinating Agency into the African Union Development Agency in conformity with the decision of the Assembly of Heads of State and Government of the African Union to rename the African Union Development Agency as the African Union Development Agency-New Partnership for Africa's Development,[21]

1. *Takes note* of the report of the Secretary-General entitled "Solving the paradoxes of development in Africa: financing, energy and food systems";[22]

2. *Also takes note* of the biennial report of the Secretary-General on the review of the implementation of commitments made towards Africa's development[23] and of the interactive multi-stakeholder dialogue organized by

---

[19] Resolution 73/195, annex.

[20] Resolution 73/291, annex.

[21] See decision Ext/Assembly/AU/Dec.1(XI) of the Assembly of Heads of State and Government of the African Union adopted at its eleventh extraordinary session, held in Addis Ababa on 17 and 18 November 2018.

[22] A/78/309.

[23] A/77/908.

the President of the General Assembly on 21 July 2023 to discuss the main findings and recommendations contained in the report;

3. *Recognizes* the efforts of the African Union Development Agency-New Partnership for Africa's Development, and in this regard reaffirms the essential role played by the Heads of State and Government Orientation Committee of the Agency, welcomes the efforts by development partners to strengthen cooperation with the Agency, and underscores the importance of coherent and coordinated implementation of Agenda 2063 and the 2030 Agenda for Sustainable Development,[24] while acknowledging that much needs to be done to overcome the challenges in their implementation;

4. *Emphasizes* the need for the United Nations development system to further cooperate with the African Union and the regional economic communities, to follow up on African development priorities in line with the 2030 Agenda and the African Union Agenda 2063 and its flagship programmes that could require United Nations financial and technical assistance within existing resources, and the need for United Nations agencies, in line with their respective mandates, to strengthen their relationship with the African Union Development Agency-New Partnership for Africa's Development;

5. *Welcomes* the progress made by African countries in fulfilling their commitments in the implementation of the New Partnership for Africa's Development[25] to deepen democracy, human rights, good governance and sound economic management, and encourages African countries, with the participation of stakeholders, including civil society, academia and the private sector, to continue their efforts towards implementing the 2030 Agenda;

6. *Encourages* African countries to strengthen and expand local and regional infrastructure, while recognizing the importance of sustainable and resilient urbanization, and quality, reliable, sustainable and resilient infrastructure, and sustainable urbanization investment, through both foreign and domestic investment, and to continue to share best practices with a view to strengthening regional and continental integration, and in this regard recognizes the need for Africa's development partners to align their efforts towards supporting the Programme for Infrastructure Development in Africa;

7. *Encourages* the efforts to improve Africa's business and investment environment and to attract investment from all sources, including from the private sector, especially in quality, reliable, sustainable and resilient infrastructure;

8. *Stresses* the importance of taking targeted measures to eradicate poverty in all its forms and dimensions, including extreme poverty, of implementing nationally appropriate social protection systems and measures for all, including social protection floors, and of achieving substantial and universal coverage of the poor and the vulnerable;

9. *Encourages* African countries to accelerate the achievement of the objective of food security and nutrition as well as the realization of the right to adequate food in Africa through healthy diets and sustainable agrifood systems with the support of Africa's development partners, and recalls the convening of the United Nations Food Systems Summit in 2021 as well as the Summit +2 Stocktaking Moment hosted by the Government of Italy in Rome from 24 to 26 July 2023, and requests the Secretary-General to step up cooperation with the African Union and relevant stakeholders to boost food security, nutrition and resilience on the continent;

10. *Calls upon* the international community to continue its support for the implementation of the Comprehensive Africa Agriculture Development Programme, which provides guidance on planning and implementing investment programmes, and calls for the expeditious implementation of the Comprehensive Africa Agriculture Development Programme and its results framework; in this regard, welcomes the establishment of a 1.5 billion United States dollar African Emergency Food Production Plan facility by the African Development Bank, and further calls upon development partners to honour their pledge of 30 billion dollars to support Africa in boosting agricultural productivity, made at the Dakar 2 Summit on Feed Africa: Food Sovereignty and Resilience, held in January 2023, and appreciates contributions of development partners to support them by providing parallel financing;

11. *Also calls upon* the international community to support the post-Malabo consultations and process, leading to a new Comprehensive Africa Agriculture Development Programme framework in 2025;

---

[24] Resolution 70/1.

[25] A/57/304, annex.

12. *Remains deeply concerned* about the recurring food insecurity and all forms of malnutrition in different regions of the world and their ongoing negative impact on health and nutrition, including in Africa, further exacerbated by the adverse impacts of climate change, volatility in global financial and commodity markets and geopolitical tensions, and in this regard underlines the urgent need for joint efforts at all levels to respond to the situation in a coherent and effective manner by aligning actions with national and regional response plans, making full use of endogenous mechanisms, including local, national and regional reserves;

13. *Welcomes* the decision of the Assembly of Heads of State and Government of the African Union to designate "Acceleration of AfCFTA implementation" as the theme of the year 2023 to promote the implementation of the African Continental Free Trade Area for the benefit of Africa's population;

14. *Calls for* effective measures and targeted investments to strengthen national health systems and to ensure access to safe drinking water, sanitation and hygiene to prevent, protect against and combat outbreaks of diseases, including the Ebola virus disease and coronavirus disease (COVID-19), recognizes in this regard that human, animal, plant and ecosystem health are interdependent, invites development partners to continue to assist African countries in their efforts to strengthen national health systems, to expand, strengthen and maintain surveillance systems in the health sector, in order to implement and comply with the International Health Regulations (2005),[26] and to eliminate diseases, while recognizing the One Health approach, and in this context calls upon development partners to support the implementation of the African Health Strategy 2016–2030 and the transition towards universal health coverage in Africa;

15. *Recalls* the political declaration on HIV and AIDS, as reflected in its resolution 75/284 of 8 June 2021, the political declaration of the third high-level meeting of the General Assembly on the prevention and control of non-communicable diseases, as reflected in its resolution 73/2 of 10 October 2018, as well as the Abuja Declaration on Roll Back Malaria in Africa,[27] and the political declarations of the high-level meetings on pandemic prevention, preparedness and response, on universal health coverage and on the fight against tuberculosis, as reflected in its resolutions 78/3, 78/4 and 78/5 of 5 October 2023, and calls upon developed countries, international health funds and other development partners to continue their support, including financial and technical support, to African countries to scale up their national efforts to fully implement, as appropriate, the actions committed to by the Heads of State and Government and their representatives;

16. *Notes* the unprecedented impact of COVID-19 on the continent's hard-won development and economic gains; welcomes the continued efforts of African leaders in mitigating the risks and impact of the pandemic on their countries and citizens; expresses its highest appreciation to all partners and international organizations for their continued support of the continent's efforts in mitigating the effects of COVID-19; notes that there is a need for additional support to reduce the effects of and recover from the pandemic to enable the continent to achieve the 2030 Agenda and Agenda 2063, and to support the implementation of the Adapted Africa Joint Continental Strategy for COVID-19 Pandemic, fully operationalize and enhance the capacity of the African Medicines Agency and the Africa Centres for Disease Control and Prevention, including to support Africa's manufacture of vaccines against COVID-19 and other viral diseases, and in this regard calls for global solidarity, particularly with regard to global equitable, affordable and timely access to vaccines, therapeutics, diagnostics and other medical products in Africa, and urges Member States and the international community to support the continental development and manufacture of safe and effective vaccines, therapeutics, diagnostics and medical products, and other relevant initiatives, including African initiatives such as the Partnerships for African Vaccine Manufacturing and the African Vaccine Acquisition Trust accelerating post-COVID-19 economic and social development;

17. *Encourages* African countries to continue their efforts in enhancing education and technical and vocational training and stresses in this regard the importance of creating a conducive environment for science, technology and innovation taking advantage of frontier technologies and investing in digitalization to strengthen connectivity, and urges all relevant stakeholders to consider ensuring appropriate financing of digital development and adequate means of implementation, including strengthened capacity-building of developing countries, especially African countries;

---

[26] World Health Organization, document WHA58/2005/REC/1, resolution 58.3, annex.

[27] See A/55/240/Add.1, annex.

18. *Welcomes* the decision of the Assembly of Heads of State and Government of the African Union to designate "Education" as the African Union theme of the year 2024, and requests the Secretary-General to organize the 2024 Africa Dialogue Series around the theme of education;

19. *Encourages* African countries to formulate and implement industrialization development plans and policies in line with their national conditions and their respective development strategies, in promoting inclusive and sustainable economic growth;

20. *Also encourages* African countries to accelerate the development of the digital infrastructure, enhance the accessibility of digital technologies and seize the development opportunities brought by the digital economy, in order to bridge the digital divides;

21. *Recognizes* the important role that African regional economic communities can play in the implementation of the mandate of the New Partnership and of Agenda 2063 and its first 10-year implementation plan, and the preparation of the second 10-year implementation plan, in close cooperation with the African Union, and in this regard encourages African countries and the international community to give regional economic communities the support necessary to strengthen their capacity;

22. *Reiterates* the need to support African countries in strengthening the capacity of national statistical offices and data systems to ensure access to high-quality, timely, reliable and disaggregated data;

23. *Recognizes* that Africa is one of the regions that contribute the least to climate change, yet is extremely vulnerable and exposed to its adverse impacts, expresses deep concern about the increasing challenges posed by drought, land degradation, desertification, the loss of biodiversity and floods, and their negative consequences on the fight against poverty, famine and hunger, and in this regard calls upon the international community, including developed countries, to continue to support Africa to address its adaptation needs through, inter alia, the development, voluntary transfer and deployment of technology on mutually agreed terms, including on concessional and preferential terms, capacity-building and the provision of adequate and predictable resources, in line with existing commitments, and highlights the need for full implementation by their respective parties of the agreed outcomes of the United Nations Framework Convention on Climate Change, the Paris Agreement,[28] and the Convention on Biological Diversity[29] and the Kunming-Montreal Global Biodiversity Framework,[30] as well as the United Nations Convention to Combat Desertification in Those Countries Experiencing Serious Drought and/or Desertification, Particularly in Africa,[31] including its 2018–2030 strategic framework,[32] and urges developed countries to fully deliver on the commitment to a goal of mobilizing jointly 100 billion dollars per year urgently and through to 2025 to address the needs of developing countries, in the context of meaningful mitigation actions and transparency on implementation, for climate action, particularly for climate adaptation, in accordance with the United Nations Framework Convention on Climate Change;

24. *Reiterates its deep concern* about the growing illicit financial flows, internationally and domestically, including those derived from trade mispricing and misinvoicing and other illegal practices, emphasizes that illicit financial flows reduce the availability of valuable resources, including for financing for development, welcomes in this regard the political declaration adopted at the thirty-second special session of the General Assembly, entitled "Our common commitment to effectively addressing challenges and implementing measures to prevent and combat corruption and strengthen international cooperation",[33] reiterates the commitment to substantially reduce illicit financial flows by 2030, with a view to eventually eliminating them, including by combating tax evasion, tax avoidance, corruption and organized crime through strengthened national institutional and policy frameworks and international cooperation in line with the Addis Ababa Action Agenda of the Third International Conference on Financing for Development,[34] and acknowledges the need to strengthen good practices on assets return and recovery;

[28] Adopted under the UNFCCC in FCCC/CP/2015/10/Add.1, decision 1/CP.21.

[29] United Nations, *Treaty Series*, vol. 1760, No. 30619.

[30] Adopted at the fifteenth meeting of the Conference of the Parties to the Convention on Biological Diversity (Part II), Montreal, Canada, 7–19 December 2022.

[31] United Nations, *Treaty Series*, vol. 1954, No. 33480.

[32] ICCD/COP(13)/21/Add.1, decision 7/COP.13, annex.

[33] Resolution S-32/1, annex.

[34] Resolution 69/313, annex.

25. *Notes* the report of the High-level Panel on International Financial Accountability, Transparency and Integrity for Achieving the 2030 Agenda,[35] recognizes the importance of scaling up international tax cooperation, welcomes the adoption of resolution 77/244 of 30 December 2022 and takes note of the adoption of resolution 78/230 of 22 December 2023, and also takes note of the report of the Secretary-General on the promotion of inclusive and effective international tax cooperation at the United Nations;[36]

26. *Notes* the Marrakech Declaration adopted by African countries at the high-level ministerial meeting on accelerating the financing of Africa's emergence, held on 12 October 2023, on the sidelines of the World Bank-International Monetary Fund Annual Meetings in Morocco, which called for a global financial architecture that is equitable and conducive to Africa's development;

27. *Recognizes* in this regard the urgent need for bold and ambitious reforms to create a stable, sustainable and inclusive international financial architecture, and reiterates that the international financial architecture, including its business models and financing capacities, must be made more fit for purpose, equitable and responsive to the financing needs of developing countries, to broaden and strengthen the voice and participation of developing countries in international economic decision-making, norm-setting and global economic governance;

28. *Urges* multilateral development banks to bring forward actions to mobilize and provide additional financing within their mandates to support developing countries to achieve the Sustainable Development Goals, supports multilateral development bank reform efforts and calls for continued tangible progress in this regard, including through securing increases to grants and concessional finance, better leveraging their capital bases and considering ways for the respective boards of the multilateral development banks to increase their capitalization, and encourages dialogue between multilateral development banks and other financial institutions;

29. *Welcomes* the special drawing rights allocation of the equivalent of 650 billion dollars of 23 August 2021, commends the achievement of the target of 100 billion dollars in pledges for rechannelling special drawing rights or equivalent contributions, recommends the exploration of further voluntary options related to special drawing rights that could serve the needs of developing member countries of the International Monetary Fund, calls for the urgent voluntary rechannelling of special drawing rights for countries most in need, including through multilateral development banks, while respecting relevant legal frameworks and preserving the reserve asset character of special drawing rights, and will explore ways for future allocations of special drawing rights to benefit those countries most in need;

30. *Welcomes* the decision of the International Monetary and Financial Committee to improve the voice and representation of sub-Saharan Africa, with the creation of a twenty-fifth chair on the International Monetary Fund Executive Board for sub-Saharan Africa;

31. *Also welcomes* the accession of the African Union as a permanent member of the Group of 20 at the New Delhi Summit held on 9 and 10 September 2023;

32. *Underscores* the importance of urgent delivery of means of implementation (capacity-building, climate finance, and technology development and transfer) to facilitate just transition pathways and of enhancing international cooperation on, and support for, just transition pathways, especially for developing country parties;

33. *Reaffirms* that achieving gender equality, empowering all women and girls, and the full realization of their human rights are essential to achieving sustained, inclusive and equitable economic growth and sustainable development, reiterates the need for gender mainstreaming, including targeted actions and investments in the formulation and implementation of all financial, economic, environmental and social policies, and recommits to adopting and strengthening sound policies and enforceable legislation and transformative actions for the promotion of gender equality and women's and girls' empowerment at all levels, to ensure women's equal rights, access and opportunities for participation and leadership in the economy and to eliminate gender-based violence, sexual exploitation and abuse and discrimination in all its forms;

34. *Welcomes* the progress that has been achieved in implementing the African Peer Review Mechanism, in particular the voluntary adherence of 42 African countries to the Mechanism and the completion of the peer review

[35] A/75/810/Rev.1, annex.

[36] A/78/235.

process in 24 countries, welcomes the progress in implementing the national programmes of action resulting from those reviews, in this regard urges African States that have not yet done so to consider joining the Mechanism process by 2023, as envisaged in the first 10-year implementation plan of Agenda 2063, takes note of the decision on its institutional reform,[37] and emphasizes African ownership of the process, and invites the international community to support the efforts of African countries, at their request, in implementing their respective national programmes of action;

35. *Notes* that the COVID-19 pandemic has reshaped the financing for development landscape in Africa and recalls that public policies and the mobilization and effective use of domestic resources, underscored by the principle of national ownership, are important to the achievement of sustainable development, including through digitalizing public financial processes, improving efficiency in public expenditures, strengthening revenue collection, sound debt management, empowering the private financial sector for development, combating illicit financial flows, improving fiscal and debt transparency and harnessing global and regional partnerships, calls upon African countries to substantially increase their fiscal space in the short term by tapping into unexplored or underutilized sources of financing, and commits to supporting the implementation of integrated national financing frameworks to align financing policies and strategies with national investment priorities, legal frameworks, and disaster risk and sustainable development strategies consistent with the 2030 Agenda, the Sendai Framework and the Paris Agreement's long-term goals;

36. *Emphasizes* that debt sustainability is essential for underpinning growth, underlining the importance of debt sustainability, debt transparency and effective debt management to the efforts to achieve the Sustainable Development Goals, stresses the need to continue to assist developing countries, including African countries, in avoiding a build-up of unsustainable debt, taking into account the challenges posed by the global economic environment and risks for debt sustainability in a growing number of developing countries, and the consequent need for coordinated policy responses, and recognizes the important role, on a case-by-case basis, of debt relief, including debt cancellation, as appropriate, and debt restructuring as debt crisis prevention, management and resolution tools;

37. *Encourages* African countries to join the Sustainable Debt Coalition, established at the twenty-seventh session of the Conference of Parties to the United Nations Framework Convention on Climate Change, as called for in Economic Commission for Africa resolution 2023/7 of 21 March 2023, to advocate for a more sustainable and inclusive framework to address the linkages between climate change and debt and identify solutions which help to build resilience;

38. *Calls upon* African countries to continue their efforts to create a domestic environment conducive to encouraging entrepreneurship, supporting micro-, small and medium-sized enterprises, especially those owned by women and youth, promoting the formalization of informal sector activities in Africa and attracting investments by, inter alia, achieving a transparent, stable and predictable investment climate, and invites Africa's development partners to promote investment by their private sector in Africa and to facilitate the development and transfer of technology to African countries on mutually agreed terms;

39. *Notes* the Algiers Declaration for Start-up Development adopted at the African Start-up Conference held in Algiers on 5 and 6 December 2022, which called for accelerating the development of Africa's start-up ecosystem;

40. *Welcomes* the convening of the twenty-eighth session of the Conference of the Parties to the United Nations Framework Convention on Climate Change, the eighteenth session of the Conference of the Parties serving as the Meeting of the Parties to the Kyoto Protocol and the fifth session of the Conference of the Parties serving as the Meeting of the Parties to the Paris Agreement, held in Dubai, United Arab Emirates, from 30 November to 13 December 2023, and urges the implementation of its decisions;

41. *Also welcomes* the convening of the Africa Climate Summit in Nairobi from 4 to 6 September 2023, takes note of the African Leaders Nairobi Declaration on Climate Change and Call to Action, and reaffirms the importance of the provision of the means of implementation to developing countries;

42. *Further welcomes* the first part of the fifteenth meeting of the Conference of the Parties to the Convention on Biological Diversity, held in Kunming, China, from 11 to 15 October 2021, and the second part of the fifteenth meeting of the Conference of the Parties to the Convention under the presidency of China, in Montreal, Canada, from

[37] See decision Ext/Assembly/AU/Dec.1(XI), sect. XI.

7 to 19 December 2022, and its outcomes, including the Kunming-Montreal Global Biodiversity Framework, urges their early, inclusive and effective implementation, and looks forward to the sixteenth meeting of the Conference of the Parties, to be held in Colombia from 21 October to 1 November 2024;

43. *Welcomes* the convening of the United Nations Conference on the Midterm Comprehensive Review of the Implementation of the Objectives of the International Decade for Action, "Water for Sustainable Development", 2018–2028, from 22 to 24 March 2023;

44. *Notes* that foreign direct investment is a major source of financing for development, that it has a critical role in achieving inclusive economic growth and sustainable development, including through the promotion of decent job creation and the eradication of poverty and hunger, and that it contributes to the active participation of the African economies in the global economy and facilitates regional economic cooperation and integration, and in this regard calls upon, as appropriate, developed countries to continue to devise source-country measures to encourage and facilitate the flow of foreign direct investment through, inter alia, the provision of export credits and other lending instruments, risk guarantees and business development services;

45. *Acknowledges* the progress made towards ensuring the free movement of persons as well as goods and services in Africa, and welcomes the entry into force of the Agreement Establishing the African Continental Free Trade Area on 30 May 2019, and the ongoing efforts to fully operationalize the Agreement, including the actual commencement of trading on 1 January 2021 aimed at doubling intra-African trade to strengthen Africa's resilience, COVID-19 recovery and achievement of the Sustainable Development Goals;

46. *Notes with concern* Africa's disproportionately low share of the volume of international trade, reiterates the need for all countries and relevant multilateral institutions to continue efforts to enhance coherence in their trade policies towards African countries, and acknowledges the importance of efforts to fully integrate African countries into the multilateral trading system and to build their capacity to compete through such initiatives as Aid for Trade and, given the world economic and financial crisis and the profound socioeconomic impact of the COVID-19 pandemic, the provision of assistance to address the adjustment challenges of trade liberalization;

47. *Emphasizes* the importance of making progress on the accession of developing countries to the World Trade Organization, recognizing the contribution that their accession would make to the full integration of those countries into the multilateral trading system, urges in this regard the facilitation of the accession process on a technical and legal basis and in a transparent manner for African countries that are in the process of accession to the World Trade Organization, and reaffirms the importance of that organization's decision on accession by the least developed countries;[38]

48. *Calls upon* Member States to keep their food markets open to maintain international trade in food and fertilizers, and underlines the importance of addressing existing and emerging global challenges, including through the facilitation of agricultural trade and by correcting and preventing trade restrictions and distortions in world agricultural markets that are inconsistent with World Trade Organization rules, such as excessive stockpiling of food, and looks forward to continuing the World Trade Organization negotiations to reform agricultural trade rules, with a view to achieving meaningful progress to address these global challenges long-term at the thirteenth Ministerial Conference of the World Trade Organization;

49. *Notes with concern* the fragile and highly uncertain global socioeconomic outlook, persisting negative effects of the COVID-19 pandemic, geopolitical tensions and conflicts, current multiple crises and increased pressure on food, energy and finance, affecting many countries around the world and their ability to achieve the Sustainable Development Goals;

50. *Encourages* Governments, relevant international and regional organizations and other relevant stakeholders to promote investments in developing sustainable, reliable, modern, inclusive and equitable energy systems, inter alia, by strengthening energy systems through cross-border grid connections, as appropriate, and to consider incorporating decentralized renewable energy solutions in energy planning, as appropriate, and recognizes that energy transitions will take different paths in different parts of the world;

51. *Reiterates* that we are setting out together on the path towards sustainable development in its three dimensions – economic, social and environmental – in a balanced and integrated manner, including through

[38] Decision WT/L/508/Add.1 of 25 July 2012.

international cooperation and partnership on the basis of mutual trust and the full benefit of all, in a spirit of global solidarity, and for the common future of present and coming generations, focusing on the needs of African countries and the achievement of the Sustainable Development Goals;

52. *Welcomes* the various important initiatives established between African countries and their development partners, and emphasizes the need for their effective implementation, and in this regard recognizes the important role that North-South, South-South and triangular cooperation can play in supporting Africa's development efforts, particularly the implementation of the New Partnership, based on African identified needs and priorities, while bearing in mind that South-South cooperation is not a substitute for but rather a complement to North-South cooperation;

53. *Reiterates* that the fulfilment of all official development assistance commitments remains crucial, including the commitment by many developed countries to achieve the target of 0.7 per cent of gross national income for official development assistance and 0.15 to 0.20 per cent of gross national income for official development assistance to the least developed countries, is encouraged by those few countries that have met or surpassed their commitment to 0.7 per cent of gross national income for official development assistance and the target of 0.15 to 0.20 per cent of gross national income for official development assistance to the least developed countries, and urges all others to step up efforts to increase their official development assistance and to make additional concrete efforts towards official development assistance targets;

54. *Emphasizes* the need to continue to hold open, inclusive and transparent discussions on the modernization of official development assistance measurement and on the proposed measure of "total official support for sustainable development", while reaffirming that any such measure will not dilute commitments already made;

55. *Requests* the United Nations system to continue to provide assistance to the New Partnership and to African countries in developing projects and programmes within the scope of the priorities of the New Partnership, and requests the Secretary-General to promote greater coherence in the work of the United Nations system in support of Agenda 2063, its related flagship project and second 10-year implementation plan, and in this regard calls upon the United Nations system to continue to mainstream the special needs of Africa in all its normative and operational activities;

56. *Invites* Member States and all relevant entities of the United Nations system, including funds, programmes, specialized agencies and regional commissions, in particular the Economic Commission for Africa, and all relevant international and regional organizations, to continue to contribute to the effectiveness and reliability of the United Nations monitoring mechanism process by cooperating in the collection of data and the evaluation of performance, and requests the President of the General Assembly to organize and preside over an interactive multi-stakeholder dialogue to discuss the main findings and recommendations contained in the report of the Secretary-General on the review of the implementation of commitments made toward Africa's development during the resumed seventy-ninth session of the General Assembly;

57. *Decides* to include an item entitled "From the New Partnership for Africa's Development to Agenda 2063: progress in the implementation of sustainable development in Africa and international support" in the provisional agenda for consideration and decision during the main part of its seventy-ninth session;

58. *Requests* the Secretary-General to submit to the General Assembly, on an annual basis, a comprehensive and action-oriented report to inform the discussions under the agenda item, including on the implementation of the present resolution, based on the provision of inputs from Governments, organizations of the United Nations system and other stakeholders in the New Partnership.

RESOLUTION 78/263

Adopted at the 57th plenary meeting, on 26 February 2024, without a vote, on the basis of draft resolution A/78/L.37, sponsored by Cuba (on behalf of the States Members of the United Nations that are members of the Group of 77 and China)

78/263. Promotion of durable peace through sustainable development in Africa

The General Assembly,

Recalling the report of the Open-ended Ad Hoc Working Group on the Causes of Conflict and the Promotion of Durable Peace and Sustainable Development in Africa,[39] its resolution 53/92 of 7 December 1998 and all subsequent annual resolutions, including resolution 77/271 of 20 February 2023, as well as all its resolutions on the New Partnership for Africa's Development,[40] its resolution 66/293 of 17 September 2012, by which it established a monitoring mechanism to review commitments made towards Africa's development, and all resolutions and decisions regarding the cooperation between the United Nations and the African Union, in particular the comprehensive strategic partnership between the two organizations,

Recalling also the 2005 World Summit Outcome,[41] through which world leaders reaffirmed their commitment to addressing the special needs of Africa, and its resolution 60/265 of 30 June 2006,

Reaffirming all other previous resolutions and outcome documents adopted by consensus relating to the causes of conflict and the promotion of durable peace and sustainable development in Africa, including the Security Council resolutions on peace and security in Africa, on women, peace and security, on youth, peace and security, on children and armed conflict, on the role of the Council in the prevention of armed conflicts, on strengthening the effectiveness of the role of the Council in conflict prevention, particularly in Africa, and on threats to international peace and security,

Reaffirming in particular Security Council resolution 2558 (2020) and General Assembly resolution 75/201 of 21 December 2020 on the review of the United Nations peacebuilding architecture, which stressed the importance of continued implementation of the resolutions on peacebuilding and sustaining peace, with emphasis on the impact made at the field level,

Emphasizing the importance of a comprehensive approach to sustaining peace, particularly through the prevention of conflict and addressing all its root causes, including by strengthening the rule of law, good governance, democracy, accountability, gender equality and respect for and protection of human rights and fundamental freedoms, as well as addressing economic and social disparities, corruption, structural inequalities, border governance, illicit trade in and proliferation of arms, and the illegal exploitation of natural resources, in all its aspects for peace, security and development in Africa, underlining the importance of sustainable and inclusive socioeconomic development for sustaining peace in Africa, through economic development, including but not limited to transnational and transregional infrastructure development, industrialization, poverty eradication, job creation, agricultural modernization and promotion of entrepreneurship, and expressing the need for continued support to African countries based on their national priorities and needs,

Reaffirming its resolution 70/1 of 25 September 2015, entitled "Transforming our world: the 2030 Agenda for Sustainable Development", in which it adopted a comprehensive, far-reaching and people-centred set of universal and transformative Sustainable Development Goals and targets, its commitment to working tirelessly for the full implementation of the Agenda by 2030, its recognition that eradicating poverty in all its forms and dimensions, including extreme poverty, is the greatest global challenge and an indispensable requirement for sustainable development, its commitment to achieving sustainable development in its three dimensions – economic, social and environmental – in a balanced and integrated manner, and to building upon the achievements of the Millennium Development Goals and seeking to address their unfinished business,

Reaffirming also its resolution 69/313 of 27 July 2015, entitled "Addis Ababa Action Agenda of the Third International Conference on Financing for Development (Addis Ababa Action Agenda)", which helps to contextualize the means of implementation of the 2030 Agenda for Sustainable Development with concrete policies and actions and to address the challenge of financing and creating an enabling environment at all levels for sustainable development,

---

[39] *Official Records of the General Assembly, Fifty-sixth Session, Supplement No. 45* (A/56/45).

[40] A/57/304, annex.

[41] Resolution 60/1.

Reaffirming further the importance of aligning international support with Africa's own priorities, aimed at the implementation of the 2030 Agenda for Sustainable Development and the African Union Agenda 2063, including but not limited to industrialization, equal access to work opportunities, youth employment, access to quality education and quality, reliable, sustainable and resilient infrastructure, the eradication of poverty, environmentally sustainable and climate-resilient economies and communities, and the reduction of inequalities,

Recognizing the capacity of the African Union and subregional organizations to address the root causes of conflict in Africa, while acknowledging the need for the provision of support by the international community and the United Nations, taking into account the responsibilities of the Organization in this regard according to the Charter of the United Nations, and reaffirming the primary responsibility of national Governments and authorities for peacebuilding,

Underscoring the importance of continuing the efforts of the African Union and subregional organizations to prevent and settle conflicts and promote human rights, democracy, the rule of law and constitutional order in Africa, while continuing to develop African capacities, including those required for the realization of sustainable development, particularly in countries emerging from conflict,

Reaffirming the commitment to ensure that there will be no tolerance for impunity for genocide, war crimes and crimes against humanity or for violations of international humanitarian law and gross violations of human rights law, and that such violations will be properly investigated and appropriately prosecuted and sanctioned, through national judicial mechanisms and institutions or, where appropriate, regional or international judicial mechanisms, and for that purpose encouraging Member States to strengthen national judicial systems and institutions,

Acknowledging the particular challenges that infectious disease outbreaks, especially the impact of the coronavirus disease (COVID-19) pandemic, pose in conflict-affected areas and their effect on health emergency and crisis management, as health systems in areas of conflict are often compromised and ill-equipped to deal with the threat posed by infectious disease outbreaks, and strongly condemning violent attacks and threats directed against medical personnel and facilities, which have long-term consequences for the civilian population and the health-care systems of the countries concerned, as well as for the neighbouring regions, and have a negative impact on sustainable development,

Reiterating the need to enable equitable access to quality, safe, efficacious and affordable COVID-19 diagnostics, therapeutics, medicines and vaccines for all, including the most vulnerable, in addition to support for strengthening health systems to ensure effective delivery, particularly in conflict-affected areas, and inviting continued, increased and accelerated provision of safe and effective vaccine doses from developed economies and all those in a position to do so to African countries in need, particularly through the Access to COVID-19 Tools (ACT) Accelerator, the COVID-19 Vaccine Global Access (COVAX) Facility and other relevant supplies and assistance as appropriate, and commends the efforts of Member States in this regard, while emphasizing the role of immunization against COVID-19 as a global public good for health,

Welcoming the work of the Peacebuilding Commission and its convening role in mobilizing attention and commitment to bringing a strategic approach and coherence to international peacebuilding efforts, and recognizing the valuable work done in country-specific, regional and thematic meetings, including the country-specific configurations of the Commission,

Welcoming also the third edition of the Aswan Forum for Sustainable Peace and Development, held in June 2022 under the theme "Africa in an era of cascading risks and climate vulnerability: pathways for a peaceful, resilient, and sustainable continent", which called for integrated and contextualized responses and a bold action agenda, and emphasized the importance of accelerating the implementation of global climate commitments and pledges, as well as scaling up support to African countries in addressing climate change, as Africa remains one of the most vulnerable continents to its devastating consequences, despite contributing least to the climate crisis,

Renewing its unwavering commitment to strengthening international cooperation to prevent and combat terrorism in all its forms and manifestations and reaffirming that any acts of terrorism are criminal and unjustifiable, regardless of their motivation, wherever, whenever and by whomsoever committed, and also recognizing that any measures taken by Member States to prevent and counter terrorism, as well as to prevent and counter violent extremism as and when conducive to terrorism, must fully comply with their obligations under international law, including the Charter of the United Nations, in particular the purposes and principles thereof, and relevant international conventions and protocols, including those related to international human rights law, international refugee law and international humanitarian law,

Encouraging the United Nations system, the African Union and subregional organizations to enhance their interaction with civil society, including women's and youth organizations, academia and research institutions, on issues relevant to the promotion of peace, security and sustainable development in Africa, and taking note with appreciation of the ongoing efforts in this regard, including by the Office of the Special Adviser on Africa as well as by the Peacebuilding Commission,

1. *Takes note* of the report of the Secretary-General on the promotion of durable peace and sustainable development in Africa;[42]

2. *Recalls* the advice submitted for the first time in 2021 by the Peacebuilding Commission on the item on the causes of conflict and the promotion of durable peace and sustainable development in Africa, as contained in the letter from the Chair of the Commission addressed to the President of the General Assembly, and further encourages the Commission to continue that good practice with a view to enhancing cooperation and synergies in support of addressing root causes of conflict in Africa;

3. *Also recalls* the adoption of the African Union Agenda 2063 and its first 10-year implementation plan (2014–2023), which outlines key African flagship projects, fast-track programmes, priority areas, specific targets and African strategies and policy measures at all levels, and urges further efforts to support the implementation of the plan;

4. *Welcomes* the unanimous adoption of General Assembly resolution 76/305 of 8 September 2022 on financing for peacebuilding, and urges all relevant stakeholders to ensure its operationalization with a view to ensuring adequate, predictable and sustained financing for peacebuilding, including in Africa, and in this regard notes that the amount of voluntary contributions has not been sufficient to meet increasing demands for the support of the Peacebuilding Fund, and affirms that other sources of funding, including assessed contributions, could be used to finance the Fund through modalities determined by the General Assembly as a means of achieving this objective, and stresses that assessed funding is not meant to be a substitute for voluntary contributions and innovative funding, and in this regard welcomes the adoption of resolution 78/257 on 22 December 2023;

5. *Also welcomes* the progress made by African countries, the African Union and subregional organizations in conflict prevention, peacemaking, peacekeeping, peacebuilding and development, calls for intensified efforts, support and a coordinated approach among national Governments, the African Union, subregional organizations, the United Nations system and relevant partners in addressing those challenges, with a view to achieving further progress towards the goal of a conflict-free Africa, and in this regard recognizes the important role played by civil society organizations, including women's organizations;

6. *Reiterates* that we are setting out together on the path towards sustainable development in its three dimensions – economic, social and environmental – in a balanced and integrated manner, including through international cooperation and partnership on the basis of mutual trust and the full benefit of all, in a spirit of global solidarity, and for the common future of present and coming generations, focusing on the needs of African countries and the achievement of the Sustainable Development Goals;

7. *Recognizes* the need for African countries to make continued efforts to create enabling environments for inclusive growth in support of sustainable development, and calls upon the international community to enhance support and fulfil its commitments to take further action in areas critical to Africa's economic and social development;

8. *Underscores* the importance of adopting a comprehensive and integrated approach to the peace and security challenges facing the continent, and requests the Secretary-General to continue to promote the coordination of United Nations entities to support a comprehensive response to Africa's peace and development challenges;

9. *Urges* continued support for measures to address the challenges of poverty eradication and hunger, decent job creation and sustainable development in Africa, including, as appropriate, domestic resource mobilization, debt relief, improved market access, regional integration and intra-African trade, including through the African Continental Free Trade Area, support for the private sector and entrepreneurship, fulfilment of commitments on official

[42] A/78/234-S/2023/553.

development assistance and increased flows of foreign direct investment and transfer of technology on mutually agreed terms;

10. *Underlines* the importance of strengthened support from development partners and the multilateral system to build and strengthen resilience, State institutions and effective governance systems, particularly in conflict-affected and post-conflict countries, including through scaling up financial assistance, technical expertise and capacity-building;

11. *Urges* Member States to commit to enhancing public health cooperation with Africa, supporting Africa in strengthening and improving health systems, namely, through capacity-building;

12. *Recognizes* the adverse effects of climate change, ecological changes and natural disasters on the achievement of sustainable development in African Member States, including drought, desertification, biodiversity loss, land degradation, flooding and food insecurity, emphasizes the importance of sustainable use of natural resources and the need for adequate risk assessment and risk management strategies, highlights the importance of supporting efforts to strengthen the implementation of initiatives aimed at enhancing resilience in Africa, in particular the Comprehensive Africa Agriculture Development Programme and other initiatives launched under the leadership of the African Union Commission such as the Great Green Wall and the Land Policy Initiative and the African Union Green Recovery Action Plan, as well as initiatives launched by African countries such as the Adaptation of African Agriculture and the Security, Stability and Sustainability initiatives, and welcomes the efforts and initiatives of the African Union on addressing climate change on the continent; and in this regard welcomes the outcomes of the twenty-seventh session of the Conference of the Parties to the United Nations Framework Convention on Climate Change (COP27), held in Sharm el-Sheikh, Egypt, in November 2022, as well as the launch of the Climate Responses for Sustaining Peace (CRSP) initiative by Egypt as President of the twenty-seventh session of the Conference of the Parties and the African Union, as well as the twenty-eighth session of the Conference of the Parties to the United Nations Framework Convention on Climate Change (COP28), held in Dubai, United Arab Emirates, in December 2023;

13. *Welcomes* the convening of the Africa Climate Summit in Nairobi from 4 to 6 September 2023, takes note of the African Leaders Nairobi Declaration on Climate Change and Call to Action, and reaffirms the importance of the provision of the means of implementation to developing countries;

14. *Also welcomes* the first part of the fifteenth meeting of the Conference of the Parties to the Convention on Biological Diversity, held in Kunming, China, from 11 to 15 October 2021, and the second part of the fifteenth meeting of the Conference of the Parties to the Convention under the presidency of China, in Montreal, Canada, from 7 to 19 December 2022, and its outcomes, including the Kunming-Montreal Global Biodiversity Framework, urges their early, inclusive and effective implementation, and looks forward to the sixteenth meeting of the Conference of the Parties, to be held in Colombia from 21 October to 1 November 2024;

15. *Reaffirms* the need to promote and protect effectively the human rights and fundamental freedoms of all migrants, regardless of their migration status, especially those of women and children, and to address international migration through international, regional or bilateral cooperation, recognizing the roles and responsibilities of countries of origin, transit and destination in promoting and protecting the human rights of all migrants, calls for respect for the principle of refugee protection in Africa and the resolution of the plight of refugees, including through support for efforts aimed at addressing the causes of refugee movement and bringing about the voluntary, dignified, safe and sustainable return and reintegration of those populations, and also calls for respect for the principle of non-refoulement of refugees in Africa;

16. *Welcomes* the progress made in improving the collection and use of disaggregated migration data, including through the establishment of migration data and knowledge centres and observatories, such as the African Migration Observatory, as well as the promotion of bilateral and regional exchanges and initiatives on migration data;

17. *Reaffirms* the convening of the intergovernmental conference held on 10 and 11 December 2018 in Marrakech, Morocco, and recalls that it adopted the Global Compact for Safe, Orderly and Regular Migration, also known as the Marrakech Compact on Migration;[43]

---

[43] Resolution 73/195, annex.

18. *Notes* the opportunities and challenges presented by Africa's demographic structure, and stresses the importance of addressing the socioeconomic dimension of youth unemployment as well as facilitating the enhanced participation of youth in decision-making processes, reaffirms the important and positive contribution of youth to the efforts for the maintenance and promotion of peace and security and the role young people play in the prevention and resolution of conflicts, including through the promotion of narratives of peace, and as a key aspect of the sustainability, inclusiveness and success of peacekeeping and peacebuilding efforts, and further notes with concern the tragic plight of children in conflict situations in Africa, in particular the unlawful recruitment and use of children by parties to armed conflicts, sexual violence as well as other violations and abuses committed against children;

19. *Recalls* its resolution 78/244 of 22 December 2023, in which it endorsed the report of the Committee for Programme and Coordination,[44] in which the Office of the Special Adviser on Africa was requested to explore the feasibility of developing deliverables and activities for the promotion of young people and ensuring their inclusion in the strategies of implementation of the 2030 Agenda for Sustainable Development[45] and Agenda 2063, underscores the relevance of addressing structural inequalities with particular focus on women and youth by ensuring equal access to education, health care, employment, participation in decision-making processes and other development needs, highlights the need to strengthen State institutions and governance systems, including through capacity-building initiatives, technical assistance and financial support, and in that regard further recalls its resolution 78/252 of 22 December 2023 and requests the Secretary-General to present in the context of the next proposed programme budget a proposal for the establishment of a fellowship for young Africans at United Nations Headquarters in New York to strengthen institutional capacities in policy analysis, design and monitoring, under the coordination of the Office of the Special Adviser on Africa;

20. *Expresses concern* that unemployment, underemployment and lack of decent work have socioeconomic implications that could serve as critical triggers for conflict, including exacerbating inequality, poor service delivery and weakening resilience, which pose threats to peace, stability and development, particularly in post-conflict and conflict-affected countries;

21. *Expresses grave concern* about the growing threat posed by terrorism and violent extremism as and when conducive to terrorism to the peace, security and social and economic development of Africa, and calls upon the Office of Counter-Terrorism, the United Nations Office on Drugs and Crime and its Terrorism Prevention Branch and relevant Global Counter-Terrorism Coordination Compact entities, within their existing mandates, to intensify cooperation, assistance and capacity-building, for African Member States, the African Union and African subregional organizations, while ensuring compliance with international law, and encourages the United Nations system and Member States to support the efforts on the establishment of the African Union Special Fund on the Prevention and Combating of Terrorism and Violent Extremism in Africa, welcomes the sixteenth extraordinary African Union summit on terrorism, held on 28 May 2022 in Equatorial Guinea, and takes note of its conclusions;

22. *Calls upon* the Office of Counter-Terrorism and relevant Global Counter-Terrorism Coordination Compact entities, within their existing mandates, to intensify cooperation, assistance and capacity-building, for African Member States, the African Union and African subregional organizations, while ensuring compliance with international law, upon their request, in preventing and combating terrorism and preventing and countering violent extremism as and when conducive to terrorism, through the implementation of relevant international and regional treaties and protocols, and in this regard welcomes in particular African initiatives, namely the African Union Plan of Action on the Prevention and Combating of Terrorism in Africa, the African Centre for Studies and Research on Terrorism (ACSRT), based in Algiers, and the Intergovernmental Authority on Development Centre of Excellence in Preventing and Countering Violent Extremism in the Horn of Africa, based in Djibouti, as well as the Community of Sahel-Saharan States Counter-Terrorism Centre, based in Cairo;

23. *Takes note* of the establishment of regional programme offices of the Office of Counter-Terrorism in Africa, in Rabat, Morocco, and Nairobi, Kenya, and welcomes their efforts in this regard, further takes note that the offices have been established to prevent and counter violent extremism conducive to terrorism and enhance counter-terrorism training and capacity-building support to Member States of the region, upon request and with the consent of the relevant Member States and in coordination with them, for delivery of programmes closer to the beneficiaries, and invites the Office of Counter-Terrorism to work in close coordination with relevant local, subregional and regional

[44] *Official Records of the General Assembly, Seventy-eighth Session, Supplement No. 16* (A/78/16).

[45] Resolution 70/1.

institutions working to counter terrorism as well as with relevant Global Counter-Terrorism Coordination Compact entities, and further invites relevant institutions dealing with counter-terrorism to coordinate, with the regional programme offices of the Office of Counter-Terrorism, in order to ensure updated and tailored training materials and programmes, while underlining the need for upholding the principle of consent of the host countries in the context of all such United Nations field engagements, in line with respective mandates, and in cooperation with the respective host countries;

24. *Recalls* the decision taken at the fourteenth extraordinary session of the Assembly of Heads of State and Government of the African Union, within the context of the African Union Agenda 2063, to extend the implementation of the African Union Master Road Map of Practical Steps for Silencing the Guns in Africa for a period of 10 years (2021–2030), with periodic reviews every two years, and to extend the commemoration and conduct of Africa Amnesty Month during September of each year for a period of 10 years (2021–2030), and calls upon Member States and the United Nations system, as appropriate, to intensify their support and cooperation with African countries, the African Union and the African regional economic communities and relevant regional mechanisms towards the timely realization of this goal;

25. *Emphasizes* that the illicit flow of arms, particularly small arms and light weapons, to rebel armed groups, terrorists and criminals contributes significantly to insecurity and violence in various parts of Africa and undermines social cohesion, public security, socioeconomic development and the normal functioning of State institutions, underlines the importance of promoting the implementation of relevant international instruments and strengthening law enforcement mechanisms, and in this regard urges Member States to take effective measures to holistically address all root causes of conflicts and redouble efforts to effectively curb the illicit flow of conventional weapons into and within Africa, including by taking the necessary steps at the national level to implement the Programme of Action to Prevent, Combat and Eradicate the Illicit Trade in Small Arms and Light Weapons in All Its Aspects;[46]

26. *Stresses* the critical importance of a regional approach to conflict prevention, including early action to address rising conflict risk and emerging violent conflict and, in particular with respect to cross-border issues such as transnational organized crime, drug trafficking, disarmament, demobilization, repatriation, resettlement and reintegration programmes, the prevention and combating of illegal exploitation of and trafficking in natural resources and high-value commodities and the illicit trade in small arms and light weapons in all its aspects, and emphasizes in this regard the central role of national Governments, the African Union and subregional organizations in addressing such issues, and welcomes the role of the African Union Mechanism for Police Cooperation (AFRIPOL), based in Algeria, in fighting the organized crimes in Africa;

27. *Notes* that in some armed conflict situations, the illicit exploitation, trafficking and trade in natural resources has contributed to the outbreak, escalation or continuation of such conflicts, and calls for the implementation of resolutions adopted on this issue to support the prevention of the illegal exploitation of natural resources;

28. *Expresses concern* over the threat of piracy and armed robbery at sea in the Gulf of Guinea to security and economic activities in the region and the continent at large, in this regard welcomes the adoption of Security Council resolution 2634 (2022) of 31 May 2022 on maritime security in the Gulf of Guinea, and commends the countries of the Gulf of Guinea region and regional bodies, including the Economic Community of Central African States, the Economic Community of West African States and the Gulf of Guinea Commission, for the collective efforts undertaken to address and prevent piracy, including the steady decline in the incidence of piracy and armed robbery in the region, armed robbery at sea and other maritime crimes, and calls for enhanced international and regional cooperation to address these threats to maritime safety and security in the Gulf of Guinea;

29. *Underscores* the critical role of regional instruments in tackling maritime insecurity on the continent of Africa, and notes that the commemoration of the tenth anniversary of the Yaoundé Architecture provides the opportunity to address gaps in its implementation in order to make it more responsive;

30. *Welcomes* the ongoing efforts of the African Union and subregional organizations to strengthen their capacity in peacekeeping operations on the continent, in accordance with Chapter VIII of the Charter of the United Nations and in close coordination with the United Nations, through the Peace and Security Council of the African Union, and in this regard takes note of the Cairo Road Map on Enhancing Peacekeeping Operations: From Mandate

[46] *Report of the United Nations Conference on the Illicit Trade in Small Arms and Light Weapons in All Its Aspects, New York, 9–20 July 2001* (A/CONF.192/15), chap. IV, para. 24.

to Exit that was endorsed by the Peace and Security Council of the African Union as an African contribution to advance United Nations peacekeeping reform efforts related to the Secretary-General's Action for Peacekeeping initiative, and further welcomes language from the communiqué as well as the ongoing efforts to develop a continental early warning system, strengthen the readiness of the African Standby Force and enhance mediation capacity and preventive diplomacy, including through the Panel of the Wise;

31. *Reaffirms* the importance of African Union-led peace support operations in the maintenance of international and regional peace and security, underscores the importance of enhancing the operational and institutional capacity to effectively discharge their respective mandates, emphasizes the need to ensure access to adequate, predictable and sustainable financing of African Union-led peace support operations, and in this regard welcomes the adoption of Security Council resolution 2719 (2023) of 21 December 2023 on a framework for African Union-led peace support operations;

32. *Welcomes* the United Nations Peacekeeping Ministerial Meeting, held in Accra, Ghana, on 5 and 6 December 2023, and notes that the Ministerial, which was the first to be held on the continent of Africa, provided an opportunity for participants to share insights on innovative ways to make modern-day peacekeeping operations more effective and responsive to the security challenges of our time, including the deteriorating security situation in some parts of Africa and globally;

33. *Recognizes* the role of the Peacebuilding Commission in ensuring that national ownership of the peacebuilding process in countries under consideration is observed and that nationally identified priorities are at the core of international and regional efforts in peacebuilding and sustaining peace in the countries under consideration, welcomes the bridging role of the Commission as a dedicated intergovernmental advisory body to bring together all the relevant actors in the United Nations system as well as international and financial institutions, representatives of national Governments, representatives of civil society and regional and subregional organizations consistent with its mandate to promote a strategic approach and coherence in international peacebuilding efforts, calls upon the Peacebuilding Commission to further enhance its relationship with regional and subregional organizations in Africa, welcomes the Peacebuilding Fund's engagement, as a timely, catalytic and risk-tolerant instrument for enhancing the impact and coherence of United Nations peacebuilding support, including with respect to cross-border initiatives that recognize the complex dynamics and regional impacts of conflicts in areas such as the Sahel, and calls upon the entirety of the United Nations system to develop cross-border initiatives that are coherent with one another (including funding from international financial institutions) and address underlying causes of regional tensions and conflict;

34. *Recalls* decision Assembly/AU/Dec.729(XXXII) of 11 February 2019 of the Assembly of Heads of State and Government of the African Union on revitalizing and operationalizing the African Union Policy on Post-Conflict Reconstruction and Development, while aligning it with the evolving international discourse on peacebuilding and sustaining peace and the actual needs of countries emerging from conflict in Africa, and calls upon the United Nations system and Member States to support the peace consolidation mechanisms and processes, including the African Peace and Security Architecture, the African Governance Architecture, the African Union Post-Conflict Reconstruction and Development Framework and the African Union Centre for Post-Conflict Reconstruction and Development, in order to fully contribute to conflict prevention, peacemaking initiatives, peacebuilding and post-conflict reconstruction;

35. *Notes with concern* that sexual violence in conflict continues and may increase even as armed conflicts draw to an end, notes the adoption by the General Assembly and the Security Council of relevant resolutions, including Council resolution 2467 (2019) of 23 April 2019, urges further progress in the implementation of policies and guidelines relating to the protection of and assistance to victims of sexual violence in conflict and post-conflict situations in Africa, including more systematic monitoring and reporting, and encourages the entities that compose United Nations Action against Sexual Violence in Conflict, as well as other relevant parts of the United Nations system, to assist the Office of the Special Representative of the Secretary-General on Sexual Violence in Conflict in the implementation of its mandate, including in Africa;

36. *Reiterates* the calls for the full, equal and meaningful participation of women in conflict prevention and resolution, and peacebuilding, consistent with Security Council resolution 1325 (2000) of 31 October 2000 and subsequent Security Council resolutions on women and peace and security, recalls the ongoing efforts of African countries and the African Union, including the work of the African Union Special Envoy on Women, Peace and Security, to ensure the protection of the rights of women and girls in conflict and post-conflict situations, also recalls the adoption and entry into force of the Protocol to the African Charter on Human and Peoples' Rights on the Rights of Women in Africa, as well as all other relevant instruments for strengthening the role of women in peace and conflict

on the continent, and further recalls in this regard the adoption of national action plans on women, peace and security by several African countries and the various initiatives of the African Union, and urges the provision of adequate international support for the implementation of these plans;

37. *Recognizes* the important contribution of the African Peer Review Mechanism since its inception in improving governance and supporting socioeconomic development in African countries, takes note of the decision adopted by the Assembly of Heads of State and Government of the African Union in January 2017 on the revitalization of the African Peer Review Mechanism, expanding the monitoring and evaluation mandate of the Mechanism, invites the United Nations system and Member States to provide voluntary substantial financial and capacity-building support to the revitalization of the Mechanism and to advance its activities, and requests the Secretary-General to develop an initiative with the African Peer Review Mechanism on the strengthening of e-governance in Africa through policy innovation and transformative technologies;

38. *Recalls* the commitment of the African leaders to Africa's political, social and economic integration agenda and to the ideal of pan-Africanism and African renaissance, as well as their effort to achieve the goal of a conflict-free Africa as affirmed in the solemn declaration adopted on 26 May 2013 on the occasion of the fiftieth anniversary of the Organization of African Unity/African Union, expresses its readiness to contribute, and calls upon all, in particular relevant United Nations entities, to help to achieve this goal through enhanced collaboration with African Union institutions, regional economic communities and regional mechanisms in accordance with their respective mandates;

39. *Welcomes* the launching by the African Union Commission and United Nations Development Programme, of the Africa Facility to Support Inclusive Transitions, on the sidelines of the fifth African Union mid-year coordination meeting, held in Nairobi on 15 July 2023;

40. *Calls upon* the United Nations system, Member States, and bilateral and multilateral partners to deliver expeditiously on their commitments and to support the full and speedy implementation of the provisions of the political declaration on Africa's development needs,[47] the 2030 Agenda and the African Union Agenda 2063, recognizing the relevance of leveraging new transformative technologies to advance sustainable development on the continent and bridge the digital divide that is undermining African countries' development efforts;

41. *Welcomes* the convening of the sixth United Nations-African Union annual conference at the level of the Secretary-General and the Chairperson of the African Union Commission at the African Union Commission headquarters on 1 December 2022, which emphasized the need to scale up joint efforts in advancing the effective implementation of the women, peace and security agenda and the youth, peace and security agenda, ending poverty and hunger, reducing inequality, promoting food and energy security and improving the health and well-being of African citizens, recalls the adoption of its resolution 71/254 of 23 December 2016 on the Framework for a Renewed United Nations-African Union Partnership on Africa's Integration and Development Agenda 2017–2027, and reaffirms the commitment to continue to deepen the strategic partnership between the United Nations and the African Union in addressing peace and security, sustainable development and human rights and implementing the 2030 Agenda and Agenda 2063 in Africa;

42. *Decides* to include the sub-item entitled "Causes of conflict and the promotion of durable peace and sustainable development in Africa" under the item entitled "From the New Partnership for Africa's Development to Agenda 2063: progress in the implementation of sustainable development in Africa and international support" in the provisional agenda for consideration and decision during the main part of its seventy-ninth session, and requests the Secretary-General to continue to monitor and report, by September 2024, to the General Assembly, and thereafter on an annual basis, on persistent and emerging challenges to the promotion of durable peace and sustainable development in Africa, including the root causes of conflict and conditions to promote sustainable development, as well as on the approach and support of the United Nations system.

RESOLUTION 78/264

Adopted at the 62nd plenary meeting, on 15 March 2024, by a recorded vote of 115 to none, with 44 abstentions,* on the basis of draft resolution A/78/L.48, sponsored by: Bolivia (Plurinational State of), China, Nicaragua, Pakistan (on behalf of the

[47] Resolution 63/1.

States Members of the United Nations that are members of the Organization of Islamic Cooperation), Philippines, Russian Federation, United Republic of Tanzania, Venezuela (Bolivarian Republic of), Zimbabwe

* *In favour:* Albania, Algeria, Australia, Azerbaijan, Bahamas, Bahrain, Bangladesh, Belarus, Bhutan, Bolivia (Plurinational State of), Bosnia and Herzegovina, Brunei Darussalam, Burkina Faso, Burundi, Cabo Verde, Cambodia, Cameroon, Canada, Chad, Chile, China, Colombia, Comoros, Costa Rica, Côte d'Ivoire, Cuba, Democratic People's Republic of Korea, Democratic Republic of the Congo, Djibouti, Dominican Republic, Egypt, El Salvador, Equatorial Guinea, Eritrea, Ethiopia, Gabon, Gambia, Ghana, Guatemala, Guinea, Guinea-Bissau, Guyana, Honduras, Iceland, Indonesia, Iran (Islamic Republic of), Iraq, Jamaica, Japan, Jordan, Kazakhstan, Kuwait, Kyrgyzstan, Lao People's Democratic Republic, Lebanon, Libya, Madagascar, Malaysia, Maldives, Mali, Mauritania, Mexico, Micronesia (Federated States of), Mongolia, Morocco, Mozambique, Myanmar, Namibia, Nepal, New Zealand, Nicaragua, Niger, Nigeria, North Macedonia, Norway, Oman, Pakistan, Palau, Panama, Papua New Guinea, Peru, Philippines, Qatar, Russian Federation, Rwanda, Saint Lucia, Saint Vincent and the Grenadines, Samoa, Saudi Arabia, Senegal, Serbia, Sierra Leone, Singapore, Somalia, South Africa, Sri Lanka, Sudan, Suriname, Syrian Arab Republic, Tajikistan, Thailand, Togo, Trinidad and Tobago, Tunisia, Türkiye, Turkmenistan, Uganda, United Arab Emirates, United Republic of Tanzania, United States of America, Uruguay, Uzbekistan, Viet Nam, Yemen, Zimbabwe

Against: None

Abstaining: Andorra, Argentina, Armenia, Austria, Belgium, Brazil, Bulgaria, Croatia, Cyprus, Czechia, Denmark, Estonia, Finland, France, Georgia, Germany, Greece, Hungary, India, Ireland, Italy, Latvia, Liechtenstein, Lithuania, Luxembourg, Malta, Monaco, Montenegro, Netherlands (Kingdom of the), Paraguay, Poland, Portugal, Republic of Korea, Republic of Moldova, Romania, San Marino, Slovakia, Slovenia, South Sudan, Spain, Sweden, Switzerland, Ukraine, United Kingdom of Great Britain and Northern Ireland

78/264. Measures to combat Islamophobia

The General Assembly,

Reaffirming the purposes and principles of the Charter of the United Nations, the Universal Declaration of Human Rights[48] and the Vienna Declaration and Programme of Action[49] for the promotion and protection of all human rights and fundamental freedoms for all persons,

Reaffirming also the positive role that the exercise of the right to freedom of opinion and expression and full respect for the freedom to seek, receive and impart information can play in strengthening democracy and combating religious intolerance, and reaffirming further that the exercise of the right to freedom of expression carries with it special duties and responsibilities, in accordance with article 19 of the International Covenant on Civil and Political Rights,[50] and recalling article 20 (2) of the Covenant, which states that any advocacy of national, racial or religious hatred that constitutes incitement to discrimination, hostility or violence shall be prohibited by law,

Deeply concerned about the prevalence of impunity in some instances, and the lack of accountability in some cases, in addressing violence against persons on the basis of religion or belief in public and private spheres, and stressing the importance of making the necessary efforts to raise awareness to address the spread of hate speech against persons on the basis of religion or belief,

Recalling its resolution 76/254 of 15 March 2022, designating 15 March as the International Day to Combat Islamophobia, and welcoming the first commemoration by the General Assembly of the International Day to Combat Islamophobia, held at United Nations Headquarters in March 2023,

Recalling also its resolutions 36/55 of 25 November 1981, in which it proclaimed the Declaration on the Elimination of All Forms of Intolerance and of Discrimination Based on Religion or Belief, 72/130 of 8 December 2017 on the International Day of Living Together in Peace, 73/296 of 28 May 2019, in which it decided to designate 22 August as the International Day Commemorating the Victims of Acts of Violence Based on Religion or Belief, 75/258 of 21 January 2021 on promoting a culture of peace and tolerance to safeguard religious sites, 77/318 of 25 July 2023 on promoting interreligious and intercultural dialogue and tolerance in countering hate speech and 78/129 of 18 December 2023 on the promotion of interreligious and intercultural dialogue, understanding and cooperation for peace,

[48] Resolution 217 A (III).

[49] A/CONF.157/24 (Part I), chap. III.

[50] See resolution 2200 A (XXI), annex.

Reaffirming the obligation of Member States to prohibit discrimination and violence on the basis of religion or belief and to implement measures to guarantee the equal and effective protection of the law,

Expressing its concern at the growing manifestations of intolerance based on religion or belief, including in the digital context, which can generate hatred and violence among individuals from and within different nations and which may have serious implications at the national, regional and international levels, and in this regard emphasizing the importance of respect for religious and cultural diversity, as well as interreligious, interfaith and intercultural dialogue aimed at promoting a culture of tolerance and respect among individuals, societies and nations,

Encouraging activities aimed at promoting interreligious and intercultural dialogue in order to enhance peace and social stability, respect for diversity and mutual respect and to create, at the global level, and also at the regional, national and local levels, an environment conducive to peace and mutual understanding,

Recognizing the leading role of the United Nations Educational, Scientific and Cultural Organization and the work of the United Nations Alliance of Civilizations in promoting intercultural dialogue and their contribution to interreligious dialogue, as well as its activities related to the culture of peace and non-violence and its focus on concrete actions at the global, regional and subregional levels,

1. *Condemns* any advocacy of religious hatred that constitutes incitement to discrimination, hostility or violence, whether it involves the use of print, audiovisual or electronic media or any other means;

2. *Also condemns* the incitement to discrimination, hostility or violence against Muslims as manifested in the increasing number of incidents of desecration of their holy book, attacks on mosques, sites and shrines and other acts of religious intolerance, negative stereotyping, hatred and violence against Muslims;

3. *Requests* the Secretary-General to appoint a United Nations Special Envoy to combat Islamophobia;

4. *Calls upon* Member States to take all necessary measures, including legislative and policy measures, to combat religious intolerance, negative stereotyping, hatred, incitement to violence and violence against Muslims and prohibit by law incitement to violence and violence against persons on the grounds of their religion or belief;

5. *Also calls upon* Member States to engage with all relevant stakeholders to promote the virtues of interreligious and intercultural dialogue and dialogue among civilizations, respect and acceptance of differences, tolerance, respect for religious and cultural diversity, peaceful coexistence and cohabitation, inclusion and respect for human rights, and to reject the spread of hate speech that constitutes incitement to discrimination, hostility and/or violence;

6. *Requests* the Secretary-General to prepare and submit a report to the General Assembly at its seventy-ninth session on the implementation of the present resolution and on measures taken by Member States and the United Nations pursuant to the present resolution to combat Islamophobia in all its forms and manifestations.

RESOLUTION 78/265

Adopted at the 63rd plenary meeting, on 21 March 2024, without a vote, on the basis of draft resolution A/78/L.49, sponsored by: Afghanistan, Albania, Algeria, Andorra, Argentina, Armenia, Australia, Austria, Bahamas, Bahrain, Bangladesh, Belgium, Bosnia and Herzegovina, Brazil, Bulgaria, Cabo Verde, Canada, Chile, China, Colombia, Costa Rica, Côte d'Ivoire, Croatia, Cyprus, Czechia, Democratic Republic of the Congo, Denmark, Djibouti, Dominican Republic, Ecuador, Egypt, Equatorial Guinea, Estonia, Ethiopia, Fiji, Finland, France, Georgia, Germany, Greece, Guatemala, Guinea-Bissau, Haiti, Hungary, Iceland, India, Indonesia, Ireland, Israel, Italy, Japan, Jordan, Kazakhstan, Kenya, Kiribati, Kuwait, Kyrgyzstan, Latvia, Lebanon, Liberia, Liechtenstein, Lithuania, Luxembourg, Malawi, Malaysia, Maldives, Malta, Marshall Islands, Monaco, Mongolia, Montenegro, Morocco, Myanmar, Nepal, Netherlands (Kingdom of the), New Zealand, Nigeria, North Macedonia, Norway, Oman, Pakistan, Palau, Papua New Guinea, Paraguay, Peru, Philippines, Poland, Portugal, Qatar, Republic of Korea, Republic of Moldova, Romania, San Marino, Saudi Arabia, Senegal, Serbia, Sierra Leone, Singapore, Slovakia, Slovenia, South Africa, South Sudan, Spain, Sri Lanka, Suriname, Sweden, Switzerland, Tajikistan, Thailand, Togo, Trinidad and Tobago, Tunisia, Türkiye, Turkmenistan, Ukraine, United Arab Emirates, United Kingdom of Great Britain and Northern Ireland, United Republic of Tanzania, United States of America, Uruguay, Uzbekistan, Viet Nam, Zambia

78/265. Seizing the opportunities of safe, secure and trustworthy artificial intelligence systems for sustainable development

The General Assembly,

Reaffirming international law, in particular the Charter of the United Nations, and recalling the Universal Declaration of Human Rights,[51]

Reaffirming also its resolution 70/1 of 25 September 2015, entitled "Transforming our world: the 2030 Agenda for Sustainable Development", its resolution 69/313 of 27 July 2015 on the Addis Ababa Action Agenda of the Third International Conference on Financing for Development, and the political declaration adopted at the high-level political forum on sustainable development convened under the auspices of the General Assembly contained in the annex to its resolution 78/1 of 29 September 2023,

Recalling its resolutions 77/320 of 25 July 2023 on the impact of rapid technological change on the achievement of the Sustainable Development Goals and targets, 78/132 of 19 December 2023 on information and communications technologies for sustainable development, 78/160 of 19 December 2023 on science, technology and innovation for sustainable development, 78/213 of 19 December 2023 on the promotion and protection of human rights in the context of digital technologies, 77/211 of 15 December 2022 on the right to privacy in the digital age, 70/125 of 16 December 2015 on the overall review of the implementation of the outcomes of the World Summit on the Information Society, all the outcomes of the World Summit on the Information Society, including the Geneva Declaration of Principles,[52] the Geneva Plan of Action,[53] the Tunis Commitment[54] and the Tunis Agenda for the Information Society,[55] and the declaration on the commemoration of the seventy-fifth anniversary of the United Nations contained in its resolution 75/1 of 21 September 2020,

Taking note of the efforts of the International Telecommunication Union, in partnership with 40 United Nations bodies, to convene the Artificial Intelligence for Good platform, including its annual summit and the launch of the International Telecommunication Union's Artificial Intelligence Repository to identify responsible and practical applications of artificial intelligence to advance the Sustainable Development Goals; and the adoption by the General Conference of the United Nations Educational, Scientific and Cultural Organization of its Recommendation on the Ethics of Artificial Intelligence of 23 November 2021,[56] its implementation plan, including the Readiness Assessment Methodology and the Ethical Impact Assessment and the Global Forum on the Ethics of Artificial Intelligence; as well as taking note of the Guiding Principles on Business and Human Rights: Implementing the United Nations "Protect, Respect and Remedy" Framework,[57] as endorsed by the Human Rights Council in its resolution 17/4 of 16 June 2011;[58] and the work of the Office of the United Nations High Commissioner for Human Rights regarding artificial intelligence,

Taking note also of the report of the Secretary-General of the United Nations entitled "Road map for digital cooperation",[59] as well as the establishment of the Office of the Secretary-General's Envoy on Technology to coordinate its implementation and the establishment by the Secretary-General of a multi-stakeholder High-level Advisory Body on Artificial Intelligence and of its interim report issued on 21 December 2023, and looking forward to its final report,

Recognizing that safe, secure and trustworthy artificial intelligence systems – which, for the purpose of this resolution, refers to artificial intelligence systems in the non-military domain, whose life cycle includes the stages: pre-design, design, development, evaluation, testing, deployment, use, sale, procurement, operation and

---

[51] Resolution 217 A (III).

[52] See A/C.2/59/3, annex.

[53] Ibid.

[54] See A/60/687.

[55] Ibid.

[56] United Nations Educational, Scientific and Cultural Organization, *Records of the General Conference, Forty-first Session, Paris, 9–24 November 2021*, vol. 1, *Resolutions*, annex VII.

[57] A/HRC/17/31, annex.

[58] See *Official Records of the General Assembly, Sixty-sixth Session, Supplement No. 53* (A/66/53), chap. III, sect. A.

[59] A/74/821.

decommissioning, are such that they are human-centric, reliable, explainable, ethical, inclusive, in full respect, promotion and protection of human rights and international law, privacy preserving, sustainable development oriented, and responsible – have the potential to accelerate and enable progress towards the achievement of all 17 Sustainable Development Goals and sustainable development in its three dimensions – economic, social and environmental – in a balanced and integrated manner; promote digital transformation; promote peace; overcome digital divides between and within countries; and promote and protect the enjoyment of human rights and fundamental freedoms for all, while keeping the human person at the centre,

Recognizing also that the improper or malicious design, development, deployment and use of artificial intelligence systems, such as without adequate safeguards or in a manner inconsistent with international law, pose risks that could hinder progress towards the achievement of the 2030 Agenda for Sustainable Development and its Sustainable Development Goals and undermine sustainable development in its three dimensions – economic, social and environmental; widen digital divides between and within countries; reinforce structural inequalities and biases; lead to discrimination; undermine information integrity and access to information; undercut the protection, promotion and enjoyment of human rights and fundamental freedoms, including the right not to be subject to unlawful or arbitrary interference with one's privacy; and increase the potential risk for accidents and compound threats from malicious actors,

Recognizing further the rapid acceleration of the design, development, deployment and use of artificial intelligence systems and rapid technological change, and their potential impact in accelerating the achievement of the Sustainable Development Goals, therefore stressing the urgency of achieving global consensus on safe, secure and trustworthy artificial intelligence systems; facilitating inclusive international cooperation to formulate and use effective, internationally interoperable safeguards, practices and standards that promote innovation and prevent the fragmentation of the governance of safe, secure and trustworthy artificial intelligence systems; and recognizing also existing artificial intelligence and other digital divides, and the varying levels of technological development between and within countries, that developing countries face unique challenges in keeping pace with this rapid acceleration, which cause obstacles to sustainable development, the need to narrow the existing disparities between developed and developing countries in terms of conditions, possibilities and capacities, therefore stressing also the urgency of strengthening capacity building and technical and financial assistance to developing countries to close digital divides between and within countries and support developing countries' effective, equitable and meaningful participation and representation in international processes and forums on the governance of artificial intelligence systems,

Recognizing also that the governance of artificial intelligence systems is an evolving area and the need for continued discussions on possible governance approaches that are appropriate, based on international law, interoperable, agile, adaptable, inclusive, responsive to the different needs and capacities of developed and developing countries alike and for the benefit of all, as the technology and our understanding of it develops,

1. *Resolves* to bridge the artificial intelligence and other digital divides between and within countries;

2. *Resolves* to promote safe, secure and trustworthy artificial intelligence systems to accelerate progress towards the full realization of the 2030 Agenda for Sustainable Development,[60] further bridging the artificial intelligence and other digital divides between and within countries; and stresses the need for the standard of safe, secure and trustworthy artificial intelligence systems to promote, not hinder, digital transformation and equitable access to their benefits in order to achieve all 17 Sustainable Development Goals and sustainable development in its three dimensions – economic, social and environmental – and address other shared global challenges, particularly for developing countries;

3. *Encourages* Member States and invites multi-stakeholders from all regions and countries, within their respective roles and responsibilities, including from the private sector, international and regional organizations, civil society, the media, academia and research institutions and technical communities and individuals, to develop and support regulatory and governance approaches and frameworks related to safe, secure and trustworthy artificial intelligence systems that create an enabling ecosystem at all levels, including for innovation, entrepreneurship and the dissemination of knowledge and technologies on mutually agreed terms, recognizing that effective partnership and cooperation between Governments and multi-stakeholders is necessary in developing such approaches and frameworks;

[60] Resolution 70/1.

4. *Calls upon* Member States and invites other stakeholders to take action to cooperate with and provide assistance to developing countries towards inclusive and equitable access to the benefits of digital transformation and safe, secure and trustworthy artificial intelligence systems, including by:

(a) Expanding participation of all countries, in particular developing countries, in digital transformation to harness the benefits and effectively participate in the development, deployment and use of safe, secure and trustworthy artificial intelligence systems, including by capacity building relating to artificial intelligence systems, recognizing that promoting knowledge sharing activities and the transfer of technology on mutually agreed terms is an important aspect of building capacity, stressing the need to close the artificial intelligence and other digital divides; and increase digital literacy;

(b) Enhancing digital infrastructure connectivity and access to technological innovations through stronger partnerships to help developing countries effectively participate throughout the life cycle of artificial intelligence systems and accelerate the inclusive and positive contribution of artificial intelligence systems to society, including towards the full realization of the 2030 Agenda and its Sustainable Development Goals, while ensuring that artificial intelligence systems around the world are safe, secure and trustworthy throughout their life cycle;

(c) Enhancing the ability of developing countries, in particular the least developed countries, to address major structural impediments and lift obstacles to accessing the benefits of new and emerging technologies and artificial intelligence innovation to achieve all 17 Sustainable Development Goals, including through scaling up the use of scientific sources, affordable technology, research and development, including through strengthened partnerships;

(d) Aiming to increase funding for Sustainable Development Goals related research and innovation related to digital technologies and safe, secure and trustworthy artificial intelligence systems and build capacity in all regions and countries to contribute to and benefit from this research;

(e) Enabling international innovation-based environments to enhance the ability of developing countries to develop technical expertise and capacities, harness data and compute resources, and national regulatory and governance approaches, frameworks and procurement capacity, and create an inclusive enabling environment at all levels for safe, secure and trustworthy artificial intelligence systems-based solutions;

(f) Urgently mobilizing means of implementation such as technology transfer on mutually agreed terms, capacity building to close the artificial intelligence and other digital divides, technical assistance and financing to developing countries related to artificial intelligence systems in accordance with developing countries' national needs, policies and priorities;

(g) Promoting the access to and design, development, deployment and use of safe, secure and trustworthy artificial intelligence systems to achieve sustainable development in its three dimensions – economic, social and environmental;

5. *Emphasizes* that human rights and fundamental freedoms must be respected, protected and promoted throughout the life cycle of artificial intelligence systems, calls upon all Member States and, where applicable, other stakeholders to refrain from or cease the use of artificial intelligence systems that are impossible to operate in compliance with international human rights law or that pose undue risks to the enjoyment of human rights, especially of those who are in vulnerable situations, and reaffirms that the same rights that people have offline must also be protected online, including throughout the life cycle of artificial intelligence systems;

6. *Encourages* all Member States, where appropriate, in line with their national priorities and circumstances and while implementing their distinct national regulatory and governance approaches and frameworks, and, where applicable, other stakeholders to promote safe, secure and trustworthy artificial intelligence systems in an inclusive and equitable manner, and for the benefit of all, and foster an enabling environment for such systems to address the world's greatest challenges, including achieving sustainable development in its three dimensions – economic, social and environmental – with specific consideration of developing countries and leaving no one behind by:

(a) Promoting the development and implementation of domestic regulatory and governance approaches and frameworks, in line with their respective national, and where applicable subnational, policies and priorities and obligations under international law, to support responsible and inclusive artificial intelligence innovation and investment for sustainable development, while simultaneously promoting safe, secure and trustworthy artificial intelligence systems;

(b) Encouraging effective measures, that promote innovation for the internationally interoperable identification, classification, evaluation, testing, prevention and mitigation of vulnerabilities and risks during the design and development and prior to the deployment and use of artificial intelligence systems;

(c) Encouraging the incorporation of feedback mechanisms to allow evidence-based discovery and reporting by end-users and third parties of technical vulnerabilities and, as appropriate, misuses of artificial intelligence systems and artificial intelligence incidents following their development, testing and deployment to address them;

(d) Raising public awareness and understanding of the core functions, capabilities, limitations and domains of appropriate civil use of artificial intelligence systems;

(e) Fostering the development, implementation and disclosure of mechanisms of risk monitoring and management, mechanisms for securing data, including personal data protection and privacy policies, as well as impact assessments as appropriate, across the life cycle of artificial intelligence systems;

(f) Strengthening investment in developing and implementing effective safeguards, including physical security, artificial intelligence systems security, and risk management across the life cycle of artificial intelligence systems;

(g) Encouraging the development and deployment of effective, accessible, adaptable, internationally interoperable technical tools, standards or practices, including reliable content authentication and provenance mechanisms – such as watermarking or labelling, where technically feasible and appropriate, that enable users to identify information manipulation, distinguish or determine the origins of authentic digital content and artificial intelligence-generated or manipulated digital content – and increasing media and information literacy;

(h) Facilitating the development and implementation of effective, internationally interoperable frameworks, practices and standards for training and testing artificial intelligence systems to enhance policymaking and to help protect individuals from all forms of discrimination, bias, misuse or other harm, and avoid reinforcing or perpetuating discriminatory or biased applications and outcomes throughout the life cycle of artificial intelligence systems, including, for example, by analysing and mitigating bias encoded in datasets and otherwise combating algorithmic discrimination and bias, while not inadvertently or disproportionally impacting the positive development, access and uses of other users and beneficiaries;

(i) Encouraging, where appropriate and relevant, the implementation of appropriate safeguards to respect intellectual property rights, including copyright-protected content, while promoting innovation;

(j) Safeguarding privacy and the protection of personal data when testing and evaluating systems, and for transparency and reporting requirements in compliance with applicable international, national and subnational legal frameworks, including on the use of personal data throughout the life cycle of artificial intelligence systems;

(k) Promoting transparency, predictability, reliability and understandability throughout the life cycle of artificial intelligence systems that make or support decisions impacting end-users, including providing notice and explanation, and promoting human oversight, such as, for example, through review of automated decisions and related processes or, where appropriate and relevant, human decision-making alternatives or effective redress and accountability for those adversely impacted by automated decisions of artificial intelligence systems;

(l) Strengthening investment in developing and implementing effective safeguards, including risk and impact assessments, throughout the life cycle of artificial intelligence systems to protect the exercise of and mitigate against the potential impact on the full and effective enjoyment of human rights and fundamental freedoms;

(m) Promoting artificial intelligence systems that advance, protect and preserve linguistic and cultural diversity, taking into account multilingualism in their training data and throughout the life cycle of the artificial intelligence system, particularly for the large language models;

(n) Intensifying information-sharing on mutually agreed terms among entities with roles across the life cycle of artificial intelligence systems to identify, understand and act using scientific and evidence-based best practices, policies and approaches to artificial intelligence systems to maximize the benefits while mitigating the potential risks across the life cycle of artificial intelligence systems, including advanced artificial intelligence systems;

(o) Encouraging research and international cooperation to understand, balance and address the potential benefits and risks related to the role of artificial intelligence systems in bridging digital divides and achieving all

17 Sustainable Development Goals, including the role of scaling up of digital solutions such as open-source artificial intelligence systems;

(p) Calling upon Member States to adopt specific measures to close the gender digital divide and to ensure that particular attention is paid to access, affordability, digital literacy, privacy and online safety, to enhance the use of digital technologies, including artificial intelligence systems, and to mainstream a disability, gender and racial equality perspective in policy decisions and the frameworks that guide them;

(q) Encouraging research and international cooperation to develop measures for the identification and assessment of the impacts of the deployment of artificial intelligence systems on labour markets, and providing support for the mitigation of potential negative consequences for workforces, especially in developing countries, in particular the least developed countries, and fostering programmes aimed at digital training, capacity building, supporting innovation and enhancing access to benefits of artificial intelligence systems;

7. *Recognizes also* that data is fundamental to the development and operation of artificial intelligence systems; emphasizes that the fair, inclusive, responsible and effective data governance, improving data generation, accessibility and infrastructure, and the use of digital public goods are essential to harnessing the potential of safe, secure and trustworthy artificial intelligence systems for sustainable development, and urges Member States to share best practices on data governance and to promote international cooperation, collaboration and assistance on data governance for greater consistency and interoperability, where feasible, of approaches for advancing trusted cross-border data flows for safe, secure and trustworthy artificial intelligence systems, and make its development more inclusive, equitable, effective and beneficial to all;

8. *Acknowledges* the importance of continuing the discussion on developments in the area of artificial intelligence governance so that international approaches keep pace with the evolution of artificial intelligence systems and their uses; and encourages continued efforts by the international community to promote inclusive research, mapping and analysis that benefit all parties on the potential impacts and applications that artificial intelligence systems and rapid technological change can have in the development of existing and new and emerging technologies and on accelerating the achievement of all 17 Sustainable Development Goals, and to inform how to develop, promote and implement effective, internationally interoperable safeguards, practices, standards and tools for artificial intelligence designers, developers, evaluators, deployers, users and other stakeholders for safe, secure and trustworthy artificial intelligence systems; as well as stresses the need for Governments, the private sector, civil society, international and regional organizations, academia and research institutions and technical communities and all other stakeholders to continue to work together, as appropriate; as well as acknowledges the need for more cohesive, effective, coordinated and inclusive engagement and participation of all communities, particularly from developing countries, in the inclusive governance of safe, secure and trustworthy artificial intelligence systems;

9. *Encourages* the private sector to adhere to applicable international and domestic laws and act in line with the United Nations Guiding Principles on Business and Human Rights: Implementing the United Nations "Protect, Respect and Remedy" Framework; acknowledges the importance of more inclusive and equitable access to the benefits of safe, secure and trustworthy artificial intelligence systems; and recognizes the need for increased collaboration, including between and within the public and private sectors and civil society, academia and research institutions and technical communities, to provide and promote fair, open, inclusive and non-discriminatory business environment, economic and commercial activities, competitive ecosystems and marketplaces across the life cycle of safe, secure and trustworthy artificial intelligence; as well as encourages Member States to develop policies and regulations to promote competition in safe, secure and trustworthy artificial intelligence systems and related technologies, including by supporting and enabling new opportunities for small businesses and entrepreneurs and technical talent, and enabling fair competition in the artificial intelligence marketplace, through critical investment, especially for developing countries;

10. *Calls upon* specialized agencies, funds, programmes, other entities, bodies and offices, and related organizations of the United Nations system, within their respective mandates and resources, to continue to assess and enhance their response to leverage the opportunities and address the challenges posed by artificial intelligence systems in a collaborative, coordinated and inclusive manner, through appropriate inter-agency mechanisms, including by conducting research, mapping and analysis that benefit all parties on the potential impacts and applications; reporting on progress and challenges in addressing issues; and cooperating with and assisting developing countries in capacity building, access and sharing the benefits of safe, secure and trustworthy artificial intelligence systems in achieving all

17 Sustainable Development Goals and sustainable development in its three dimensions – economic, social and environmental; stressing the need to close artificial intelligence and other digital divides between and within countries;

11. *Recalls* its resolution 76/307 of 8 September 2022 and its decision 77/568 of 1 September 2023 on the modalities and the scope of the Summit of the Future and, in this regard, looks forward to the development of a global digital compact;

12. *Looks forward also* to the overall review by the General Assembly, in 2025, of the progress made since the World Summit on the Information Society;

13. *Acknowledges* that the United Nations system, consistent with its mandate, uniquely contributes to reaching global consensus on safe, secure and trustworthy artificial intelligence systems, that is consistent with international law, in particular the Charter of the United Nations; the Universal Declaration of Human Rights; and the 2030 Agenda for Sustainable Development, including by promoting inclusive international cooperation and facilitating the inclusion, participation and representation of developing countries in deliberations.

RESOLUTION 78/266

Adopted at the 63rd plenary meeting, on 21 March 2024, without a vote, on the basis of draft resolution A/78/L.47, sponsored by: Afghanistan, Algeria, Armenia, Austria, Azerbaijan, Bahrain, Bangladesh, Belarus, Bolivia (Plurinational State of), Bosnia and Herzegovina, Botswana, Brazil, Burkina Faso, Cambodia, China, Colombia, Côte d'Ivoire, Cyprus, Djibouti, Egypt, Equatorial Guinea, Georgia, Germany, Greece, Guatemala, Guinea-Bissau, Hungary, India, Indonesia, Iran (Islamic Republic of), Israel, Jordan, Kazakhstan, Kuwait, Kyrgyzstan, Lao People's Democratic Republic, Latvia, Lebanon, Lesotho, Liberia, Maldives, Marshall Islands, Mongolia, Montenegro, Morocco, Mozambique, Myanmar, Nepal, Nicaragua, Nigeria, Oman, Pakistan, Palau, Panama, Paraguay, Peru, Philippines, Portugal, Qatar, Republic of Korea, Russian Federation, Rwanda, Samoa, Saudi Arabia, Senegal, Serbia, Seychelles, Singapore, Slovenia, Spain, Sri Lanka, Sudan, Suriname, Tajikistan, Thailand, Timor-Leste, Togo, Tunisia, Türkiye, Turkmenistan, United Arab Emirates, United Republic of Tanzania, Uzbekistan, Vanuatu, Venezuela (Bolivarian Republic of), Zimbabwe

78/266. International Year of Peace and Trust, 2025

The General Assembly,

Recognizing the important role of the United Nations in developing friendly relations among nations,

Reaffirming the Charter of the United Nations and its purposes and principles, and especially the commitment to settle disputes through peaceful means and the determination to save succeeding generations from the scourge of war,

Acknowledging that the approach of multilateralism and diplomacy could reinforce the advancement of the three pillars of the United Nations, namely, sustainable development, peace and security, and human rights, which are interconnected and mutually reinforcing, while observing respective mandates and the Charter,

Recalling its resolution 73/338 of 12 September 2019, by which it declared 2021 the International Year of Peace and Trust, and its resolution 76/299 of 28 July 2022, in which it noted the proclamation every five years of the United Nations International Year of Peace and Trust in order to focus the efforts of the United Nations and its Member States, with a view to promoting the ideals of peace and trust and demonstrating by all possible means their commitment to peace and trust,

Reaffirming the United Nations Millennium Declaration[61] and its resolution 70/1 of 25 September 2015, entitled "Transforming our world: the 2030 Agenda for Sustainable Development",

Recognizing the importance of the Declaration and Programme of Action on a Culture of Peace,[62] which serve as the universal mandate for the international community, particularly the United Nations system, for the promotion of a culture of peace and non-violence that benefits humanity, in particular future generations,

---

[61] Resolution 55/2.

[62] Resolutions 53/243 A and B.

Recognizing also that all efforts made by the United Nations system in general and the international community at large for the prevention of conflicts, the peaceful settlement of disputes, peacekeeping, peacebuilding, mediation, disarmament, sustainable development, the promotion of human dignity and human rights, social inclusion, democracy, the rule of law, good governance and gender equality at the national and international levels contribute greatly to a culture of peace,

Acknowledging that peace and trust entail accepting differences and having the ability to listen to, recognize, respect and appreciate others, as well as living in a peaceful and united way,

Recognizing the role of international, regional and subregional organizations, in accordance with their mandates, in the promotion and preservation of peace,

Recognizing also that peace not only is the absence of conflict, but also requires a positive, dynamic participatory process where dialogue is encouraged and conflicts are solved in a spirit of mutual understanding and cooperation,

Recognizing further the urgent need to promote and strengthen preventive diplomacy, inter alia, through multilateralism and political dialogue, and the important role of the United Nations in this regard,

Stressing the importance of preventive diplomacy in supporting the efforts of the United Nations to promote the peaceful settlement of conflicts, in order to preserve peace,

Recalling its resolution 72/130 of 8 December 2017, by which it declared 16 May as the International Day of Living Together in Peace, which constitutes a means of regularly mobilizing the efforts of the international community to promote peace, tolerance, inclusion, understanding and solidarity,

Recalling also its resolution 75/309 of 21 July 2021, by which it proclaimed 18 June as the International Day for Countering Hate Speech, as an observance that mobilizes annually the international community and the United Nations to promote peace, tolerance, inclusion, understanding and solidarity,

Emphasizing the role of women and youth, as well as the contribution of children and older persons in advancing a culture of peace, and in particular the importance of the active participation of women in the prevention and resolution of conflicts and in activities promoting a culture of peace, including in post-conflict situations,

Recognizing the importance of developing more peaceful societies through advancing equality, tolerance, human development and promoting human rights, and in this regard calling for investment in education, including through effective policies and practices, towards promoting respect, reconciliation and a culture of peace and non-violence,

Encouraging the continued and increasing efforts and activities on the part of civil society organizations throughout the world in advancing a culture of peace, as envisaged in the Declaration and Programme of Action on a Culture of Peace,

Emphasizing that the policy of neutrality declared and pursued by some States Members of the United Nations plays an important role in the development of peaceful, trust-based, friendly and mutually beneficial relations among the countries of the world and contributes to the strengthening of international peace and security at the regional and global levels,

Recalling its resolutions declaring zones of peace in Central Asia,[63] the South Atlantic[64] and the Indian Ocean,[65] and emphasizing the importance of these zones in maintaining stability and security in those regions,

Recognizing the capacity of the African Union and subregional organizations to address the root causes of conflict in Africa, while acknowledging the need for the provision of support by the international community and the United Nations, taking into account the responsibilities of the Organization in this regard according to the Charter of the United Nations, and reaffirming the primary responsibility of national Governments and authorities for peacebuilding,

[63] Resolution 76/299.

[64] Resolution 41/11.

[65] Resolution 2832 (XXVI).

Reaffirming its resolutions 53/199 of 15 December 1998 and 61/185 of 20 December 2006 on the proclamation of international years, and Economic and Social Council resolution 1980/67 of 25 July 1980 on international years and anniversaries, in particular paragraphs 1 to 10 of the annex thereto on the agreed criteria for the proclamation of international years, as well as paragraphs 13 and 14, in which it is stated that an international day or year should not be proclaimed before the basic arrangements for its organization and financing have been made,

1. *Proclaims* 2025 the International Year of Peace and Trust;

2. *Underlines* that the International Year of Peace and Trust constitutes a means of mobilizing the efforts of the international community to promote peace and trust among nations based on, inter alia, political dialogue, mutual understanding and cooperation, in order to build sustainable peace, solidarity and harmony;

3. *Reiterates* that the objective of the effective implementation of the Programme of Action on a Culture of Peace is to strengthen further the global movement for a culture of peace, and calls upon all concerned to renew their attention to this objective;

4. *Calls upon* the international community to resolve conflicts through inclusive dialogue and negotiation in order to ensure the strengthening of peace and trust in relations between Member States as a value that promotes sustainable development, peace and security, and human rights;

5. *Invites* the United Nations Educational, Scientific and Cultural Organization and the Department of Political and Peacebuilding Affairs of the Secretariat, mindful of the provisions contained in the annex to Economic and Social Council resolution 1980/67, to facilitate the implementation of the International Year;

6. *Encourages* all Member States, organizations of the United Nations system and other international, regional and subregional organizations, as well as other relevant stakeholders, including civil society, the private sector, academia and individuals, to observe the International Year of Peace and Trust, in an appropriate manner and to disseminate the advantages of peace and trust, including through educational and public awareness-raising activities;

7. *Takes note with appreciation* of the proposal of Turkmenistan to host the International Forum of Peace and Trust in December 2025, as a culminating event for the commemoration of the International Year;

8. *Stresses* that the cost of all activities that may arise from the implementation of the present resolution should be met from voluntary contributions;

9. *Invites* all relevant stakeholders to make voluntary contributions to the trust fund of the International Year and to provide other forms of support for its observance;

10. *Requests* the Secretary-General to bring the present resolution to the attention of all Member States, organizations of the United Nations system and other international and regional organizations, as well as relevant stakeholders, including civil society, the private sector, academia and individuals, for appropriate observance.

RESOLUTION 78/267

Adopted at the 63rd plenary meeting, on 21 March 2024, without a vote, on the basis of draft resolution A/78/L.45, sponsored by: Albania, Andorra, Argentina, Austria, Azerbaijan, Bahrain, Belarus, Belgium, Bosnia and Herzegovina, Bulgaria, Cambodia, Colombia, Croatia, Cyprus, Czechia, Dominican Republic, Ecuador, El Salvador, Equatorial Guinea, Georgia, Germany, Greece, Guatemala, Guinea-Bissau, Hungary, Indonesia, Israel, Italy, Jamaica, Japan, Kazakhstan, Kuwait, Kyrgyzstan, Latvia, Liechtenstein, Luxembourg, Maldives, Malta, Monaco, Montenegro, Morocco, Myanmar, Netherlands (Kingdom of the), Nigeria, North Macedonia, Paraguay, Peru, Philippines, Poland, Portugal, Qatar, Republic of Moldova, Romania, San Marino, Saudi Arabia, Slovakia, Slovenia, South Africa, Spain, Suriname, Tunisia, Ukraine, United Arab Emirates, United Republic of Tanzania, Uruguay, Uzbekistan, Zambia

78/267. International Day for the Prevention of and Fight against All Forms of Transnational Organized Crime

The General Assembly,

Guided by the Charter of the United Nations,

Recalling previous relevant resolutions of the General Assembly, in particular its resolutions 55/25 of 15 November 2000 and 55/255 of 31 May 2001, by which it adopted the United Nations Convention against Transnational Organized Crime and the Protocols thereto,[66] as well as its resolution 78/229 of 19 December 2023, entitled "Strengthening the United Nations crime prevention and criminal justice programme, in particular its technical cooperation capacity",

Recalling also previous relevant resolutions of the Economic and Social Council, the Commission on Crime Prevention and Criminal Justice and the Conference of the Parties to the United Nations Convention against Transnational Organized Crime, in particular its resolution 10/4 of 16 October 2020, entitled "Celebrating the twentieth anniversary of the adoption of the United Nations Convention against Transnational Organized Crime and promoting its effective implementation",[67]

Seriously concerned about the negative impact of transnational organized crime on security, stability, the rule of law and sustainable development,

Recognizing the importance of the prevention of and fight against transnational organized crime for the implementation of the 2030 Agenda for Sustainable Development,[68]

Reaffirming the importance of the Convention and the Protocols thereto as the main global tools available to the international community to prevent and fight all forms and manifestations of transnational organized crime, and protect the victims,

Emphasizing the particular relevance of the Convention as a legal basis for international cooperation in extradition and mutual legal assistance, as well as for other forms of judicial and law enforcement cooperation,

Recognizing the primary role and responsibility of States in preventing and combating transnational organized crime and in defining their crime prevention policies and strategies in this regard, and recalling the commitment of States parties to the Convention to carry out those obligations in a manner consistent with article 4 thereof,

Emphasizing that transnational organized crime must be addressed with full respect for the principle of the sovereignty of States and in accordance with the rule of law as part of a comprehensive response to promote durable solutions through the promotion of human rights and more equitable socioeconomic conditions,

Recognizing that technical assistance and economic development are fundamental to ensuring the effective implementation of the provisions of the Convention and the Protocols thereto, and recalling in this regard article 30 of the Convention,

Commemorating all victims of organized crime, including those who have lost their lives fighting such crime, in particular law enforcement and judicial personnel, and paying special tribute to all those persons, such as Judge Giovanni Falcone, whose work and sacrifice paved the way for the adoption of the Convention, and affirming that their legacy lives on through our global commitment to preventing and combating organized crime,

Recalling the important roles of civil society, non-governmental and community-based organizations, the private sector and academia in the prevention of and fight against transnational organized crime and the contributions that they can provide to such efforts,

Reaffirming its resolutions 53/199 of 15 December 1998 and 61/185 of 20 December 2006 on the proclamation of international years, and Economic and Social Council resolution 1980/67 of 25 July 1980 on international years and anniversaries, in particular paragraphs 1 to 10 of the annex thereto on the agreed criteria for the proclamation of international years, as well as paragraphs 13 and 14, in which it is stated that an international day or year should not be proclaimed before the basic arrangements for its organization and financing have been made,

1. *Decides* to declare 15 November the International Day for the Prevention of and Fight against All Forms of Transnational Organized Crime, in order to raise awareness of the threats posed by all forms of transnational organized crime and to enhance international cooperation in this regard;

---

[66] United Nations, *Treaty Series*, vols. 2225, 2237, 2241 and 2326, No. 39574.

[67] See CTOC/COP/2020/10, sect. I.A.

[68] Resolution 70/1.

2. *Invites* all Member States, the organizations of the United Nations system and other global and regional organizations, within existing resources, as well as other relevant stakeholders, including civil society, the private sector, academia and the media, to commemorate the International Day in an appropriate manner, including through educational and public awareness-raising activities, and to share best practices in this regard;

3. *Invites* the United Nations Office on Drugs and Crime, in collaboration with other relevant entities, to facilitate the observance of the International Day;

4. *Stresses* that the cost of all activities that may arise from the implementation of the present resolution shall be met from voluntary contributions;

5. *Requests* the Secretary-General to bring the present resolution to the attention of all Member States, the organizations of the United Nations system and civil society organizations for appropriate observance of the International Day.

RESOLUTION 78/268

Adopted at the 64th plenary meeting, on 25 March 2024, without a vote, on the basis of draft resolution A/78/L.53, sponsored by: Algeria, Andorra, Antigua and Barbuda, Armenia, Austria, Bahamas, Bahrain, Bangladesh, Barbados, Belgium, Belize, Bolivia (Plurinational State of), Bosnia and Herzegovina, Brazil, Brunei Darussalam, Bulgaria, Burkina Faso, Cabo Verde, Cambodia, Central African Republic, Chad, Chile, China, Colombia, Costa Rica, Croatia, Cuba, Cyprus, Czechia, Denmark, Djibouti, Dominican Republic, Ecuador, Egypt, El Salvador, Equatorial Guinea, Estonia, Eswatini, Fiji, Finland, France, Gambia, Georgia, Germany, Ghana, Greece, Grenada, Guatemala, Guinea-Bissau, Guyana, Haiti, Honduras, Hungary, Iceland, Indonesia, Ireland, Italy, Jamaica, Japan, Jordan, Kazakhstan, Kenya, Kiribati, Kuwait, Kyrgyzstan, Lao People's Democratic Republic, Latvia, Lebanon, Lesotho, Liberia, Libya, Liechtenstein, Lithuania, Luxembourg, Malawi, Malaysia, Maldives, Malta, Mauritania, Mauritius, Monaco, Mongolia, Montenegro, Morocco, Mozambique, Myanmar, Nepal, Netherlands (Kingdom of the), New Zealand, Nicaragua, Nigeria, North Macedonia, Oman, Pakistan, Palau, Panama, Paraguay, Peru, Philippines, Poland, Portugal, Qatar, Republic of Moldova, Romania, Saint Lucia, Saint Vincent and the Grenadines, Samoa, San Marino, Saudi Arabia, Senegal, Serbia, Singapore, Slovakia, Slovenia, Somalia, South Africa, Spain, Sri Lanka, Suriname, Sweden, Tajikistan, Thailand, Timor-Leste, Trinidad and Tobago, Tunisia, Türkiye, Turkmenistan, Uganda, Ukraine, United Arab Emirates, United Republic of Tanzania, United States of America, Uruguay, Uzbekistan, Vanuatu, Venezuela (Bolivarian Republic of), Viet Nam, Zambia

78/268. International Day of Play

The General Assembly,

Recalling its resolutions 53/199 of 15 December 1998 and 61/185 of 20 December 2006 on the proclamation of international years, and Economic and Social Council resolution 1980/67 of 25 July 1980 on international years and anniversaries, in particular paragraphs 1 to 10 of the annex thereto on the agreed criteria for the proclamation of international years, as well as paragraphs 13 and 14, in which it is stated that an international year should not be proclaimed before the basic arrangements for its organization and financing have been made,

Reaffirming the Universal Declaration of Human Rights,[69] the Convention on the Rights of the Child[70] and the Optional Protocols thereto,[71] and the Convention on the Rights of Persons with Disabilities,[72] and recalling all other relevant international human rights instruments,

Reaffirming also its resolution 70/1 of 25 September 2015, entitled "Transforming our world: the 2030 Agenda for Sustainable Development", in which it adopted a comprehensive, far-reaching and people-centred set of universal and transformative Sustainable Development Goals and targets, its commitment to working tirelessly for the full implementation of the Agenda by 2030, its recognition that eradicating poverty in all its forms and dimensions, including extreme poverty, is the greatest global challenge and an indispensable requirement for sustainable development, its commitment to achieving sustainable development in its three dimensions – economic, social and

[69] Resolution 217 A (III).

[70] United Nations, *Treaty Series*, vol. 1577, No. 27531.

[71] Ibid., vols. 2171, 2173 and 2983, No. 27531.

[72] Ibid., vol. 2515, No. 44910.

environmental – in a balanced and integrated manner, and to building upon the achievements of the Millennium Development Goals and seeking to address their unfinished business,

Recalling its resolution 75/131 of 14 December 2020, entitled "United Nations Decade of Healthy Ageing (2021–2030)",

Recognizing the role of play in building essential and transferable physical, social, cognitive, communication and emotional life skills at all ages, and its positive impact on promoting tolerance and resilience and facilitating social inclusion, conflict prevention and peacebuilding,

Recognizing also the importance of access to play and recreational activities and their contributions to the physical and psychosocial well-being and development of children and youth, regardless of race, colour, sex, language, religion, political or other opinion, national, ethnic or social origin, property, disability, birth or other status,

Acknowledging that play and recreation are essential to the health and well-being of children and promote the development of creativity, imagination, self-confidence, self-efficacy and sense of responsibility, as well as physical, social, cognitive, communication and emotional strength and skills,

1. *Decides* to proclaim 11 June as the International Day of Play, to be observed annually;

2. *Invites* all States Members of the United Nations, members of the specialized agencies and observers of the General Assembly, as well as the organizations of the United Nations system, other international, regional and subregional organizations and other relevant stakeholders, including civil society, the private sector and academia, to observe the International Day of Play in an appropriate manner through activities aimed at education and awareness-raising of the importance of play;

3. *Invites* the United Nations Children's Fund and the United Nations Educational, Scientific and Cultural Organization to facilitate the observance of the International Day of Play, mindful of the criteria set out in the annex to Economic and Social Council resolution 1980/67;

4. *Stresses* that the costs of all activities that may arise from the implementation of the present resolution should be met through voluntary contributions, including from the private sector;

5. *Requests* the Secretary-General to bring the present resolution to the attention of all States Members of the United Nations, members of the specialized agencies and observers of the General Assembly, as well as the organizations of the United Nations system and other relevant stakeholders, for appropriate observance of the International Day of Play.

RESOLUTION 78/269

Adopted at the 64th plenary meeting, on 25 March 2024, without a vote, on the basis of draft resolution A/78/L.50, submitted by the President of the General Assembly, and as orally revised

78/269. Scope, modalities, format and organization of the high-level meeting on antimicrobial resistance convened by the President of the General Assembly

The General Assembly,

Recalling its resolution 76/257 of 29 March 2022, entitled "Elevating pandemic prevention, preparedness and response to the highest level of political leadership", in which it decided to hold a high-level meeting in 2024 on antimicrobial resistance and requested the President of the General Assembly to appoint two co-facilitators to present options and modalities for the conduct of such a meeting, including potential deliverables, in collaboration with the World Health Organization, the Food and Agriculture Organization of the United Nations, the World Organisation for Animal Health and the United Nations Environment Programme, the Quadripartite organizations, and with the support of the Global Leaders Group on Antimicrobial Resistance,

Reaffirming its commitment to the political declaration of the high-level meeting of the General Assembly on antimicrobial resistance in 2016,[73] in which it reiterated that antimicrobial resistance challenges the sustainability and

[73] Resolution 71/3.

effectiveness of the public health response to communicable diseases and epidemics, as well as imperils the gains in health and development and the attainment of the 2030 Agenda for Sustainable Development,[74]

Acknowledging that, owing to antimicrobial resistance, many achievements of the twentieth century are being gravely challenged, in particular the reduction in illness and death from infectious diseases achieved through social and economic development; access to health services and to quality, safe, efficacious and affordable medicines; hygiene, safe water and sanitation; disease prevention in community and health-care settings, including immunization; nutrition and healthy food; improvements in human and veterinary medicine; and the introduction of new antimicrobial and other medicines,

Recognizing the importance of addressing growing antimicrobial resistance to contribute to the achievement of the 2030 Agenda for Sustainable Development,

Mindful of the need to summon and maintain strong national, regional and international political commitment to addressing antimicrobial resistance comprehensively and multisectorally, and to increase and improve awareness of antimicrobial resistance,

Taking note of the 2019 report of the Secretary-General on the implementation of the political declaration of the high-level meeting of the General Assembly on antimicrobial resistance,[75] the Strategic Framework for collaboration on antimicrobial resistance of the Quadripartite organizations and the work of the Quadripartite Joint Secretariat on Antimicrobial Resistance, which consolidates their cooperation,

Taking note also of the High-level Interactive Dialogue on Antimicrobial Resistance, convened by the President of the General Assembly in 2021, and of the Call to Action on Antimicrobial Resistance – 2021,[76]

Taking note further of the contributions by the Ministerial Conferences on Antimicrobial Resistance in 2014 and 2019 in the Netherlands, the Third Global High-level Ministerial Conference on Antimicrobial Resistance in 2022 in Oman, during which 47 Member States endorsed the Muscat Ministerial Manifesto, the forthcoming Fourth Global High-level Ministerial Conference on Antimicrobial Resistance in Saudi Arabia, and other planned ministerial conferences in 2024,

Recalling the organization of the 2023 high-level meetings of the General Assembly on pandemic prevention, preparedness and response, on universal health coverage, and on the fight against tuberculosis and the adoption of the three political declarations,[77]

Emphasizing the important role and the responsibilities of Governments, as well as the role of relevant intergovernmental organizations, particularly the World Health Organization in coordination with the Food and Agriculture Organization of the United Nations, the United Nations Environment Programme and the World Organisation for Animal Health within their mandates and as appropriate, in preventing, addressing and responding to the challenges of antimicrobial resistance, and the essential need for multisectoral and cross-sectoral efforts and the engagement of all relevant sectors of society, such as human and veterinary medicine, agriculture, finance, environment, development, research, education and consumers, to generate an effective response, including towards a "One Health" approach,

Recalling World Health Assembly resolution 68.7 of 26 May 2015, entitled "Global action plan on antimicrobial resistance",[78] and World Health Assembly resolution 72.5 of 28 May 2019, entitled "Antimicrobial resistance",[79] which reflect a global consensus that antimicrobial resistance poses a significant public health challenge, and emphasize the paramount significance of achieving the five strategic objectives of the global action plan,

Taking note of the report of the Inter-Agency Coordination Group on Antimicrobial Resistance and its recommendations to the Secretary-General of April 2019,

---

[74] Resolution 70/1.

[75] A/73/869.

[76] A/75/903, annex.

[77] Resolution 78/3, annex, resolution 78/4, annex, and resolution 78/5, annex.

[78] See World Health Organization, document WHA68/2015/REC/1.

[79] See World Health Organization, document WHA72/2019/REC/1.

1. *Decides* that the one-day high-level meeting on antimicrobial resistance to be convened by the President of the General Assembly shall be held at United Nations Headquarters in New York on 26 September 2024 during the general debate of the Assembly at its seventy-ninth session, from 10 a.m. to 6 p.m., and shall consist of an opening segment, a plenary segment for general discussion, two multi-stakeholder panels and a brief closing segment;

2. *Also decides* that the overall theme of the high-level meeting will be "Investing in the present and securing our future together: accelerating multisectoral global, regional and national actions to address antimicrobial resistance";

3. *Further decides* that:

(a) The opening segment, to be held from 10 to 10.45 a.m., will feature statements by the President of the General Assembly, the President of the Economic and Social Council, the Secretary-General, the Director General of the World Health Organization, the Director General of the Food and Agriculture Organization of the United Nations, the Executive Director of the United Nations Environment Programme, the Director General of the World Organisation for Animal Health, the President of the World Bank, a representative of the Global Leaders Group on Antimicrobial Resistance, as well as a person affected by antimicrobial resistance, selected in consultation with Member States by the President of the General Assembly and giving due consideration to gender balance and geographical representation;

(b) The plenary segment, to be held from 10.45 a.m. to 5.30 p.m., will comprise statements by Member States and observers of the General Assembly; a list of speakers will be established in accordance with established practices of the Assembly, and the time limits for these statements will be three minutes for individual delegations and five minutes for statements made on behalf of a group of States;

(c) The closing segment, to be held from 5.30 to 6 p.m., will comprise summaries of the multi-stakeholder panels and concluding remarks by the President of the General Assembly and a representative of the Global Leaders Group on Antimicrobial Resistance, as well as a person affected by antimicrobial resistance;

4. *Decides* that the organizational arrangements for the two multi-stakeholder panels will be as follows:

(a) Two multi-stakeholder panels will be held in parallel to the plenary segment, one from 11 a.m. to 1 p.m. and the other from 3 to 5 p.m.;

(b) The multi-stakeholder panels will address the following themes:

Panel 1: Addressing the urgent global risk of antimicrobial resistance across the human, animal, plant and environmental sectors through equity, access, building awareness and innovation;

Panel 2: Addressing human health, animal health, agrifood systems and protecting the environment to tackle antimicrobial resistance, through surveillance, capacity-building, sustainable resources, financing and investment;

(c) Each of the two multi-stakeholder panels will be co-chaired by two representatives, one from a developed country and one from a developing country, to be appointed by the President of the General Assembly from among the Heads of State or Government attending the high-level meeting, in consultation with Member States, taking into account gender balance, level of development and geographical representation;

(d) The President of the General Assembly may invite parliamentarians, local governments, the heads or senior representatives of relevant United Nations entities, including the World Health Organization, the Food and Agriculture Organization of the United Nations, the United Nations Environment Programme as well as the World Organisation for Animal Health, and international financial institutions, development partners, civil society, the private sector, academia, medical and scientific associations, Indigenous Peoples, representative organizations of people affected by antimicrobial resistance, persons with disabilities and community organizations to serve as speakers on the panels, taking into account gender balance, level of development, geographical representation and the representation of youth and older persons;

5. *Also decides* that the high-level meeting shall approve a concise and action-oriented political declaration with a shared vision including the consideration of measurable targets and objectives on, inter alia, mobilizing political will and action at the national, regional and international levels to address the drivers, sources and challenges of

antimicrobial resistance, agreed in advance by consensus through intergovernmental negotiations, to be submitted by the President of the General Assembly for adoption by the Assembly;

6. *Requests* the President of the General Assembly, with the support of the World Health Organization, the Food and Agriculture Organization of the United Nations, the United Nations Environment Programme, the World Organisation for Animal Health and other relevant partners, to organize and preside over an interactive multi-stakeholder hearing, before the end of June 2024, with the active participation of regional organizations, non-governmental organizations in consultative status with the Economic and Social Council, invited civil society organizations, philanthropic foundations, academia, medical associations, the private sector including the agriculture and food industry, broader communities, ensuring the participation and voices of women, children, youth, Indigenous Peoples, and people of African descent, as well as appropriate senior-level representatives of Member States, observers of the General Assembly, parliamentarians, representatives of local governments, and relevant United Nations entities, as part of the preparatory process for the high-level meeting, and also requests the President to prepare a summary of the hearing prior to the high-level meeting;

7. *Encourages* all Member States and members of the United Nations specialized agencies to participate in the high-level meeting, including the multi-stakeholder panels, at the highest possible level, preferably at the level of Heads of State and Government, and invites all observers of the General Assembly to be represented at the highest possible level;

8. *Invites* the United Nations system, including funds, programmes and specialized agencies, including the World Health Organization, the Food and Agriculture Organization of the United Nations, the United Nations Environment Programme as well as the World Organisation for Animal Health, the Global Leaders Group on Antimicrobial Resistance, the Inter-Parliamentary Union, regional commissions and relevant envoys of the Secretary-General, to participate in the high-level meeting, as appropriate, and urges them to consider relevant initiatives, such as the 2021 Call to Action on Antimicrobial Resistance, in support of the preparatory process and the high-level meeting, particularly with regard to sharing evidence and good practices, challenges and lessons learned;

9. *Invites* non-governmental organizations with relevant expertise that are in consultative status with the Economic and Social Council to register with the Secretariat to attend the high-level meeting and participate in the interactive multi-stakeholder hearing and the multi-stakeholder panels;

10. *Invites* members of civil society, non-governmental organizations, the private sector, academia, including research institutes, development partners and other relevant initiatives to make a fundamental contribution to the process in terms of raising awareness of the importance of addressing antimicrobial resistance;

11. *Requests* the President of the General Assembly to draw up a list of representatives of other relevant non-governmental organizations, civil society organizations, academic institutions and the private sector who may participate in the high-level meeting, including its panel discussions, taking into account the principles of transparency and equitable geographical representation, with due regard for gender parity, to submit the proposed list to Member States for their consideration on a non-objection basis[80] and to bring the list to the attention of the Assembly for a final decision by the Assembly on participation in the high-level meeting;

12. *Encourages* Member States and members of the United Nations specialized agencies to include in their delegations to the high-level meeting ministers from all relevant ministries, as appropriate, representatives such as parliamentarians, mayors and governors, representatives of civil society, including non-governmental organizations, Indigenous Peoples, people of African descent, community organizations and faith-based organizations, academic institutions and the private sector with expertise in antimicrobial resistance, philanthropic foundations, and networks representing people affected by antimicrobial resistance, with due regard to gender balance and geographical representation;

13. *Decides* that the proceedings of the high-level meeting and the multi-stakeholder hearing shall be webcast, and encourages the President of the General Assembly, the Secretary-General and the Director General of the World Health Organization, the Director General of the Food and Agriculture Organization of the United Nations, the

[80] The list will include proposed as well as final names. The general basis of any objections, if requested by one or more States Members of the United Nations or States members of the specialized agencies, will be made known to the Office of the President of the General Assembly and the requester.

Executive Director of the United Nations Environment Programme and the Director General of the World Organisation for Animal Health to give the highest visibility to the high-level meeting, through all relevant media platforms and information and communications technologies.

RESOLUTION 78/270

Adopted at the 65th plenary meeting, on 3 April 2024, without a vote, on the basis of draft resolution A/78/L.54, sponsored by: Albania, Angola, Armenia, Austria, Belgium, Bosnia and Herzegovina, Botswana, Bulgaria, Burkina Faso, Burundi, Chile, Côte d'Ivoire, Croatia, Cyprus, Czechia, Democratic Republic of the Congo, Equatorial Guinea, Estonia, Finland, France, Germany, Greece, Guinea-Bissau, Guyana, Hungary, India, Italy, Japan, Latvia, Liberia, Luxembourg, Malawi, Mali, Malta, Mauritania, Montenegro, Mozambique, Namibia, Netherlands (Kingdom of the), Nicaragua, North Macedonia, Poland, Portugal, Russian Federation, Senegal, Singapore, Slovakia, Slovenia, South Africa, Sweden, Switzerland, Timor-Leste, United Arab Emirates, United Republic of Tanzania, Zimbabwe

78/270. The role of diamonds in fuelling conflict: breaking the link between the illicit transaction of rough diamonds and armed conflict as a contribution to prevention and settlement of conflicts

The General Assembly,

Recognizing that the trade in conflict diamonds continues to be a matter of serious international concern, which can be directly linked to the fuelling of armed conflict, the activities of rebel movements aimed at undermining or overthrowing legitimate Governments and the illicit traffic in and proliferation of armaments, especially small arms and light weapons,

Recognizing also the devastating impact of conflicts fuelled by the trade in conflict diamonds on peace and the safety and security of people in affected countries, and the systematic and gross human rights violations that have been perpetrated in such conflicts,

Expressing deep concern regarding the unprecedented challenges faced by the Kimberley Process arising from ongoing geopolitical tensions and conflicts,

Noting the negative impact of such conflicts on regional stability and the obligations placed upon States by the Charter of the United Nations regarding the maintenance of international peace and security, and recognizing that continued action to curb the trade in conflict diamonds is imperative,

Noting also that the Kimberley Process remains a unique tripartite initiative that brings together stakeholders in Government, industry and civil society in its quest to prevent conflict diamonds from entering the diamond trade and has had a valuable development impact in improving the lives of people in some diamond-mining communities and contributing to the achievement of the 2030 Agenda for Sustainable Development[81] and the Sustainable Development Goals,

Noting with appreciation that the Kimberley Process, as an international initiative led by participants, has pursued its deliberations on an inclusive basis involving concerned stakeholders, including producing, exporting and importing States, the diamond industry and civil society, as well as applicant States and international organizations,

Recalling that conflict prevention and the elimination of conflict diamonds from legitimate trade is the primary objective of the Kimberley Process, and stressing the need to continue its activities in order to achieve this objective,

Welcoming the important contribution of the Kimberley Process, which was initiated by African diamond-producing countries and supported by other Kimberley Process participants, and calling for the consistent implementation of commitments made by Kimberley Process participants and the diamond industry and civil society organizations, as observers,

Acknowledging the role that the Kimberley Process has played, in the past 21 years, in stemming the flow of conflict diamonds and the significant development impact it has had in improving the lives of many people dependent on the trade in diamonds, and noting that the plenary meeting of the Kimberley Process, in looking towards the future,

[81] Resolution 70/1.

committed to continue to ensure that the Kimberley Process remains relevant as a credible tool in curbing the flow of conflict diamonds, capturing the evolving nature of conflicts and realities on the ground,

Acknowledging also that the diamond sector is an important catalyst for promoting economic and social development, which are necessary for poverty reduction and achieving the Sustainable Development Goals in many producing countries, particularly in developing countries,

Bearing in mind the positive benefits of the legitimate diamond trade to producing countries, workers and their communities, and underlining the need for continued regional and international action to prevent the problem of conflict diamonds from negatively affecting the trade in legitimate diamonds, which makes a critical contribution to the economies of producing, exporting and importing States,

Noting that the total elimination of conflict diamonds from the diamond market continues to be the primary objective of the Kimberley Process, and stressing the need for the Kimberley Process to continue evolving to meet the social and environmental challenges in line with the 2030 Agenda and the Sustainable Development Goals,

Recognizing that the Kimberley Process promotes legitimate rough diamond trade, and recalling the positive benefits of legitimate diamond trade to producing countries, including its transparency and accountability throughout the diamond industry, and the contribution it has made to the economies of producing, exporting and importing States, and therefore underlining the need for continued international action with regard to the ethical exploitation, sale and trade of rough diamonds,

Expressing appreciation for the continuous efforts made by Botswana in supporting the operationalization of the Kimberley Process secretariat in Gaborone,

Welcoming the efforts to enhance regional cooperation on Kimberley Process matters, including among artisanal and alluvial diamond-producing countries in Central Africa and the Mano River Union, and encouraging the sharing of lessons and increased capacity-building for the Certification Scheme,

Recalling the Charter and all the relevant resolutions of the General Assembly and of the Security Council related to conflict diamonds, and determined to contribute to and support the implementation of the measures provided for in those resolutions,

Recalling also General Assembly resolution 55/56 of 1 December 2001 and Security Council resolution 1459 (2003) of 28 January 2003, in which the Assembly and the Council strongly supported the Kimberley Process Certification Scheme as a valuable contribution in breaking the link between the illicit transaction of rough diamonds and armed conflict as a contribution to prevention and settlement of conflicts,

Noting that the implementation of the Kimberley Process Certification Scheme continues to have a positive impact in reducing the opportunity for conflict diamonds to play a role in fuelling armed conflict and helps to protect legitimate trade and ensure the effective implementation of the relevant resolutions on trade in conflict diamonds,

Acknowledging that lessons learned from the Peacebuilding Commission may be useful for some Kimberley Process participants and that some Kimberley Process participants may also have experiences to share with respect to peacebuilding, as appropriate,

Recognizing that the ongoing and regular review and reform of the Kimberley Process is necessary to keep pace with and aim to address the ongoing threat of instability, conflict and contemporary challenges in the diamond trade in order for the Kimberley Process to continue to fulfil its mandate in the regulation of the trade of rough diamonds and the prevention of conflicts,

Welcoming the decision of the 59 Kimberley Process participants, representing 85 countries, including the 27 States members of the European Union represented by the European Commission, to address the problem of conflict diamonds by participating in the Kimberley Process and implementing the Kimberley Process Certification Scheme,

Recognizing that State sovereignty should be fully respected and that the principles of equality, mutual benefits and consensus should be adhered to, and welcoming the implementation of the Kimberley Process Certification Scheme in such a way as not to impede the legitimate trade in diamonds or impose an undue burden on Governments or industry, particularly smaller producers, and not to hinder the development of the diamond industry,

Recognizing also that the Kimberley Process Certification Scheme, which came into effect on 1 January 2003, will be credible only if all participants have the requisite national legislation coupled with effective and credible internal systems of control designed to eliminate the presence of conflict diamonds in the chain of producing, exporting and importing rough diamonds within their own territories and across their borders, while taking into account that differences in production methods and trading practices, as well as differences in the institutional controls thereof, may require different approaches to meeting minimum standards, and encouraging all participants to work towards overall compliance with the Kimberley Process standards,

Welcoming the voluntary system of industry self-regulation through the System of Warranties, in accordance with the Kimberley Process Certification Scheme core document, that supports the effectiveness of the Certification Scheme,

Noting that the Kimberley Process established the Ad Hoc Committee on Review and Reform of the Kimberley Process, as articulated under paragraph 20 of the Kimberley Process Certification Scheme core document,

Expressing appreciation to Zimbabwe, as the 2023 Chair of the Kimberley Process, for its efforts in promoting the continuation of work, and for hosting the nineteenth plenary meeting of the Kimberley Process in Victoria Falls, from 6 to 10 November 2023, in a hybrid format,

Noting with regret that the 2023 Kimberley Process plenary meeting ended without consensus on a communiqué,

1. *Recognizes* that the Kimberley Process Certification Scheme helps to ensure the effective implementation of relevant resolutions of the Security Council containing sanctions on the trade in conflict diamonds and contributes to the prevention of conflicts fuelled by diamonds, and calls for the full implementation of existing Council measures targeting the illicit trade in rough diamonds, particularly diamonds which play a role in fuelling conflicts;

2. *Also recognizes* the important contributions that the international efforts to address the problem of conflict diamonds, including the Kimberley Process, have made and can make to the settlement of conflicts and the consolidation of peace;

3. *Notes* that the annual reporting process on Kimberley Process Certification Scheme implementation is the main comprehensive and regular source of information on the implementation of the Kimberley Process provided by participants, and calls upon participants to submit consistent and substantive annual reports in order to conform to this requirement;

4. *Also notes* the adoption of the administrative decision on the Ad Hoc Committee on Review and Reform, in particular its paragraph 4.1, whereby the Kimberley Process entrusted the Committee:

(a) To review and propose, for the plenary's adoption, a definition of "conflict diamonds" which captures the evolving nature of conflicts and the realities on the ground;

(b) To strengthen Kimberley Process Certification Scheme implementation with regard to technical assistance between participants in rough diamond mining and trading;

(c) To consider conducting a structural review of the Kimberley Process with a view to addressing challenges facing communities impacted by diamond mining activities, through corporate social responsibility and support for artisanal and small-scale mining communities;

(d) To clarify the Kimberley Process position on total country compliance or partial compliance zoning in producing countries;

(e) To consider strengthening Kimberley Process governance;

5. *Reaffirms* the commitment of the Kimberley Process to continue its cooperation with the World Customs Organization and the intention to work on reviewing the explanatory notes of the harmonized system code to further engage with the World Customs Organization on processes and technologies now used in diamond cutting and polishing;

6. *Welcomes* the decision by the 2022 plenary meeting of the Kimberley Process to establish the Kimberley Process secretariat in Gaborone;

7. *Stresses* the decision by the plenary that, while financial contributions to the Kimberley Process secretariat are not mandatory for Kimberley Process members, such contributions are critical to the proper functioning of the

Kimberley Process secretariat, and therefore encourages Member States to also voluntarily support the operationalization of the secretariat;

8. *Recalls* its resolution 77/277 of 29 March 2023, in which it noted the plenary's views of the Kimberley Process as an effective multilateral tool for conflict prevention in stemming the flow of conflict diamonds, and its valuable development impact in improving the lives of people in some diamond-producing countries and its contribution to the 2030 Agenda for Sustainable Development and the Sustainable Development Goals;

9. *Reaffirms* the importance of the tripartite nature of the Kimberley Process, stresses that the widest possible participation in the Kimberley Process Certification Scheme is essential, and therefore encourages participants to contribute to the work of the Kimberley Process by participating actively in the Certification Scheme and ensuring compliance with its undertakings and the effective implementation of its measures, underscores the importance of the Civil Society Coalition and its members to the Kimberley Process, and acknowledges the importance of supporting additional applications for membership by civil society organizations;

10. *Recalls* the central place of mining communities in the Kimberley Process and the need to devote particular attention to engaging Kimberley Process stakeholders and communities, especially artisanal miners, in governance structures, developing best practices, and promoting the rule of law;

11. *Reaffirms* the importance of enhancing cooperation with and assistance to participants in Kimberley Process matters, including with a regional dimension, focusing on the implementation of best practices, capacity-building and compliance with Kimberley Process standards, rules and procedures;

12. *Encourages* the continued implementation of the Declaration on Supporting Principles for Responsible Diamond Sourcing as Best Practices for the benefit of the global diamond industry and communities;

13. *Recognizes* the value of engaging with relevant external organizations to support the work of the Kimberley Process and its working bodies;

14. *Encourages* further strengthening of the Kimberley Process to enhance its effectiveness in addressing challenges posed to the diamond industry and related communities, including from instability and conflict, and to ensure that the Kimberley Process remains relevant for the future and continues to contribute to international peace and security and the achievement of the 2030 Agenda and the Sustainable Development Goals, and looks forward to further exploring and advancing the ways in which the Kimberley Process contributes to peacebuilding and sustaining peace;

15. *Acknowledges with great appreciation* the important contribution that Zimbabwe, as Chair of the Kimberley Process in 2023, made to the efforts to curb the trade in conflict diamonds, and welcomes the succession of the United Arab Emirates as Chair of the Kimberley Process for 2024;

16. *Requests* the Chair of the Kimberley Process to submit to the General Assembly at its seventy-ninth session a report on the implementation of the Kimberley Process;

17. *Decides* to include in the provisional agenda of its seventy-ninth session the item entitled "The role of diamonds in fuelling conflict".

RESOLUTION 78/271

Adopted at the 69th plenary meeting, on 11 April 2024, without a vote, on the basis of draft resolution A/78/L.58, submitted by the President of the General Assembly

78/271. Further modalities of the Fourth International Conference on Financing for Development

The General Assembly,

Recalling its resolution 78/231 of 22 December 2023, in which it decided to convene the Fourth International Conference on Financing for Development in 2025 and welcomed the offer by the Government of Spain to host the Conference,

1. *Decides* that the Fourth International Conference on Financing for Development:

(a) Shall be held in Spain from 30 June to 3 July 2025, and that the Conference shall be held at the highest possible political level, including Heads of State or Government, relevant ministers, including ministers for finance, foreign affairs and development cooperation and special representatives and other representatives, as appropriate;

(b) Shall result in an intergovernmentally negotiated and agreed outcome and shall also result in summaries of the plenary meetings, round tables and other deliberations of the Conference, to be included in the report of the Conference;

2. *Also decides* that the Conference and its preparatory process shall be open to participation by all States Members of the United Nations or States members of the specialized agencies and observers in the General Assembly, in accordance with arrangements utilized for previous international conferences on financing for development, and looks forward to the efforts of the hosting Governments and the Secretariat to facilitate the participation of all States Members of the United Nations or States members of the specialized agencies and observers in the General Assembly, as needed and appropriate;

3. *Further decides*:

(a) To invite other relevant intergovernmental organizations, international financial institutions and other interested international bodies that were accredited to the previous international conferences on financing for development held in Monterrey, Mexico, in Doha and in Addis Ababa or to their follow-up processes, as well as relevant organizations and bodies of the United Nations system, including associate members of the regional commissions,[82] to participate in the deliberations of the Conference and its preparatory process, as appropriate, in accordance with the rules of procedure of the Conference;

(b) To invite interested intergovernmental organizations that were not accredited to the conferences and meetings referred to in paragraph 3 (a) above to apply for accreditation following the established accreditation procedure, subject to the approval of the Preparatory Committee for the Conference or the General Assembly;

4. *Stresses* the importance of the effective participation of all relevant stakeholders, including civil society, academia and the private sector, in the Conference and its preparatory process, and decides:

(a) To invite non-governmental organizations that are in consultative status with the Economic and Social Council, as well as those that were accredited to the conferences and meetings referred to in paragraph 3 (a) above, to register with the Secretariat in order to participate in the Conference and its preparatory process;

(b) To request the President of the General Assembly to draw up a list of representatives of other relevant non-governmental organizations, civil society organizations, academic institutions and the private sector who may participate in the Conference and its preparatory process, taking into account the principles of transparency and of equitable geographical representation and with due regard for gender parity, and to submit the proposed list to Member States for their consideration on a non-objection basis and bring the list to the attention of the Assembly for a final decision by the Assembly on participation in the Conference and its preparatory process;[83]

5. *Decides* that substantive preparations should be carried out in a most effective, well-structured and broad participatory manner and that, for this purpose, the Department of Economic and Social Affairs of the Secretariat, through its Financing for Sustainable Development Office, and the relevant organizations of the United Nations system, including the regional commissions, within their respective mandates and available resources, should provide the necessary support to the Conference and its preparatory process;

6. *Invites* the regional commissions, with the support of regional development banks and other relevant entities, to hold regional consultations, as appropriate, the outcome of which could serve as input to the preparations for the Conference;

[82] American Samoa, Anguilla, Aruba, Bermuda, the British Virgin Islands, the Cayman Islands, the Commonwealth of the Northern Mariana Islands, Curaçao, French Polynesia, Guam, Montserrat, New Caledonia, Puerto Rico, Sint Maarten, the Turks and Caicos Islands and the United States Virgin Islands.

[83] The list will include proposed as well as final names. The general basis of any objections, if requested by one or more States Members of the United Nations or States members of the specialized agencies, will be made known to the Office of the President of the General Assembly and the requester.

7. *Invites* the Economic and Social Council to contribute to the preparations for the Conference, as appropriate, including through its forum on financing for development follow-up and the special high-level meeting with the World Bank, the International Monetary Fund, the World Trade Organization and the United Nations Conference on Trade and Development to be held during the forum in 2024.

RESOLUTION 78/272

Adopted at the 73rd plenary meeting, on 24 April 2024, by a recorded vote of 164 to 2, with 2 abstentions,* on the basis of draft resolution A/78/L.41, sponsored by Singapore

* *In favour:* Albania, Algeria, Andorra, Antigua and Barbuda, Argentina, Armenia, Australia, Austria, Bahamas, Bahrain, Bangladesh, Barbados, Belarus, Belgium, Belize, Bhutan, Bolivia (Plurinational State of), Bosnia and Herzegovina, Botswana, Brazil, Brunei Darussalam, Bulgaria, Burundi, Cabo Verde, Cambodia, Cameroon, Canada, Chad, Chile, China, Colombia, Comoros, Congo, Costa Rica, Côte d'Ivoire, Croatia, Cuba, Cyprus, Czechia, Democratic Republic of the Congo, Denmark, Djibouti, Dominica, Dominican Republic, Egypt, El Salvador, Equatorial Guinea, Eritrea, Estonia, Eswatini, Ethiopia, Fiji, Finland, France, Gabon, Gambia, Georgia, Germany, Ghana, Greece, Grenada, Guatemala, Guinea, Guyana, Haiti, Honduras, Hungary, Iceland, India, Indonesia, Iran (Islamic Republic of), Iraq, Ireland, Israel, Italy, Jamaica, Japan, Jordan, Kenya, Kuwait, Lao People's Democratic Republic, Latvia, Lebanon, Lesotho, Liechtenstein, Lithuania, Luxembourg, Madagascar, Malawi, Malaysia, Maldives, Mali, Malta, Marshall Islands, Mauritania, Mauritius, Mexico, Micronesia (Federated States of), Monaco, Mongolia, Montenegro, Morocco, Mozambique, Myanmar, Namibia, Nauru, Nepal, Netherlands (Kingdom of the), New Zealand, Nigeria, North Macedonia, Norway, Oman, Pakistan, Palau, Panama, Papua New Guinea, Paraguay, Peru, Philippines, Poland, Portugal, Qatar, Republic of Korea, Republic of Moldova, Romania, Rwanda, Saint Kitts and Nevis, Saint Lucia, Saint Vincent and the Grenadines, Samoa, San Marino, Saudi Arabia, Senegal, Seychelles, Sierra Leone, Singapore, Slovakia, Slovenia, Solomon Islands, South Africa, Spain, Sri Lanka, Sudan, Suriname, Sweden, Switzerland, Thailand, Timor-Leste, Trinidad and Tobago, Tunisia, Tuvalu, Uganda, Ukraine, United Arab Emirates, United Kingdom of Great Britain and Northern Ireland, United Republic of Tanzania, United States of America, Uruguay, Vanuatu, Viet Nam, Yemen, Zambia, Zimbabwe
Against: Russian Federation, Syrian Arab Republic
Abstaining: Angola, Togo

78/272. Agreement under the United Nations Convention on the Law of the Sea on the Conservation and Sustainable Use of Marine Biological Diversity of Areas beyond National Jurisdiction

The General Assembly,

Recalling its resolution 72/249 of 24 December 2017, in which it decided to convene an intergovernmental conference, under the auspices of the United Nations, to consider the recommendations of the Preparatory Committee established by resolution 69/292 of 19 June 2015 on the elements and to elaborate the text of an international legally binding instrument under the United Nations Convention on the Law of the Sea[84] on the conservation and sustainable use of marine biological diversity of areas beyond national jurisdiction, with a view to developing the instrument as soon as possible, and relevant resolutions and decisions relating to the convening of the fourth and fifth sessions of the conference, the resumed fifth session of the conference and the further resumed fifth session of the conference,[85]

Recalling also the adoption by the conference, on 19 June 2023, of the Agreement under the United Nations Convention on the Law of the Sea on the Conservation and Sustainable Use of Marine Biological Diversity of Areas beyond National Jurisdiction,[86] by consensus,

Recalling further that, pursuant to article 47, paragraph 2, of the Agreement, the first meeting of the Conference of the Parties established under article 47, paragraph 1, of the Agreement shall be convened by the Secretary-General of the United Nations no later than one year after the entry into force of the Agreement,

Noting that, in a letter dated 30 June 2023 addressed to the President of the General Assembly, the President of the conference drew attention to the desire expressed by several delegations that efforts be undertaken with a view to supporting the early entry into force of the Agreement as well as its early implementation, including through a preparatory process such as a preparatory commission, and the President also observed that a preparatory process, to be established under the auspices of the Assembly, to carry out the required preparations for the first meeting of the

[84] United Nations, *Treaty Series*, vol. 1833, No. 31363.

[85] Resolutions 75/239 and 77/248 and decisions 74/543, 75/570, 76/564 and 77/556.

[86] A/CONF.232/2023/4.

Conference of the Parties to the Agreement and to provide guidance on the work of the interim secretariat under the Agreement until the convening of that meeting would be very helpful,[87]

Recalling its resolution 77/321 of 1 August 2023 on the Agreement,

Noting that the Agreement was opened for signature in New York at United Nations Headquarters on 20 September 2023,

Noting also the number of signatories that the Agreement has to date,

Recognizing the need to prepare for the entry into force of the Agreement and for the convening of the first meeting of the Conference of the Parties to the Agreement,

1. *Welcomes* the opening for signature of the Agreement under the United Nations Convention on the Law of the Sea on the Conservation and Sustainable Use of Marine Biological Diversity of Areas beyond National Jurisdiction;

2. *Emphasizes* the importance of the early entry into force and effective implementation of the Agreement;

3. *Decides* to establish a preparatory commission, which shall meet at United Nations Headquarters unless otherwise decided, on dates to be determined, to prepare for the entry into force of the Agreement and to prepare for the convening of the first meeting of the Conference of the Parties to the Agreement, at the conclusion of which the commission will cease to exist;

4. *Also decides* that the commission shall be open to all States Members of the United Nations, members of the specialized agencies and parties to the United Nations Convention on the Law of the Sea;

5. *Further decides* to invite to the commission representatives of organizations and other entities that have received a standing invitation from the General Assembly pursuant to its relevant resolutions to participate, in the capacity of observer, in its sessions and work, on the understanding that such representatives would participate in the work of the commission in that capacity, and to invite, as observers to the commission, representatives of interested global and regional intergovernmental organizations and other interested international bodies that were invited to participate in relevant conferences and summits,[88] associate members of the regional commissions[89] and representatives of relevant specialized agencies, as well as other organs, organizations, funds and programmes of the United Nations system;

6. *Decides* that attendance at the meetings of the commission as observers will also be opened to relevant non-governmental organizations in consultative status with the Economic and Social Council in accordance with the provisions of Council resolution 1996/31 of 25 July 1996, as well as to those that were accredited to relevant conferences and summits referred to in paragraph 5 of the present resolution, on the understanding that participation means attending formal meetings, unless otherwise decided by the commission in specific situations, receiving copies of the official documents, making available their materials to delegates and addressing the meetings, through a limited number of their representatives, as appropriate;

7. *Also decides* that, subject to paragraphs 8 and 9 of the present resolution, the rules and the established practice applicable to the procedure of the intergovernmental conference on an international legally binding instrument under the United Nations Convention on the Law of the Sea on the conservation and sustainable use of marine biological diversity of areas beyond national jurisdiction, as reflected in paragraphs 17, 18 and 19 of resolution 72/249, shall apply mutatis mutandis to the procedure of the commission unless otherwise agreed by the commission;

[87] See A/77/945.

[88] Reference is made to the following relevant conferences and summits: the World Summit on Sustainable Development, the United Nations Conference on Sustainable Development, the United Nations conferences on the sustainable development of small island developing States, the United Nations Conference on Straddling Fish Stocks and Highly Migratory Fish Stocks, the Review Conference on the Agreement for the Implementation of the Provisions of the United Nations Convention on the Law of the Sea of 10 December 1982 relating to the Conservation and Management of Straddling Fish Stocks and Highly Migratory Fish Stocks, as well as the United Nations Conferences to Support the Implementation of Sustainable Development Goal 14: Conserve and sustainably use the oceans, seas and marine resources for sustainable development.

[89] American Samoa, Anguilla, Aruba, Bermuda, the British Virgin Islands, the Cayman Islands, the Commonwealth of the Northern Mariana Islands, Curaçao, French Polynesia, Guam, Montserrat, New Caledonia, Puerto Rico, Sint Maarten, the Turks and Caicos Islands and the United States Virgin Islands.

8. *Further decides* that, after 20 September 2025 or the date of entry into force of the Agreement, whichever comes earlier, the taking of decisions by the commission shall only be by States and regional economic integration organizations that have signed the Agreement or have ratified, approved, accepted or acceded to the Agreement;

9. *Decides* that the commission will take decisions on any recommendations to the Conference of Parties to the Agreement at the final meeting of the commission;

10. *Also decides* that the commission shall be chaired by Co-Chairs, one from a developed country and one from a developing country, taking into account gender balance, and requests the President of the General Assembly to undertake consultations, in an open and transparent manner, for the nomination of the Co-Chairs-designate of the commission;

11. *Further decides* that the commission shall hold a three-day organizational meeting in the first half of 2024 with full conference services, including documentation, to discuss organizational matters, including the election of the Co-Chairs and a Bureau of the commission consisting of up to 15 members with up to 3 members from each regional group and taking into account gender balance, the dates of the meetings of the commission and the programme of work of the commission;

12. *Decides* that the commission shall prepare a final report on all matters within its mandate for presentation to the Conference of the Parties to the Agreement at its first meeting;

13. *Requests* the Secretary-General to provide the commission with the assistance necessary for the performance of its work, including secretariat services and the provision of essential background information and relevant documents, and to arrange for support to be provided by the Division for Ocean Affairs and the Law of the Sea of the Office of Legal Affairs in cooperation with other relevant departments of the Secretariat;

14. *Also requests* the Secretary-General to continue to administer the voluntary trust fund established pursuant to resolution 69/292 for the purpose of assisting developing countries, in particular the least developed countries, landlocked developing countries and small island developing States, in attending the meetings of the commission, and authorizes the Secretary-General to expand the assistance provided by the trust fund to include daily subsistence allowance in addition to defraying the costs of economy-class travel, limiting requests for assistance from the trust fund to one delegate per State for each meeting of the commission;

15. *Invites* Member States, international financial institutions, donor agencies, intergovernmental organizations, non-governmental organizations and natural and juridical persons to make financial contributions to the voluntary trust fund;

16. *Invites* States to provide information to the Secretary-General on their capacity-building and technical assistance needs with a view to becoming parties to the Agreement to inform the further development and provision of capacity-building and technical assistance activities of the Division in support of requesting States becoming parties to the Agreement and the effective implementation of the Agreement;

17. *Decides* to include in the provisional agenda of its seventy-ninth session, under the item entitled "Oceans and the law of the sea", the sub-item entitled "Agreement under the United Nations Convention on the Law of the Sea on the Conservation and Sustainable Use of Marine Biological Diversity of Areas beyond National Jurisdiction".

RESOLUTION 78/277

Adopted at the 77th plenary meeting, on 2 May 2024, without a vote, on the basis of draft resolution A/78/L.57, sponsored by: Algeria, Angola, Armenia, Austria, Azerbaijan, Bahrain, Bangladesh, Belarus, Belize, Bolivia (Plurinational State of), Bosnia and Herzegovina, Brunei Darussalam, Bulgaria, Burkina Faso, Cabo Verde, Cambodia, Cameroon, Canada, Chad, China, Colombia, Costa Rica, Côte d'Ivoire, Croatia, Denmark, Dominican Republic, Ecuador, Egypt, Equatorial Guinea, Eritrea, Fiji, Finland, Gambia, Germany, Greece, Guatemala, Guyana, Honduras, Hungary, Iceland, India, Indonesia, Japan, Jordan, Kazakhstan, Kenya, Kiribati, Kuwait, Kyrgyzstan, Latvia, Lebanon, Luxembourg, Malawi, Malaysia, Maldives, Mali, Mauritius, Mexico, Mongolia, Montenegro, Morocco, Mozambique, Myanmar, Namibia, Nepal, Netherlands (Kingdom of the), Nicaragua, Nigeria, North Macedonia, Oman, Pakistan, Palau, Papua New Guinea, Paraguay, Peru, Philippines, Portugal, Qatar, Republic of Korea, Russian Federation, Rwanda, San Marino, Saudi Arabia, Senegal, Serbia, Sierra Leone, Singapore, Slovenia, South Africa, Spain, Sri Lanka, Sudan, Suriname, Sweden, Tajikistan, Thailand, Timor-Leste, Togo, Trinidad and Tobago, Tunisia, Türkiye, Turkmenistan, Uganda, Ukraine, United Arab Emirates, United Republic of Tanzania, Uruguay, Uzbekistan, Vanuatu, Venezuela (Bolivarian Republic of), Viet Nam, Yemen, State of Palestine

78/277. Follow-up to the Declaration and Programme of Action on a Culture of Peace

The General Assembly,

Bearing in mind the Charter of the United Nations, including the purposes and principles contained therein, and especially the dedication to saving succeeding generations from the scourge of war,

Recalling the Constitution of the United Nations Educational, Scientific and Cultural Organization, which states that, "since wars begin in the minds of men, it is in the minds of men that the defences of peace must be constructed",

Recognizing the importance of the Declaration and Programme of Action on a Culture of Peace, adopted by the General Assembly on 13 September 1999,[90] which serve as the universal mandate for the international community, particularly the United Nations system, for the promotion of a culture of peace and non-violence that benefits humanity, in particular future generations,

Recalling all its previous resolutions on a culture of peace,

Recalling also the United Nations Millennium Declaration[91] and the 2030 Agenda for Sustainable Development,[92] which call for the active promotion of a culture of peace,

Recalling further its resolutions 75/201 of 21 December 2020 and 70/262 of 27 April 2016 on the review of the United Nations peacebuilding architecture, 72/276 of 26 April 2018 on the follow-up to the report of the Secretary-General on peacebuilding and sustaining peace and 76/305 of 8 September 2022 on financing for peacebuilding,

Recalling its resolutions declaring zones of peace in Central Asia,[93] the South Atlantic[94] and the Indian Ocean,[95] and emphasizing the importance of these zones in maintaining stability and security in those regions,

Recalling also its resolutions on terrorism and violent extremism, as and when conducive to terrorism, including resolutions 72/241 of 20 December 2017 on a world against violence and violent extremism and 77/298 of 30 June 2023 on the eighth review of the United Nations Global Counter-Terrorism Strategy, the Secretary-General's Plan of Action to Prevent Violent Extremism and the establishment of the Office of Counter-Terrorism under resolution 71/291 of 15 June 2017,

Recalling further the 2005 World Summit Outcome adopted at the high-level plenary meeting of the General Assembly,[96]

Welcoming the observance of 10 December as Human Rights Day,[97] 9 December as the International Day of Commemoration and Dignity of the Victims of the Crime of Genocide and of the Prevention of This Crime,[98] 2 October as the International Day of Non-Violence,[99] 18 June as the International Day for Countering Hate Speech,[100] 16 May as the International Day of Living Together in Peace,[101] 21 August as the International Day of Remembrance of and Tribute to the Victims of Terrorism,[102] 4 February as the International Day of Human Fraternity,[103] 22 August as the International Day Commemorating the Victims of Acts of Violence Based on Religion

---

[90] Resolutions 53/243 A and B.
[91] Resolution 55/2.
[92] Resolution 70/1.
[93] Resolution 76/299.
[94] Resolution 41/11.
[95] Resolution 2832 (XXVI).
[96] Resolution 60/1.
[97] Resolution 423 (V).
[98] Resolution 69/323.
[99] Resolution 61/271.
[100] Resolution 75/309.
[101] Resolution 72/130.
[102] Resolution 72/165.
[103] Resolution 75/200.

or Belief,[104] 5 April as the International Day of Conscience,[105] 15 March as the International Day to Combat Islamophobia[106] and 27 January as the International Day of Commemoration in Memory of the Victims of the Holocaust,[107] as proclaimed by the United Nations,

Recognizing that all efforts made by the United Nations system in general and the international community at large for the prevention of conflicts, the peaceful settlement of disputes, peacekeeping, peacebuilding, mediation, disarmament, sustainable development, the promotion of human dignity and human rights, social inclusion, democracy, the rule of law, good governance and gender equality at the national and international levels contribute greatly to a culture of peace,

Taking note of the United Nations Strategy and Plan of Action on Hate Speech, in which it is proposed that the United Nations system establish and strengthen partnerships with new and traditional media to promote the values of tolerance, non-discrimination, pluralism and freedom of opinion and expression, and to address hate speech narratives,

Recognizing that efforts towards peacebuilding and sustaining peace need to take into account the promotion of a culture of peace and vice versa,

Recalling its resolution 76/6 of 15 November 2021 on the report of the Secretary-General entitled "Our Common Agenda",[108] and its follow-up processes,

Recognizing that the collective well-being, safety, security and prosperity of our nations and peoples are deeply intertwined, which requires us to work urgently and together in accordance with the Charter to address global risks and challenges, find viable solutions and accelerate the implementation of agreed frameworks, including the 2030 Agenda for Sustainable Development and the Sustainable Development Goals and the Addis Ababa Action Agenda of the Third International Conference on Financing for Development,[109] as well as the United Nations Framework Convention on Climate Change[110] and the Paris Agreement,[111]

Recognizing also that the open, constructive and respectful debate of ideas, as well as interreligious, interfaith and intercultural dialogue at the local, national, regional and international levels, involving civil society, can play a positive role in fostering democratic participation, ensuring equality of access to education for women, especially girls, combating hatred, incitement and violence based on religion or belief as well as racism, hate speech and other forms of intolerance, and advancing human dignity, human fraternity, tolerance and solidarity,

Recognizing further the importance of respect and understanding for religious and cultural diversity throughout the world, of choosing dialogue and negotiations over confrontation and of working together and not against each other,

Recalling the report of the Secretary-General,[112] which provides an overview of the actions taken across the United Nations system and by Member States to implement the Programme of Action and to promote a culture of peace and non-violence since the adoption by the General Assembly of its resolution 76/68 of 9 December 2021,

Recalling also its proclamation of the period 2022–2032 as the International Decade of Indigenous Languages,

Recalling further the proclamations by the United Nations Educational, Scientific and Cultural Organization, in particular of 21 February as International Mother Language Day, which aims at protecting, promoting and preserving linguistic and cultural diversity and multilingualism, in order to foster and enrich a culture of peace, social harmony, cross-cultural dialogue and mutual understanding, of 30 April as International Jazz Day, which aims to develop and increase intercultural exchanges and understanding between cultures for the purpose of mutual comprehension, tolerance and the promotion of a culture of peace, and of 21 March as the International Day of Nowruz, which

[104] Resolution 73/296.

[105] Resolution 73/329.

[106] Resolution 76/254.

[107] Resolution 60/7.

[108] A/75/982.

[109] Resolution 69/313, annex.

[110] United Nations, *Treaty Series*, vol. 1771, No. 30822.

[111] See FCCC/CP/2015/10/Add.1, decision 1/CP.21, annex.

[112] A/77/614.

promotes values of peace and solidarity between generations and within families as well as reconciliation and neighbourliness, thus contributing to cultural diversity and friendship among peoples and different communities,

Taking note of the Transforming Education Summit, convened by the Secretary-General from 16 to 19 September 2022 in New York, as well as its pre-Summit, hosted by the United Nations Educational, Scientific and Cultural Organization from 28 to 30 June 2022 in Paris,

Taking note also of Member States' engagement throughout the Transforming Education Summit process, including through national consultations, and inviting the United Nations Educational, Scientific and Cultural Organization and relevant stakeholders, including the Sustainable Development Goal 4-Education 2030 High-level Steering Committee, to support Member States, upon their request, in the country-level implementation of their national commitments made during the Transforming Education Summit process,

Welcoming the efforts of the international community to enhance understanding through constructive dialogue among civilizations, in particular through various initiatives at the local, national, regional and international levels,

Expressing its appreciation for the ongoing efforts of the United Nations Alliance of Civilizations in promoting a culture of peace through a number of practical projects in the areas of youth, education, media and migrations, in collaboration with Governments, international organizations, foundations and civil society groups, as well as media and the private sector,

Taking note of the ninth United Nations Alliance of Civilizations Forum, held in Fez, Morocco, on 22 and 23 November 2022 on the theme "Towards an alliance of peace: living together as one humanity",

Recalling the General Assembly High-level Forum held on 13 September 2019 on the occasion of the twentieth anniversary of the adoption of the Declaration and Programme of Action and the Chair's summary of the meeting on the theme "The Culture of Peace: empowering and transforming humanity",

Welcoming the General Assembly High-level Forum on the Culture of Peace held on 31 August 2023 on the theme "Promoting a Culture of Peace in the digital era", at which Member States and observers of the General Assembly and other stakeholders, such as civil society, private sector and other relevant stakeholders, renewed their commitments to the full and effective implementation of the Declaration and Programme of Action in the context of rapid technological change,

Taking note of the outcome document of the international conference entitled "Dialogue is a Guarantee of Peace", held in Ashgabat on 11 December 2022,[113] and the Declaration of the Seventh Congress of the Leaders of World and Traditional Religions, held in Astana on 14 and 15 September 2022,[114]

Noting with appreciation that the Declaration and Programme of Action continue to find relevance across the three pillars of the United Nations, which are interconnected and mutually reinforcing, in addressing contemporary global challenges,

Recalling the high-level plenary meeting of the General Assembly, known as the Nelson Mandela Peace Summit, convened by the President of the Assembly on 24 September 2018, and the adoption of its political declaration,[115]

Recognizing the urgent need to promote and strengthen preventive diplomacy, inter alia, through multilateralism, international cooperation and political dialogue, and stressing the crucial role of the United Nations in this regard,

Recognizing also the role of women and youth, as well as the contribution of children and older persons in advancing a culture of peace, and in particular the importance of ensuring gender equality and the empowerment of women and girls, with the aim of advancing the full, equal and meaningful participation of women in the prevention and resolution of conflicts, in peacebuilding, as well as in activities promoting a culture of peace, including in post-conflict situations,

[113] A/77/651, annex.

[114] A/77/360, annex.

[115] Resolution 73/1.

Noting the important and positive contribution of youth in efforts to counter terrorism and prevent violent extremism as and when conducive to terrorism, as well as for the promotion of peace and security, sustainable development and human rights, and the importance of the full, effective, constructive and inclusive participation of youth in decision-making, and noting in this regard the establishment of the United Nations Youth Office,

Recalling the adoption by the General Conference of the United Nations Educational, Scientific and Cultural Organization at its thirty-sixth session of a programme of action for a culture of peace and non-violence, and noting that the objectives of that programme of action are in line with the Declaration and Programme of Action on a Culture of Peace adopted by the General Assembly,

Recognizing the activities of the United Nations Educational, Scientific and Cultural Organization related to the culture of peace and non-violence and their focus on concrete actions at the global, regional and subregional levels, and noting its support for the Member States, upon their request, in promoting the culture of peace at the national level,

Noting with deep concern that the coronavirus disease (COVID-19) pandemic has led to a rise in hate speech, stigmatization, racism and xenophobia, exacerbated pre-existing inequalities in income, opportunities, access to information and communications technologies, health coverage and social protection, deepened gender inequality, and created new challenges with regard to access to health-care services and vaccines,

Recognizing that the digital sphere and its ongoing transformation are an important area for global action on building a culture of peace,

Noting the initiatives of civil society, in collaboration with Governments, to strengthen civilian capacities to enhance the physical safety of vulnerable populations under threat of violence and to promote the peaceful settlement of disputes,

Encouraging the continued and increasing efforts and activities on the part of civil society organizations throughout the world in advancing a culture of peace as envisaged in the Declaration and Programme of Action,

1. *Reiterates* that the objective of the effective implementation of the Programme of Action on a Culture of Peace is to strengthen further the global movement for a culture of peace, and calls upon all concerned to renew their attention to this objective;

2. *Invites* Member States to continue to place greater emphasis on and expand their activities promoting a culture of peace at the national, regional and international levels and to ensure that peace and non-violence are fostered at all levels;

3. *Invites* the entities of the United Nations system, within their existing mandates, to integrate, as appropriate, the eight action areas of the Programme of Action into their programmes of activities, focusing on promoting a culture of peace and non-violence at the national, regional and international levels;

4. *Commends* the United Nations Educational, Scientific and Cultural Organization for strengthening efforts to mobilize all relevant stakeholders within and outside the United Nations system in support of a culture of peace, and invites the Organization to continue to enhance communication and outreach, including through the culture of peace website;

5. *Commends* the practical initiatives and actions by relevant United Nations bodies, including the United Nations Children's Fund, the United Nations Entity for Gender Equality and the Empowerment of Women (UN-Women) and the University for Peace, as well as their activities in further promoting a culture of peace and non-violence, in particular the promotion of peace education and activities related to specific areas identified in the Programme of Action, and encourages them to continue and further strengthen and expand their efforts;

6. *Stresses* the importance of addressing the underlying drivers of violence and conflict to promote a culture of peace;

7. *Encourages* Member States, United Nations entities and other relevant actors to adopt a holistic approach to the cross-cutting dimensions of peace, development, humanitarian action and human rights in order to prevent the recurrence of conflict and violence and build lasting peace;

8. *Underlines* that early childhood development contributes to the development of more peaceful societies through advancing equality, tolerance, human development and promoting human rights, and calls for investment in early childhood education, including through effective policies and practices, towards promoting a culture of peace;

9. *Encourages* Member States, United Nations entities, regional and subregional organizations and relevant actors to consider instituting mechanisms to involve youth in the promotion of a culture of peace, tolerance and intercultural and interreligious dialogue and develop, as appropriate, an understanding of respect for human dignity, pluralism and diversity, including, as appropriate, through education programmes, that could discourage their participation in acts of terrorism, violent extremism as and when conducive to terrorism, violence, xenophobia and all forms of discrimination;

10. *Encourages* the United Nations Alliance of Civilizations to increase its activities that focus on peace education and global citizenship education in order to enhance an understanding among young people of values such as peace, tolerance, openness, inclusion and mutual respect, which are essential in developing a culture of peace;

11. *Encourages* the United Nations peacebuilding architecture to continue to promote peacebuilding and sustaining peace activities, as outlined in its resolutions 72/276 and 75/201, and to advance a culture of peace and non-violence in post-conflict peacebuilding efforts at the country level, and recognizes the important role of the Peacebuilding Commission in this regard;

12. *Emphasizes* the critical importance of an inclusive, resilient and sustainable recovery from the COVID-19 pandemic, and in this regard calls upon States to promote the values of a culture of peace, inter alia, in countering rising inequalities, discrimination, exclusion, hate crimes and violence;

13. *Urges* the appropriate authorities to provide age-appropriate education in children's schools that builds a culture of peace and non-violence, including lessons in mutual understanding, respect, tolerance, active and global citizenship and human rights;

14. *Encourages* the involvement of media, especially the mass media, in promoting a culture of peace and non-violence, with particular regard to children and young people;

15. *Commends* civil society, non-governmental organizations and young people for their activities in further promoting a culture of peace and non-violence, including through their campaign to raise awareness on a culture of peace and the peaceful settlement of disputes;

16. *Encourages* civil society and non-governmental organizations to further strengthen their efforts to promote a culture of peace, inter alia, by adopting their own programme of activities to complement the initiatives of Member States, the United Nations system and other international and regional organizations, in line with the Declaration and Programme of Action;

17. *Invites* Member States, all entities of the United Nations system and civil society organizations to accord increasing attention to their observance of the International Day of Peace on 21 September each year as a day of global ceasefire and non-violence, in accordance with its resolution 55/282 of 7 September 2001, and of the International Day of Non-Violence on 2 October, in accordance with its resolution 61/271 of 15 June 2007;

18. *Notes* that 2024 will mark the twenty-fifth anniversary of the adoption of the Declaration on a Culture of Peace by the United Nations at the fifty-third session of the General Assembly in 1999;

19. *Invites* Member States, United Nations entities, international and regional organizations and other relevant stakeholders, including civil society, the private sector, academia and the media, to commemorate the anniversary in an appropriate manner, including through educational and public awareness-raising activities;

20. *Requests* the President of the General Assembly to convene, within existing resources, a day-long high-level forum during its seventy-eighth session to commemorate the twenty-fifth anniversary of the adoption of the Declaration and Programme of Action on a Culture of Peace;

21. *Invites* the Secretary-General, within existing resources, in consultation with the Member States and taking into account the observations of civil society organizations, to explore mechanisms and strategies, in particular strategies in the sphere of information and communications technology, for the implementation of the Declaration and Programme of Action and to initiate outreach efforts to increase global awareness of the Programme of Action and its

eight areas of action aimed at their implementation, including through public information activities by the Department of Global Communications of the Secretariat;

22. *Requests* the Secretary-General to submit to the General Assembly at its seventy-ninth session a report, within existing resources, on actions taken by Member States, on the basis of information provided by them, and those taken system-wide by all concerned entities of the United Nations to implement the present resolution;

23. *Decides* to include in the provisional agenda of its seventy-ninth session the item entitled "Culture of peace".

RESOLUTION 78/278

Adopted at the 77th plenary meeting, on 2 May 2024, without a vote, on the basis of draft resolution A/78/L.60, sponsored by: Afghanistan, Azerbaijan, Bangladesh, Belarus, Bosnia and Herzegovina, China, Cuba, Egypt, Germany, Hungary, Indonesia, Israel, Jordan, Kazakhstan, Kyrgyzstan, Lebanon, Libya, Nicaragua, Pakistan, Paraguay, Portugal, Senegal, Singapore, Tajikistan, Turkmenistan, Uzbekistan

78/278. International Day of the Markhor

The General Assembly,

Reaffirming its resolution 70/1 of 25 September 2015, entitled "Transforming our world: the 2030 Agenda for Sustainable Development", by which it adopted a comprehensive, far-reaching and people-centred set of universal and transformative Sustainable Development Goals and targets,

Reaffirming also its resolutions 53/199 of 15 December 1998 and 61/185 of 20 December 2006 on the proclamation of international years, and Economic and Social Council resolution 1980/67 of 25 July 1980 on international years and anniversaries, in particular paragraphs 1 to 10 of the annex thereto on the agreed criteria for the proclamation of international years, as well as paragraphs 13 and 14, in which it is stated that an international day or year should not be proclaimed before the basic arrangements for its organization and financing have been made,

Reaffirming further the intrinsic value of wildlife and its various contributions, including its ecological, genetic, social, economic, scientific, educational, cultural, recreational and aesthetic contributions to sustainable development and human well-being, and recognizing that wild fauna in their many beautiful and varied forms are an irreplaceable part of the natural systems of the Earth which must be protected for this generation and the generations to come,

Stressing the urgent need to address the unprecedented global decline in biodiversity, including by preventing the extinction of threatened species, improving and sustaining their conservation status and restoring and safeguarding ecosystems that provide essential functions and services, including services related to water, health, livelihoods and well-being,

Underlining that the markhor (*Capra falconeri*) is an iconic and ecologically significant species found across the mountainous regions of Central and South Asia, including Afghanistan, India, Pakistan, Tajikistan, Turkmenistan and Uzbekistan, and recognizing that the markhor was categorized as "near threatened" in 2014 and is on the International Union for Conservation of Nature Red List of Threatened Species, and has been included in appendix I to the Convention on International Trade in Endangered Species of Wild Fauna and Flora[116] since 1992,

Recognizing that preserving the markhor and its natural habitat is an ecological imperative and a significant opportunity to bolster the regional economy, foster conservation efforts and promote sustainable tourism and economic growth and that conservation efforts will benefit the ecosystem,

Stressing that, besides its ecological value, the markhor is a valuable species that contributes to the local economy and conservation initiatives,

Recognizing national and regional initiatives for range State cooperation, transboundary approaches and mechanisms at the regional level to foster conservation of the markhor,

[116] United Nations, *Treaty Series*, vol. 993, No. 14537.

Noting the upcoming Ninth World Conference on Mountain Ungulates, to be held in Dushanbe from 12 to 15 October 2024,

Recognizing that the greatest threats to the survival of the markhor are habitat loss, illegal hunting, including poaching, and climate change,

Recalling its resolution 78/155 of 19 December 2023, entitled "Implementation of the Convention on Biological Diversity and its contribution to sustainable development", in which it called upon parties to the Convention and stakeholders to strengthen international cooperation measures for the fulfilment of obligations contained in the Convention,

Recognizing efforts for the conservation of the markhor, including the establishment of breeding programmes and the development of a regional strategy and national action plans for the conservation of the markhor in some range States that aim to protect the species throughout its range,

1. *Decides* to proclaim 24 May the International Day of the Markhor;

2. *Invites* all Member States, organizations of the United Nations system, other international and regional organizations, civil society, non-governmental organizations, individuals and other relevant stakeholders to observe the International Day of the Markhor, as appropriate;

3. *Invites* all relevant stakeholders to give due consideration to enhancing international and regional cooperation in support of efforts to conserve the markhor, given its role in the overall ecosystem;

4. *Invites* the United Nations Environment Programme to facilitate the observance of the International Day of the Markhor, mindful of the provisions contained in the annex to Economic and Social Council resolution 1980/67;

5. *Stresses* that the cost of all activities that may arise from the implementation of the present resolution should be met from voluntary contributions and that such activities would be subject to the availability and provision of voluntary contributions;

6. *Requests* the Secretary-General to bring the present resolution to the attention of all Member States, the organizations of the United Nations system and civil society organizations for appropriate observance.

RESOLUTION 78/279

Adopted at the 77th plenary meeting, on 2 May 2024, without a vote, on the basis of draft resolution A/78/L.59, sponsored by: Albania, Algeria, Andorra, Argentina, Armenia, Australia, Austria, Azerbaijan, Bangladesh, Barbados, Belgium, Bolivia (Plurinational State of), Bosnia and Herzegovina, Botswana, Brazil, Bulgaria, Burkina Faso, Burundi, Cabo Verde, Cambodia, Canada, Chile, China, Colombia, Costa Rica, Croatia, Cyprus, Czechia, Democratic Republic of the Congo, Djibouti, Dominican Republic, Ecuador, Egypt, El Salvador, Eritrea, Estonia, Eswatini, Fiji, Finland, France, Gabon, Gambia, Georgia, Germany, Greece, Guatemala, Guyana, Haiti, Honduras, Hungary, Iceland, India, Indonesia, Ireland, Israel, Italy, Jamaica, Japan, Jordan, Kazakhstan, Kenya, Kyrgyzstan, Lao People's Democratic Republic, Latvia, Lebanon, Lesotho, Liberia, Liechtenstein, Lithuania, Luxembourg, Malaysia, Malta, Mongolia, Montenegro, Morocco, Mozambique, Myanmar, Nepal, Netherlands (Kingdom of the), New Zealand, North Macedonia, Norway, Pakistan, Palau, Panama, Papua New Guinea, Paraguay, Peru, Philippines, Poland, Portugal, Qatar, Republic of Korea, Republic of Moldova, Romania, San Marino, Saudi Arabia, Senegal, Serbia, Singapore, Slovenia, South Africa, Spain, Sri Lanka, Suriname, Sweden, Tajikistan, Thailand, Timor-Leste, Trinidad and Tobago, Tunisia, Türkiye, Turkmenistan, Uganda, Ukraine, United Arab Emirates, United Kingdom of Great Britain and Northern Ireland, United Republic of Tanzania, United States of America, Uruguay, Uzbekistan, Viet Nam, Yemen, Zambia

78/279. International Year of the Woman Farmer, 2026

The General Assembly,

Reaffirming its resolution 70/1 of 25 September 2015, entitled "Transforming our world: the 2030 Agenda for Sustainable Development", in which it adopted a comprehensive, far-reaching and people-centred set of universal and transformative Sustainable Development Goals and targets, its commitment to working tirelessly for the full implementation of the Agenda by 2030, its recognition that eradicating poverty in all its forms and dimensions, including extreme poverty, is the greatest global challenge and an indispensable requirement for sustainable development, its commitment to achieving sustainable development in its three dimensions – economic, social and environmental – in a balanced and integrated manner, and to building upon the achievements of the Millennium Development Goals and seeking to address their unfinished business,

Reaffirming also its resolutions 53/199 of 15 December 1998 and 61/185 of 20 December 2006 on the proclamation of international years, and Economic and Social Council resolution 1980/67 of 25 July 1980 on international years and anniversaries,

Recalling its resolutions 77/181 of 14 December 2022 on women in development, 78/168 of 19 December 2023 on agriculture development, food security and nutrition and 62/136 of 18 December 2007 and 78/181 of 19 December 2023 on the improvement of the situation of women and girls in rural areas,

Recalling also its resolution 72/239 of 20 December 2017, by which it proclaimed the United Nations Decade of Family Farming (2019–2028), and the global launch of the Decade in Rome on 29 May 2019, and cognizant of the important contributions that women farmers, particularly small-scale producers, make to bolstering food security at all levels,

Recalling further its resolution 76/253 of 17 March 2022, by which it declared 2026 the International Year of Rangelands and Pastoralists, to acknowledge that rangelands and pastoralism are currently facing urgent and different challenges around the world and to emphasize that well-developed and fair production pastoral value chains can provide equitable economic opportunities for all and contribute to ending extreme poverty,

Taking note of the 2023 report of the Food and Agricultural Organization of the United Nations entitled *The Status of Women in Agrifood Systems*,

Taking note also of the Voluntary Guidelines on Gender Equality and Women's and Girls' Empowerment in the Context of Food Security and Nutrition of the Committee on World Food Security endorsed at the fifty-first session of the Committee, held in Rome from 23 to 27 October and on 25 November 2023,

Taking note with appreciation of the 2021 United Nations Food Systems Summit, convened by the Secretary-General on 23 and 24 September 2021, as well as its pre-Summit, held from 26 to 28 July 2021 in Rome, and the United Nations Food Systems Summit +2 Stocktaking Moment, convened by the Secretary-General and hosted by the Government of Italy in Rome from 24 to 26 July 2023,

Stressing that progress in achieving the Sustainable Development Goals, including Goal 1 (End poverty in all its forms everywhere), Goal 2 (End hunger, achieve food security and improved nutrition and promote sustainable agriculture) and Goal 5 (Achieve gender equality and empower all women and girls), have been hampered, in part, owing to recent global shocks and stressors that are compounding gender inequality across agrifood systems,

Acknowledging the important contributions of all women working in agrifood systems throughout value chains, including, inter alia, farmers, producers, peasants, family and smallholder farmers, fishers, fish workers, beekeepers, pastoralists, processors, traders, formal and informal workers, and entrepreneurs, as well as Indigenous women and women in local communities, to achieving food security, improving nutrition and eradicating poverty in all its forms and dimensions, including extreme poverty and rural poverty,

Stressing that peasant women and other rural women play a significant role in the economic survival of their families and in contributing to the rural and national economy, including through their work in the non-monetized sectors of the economy, but are often denied tenure and ownership of land, equal access to land, productive resources, financial services, information, employment or social protection, and are often victims of violence and discrimination in a variety of forms and manifestations,

Noting with concern that women farmers' access to, ownership of and control over productive resources, assets, inputs and services, including land, training and capacity-building, credit and technology, varies greatly across and within countries and regions, and reaffirming that addressing these concerns has the potential to bolster food security and nutrition at the local, national and global levels and stimulate economic growth,

Stressing the importance of promoting rural women's economic empowerment by realizing their right to work and rights at work, building their capacities and skills to manage enterprises and cooperatives, facilitating formalization and ensuring their financial and digital inclusion and equal access to natural resources and economic and productive resources, including access to, use of, ownership of and control over land, including diverse types of land tenure, property and appropriate new technology, as well as inheritance rights, developing specific assistance programmes and advisory services to promote economic skills of rural women in banking, modern trading and financial procedures, including financial literacy and consumer protection, and providing affordable microcredit and other financial and business services to a greater number of women in rural areas, in particular female heads of households, for their economic empowerment,

Recognizing the need to empower all women and girls through inclusive and equitable quality education and training to promote on-farm activities that improve sustainable production and build resilience,

Recognizing also that supporting women farmers is critical to accelerating the transition to more sustainable agrifood systems through productivity growth that optimizes agricultural sustainability across social, economic and environmental dimensions,

Recognizing further that the observance of an International Year of the Woman Farmer in 2026 by the international community would contribute significantly to raising awareness of these issues,

1. *Decides* to declare 2026 the International Year of the Woman Farmer;

2. *Invites* all Member States, organizations of the United Nations system, other international and regional organizations and other relevant stakeholders, including civil society, the private sector, Indigenous Peoples, local communities and academia, to observe the International Year, as appropriate, through activities aimed at raising awareness of and directing policy attention to the barriers and challenges that women farmers face across agrifood systems, as well as the initiatives, policies and actions that can and are being taken to address these issues and achieve gender equality and the empowerment of all women in agriculture;

3. *Invites* the Food and Agriculture Organization of the United Nations, in collaboration with the other United Nations Rome-based agencies, mindful of the provisions contained in the annex to Economic and Social Council resolution 1980/67, to facilitate the implementation of the present resolution and observe the International Year;

4. *Also invites* the Food and Agriculture Organization of the United Nations, mindful of the provisions of paragraphs 23 to 27 of the annex to Economic and Social Council resolution 1980/67, to inform the General Assembly at its eighty-second session regarding the implementation of the present resolution, including an evaluation of the observance of the International Year;

5. *Stresses* that the costs of all the activities that may arise from the implementation of the present resolution should be met through voluntary contributions, including from the private sector;

6. *Invites* all relevant stakeholders to contribute to and support the implementation of the present resolution;

7. *Requests* the Secretary-General to bring the present resolution to the attention of all Member States, the organizations of the United Nations system and other relevant stakeholders, including civil society, the private sector and academia, for appropriate observance.

RESOLUTION 78/280

Adopted at the 77th plenary meeting, on 2 May 2024, without a vote, on the basis of draft resolution A/78/L.62, as amended in A/78/L.66, sponsored by: Angola, Brazil, Cambodia, Chad, Djibouti, El Salvador, Eswatini, France, Indonesia, Mali, Norway, Philippines, Rwanda, Senegal, South Africa, Thailand, Timor-Leste, Tunisia, Uganda, Viet Nam

78/280. Global health and foreign policy: addressing global health challenges in the foreign policy space

The General Assembly,

Recalling its resolutions 63/33 of 26 November 2008, 64/108 of 10 December 2009, 65/95 of 9 December 2010, 66/115 of 12 December 2011, 67/81 of 12 December 2012, 68/98 of 11 December 2013, 69/132 of 11 December 2014, 70/183 of 17 December 2015, 71/159 of 15 December 2016, 72/139 of 12 December 2017, 73/132 of 13 December 2018, 74/20 of 11 December 2019, 75/130 of 14 December 2020 and 76/257 of 29 March 2022,

Reaffirming its resolution 70/1 of 25 September 2015, entitled "Transforming our world: the 2030 Agenda for Sustainable Development", in which it adopted a wide, far-reaching and people-centred set of universal and transformative Sustainable Development Goals and targets, its commitment to working tirelessly for the full implementation of the Agenda by 2030, its recognition that eradicating poverty in all its forms and dimensions, including extreme poverty, is the greatest global challenge and an indispensable requirement for sustainable development, its commitment to achieving sustainable development goals that are integrated and indivisible and balanced in its three dimensions – economic, social and environmental – and its commitment to building upon the achievements of the Millennium Development Goals and seeking to address their unfinished business, recommitting that no one will be left behind and endeavouring to reach the furthest behind first,

Reaffirming also its resolution 69/313 of 27 July 2015 on the Addis Ababa Action Agenda of the Third International Conference on Financing for Development, which is an integral part of the 2030 Agenda for Sustainable Development, supports and complements it, helps to contextualize its means of implementation targets with concrete policies and actions, and reaffirms the strong political commitment to address the challenge of financing and creating an enabling environment at all levels for sustainable development in the spirit of global partnership and solidarity,

Recognizing that universal health coverage is fundamental for achieving the Sustainable Development Goals related not only to health and well-being, but also to eradicating poverty in all its forms and dimensions, ensuring quality education, achieving gender equality and the empowerment of all women and girls, providing decent work and economic growth, as well as the elimination of all forms of violence against women and girls, reducing inequalities, ensuring just, peaceful and inclusive societies and to building and fostering partnerships, recognizing the interdependence between global health and development, while reaching the goals and targets included throughout the 2030 Agenda is critical for the attainment of healthy lives and well-being for all, with a focus on health outcomes throughout the life course,

Recalling the Universal Declaration of Human Rights,[117] the International Covenant on Economic, Social and Cultural Rights,[118] the International Convention on the Elimination of All Forms of Racial Discrimination,[119] the Convention on the Elimination of All Forms of Discrimination against Women,[120] the Convention on the Rights of the Child,[121] the Convention on the Rights of Persons with Disabilities,[122] the International Covenant on Civil and Political Rights[123] and relevant provisions of international humanitarian law,

Recognizing that the year 2023 marked the seventy-fifth anniversaries of the World Health Organization and the Universal Declaration of Human Rights, as well as the thirtieth anniversary of the Vienna Declaration and Programme of Action,[124]

Recalling that health is a precondition for and an outcome and indicator of all three dimensions of sustainable development – economic, social and environmental – and that, despite progress made, challenges in global health, including major inequities and vulnerabilities within and among countries, regions and populations, still remain and demand persistent attention,

Recalling also that in the Constitution of the World Health Organization[125] health is defined as a state of complete physical, mental and social well-being and not merely the absence of disease or infirmity, and it is declared that the enjoyment of the highest attainable standard of health is one of the fundamental rights of every human being without distinction of race, religion, political belief, economic or social condition,

Recalling further that in the Constitution of the World Health Organization it is stated that unequal development in different countries in the promotion of health and control of disease, especially communicable disease, is a common danger,

Recognizing the leading role of the World Health Organization, as the primary specialized agency for health, including its roles and functions with regard to health policy in accordance with its mandate, and welcoming ongoing processes to improve the sustainable financing of the World Health Organization, including the adoption of the

[117] Resolution 217 A (III).

[118] See resolution 2200 A (XXI), annex.

[119] United Nations, *Treaty Series*, vol. 660, No. 9464.

[120] Ibid., vol. 1249, No. 20378.

[121] Ibid., vol. 1577, No. 27531.

[122] Ibid., vol. 2515, No. 44910.

[123] See resolution 2200 A (XXI), annex.

[124] A/CONF.157/24 (Part I), chap. III.

[125] United Nations, *Treaty Series*, vol. 14, No. 221.

recommendations of the Working Group on Sustainable Financing by the World Health Assembly at its seventy-fifth session,[126]

Underlining the significant role of the Foreign Policy and Global Health Initiative in promoting synergies between foreign policy and global health, as well as the contribution of the Oslo Ministerial Declaration of 20 March 2007, entitled "Global health: a pressing foreign policy issue of our time",[127] which was reaffirmed, with renewed actions and commitments, in the ministerial communiqué of the Initiative entitled "Renewing 10 years of concerted efforts and preparing for new challenges", of 22 September 2017,[128]

Underlining also that in the Oslo Declaration it is acknowledged that investment in health is fundamental to economic growth and development, and in this regard recalling that health inequities arise, as stated in the Rio Political Declaration on Social Determinants of Health, from the societal conditions in which people are born, grow, live, work and age, referred to as social determinants of health,

Recognizing the close relationship between foreign policy and global health and their interdependence, and noting that foreign policy can help to sustain political momentum, advance international cooperation and find solutions to health and other interlocking challenges based on the principles of global solidarity and equity,

Underscoring the importance of enhanced international cooperation to support the efforts of Member States to achieve health goals, including the target of achieving universal health coverage, including financial risk protection, access to quality essential health-care services and access to safe, effective, quality and affordable essential medicines and vaccines for all,

Underlining the primary responsibility of States to promote universal health coverage that comprises universal and equitable access to quality health services and ensures affordable and quality service delivery, especially through primary health care and social protection mechanisms, with the support of the international community and with a view to providing access to health services for all, in particular women and children and those who are in vulnerable situations or marginalized,

Reaffirming the importance of national ownership and the primary role and responsibility of governments at all levels to determine their own path towards achieving universal health coverage, in accordance with national contexts and priorities, and underscoring the importance of political leadership for universal health coverage beyond the health sector in order to pursue whole-of-government and whole-of-society approaches, as well as health-in-all-policies approaches, equity-based approaches and life-course approaches,

Recognizing that primary health care is the cornerstone of a sustainable health system for universal health coverage and health-related Sustainable Development Goals, in particular Goal 3.8, as declared in the 1978 Declaration of Alma-Ata, the 2030 Agenda and reaffirmed in the 2018 Declaration of Astana as adopted at the Global Conference on Primary Health Care in Astana,

Recognizing also that social protection is an important tool to act on social and economic determinants of health, such as poverty, inequality, social exclusion and social insecurity, and that it protects people and communities in need of health-care services from hardship and from an increased risk of poverty due to the financial consequences of illness and disability,

Recognizing further that humanitarian emergencies have a devastating impact on health systems, leaving people, especially people in vulnerable situations, without full access to health-care services and exposing them to preventable diseases and other health risks,

Recalling the consequence of the adverse impact of climate change, natural disasters, extreme weather events as well as other environmental determinants of health, such as clean air, safe drinking water, sanitation, safe, sufficient and nutritious food and secure shelter, for health, and in this regard underscoring the need to foster health in climate change adaptation efforts, underlining that resilient and people-centred health systems are necessary to protect the

[126] See World Health Organization, document WHA75/2022/REC/1, decision 75(8).

[127] A/63/591, annex.

[128] A/72/559, annex.

health of all people, in particular those who are vulnerable or in vulnerable situations, particularly those living in small island developing States,

Underlining the need to strengthen pandemic prevention, preparedness and response, including for ongoing global epidemics such as HIV/AIDS, tuberculosis and malaria, as well as neglected tropical diseases and preventable diseases, by sharing experience and best practices, and raise the level of preparedness, including enabling diagnostics of drivers of outbreaks in animals of zoonotic potential, surveillance and early warning systems, in order to have the earliest and most adequate response to any outbreak that may arise, recognizing the necessity of a One Health approach that fosters cooperation between the human, animal and plant health, as well as other relevant sectors, including through strengthened cooperation and collaboration among the World Health Organization, the Food and Agriculture Organization of the United Nations, the World Organization for Animal Health and the United Nations Environment Programme,

Recognizing the present and ever-increasing urgent global risk of antimicrobial resistance, which kills 1.27 million people a year, about 20 per cent of whom are children under 5, and emphasizing that antimicrobial resistance could result in 1 trillion United States dollars of additional health-care costs by 2050 and 1 trillion to 3.4 trillion dollars of gross domestic product losses per year by 2030,

Recognizing also the need to strengthen the capacity of all countries, in particular developing countries, for early warning, risk reduction and management of national and global health risks, guided by target 3.d of the 2030 Agenda,

Recalling the political declaration of the high-level meeting on the midterm review of the Sendai Framework for Disaster Reduction 2015–2030[129] and the Bali Agenda for Resilience resulting from the seventh session of the Global Platform for Disaster Risk Reduction, which highlighted the importance of strengthening of community engagement in preparing for and responding to disaster, including outbreaks of infectious disease, including strengthening capacity-building and funding for local governments and local communities to prevent, prepare for and respond to outbreaks and other disasters,

Recognizing that health is an investment in human capital and social and economic development towards the full realization of human potential and significantly contributes to the promotion and protection of human rights and dignity as well as the empowerment of all people,

Recalling the need to further strengthen cooperation to recruit, train, develop and retain a skilled health workforce, which is an important element of strong and resilient health systems, as part of health emergency prevention and preparedness strategies, guided by target 3.c of the 2030 Agenda and the World Health Organization Global Code of Practice on the International Recruitment of Health Personnel,[130] and noting with concern that highly trained and skilled health personnel from developing countries continue to emigrate at an increasing rate to certain countries, which weakens health systems in countries of origin, while taking into account individual rights of health personnel to work in any country in accordance with applicable laws, and taking into account that nothing should be interpreted as limiting the freedom of health personnel to migrate to countries that wish to employ them,

Noting the negative impact of misinformation, disinformation and stigmatization on preparedness and response to health emergencies, and on people's physical and mental health, and the need to counter misinformation, disinformation and stigmatization in the context of health emergencies, and recognizing that for all stakeholders to be part of the response, they need to have access to timely and accurate information and to be involved in decisions that affect them,

Emphasizing the need to tackle health-related inequities and inequalities within and among countries, as well as social and economic injustices that were exacerbated by the coronavirus disease (COVID-19) pandemic, through political commitment, policies and international cooperation, including those that address social, economic and environmental and other determinants of health,

Noting the discussions on innovative options to enhance the global effort towards the production and equitable distribution of medicines and other health technologies through local and regional production, welcoming the establishment of technology transfer hubs for mRNA vaccines to develop and strengthen local and regional production

[129] Resolution 77/289, annex.

[130] World Health Organization, document WHA63/2010/REC/1, annex 5.

chains in developing countries, and emphasizing the need to enhance the manufacturing and research capacity of countries through innovation and transfer of technology and know-how with the support of developed countries and advanced industries,

Underlining the urgency of having strong and resilient health systems, reaching those who are vulnerable or in vulnerable situations, including those in humanitarian settings as well as health emergencies, and capable of effectively implementing the International Health Regulations (2005)[131] in the context of health emergencies, ensuring pandemic prevention, preparedness and the detection of and response to any outbreaks, infectious disease and other health threats,

Recognizing that armed conflicts have a devastating impact on health systems, leaving persons, especially persons in vulnerable situations, refugees, internally displaced persons and those living in occupied territories or conflict-affected areas, without full access to essential health care and exposing them to preventable diseases and other health risks, and exacerbate health needs, including for mental health and psychosocial support, rehabilitation, treatment for chronic diseases and others such as cancer, HIV/AIDS and tuberculosis,

Highlighting that the COVID-19 pandemic has been one of the greatest global challenges in the history of the United Nations, and noting with deep concern its impact on health and the loss of life, mental health and well-being, as well as the negative impact on global humanitarian needs, gender equality and the empowerment of all women and girls, the enjoyment of human rights and across all spheres of society, including on livelihoods, food security and nutrition, and education, the exacerbation of poverty, hunger and malnutrition, disruption to economies, trade, societies and environments, and the exacerbation of economic and social inequalities within and among countries, particularly between developing and developed countries, which is reversing hard-won development gains and hampering progress towards achieving the 2030 Agenda and all its Goals and targets,

Expressing deep concern about the uneven access of developing countries, particularly African countries, to safe, quality, efficacious, effective, accessible and affordable vaccines against COVID-19, emphasizing the need to enhance the capacities of developing countries to achieve universal health coverage and have equitable access to vaccines and health technologies and means to respond to and recover from the COVID-19 and other pandemics, reaffirming the need to strengthen the support for national, regional and multilateral initiatives that aim to accelerate the development and production of and equitable access to COVID-19 diagnostics, therapeutics and vaccines, and taking note of the Declaration on the Right to Development,[132]

Recalling that, while the World Health Organization has declared an end to COVID-19 as a public health emergency of international concern, the threat of future pandemics remains, and the world needs a stronger, better coordinated, inclusive and more agile global health architecture for pandemic prevention, preparedness, response and recovery to stop the severe impact of future outbreaks,

Recognizing that the COVID-19 pandemic has disproportionately impacted the poor and those in vulnerable situations, with repercussions on health and development gains, thus hampering the achievement of the Sustainable Development Goals and universal health coverage,

Recalling World Health Assembly decision SSA2(5) of 1 December 2021, in which it established an intergovernmental negotiating body to draft and negotiate a World Health Organization convention, agreement or other international instrument on pandemic prevention, preparedness and response, with the aim of strengthening the global health architecture and with a whole-of-government and whole-of-society approach, and noting the progress made, including the agreement that the new international instrument should be legally binding, guided by equity and solidarity,

Emphasizing the need for universal, equitable and timely access to affordable medical and health products to enable rapid and effective response to health emergencies and pandemics, while seriously concerned about the high prices of some health products and the inequitable access within and among States, as well as the financial hardships associated with high prices, which continue to impede progress towards achieving universal health coverage for all,

---

[131] World Health Organization, document WHA58/2005/REC/1, resolution 58.3, annex.

[132] Resolution 41/128, annex.

Recognizing that the COVID-19 pandemic has highlighted the relevance of digitalization in strengthening health systems and providing accessible and equitable health-care services for all, as well as its impact on improving the quality of health-care delivery through information systems that support clinical and management decision-making and planning, to facilitate continuity of care through the creation of longitudinal electronic health records, to enable real-time surveillance and to serve as a basis for precision medicine and personalized health care,

Noting that the current legal frameworks and funding mechanisms are fragmented and rely heavily on bilateral funding and debt, and that there is a need to invest in public health and mobilize international and domestic resources, including to assist developing countries,

Welcoming the launch of the Pandemic Fund in November 2022 as one of the mechanisms to finance critical investments to strengthen national, regional and global pandemic prevention, preparedness and response capacities with a focus on developing countries, and recalling that financing effective national, regional and global health emergency preparedness will require approximately 30 billion dollars per year, including an estimated gap of 10 billion dollars, in new external financing per year outside current official development assistance levels,

Encouraging the promotion of increased access to affordable, safe, effective and quality medicines, including generics, vaccines, diagnostics and health technologies, reaffirming the World Trade Organization Agreement on Trade-Related Aspects of Intellectual Property Rights (TRIPS Agreement) as amended, and also reaffirming the 2001 World Trade Organization Doha Declaration on the TRIPS Agreement and Public Health, which recognizes that intellectual property rights should be interpreted and implemented in a manner supportive of the right of Member States to protect public health and, in particular, to promote access to medicines for all, and noting the need for appropriate incentives in the development of new health products,

Reaffirming the right to use, to the fullest extent, the provisions contained in the World Trade Organization Agreement on Trade-Related Aspects of Intellectual Property Rights (TRIPS Agreement), which provides flexibilities for the protection of public health and promotes access to medicines for all, in particular for developing countries, and the World Trade Organization Doha Declaration on the TRIPS Agreement and Public Health, which recognizes that intellectual property protection is important for the development of new medicines and also recognizes the concerns about its effects on prices, while noting the discussions in the World Trade Organization and other relevant international forums, including on innovative options to enhance the global effort towards the production and timely and equitable distribution of COVID-19 vaccines, therapeutics, diagnostics and other health technologies, including through local production, and noting the outcome of the Twelfth Ministerial Conference of the World Trade Organization, including the ministerial decision on the TRIPS Agreement and the ministerial declaration on the World Trade Organization response to the COVID-19 pandemic and preparedness for future pandemics, while noting discussions in the World Trade Organization on a possible extension of the decision to cover the production and supply of COVID-19 diagnostics and therapeutics,

Seriously concerned that the supply of health products and technologies is dependent on manufacturing facilities concentrated in few countries and that the lack of national or regional production capacities, adequate infrastructure and logistics expertise to store, distribute and deliver diagnostics, medicines, vaccines and other health products and technologies, particularly in developing countries, among other factors, hampers efforts to achieve diagnosis, treatment and vaccination targets for several diseases, at the right time, safely and efficiently, especially in the context of health emergencies,

Stressing the urgent need to reinforce actions and initiatives, including research and development, to tackle known health challenges, including preventable maternal, newborn and child deaths, and ongoing epidemics, such as HIV/AIDS, tuberculosis and malaria, and non-communicable and neglected tropical diseases, which disproportionately affect developing countries and are, in general, determined by social determinants of health,

Recognizing that the human and economic cost of non-communicable diseases contributes to poverty and inequities and threatens the health of peoples and the development of countries, and in this regard reaffirming the commitments to mobilize and allocate adequate, predictable and sustained resources for national responses to prevent and control non-communicable diseases, including through international cooperation and official development assistance,

Welcoming the organization and recalling the political declarations of the 2023 high-level meetings of the General Assembly on pandemic prevention, preparedness and response, on universal health coverage and on the fight against tuberculosis,[133] which highlighted the importance of cooperation, equity and solidarity in scaling up the global effort to leave no one behind and to build a healthier world for all,

Recalling the 2023 political declaration of the high-level political forum on sustainable development convened under the auspices of the General Assembly (Sustainable Development Goals Summit),[134]

Noting that challenges in global health still remain and demand persistent attention and that this urgently requires the fulfilment of commitments to strengthen the global partnership for development, and re-emphasizes in particular North-South cooperation, the importance of South-South and triangular cooperation and the exchange of best practices, as well as capacity-building, research and development, and the transfer of technology on mutually agreed terms to address health inequities in the context of poverty eradication and sustainable development, in line with national priorities,

Noting with concern that access to the benefits of research and innovation, such as quality, safe, efficacious and affordable diagnostics and treatment, remains challenging, especially for developing countries,

Welcoming international cooperation initiatives by the World Health Organization towards the development of and equitable access to COVID-19, malaria, tuberculosis, cholera and HIV/AIDS vaccines in developing countries, inter alia, through the mRNA vaccine technology transfer hub based in South Africa, working with 15 partners across the world, in collaboration with Medicines Patent Pool,

1. *Urges* Member States to continue to consider health issues in the formulation of foreign policy;

2. *Encourages* Member States to strengthen regional and international cooperation, multilateralism, global solidarity, coordination and health governance, towards the progressive realization of the right to the enjoyment of the highest attainable standard of physical and mental health for all, without distinction of any kind;

3. *Calls upon* Member States to continue to contribute actively to the Intergovernmental Negotiating Body to draft and negotiate a legally binding World Health Organization convention, agreement or other international instrument on pandemic prevention, preparedness and response, as well as the amendments to the International Health Regulations (2005) to achieve a timely completion of both processes by the seventy-seventh session of the World Health Assembly in May 2024;

4. *Urges* Member States to cooperate, including through technical and financial support to capacity-building and access to technology in acknowledgement of their different levels of development and capacities, to ensure that all States, in particular developing countries, can effectively implement measures to prevent, prepare for and respond to pandemics and other health emergencies, in accordance with the International Health Regulations (2005);

5. *Also urges* Member States to commit to strengthening women's full, effective and meaningful participation in leadership and decision-making processes in pandemics and other health emergencies at all levels, and to mainstream a gender perspective into all policies and programmes, including in budgetary responses;

6. *Calls upon* Member States, as appropriate, to establish stronger regional capacities for research and development, manufacturing, regulation and procurement of needed tools for equitable and effective access to vaccines, therapeutics, diagnostics and essential supplies, as well as for clinical trials, and to increase global supply through, inter alia, facilitating transfer of technology within the framework of relevant multilateral agreements, while strengthening their leadership, commitment and support in promoting the establishment and strengthening of quality and sustainable local production of medicines and other health technologies that follows good manufacturing practices;

7. *Urges* Member States, where appropriate, based on the national context, to apply a holistic approach in strengthening local and regional production by considering, for example, promoting research and development, transparency of markets for medicines and other health products and technologies, strengthening of regulatory systems, access to sustainable and affordable financing, development of skilled human resources, access to technology transfer on mutually agreed terms for production and needs-based innovation, the aggregation of national and regional demand, and appropriate incentives for private sector investment;

[133] Resolution 78/3, annex, resolution 78/4, annex, and resolution 78/5, annex.

[134] Resolution 78/1, annex.

8. *Also urges* Member States to ensure that digital health interventions complement and enhance health system functions through mechanisms such as accelerating exchange of information, recognizes that digital health interventions are not a substitute for functioning health systems, that there are significant limitations to what digital health is able to address, and that it can never replace the fundamental components needed by health systems such as health workforce, financing, leadership and governance, and access to essential medicines, and in this regard acknowledges the pressing need to address the major impediments that developing countries face in accessing and developing digital technologies, and highlights the importance of financing and capacity-building;

9. *Urges* the sustainable, affordable, fair, equitable, effective, efficient and timely access to medical countermeasures, including vaccines, therapeutics, diagnostics and other health products, and calls upon the World Health Organization to coordinate this with relevant partners, ensuring coherence with the ongoing discussions of the Intergovernmental Negotiating Body and the Working Group on Amendments to the International Health Regulations (2005) in Geneva;

10. *Calls upon* Member States to remove trade barriers, strengthen supply chains, facilitate the movement of medical and public health goods, and diversify manufacturing capacities across regions, especially during pandemics and other health emergencies among and within countries;

11. *Urges* Member States to prioritize, by increasing or maintaining, as appropriate, domestic and international financing for health, to contribute to the sustainable financing of the multilateral system, including the World Health Organization consistent with decisions of the World Health Assembly, and to continue to support the planning of a World Health Organization investment round as part of a more predictably and sustainably financed Organization;

12. *Encourages* Member States to support the Pandemic Fund and in mobilizing additional external resources for pandemic prevention, preparedness and response, including from new donors, and in helping countries to become more resilient to future pandemics and other health emergencies;

13. *Calls upon* the international community to mobilize the means necessary to support Africa's efforts to prevent, prepare for and respond to outbreaks and epidemics that account for over 100 major public health emergency events annually;

14. *Calls upon* Member States to further implement and reinforce an integrated One Health approach that fosters cooperation and collaboration between the human health, animal health and plant health, as well as environmental and other relevant sectors, taking into account the relevant guidance recommended by the World Health Organization, the Food and Agriculture Organization of the United Nations, the World Organization for Animal Health and United Nations Environment Programme, the Quadripartite organizations, and exchanging reliable information and scientific knowledge in a timely manner;

15. *Calls for* international cooperation and coordination in alignment with the Quadripartite One Health Joint Plan of Action (2022–2026), as appropriate, to support building regional, national and community-level capacities, including through the use of a One Health approach, and enable diagnostics of comprehensively addressing outbreaks in animals, the environment and humans during both inter-pandemic and pandemic times;

16. *Calls upon* Member States to strengthen the resilience of their health systems and universal health coverage as an integral part of their systems for effective and sustainable prevention, preparedness and response to pandemics and other public health and humanitarian emergencies, while maintaining access to essential health services, including routine immunization, or to quickly reinstate them after disruption;

17. *Urges* Member States to strengthen international cooperation to support efforts to finance, build, strengthen and maintain capacity in developing countries to improve water, sanitation, hygiene, waste and electricity services in health-care facilities;

18. *Encourages* Member States to accelerate action to address the global shortfall of health and care workers and encourage the development of nationally costed health workforce plans in accordance with the Global Strategy on Human Resources for Health: Workforce 2030 by investing in education, employment and retention, strengthening the institutional capacity for health workforce governance, leadership, disaggregated data and planning, gender equality, addressing causes of health worker migration as well as departure from the health workforce and protecting and supporting all health and care workers from all forms of discrimination, harassment, violence and attacks, and to

promote a decent and safe working environment and conditions at all times as well as ensure their physical and mental health;

19. *Urges* Member States to implement their commitment to provide better opportunities and decent work for women to ensure their role and leadership in the health sector, with a view to increasing the meaningful representation, engagement, participation and empowerment of all women in the workforce at all levels, including in decision-making positions, and take measures towards fair employment practices and eliminating biases against women, and address inequalities, including the gender pay gap, by appropriately remunerating health workers and care workers in the health sector, including community health workers;

20. *Calls upon* Member States to strengthen national efforts, international cooperation and global solidarity to accelerate the achievement of universal health coverage by 2030, with primary health care as a cornerstone, and leave no one behind to ensure healthy lives and promote well-being for all throughout the life course, while reducing catastrophic out-of-pocket health expenditure and eliminating impoverishment due to health-related expenses by 2030;

21. *Also calls upon* Member States to take measures to significantly reduce maternal, perinatal, neonatal, infant and child mortality and morbidity and increase access to quality health-care services for newborns, infants and children, as well as all women before, during and after pregnancy and childbirth, including through providing antenatal and postnatal care, sufficient numbers of skilled birth attendants and adequately supplied birthing facilities;

22. *Urges* timely, equitable and unhindered access to safe, affordable, effective and quality medicines, vaccines, diagnostics and therapeutics and other health products and technologies as one of the fundamental elements for the full realization of the right of everyone to the enjoyment of the highest attainable standard of physical and mental health and the correspondent objectives of universal health coverage and health for all, without discrimination, with special attention to reaching those furthest behind first;

23. *Urges* Member States to ensure, by 2030, universal access to sexual and reproductive health-care services, including for family planning, information and education and the integration of reproductive health into national strategies and programmes, and ensure universal access to sexual and reproductive health and reproductive rights as agreed in accordance with the Programme of Action of the International Conference on Population and Development[135] and the Beijing Platform for Action[136] and the outcome documents of their review conferences;

24. *Also urges* Member States to ensure safe, timely and unhindered access of humanitarian personnel and medical personnel responding to pandemics and other health emergencies, as well as their means of transport, supplies and equipment, and to support, facilitate and enable transportation and logistical supply lines, in order to allow such personnel to efficiently and safely perform their task of assisting affected populations, and in this regard also reaffirms the need to take the necessary measures to respect and protect such personnel, hospitals and other medical facilities consistent with international humanitarian law;

25. *Encourages* Member States to strengthen health literacy and address the negative impact of misinformation, disinformation and stigmatization on public health measures and people's physical and mental health, including on social media platforms, and foster trust in health systems and vaccine confidence, particularly by promoting access to timely and accurate information;

26. *Calls upon* Member States to scale up investments for the tuberculosis response, research and innovation to reduce the number of people falling ill, including by incorporating lessons learned from the response to the COVID-19 pandemic, and achieve the targets agreed in the 2030 Agenda for Sustainable Development[137] and in the End TB Strategy;[138]

27. *Urges* Member States to commit to strengthening research capacity and collaboration through improving tuberculosis research platforms and networks across the public and private sectors, noting platforms and networks

---

[135] *Report of the International Conference on Population and Development, Cairo, 5–13 September 1994* (United Nations publication, Sales No. E.95.XIII.18), chap. I, resolution 1, annex.

[136] *Report of the Fourth World Conference on Women, Beijing, 4–15 September 1995* (United Nations publication, Sales No. E.96.IV.13), chap. I, resolution 1, annex II.

[137] Resolution 70/1.

[138] See World Health Organization, document WHA67/2014/REC/1, resolution 67.1.

such as the BRICS Tuberculosis Research Network in basic science, clinical research and development, including pre-clinical and clinical trials, as well as operational, qualitative and applied research, to advance effective tuberculosis prevention, diagnosis, treatment and care and actions on the economic and social determinants and impacts of the disease;

28. *Calls upon* Member States to commit to reinforcing actions and multilateral initiatives like the Global Fund to fight AIDS, Tuberculosis and Malaria, Unitaid and Gavi, the Vaccine Alliance, including through outreach to the private sector and philanthropic entities with a mission to end ongoing health emergencies and health challenges, such as tuberculosis, HIV/AIDS, malaria, neglected tropical diseases and other preventable diseases that disproportionately affect developing countries;

29. *Also calls upon* Member States to strengthen the meaningful engagement of parliaments, civil society, the educational system and local communities, young people, women and, as appropriate, girls in all aspects of the response to health challenges and health emergencies, to ensure that the response is equitable, inclusive, people-centred and promotes gender equality and respects human rights, including with regard to policymaking forums, planning, care delivery, and national multisectoral accountability and review mechanisms as appropriate, and increase and sustain investment for initiatives, in particular at the community level, and in line with national contexts;

30. *Urges* Member States to strengthen the capacity of health systems for monitoring and minimizing the public health impacts of climate change through adequate preventive measures, preparedness, timely response and effective management of natural disasters, and to develop health measures and integrate them into plans for adaptation to climate change as appropriate;

31. *Invites* the World Health Organization to continue to provide quality and effectively disseminated normative guidance and technical support to Member States, upon their request, in order to build capacity, strengthen health systems and prevention, preparedness and response to health emergencies, promote training, recruitment, development and retention of human resources for health systems and technology transfer on mutually agreed terms with a particular focus on developing countries, and notes with appreciation the creation of the World Health Organization Academy in this regard;

32. *Requests* the President of the General Assembly to convene, in 2025, within existing resources, a one-day high-level interactive dialogue on the social, economic and environmental determinants of health and to draft and circulate a summary of the meeting;

33. *Requests* the Secretary-General, in close collaboration with the Director General of the World Health Organization as well as with relevant international organizations, to report to the General Assembly at its seventy-ninth session, under the item entitled "Global health and foreign policy", on improving international cooperation and multilateral efforts to address global health challenges and promote equity in health for the achievement of the 2030 Agenda.

RESOLUTION 78/281

Adopted at the 80th plenary meeting, on 7 May 2024, without a vote, on the basis of draft resolution A/78/L.56, sponsored by: Afghanistan, Albania, Algeria, Andorra, Angola, Antigua and Barbuda, Argentina, Armenia, Austria, Azerbaijan, Bahamas, Bahrain, Bangladesh, Barbados, Belarus, Belgium, Belize, Benin, Bhutan, Bolivia (Plurinational State of), Bosnia and Herzegovina, Botswana, Brazil, Bulgaria, Burkina Faso, Burundi, Cabo Verde, Cambodia, Cameroon, Canada, Central African Republic, Chad, China, Colombia, Comoros, Congo, Costa Rica, Côte d'Ivoire, Croatia, Cuba, Czechia, Democratic People's Republic of Korea, Democratic Republic of the Congo, Denmark, Djibouti, Dominica, Dominican Republic, Ecuador, Egypt, El Salvador, Equatorial Guinea, Eritrea, Eswatini, Ethiopia, Finland, France, Gabon, Gambia, Georgia, Germany, Ghana, Greece, Guatemala, Guinea-Bissau, Guyana, Haiti, Honduras, Hungary, Iceland, India, Indonesia, Iran (Islamic Republic of), Iraq, Ireland, Italy, Jamaica, Japan, Jordan, Kazakhstan, Kenya, Kiribati, Kuwait, Kyrgyzstan, Lao People's Democratic Republic, Latvia, Lebanon, Lesotho, Liberia, Libya, Liechtenstein, Luxembourg, Malaysia, Maldives, Mali, Malta, Marshall Islands, Mauritania, Mauritius, Micronesia (Federated States of), Monaco, Mongolia, Montenegro, Morocco, Mozambique, Myanmar, Namibia, Nepal, Netherlands (Kingdom of the), Nicaragua, Niger, Nigeria, North Macedonia, Norway, Oman, Pakistan, Palau, Panama, Paraguay, Peru, Philippines, Portugal, Qatar, Republic of Korea, Republic of Moldova, Romania, Russian Federation, Rwanda, Saint Kitts and Nevis, Saint Lucia, Saint Vincent and the Grenadines, Samoa, San Marino, Saudi Arabia, Senegal, Serbia, Seychelles, Sierra Leone, Singapore, Slovakia, Slovenia, Solomon Islands, Somalia, South Africa, Spain, Sri Lanka, Sudan, Suriname, Sweden, Syrian Arab Republic, Tajikistan, Thailand, Timor-Leste, Togo, Trinidad and Tobago, Tunisia, Türkiye, Turkmenistan, Tuvalu, Uganda, United Arab Emirates, United Kingdom of Great Britain and

Northern Ireland, United Republic of Tanzania, Uruguay, Uzbekistan, Vanuatu, Venezuela (Bolivarian Republic of), Viet Nam, Yemen, Zambia, State of Palestine

78/281. World Football Day

The General Assembly,

Recalling its resolution 77/27 of 1 December 2022, in which it reaffirmed that sport is an important enabler of sustainable development and recognized the growing contribution of sport to the realization of development and peace, the promotion of tolerance and respect, and the empowerment of women and girls, young people, individuals and communities, and persons with disabilities, as well as to the achievement of physical and mental health, education and social inclusion objectives,

Recalling also its resolutions on sport as a means to promote education, health, development and peace, in particular resolution 58/5 of 3 November 2003, in which it proclaimed 2005 the International Year for Sport and Physical Education, and resolutions 59/10 of 27 October 2004, 60/9 of 3 November 2005, 61/10 of 3 November 2006, 62/271 of 23 July 2008, 63/135 of 11 December 2008, 65/4 of 18 October 2010, 67/17 of 28 November 2012, 69/6 of 31 October 2014, 71/160 of 16 December 2016, 73/24 of 3 December 2018, 75/18 of 1 December 2020 and 76/259 of 8 April 2022,

Recognizing the valuable contribution of sport in promoting education, sustainable development, peace, gender equality, cooperation, solidarity, fairness, social inclusion and health at the local, regional and international levels, and noting that, as declared in the 2005 World Summit Outcome,[139] sports can contribute to an atmosphere of tolerance and understanding among peoples and nations,

Recalling its resolution 67/296 of 23 August 2013, in which it proclaimed 6 April the International Day of Sport for Development and Peace,

Reaffirming its resolutions 53/199 of 15 December 1998 and 61/185 of 20 December 2006 on the proclamation of international years, and Economic and Social Council resolution 1980/67 of 25 July 1980 on international years and anniversaries,

Recognizing that major international sporting events should be organized in the spirit of peace, mutual understanding, international cooperation, friendship, and tolerance, and without discrimination, and that the unifying and conciliative nature of such events should be respected,

Recognizing also the fundamental role of the Fédération Internationale de Football Association and the important role of regional and national football federations, as well as relevant associations, in promoting the game of football,

Encouraging all Member States and relevant international and regional organizations to facilitate the participation of the athletes in sporting events and competitions,

Recognizing that sports, the arts and physical activity have the power to change perceptions, prejudices and behaviours, as well as to inspire people, break down racial and political barriers, combat discrimination and defuse conflict, as reflected in the political declaration adopted at the Nelson Mandela Peace Summit in 2018,[140]

Noting that sport, including sport for persons with disabilities, has a vital role in promoting peace, development and respect for human rights,

Noting also that sport is a potential tool for raising public awareness on issues such as climate change and health through high-profile events, athletes and teams,

Encouraging Member States involved in delivering mega sporting events to respect applicable laws and international principles, including the Guiding Principles on Business and Human Rights: Implementing the United Nations "Protect, Respect and Remedy" Framework, as well as the fundamental values of Olympism and the International Olympic Movement and other international sport governing organizations,

---

[139] Resolution 60/1.

[140] Resolution 73/1.

Acknowledging the global reach of football and its impact in various spheres, including commerce, peace and diplomacy, and recognizing that football creates a space for cooperation,

Welcoming the Football for the Goals initiative, a platform for the global football community to engage with and advocate for the Sustainable Development Goals and build on sustainability practices,

Recalling that the goal of establishing international days is to create special time and space everywhere around the world to educate the general public on issues of concern, to mobilize political will and resources to address global problems, and to celebrate and reinforce achievements of humanity, and recognizing the global impact of designated international days as springboards for awareness-raising actions,

1. *Commends* countries that have hosted and will host significant international football events and encourages them to ensure that these events leave a lasting legacy for global peace, sportsmanship and fair play;

2. *Emphasizes* that sport, including sport for persons with disabilities, has an important role to play in the promotion of peace and development, respect for human rights, the fight against racism and racial discrimination, gender equality and the empowerment of women and girls, in particular football, given its universal popularity;

3. *Encourages* all Member States to support sport, including football, in its role as a tool to promote peace, development, the empowerment of women and girls, and the achievement of the Sustainable Development Goals, fostering social inclusion, intercultural dialogue and dialogue among civilizations;

4. *Also encourages* Member States to adopt policies and programmes for the promotion of sport and physical activities, including football, at the national and local levels as a means to enhance physical and mental health and well-being and to cultivate a sporting culture in society;

5. *Decides* to proclaim 25 May as World Football Day, as 2024 marks the 100th anniversary of the first international football tournament in history with the representation of all regions as part of the 1924 Summer Olympic Games, held in Paris;

6. *Invites* all States Members of the United Nations, members of the specialized agencies and observers of the General Assembly, as well as organizations of the United Nations system, in particular the Division for Inclusive Social Development of the Department of Economic and Social Affairs of the Secretariat, other international and regional organizations, academia, civil society, the private sector and other relevant stakeholders to observe World Football Day in an appropriate manner and in accordance with national priorities, and to disseminate the advantages of football for all, including through educational and public awareness-raising activities;

7. *Stresses* that the cost of all activities that may arise from the implementation of the present resolution should be met through voluntary contributions;

8. *Requests* the Secretary-General to bring the present resolution to the attention of all Member States, the organizations of the United Nations system and other relevant stakeholders for appropriate observance.

RESOLUTION 78/282

Adopted at the 82nd plenary meeting, on 23 May 2024, by a recorded vote of 84 to 19, with 68 abstentions,* on the basis of draft resolution A/78/L.67/Rev.1, sponsored by: Albania, Andorra, Australia, Austria, Bangladesh, Belgium, Bosnia and Herzegovina, Bulgaria, Canada, Chile, Croatia, Denmark, Estonia, Finland, France, Germany, Iceland, Ireland, Italy, Jordan, Latvia, Liechtenstein, Lithuania, Luxembourg, Malaysia, Marshall Islands, Micronesia (Federated States of), Netherlands (Kingdom of the), New Zealand, North Macedonia, Norway, Poland, Rwanda, Slovenia, Sweden, Türkiye, United Kingdom of Great Britain and Northern Ireland, United States of America

* *In favour:* Albania, Andorra, Australia, Austria, Bangladesh, Belgium, Bosnia and Herzegovina, Brunei Darussalam, Bulgaria, Cabo Verde, Canada, Chad, Chile, Colombia, Costa Rica, Croatia, Czechia, Denmark, Djibouti, Ecuador, Egypt, El Salvador, Estonia, Fiji, Finland, France, Gambia, Germany, Guinea-Bissau, Guyana, Iceland, Indonesia, Iran (Islamic Republic of), Iraq, Ireland, Italy, Japan, Jordan, Kuwait, Latvia, Libya, Liechtenstein, Lithuania, Luxembourg, Malawi, Malaysia, Malta, Mauritania, Micronesia (Federated States of), Montenegro, Myanmar, Netherlands (Kingdom of the), New Zealand, Niger, North Macedonia, Norway, Pakistan, Palau, Poland, Portugal, Qatar, Republic of Korea, Republic of Moldova, Romania, Rwanda, San Marino, Saudi Arabia, Senegal, Sierra Leone, Singapore, Slovenia, South Africa, Spain, Sweden, Switzerland, Tunisia, Türkiye, Ukraine, United Kingdom of Great Britain and Northern Ireland, United Republic of Tanzania, United States of America, Uruguay, Yemen, Zambia

Against: Antigua and Barbuda, Belarus, China, Comoros, Cuba, Democratic People's Republic of Korea, Democratic Republic of the Congo, Dominica, Eritrea, Eswatini, Grenada, Hungary, Mali, Nauru, Nicaragua, Russian Federation, Sao Tome and Principe, Serbia, Syrian Arab Republic

Abstaining: Algeria, Angola, Argentina, Armenia, Bahamas, Bahrain, Barbados, Benin, Bhutan, Botswana, Brazil, Burundi, Cambodia, Cameroon, Congo, Côte d'Ivoire, Cyprus, Dominican Republic, Equatorial Guinea, Ethiopia, Gabon, Georgia, Ghana, Greece, Guatemala, Guinea, Haiti, Honduras, India, Jamaica, Kazakhstan, Kenya, Kiribati, Lao People's Democratic Republic, Lebanon, Lesotho, Madagascar, Maldives, Mexico, Mongolia, Mozambique, Namibia, Nepal, Nigeria, Oman, Panama, Papua New Guinea, Paraguay, Peru, Philippines, Saint Kitts and Nevis, Saint Lucia, Saint Vincent and the Grenadines, Seychelles, Slovakia, Solomon Islands, South Sudan, Sri Lanka, Sudan, Suriname, Tajikistan, Thailand, Togo, Trinidad and Tobago, Tuvalu, Uganda, United Arab Emirates, Viet Nam

78/282. International Day of Reflection and Commemoration of the 1995 Genocide in Srebrenica

The General Assembly,

Guided by the Charter of the United Nations, the Universal Declaration of Human Rights[141] and the Convention on the Prevention and Punishment of the Crime of Genocide,[142]

Recalling Security Council resolution 819 (1993) of 16 April 1993 declaring Srebrenica a safe area, resolution 827 (1993) of 25 May 1993 concerning the establishment of the International Tribunal for the Former Yugoslavia and resolution 1966 (2010) of 22 December 2010 concerning the establishment of the International Residual Mechanism for Criminal Tribunals,

Recalling also all judgments of the International Tribunal for the Former Yugoslavia, in particular eight that contain guilty verdicts for the crime of genocide against Bosnian Muslims committed at Srebrenica in 1995, most notably the Tribunal Appeals Chamber judgment of 19 April 2004 (*The Prosecutor v. Krstić*), the International Residual Mechanism for Criminal Tribunals Appeals Chamber judgment of 8 June 2021 (*The Prosecutor v. Mladić*) and the Mechanism Appeals Chamber judgment of 20 March 2019 (*The Prosecutor v. Karadžić*), as well as the judgment of the International Court of Justice of 26 February 2007, in which the Court determined that the acts committed in Srebrenica constituted acts of genocide,

Reaffirming its strong opposition to impunity for genocide, crimes against humanity, war crimes or other violations of international humanitarian law and international human rights law, and emphasizing in this context the responsibility of States to end impunity and, to that end, to thoroughly investigate and prosecute, in accordance with their relevant international legal obligations and their domestic law, persons responsible for such acts, in order to avoid their recurrence and to seek sustainable peace, justice, truth and reconciliation, for which the participation of victims and survivors as well as their family members is central,

Welcoming the important progress made by international courts in recent years with respect to the fight against impunity and in ensuring accountability for genocide, crimes against humanity, war crimes and other egregious crimes achieved through the international criminal justice system,

Recognizing in this regard the particular contribution of the International Tribunal for the Former Yugoslavia, and emphasizing the importance of the international community being prepared to take collective action through the Security Council, in accordance with the Charter, and on a case-by-case basis to further ensure accountability for and the prevention of genocide,

Reiterating that criminal accountability under international law for the crime of genocide is individualized and cannot be attributed to any ethnic, religious or other group or community as a whole,

Taking note of the role of the Special Advisers to the Secretary-General on the Prevention of Genocide and on the Responsibility to Protect, and noting the importance of regular briefings on human rights and international humanitarian law violations as well as on hate speech and incitement in raising early awareness of potential genocide,

Noting that the prosecution of persons responsible for genocide and other international crimes in national justice systems, including the Court of Bosnia and Herzegovina, and the International Tribunal for the Former Yugoslavia as well as the International Residual Mechanism for Criminal Tribunals, remains central to the process of national

---

[141] Resolution 217 A (III).

[142] Resolution 260 A (III), annex.

reconciliation and trust-building and to the restoration and maintenance of peace in Bosnia and Herzegovina, and recognizing that strong regional cooperation between national prosecutors' offices is essential in fostering peace, justice, truth and reconciliation among countries in the region,

Reiterating the unwavering commitment to maintaining stability and fostering unity in diversity in Bosnia and Herzegovina,

Noting that 2025 will mark the thirtieth anniversary of the genocide in Srebrenica, in which at least 8,372 lives were lost, thousands were displaced and families and communities were devastated,

1. *Decides* to designate 11 July as the International Day of Reflection and Commemoration of the 1995 Genocide in Srebrenica, to be observed annually;

2. *Condemns without reservation* any denial of the Srebrenica genocide as a historical event, and urges Member States to preserve the established facts, including through their educational systems by developing appropriate programmes, also in remembrance, towards preventing denial and distortion, and occurrence of genocides in the future;

3. *Also condemns without reservation* actions that glorify those convicted of war crimes, crimes against humanity and genocide by international courts, including those responsible for the Srebrenica genocide;

4. *Emphasizes* the importance of completing the process of finding and identifying the remaining victims of the Srebrenica genocide and according them dignified burials, and calls for the continued prosecution of those perpetrators of the Srebrenica genocide who have yet to face justice;

5. *Urges* all States to fully adhere to their obligations under the Convention on the Prevention and Punishment of the Crime of Genocide, as applicable, and customary international law on the prevention and punishment of genocide, with due regard to relevant decisions of the International Court of Justice;

6. Reques*ts the S*ecretary-General to establish an outreach programme entitled "The Srebrenica Genocide and the United Nations", starting its activities with preparations for the thirtieth anniversary in 2025, and also requests the Secretary-General to bring the present resolution to the attention of all Member States, organizations of the United Nations system and civil society organizations for appropriate observance;

7. *Invites* all Member States, organizations of the United Nations system, other international and regional organizations and civil society, including non-governmental organizations, academic institutions and other relevant stakeholders to observe the International Day, including special observances and activities in memory and honour of the victims of the 1995 genocide in Srebrenica, as well as appropriate education and public awareness-raising activities.

RESOLUTION 78/283

Adopted at the 85th plenary meeting, on 4 June 2024, by a recorded vote of 103 to 9, with 53 abstentions,* on the basis of draft resolution A/78/L.74, sponsored by: Albania, Andorra, Antigua and Barbuda, Australia, Austria, Belgium, Bulgaria, Cabo Verde, Canada, Costa Rica, Croatia, Czechia, Democratic Republic of the Congo, Denmark, Djibouti, Estonia, Fiji, Finland, France, Georgia, Germany, Greece, Guatemala, Hungary, Iceland, Ireland, Italy, Japan, Kiribati, Latvia, Liberia, Liechtenstein, Lithuania, Luxembourg, Malawi, Malta, Marshall Islands, Mexico, Micronesia (Federated States of), Monaco, Montenegro, Netherlands (Kingdom of the), New Zealand, North Macedonia, Norway, Palau, Papua New Guinea, Poland, Portugal, Republic of Moldova, Romania, San Marino, Slovakia, Slovenia, Spain, Sweden, Tonga, Trinidad and Tobago, Türkiye, Tuvalu, Ukraine, United Kingdom of Great Britain and Northern Ireland, United States of America, Vanuatu

* *In favour:* Albania, Andorra, Antigua and Barbuda, Argentina, Armenia, Australia, Austria, Azerbaijan, Bahamas, Barbados, Belgium, Belize, Bosnia and Herzegovina, Botswana, Bulgaria, Cabo Verde, Canada, Chile, Colombia, Costa Rica, Côte d'Ivoire, Croatia, Cyprus, Czechia, Democratic Republic of the Congo, Denmark, Djibouti, Dominica, Dominican Republic, Ecuador, Estonia, Fiji, Finland, France, Gambia, Georgia, Germany, Ghana, Greece, Grenada, Guatemala, Guyana, Haiti, Honduras, Hungary, Iceland, Ireland, Italy, Jamaica, Japan, Kiribati, Latvia, Liberia, Liechtenstein, Lithuania, Luxembourg, Malawi, Maldives, Malta, Marshall Islands, Mauritius, Mexico, Micronesia (Federated States of), Monaco, Montenegro, Myanmar, Netherlands (Kingdom of the), New Zealand, North Macedonia, Norway, Palau, Panama, Papua New Guinea, Peru, Philippines, Poland, Portugal, Republic of Moldova, Romania, Saint Kitts and Nevis, Saint Lucia, Saint Vincent and the Grenadines, Samoa, San Marino, Singapore, Slovakia, Slovenia, Solomon Islands, South Africa, Spain, Suriname, Sweden, Timor-Leste, Tonga, Trinidad and Tobago, Türkiye, Tuvalu, Ukraine, United Kingdom of Great Britain and Northern Ireland, United States of America, Uruguay, Vanuatu, Zambia

Against: Belarus, Burundi, Cuba, Democratic People's Republic of Korea, Mali, Nicaragua, Russian Federation, Syrian Arab Republic, Zimbabwe

Abstaining: Algeria, Bahrain, Bangladesh, Benin, Bhutan, Brazil, Brunei Darussalam, Cambodia, Cameroon, China, Egypt, El Salvador, Eritrea, Ethiopia, Gabon, Guinea-Bissau, India, Indonesia, Iran (Islamic Republic of), Iraq, Israel, Kazakhstan, Kenya, Kuwait, Kyrgyzstan, Lebanon, Libya, Madagascar, Malaysia, Mauritania, Mongolia, Morocco, Mozambique, Namibia, Nepal, Niger, Oman, Pakistan, Paraguay, Qatar, Republic of Korea, Saudi Arabia, Senegal, Serbia, Sri Lanka, Switzerland, Tajikistan, Thailand, Togo, United Arab Emirates, United Republic of Tanzania, Uzbekistan, Yemen

78/283. Status of internally displaced persons and refugees from Abkhazia, Georgia, and the Tskhinvali region/South Ossetia, Georgia

The General Assembly,

Recalling all its relevant resolutions on the protection of and assistance to internally displaced persons, including its resolutions 62/153 of 18 December 2007, 62/249 of 15 May 2008, 63/307 of 9 September 2009, 64/162 of 18 December 2009, 64/296 of 7 September 2010, 65/287 of 29 June 2011, 66/165 of 19 December 2011, 66/283 of 3 July 2012, 67/268 of 13 June 2013, 68/180 of 18 December 2013, 68/274 of 5 June 2014, 69/286 of 3 June 2015, 70/165 of 17 December 2015, 70/265 of 7 June 2016, 71/290 of 1 June 2017, 72/182 of 19 December 2017, 72/280 of 12 June 2018, 73/298 of 4 June 2019, 74/160 of 18 December 2019, 74/300 of 3 September 2020, 75/285 of 16 June 2021, 76/167 of 16 December 2021, 76/267 of 8 June 2022, 77/293 of 7 June 2023 and 78/205 of 19 December 2023,

Recalling also all relevant Security Council resolutions on Georgia relating to the need for all parties to work towards a comprehensive peace and the return of internally displaced persons and refugees to their places of origin, and stressing the importance of their full and timely implementation,

Recognizing the Guiding Principles on Internal Displacement[143] as the key international framework for the protection of internally displaced persons,

Concerned by forced demographic changes resulting from the conflicts in Georgia,

Concerned also by the humanitarian situation caused by armed conflict in August 2008, which resulted in the further forced displacement of civilians,

Mindful of the urgent need to find a solution to the problems related to forced displacement in Georgia,

Underlining the importance of the discussions that commenced in Geneva on 15 October 2008 and of continuing to address the issue of the voluntary, safe, dignified and unhindered return of internally displaced persons and refugees on the basis of internationally recognized principles and conflict-settlement practices,

Taking note of the report of the Secretary-General concerning the implementation of resolution 77/293,[144]

1. *Recognizes* the right of return of all internally displaced persons and refugees and their descendants, regardless of ethnicity, to their homes throughout Georgia, including in Abkhazia and the Tskhinvali region/South Ossetia;

2. *Stresses* the need to respect the property rights of all internally displaced persons and refugees affected by the conflicts in Georgia and to refrain from obtaining property in violation of those rights;

3. *Reaffirms* the unacceptability of forced demographic changes;

4. *Underlines* the urgent need for unimpeded access for humanitarian activities to all internally displaced persons, refugees and other persons residing in all conflict-affected areas throughout Georgia;

5. *Calls upon* all participants in the Geneva discussions to intensify their efforts to establish a durable peace, to commit to enhanced confidence-building measures and to take immediate steps to ensure respect for human rights and create favourable security conditions conducive to the voluntary, safe, dignified and unhindered return of all internally displaced persons and refugees to their places of origin;

[143] E/CN.4/1998/53/Add.2, annex.

[144] A/78/864.

6. *Underlines* the need for the development of a timetable to ensure the voluntary, safe, dignified and unhindered return of all internally displaced persons and refugees affected by the conflicts in Georgia to their homes;

7. *Requests* the Secretary-General to submit to the General Assembly at its seventy-ninth session a comprehensive report on the implementation of the present resolution;

8. *Decides* to include in the provisional agenda of its seventy-ninth session the item entitled "Protracted conflicts in the GUAM area and their implications for international peace, security and development".

RESOLUTION 78/284

Adopted at the 85th plenary meeting, on 4 June 2024, without a vote, on the basis of draft resolution A/78/L.68, sponsored by: Afghanistan, Algeria, Armenia, Azerbaijan, Bahrain, Belarus, China, Congo, Djibouti, Egypt, Indonesia, Iran (Islamic Republic of), Japan, Jordan, Kazakhstan, Kiribati, Kuwait, Kyrgyzstan, Morocco, Nicaragua, Oman, Pakistan, Philippines, Qatar, Russian Federation, Saudi Arabia, Senegal, Singapore, Tajikistan, Türkiye, Turkmenistan, United Arab Emirates, Uzbekistan

78/284. Central Asia's unified resolve and cooperation to effectively address and counter drug-related challenges

The General Assembly,

Guided by the Charter of the United Nations,

Underscoring that the Single Convention on Narcotic Drugs of 1961 as amended by the 1972 Protocol,[145] the Convention on Psychotropic Substances of 1971,[146] the United Nations Convention against Illicit Traffic in Narcotic Drugs and Psychotropic Substances of 1988[147] and other relevant instruments constitute the cornerstone of the international drug control system,

Reaffirming its commitment to the goals and objectives of the three international drug control conventions, including concern about the health and welfare of humankind as well as the individual and public health-related, social and safety problems resulting from the abuse of narcotic drugs and psychotropic substances, in particular among children and young people, and drug-related crime, and reaffirming its determination to prevent and treat the abuse of such substances and prevent and counter their illicit cultivation, production, manufacturing and trafficking,

Reaffirming its commitment also, based on the principle of common and shared responsibility, to accelerating the full implementation of existing drug policy commitments, including the 2009 Political Declaration and Plan of Action on International Cooperation towards an Integrated and Balanced Strategy to Counter the World Drug Problem,[148] the Joint Ministerial Statement of the 2014 high-level review by the Commission on Narcotic Drugs of the implementation by Member States of the Political Declaration and Plan of Action[149] and the outcome document of the special session of the General Assembly on the world drug problem held in 2016,[150] aimed at achieving all drug policy commitments, operational recommendations and aspirational goals set out therein, as reaffirmed in the 2019 Ministerial Declaration on Strengthening Our Actions at the National, Regional and International Levels to Accelerate the Implementation of Our Joint Commitments to Address and Counter the World Drug Problem and the 2024 high-level declaration by the Commission on Narcotic Drugs on the 2024 midterm review, following up to the Ministerial Declaration of 2019,[151]

Reaffirming its unwavering commitment to effectively addressing and countering the world drug problem, which requires concerted and sustained action at the national and international levels, including accelerating the implementation of existing drug policy commitments, and ensuring that all aspects of demand reduction and related measures, supply reduction and related measures and international cooperation are addressed in full conformity with

---

[145] United Nations, *Treaty Series*, vol. 976, No. 14152.

[146] Ibid., vol. 1019, No. 14956.

[147] Ibid., vol. 1582, No. 27627.

[148] See *Official Records of the Economic and Social Council, 2009, Supplement No. 8* (E/2009/28), chap. I, sect. C.

[149] Ibid., *2014, Supplement No. 8* (E/2014/28), chap. I, sect. C.

[150] Resolution S-30/1, annex.

[151] See *Official Records of the Economic and Social Council, 2024, Supplement No. 8* (E/2024/28), chap. I, sect. B.

the purposes and principles of the Charter of the United Nations, international law and the Universal Declaration of Human Rights,[152] with full respect for the sovereignty and territorial integrity of States, the principle of non-intervention in the internal affairs of States, all human rights, fundamental freedoms, the inherent dignity of all individuals and the principles of equal rights and mutual respect among States,

Reaffirming the 2030 Agenda for Sustainable Development,[153] and reiterating that efforts to achieve the Sustainable Development Goals and to effectively address the world drug problem are complementary and mutually reinforcing,

Welcoming the increasing bilateral and regional cooperation among the countries of the region at all levels towards creating a dynamic and reinvigorated Central Asia, which provides new opportunities for United Nations engagement,

Noting the determination of Central Asian countries to address and counter the world drug problem and to actively promote a society free of drug abuse in order to help to ensure that all people can live in health, dignity and peace, with security and prosperity, and to address public health, safety and social problems resulting from drug abuse,

Recalling relevant United Nations resolutions, including General Assembly resolutions related to addressing and countering the world drug problem, as well as relevant resolutions and decisions adopted by the Commission on Narcotic Drugs,

Reaffirming the principal role of the Commission on Narcotic Drugs as the policymaking body of the United Nations system with prime responsibility for drug control matters, and the support and appreciation of the General Assembly for the efforts of the relevant United Nations entities, in particular those of the United Nations Office on Drugs and Crime as the leading entity in the United Nations system for addressing and countering the world drug problem, and reaffirming also the treaty-mandated roles of the International Narcotics Control Board and the World Health Organization,

Noting the activities and contribution of the Central Asian Regional Information and Coordination Centre for combating the illicit trafficking of narcotic drugs, psychotropic substances and their precursors in countering the illicit production of and trafficking in narcotic drugs, psychotropic substances and their precursors and coordinating efforts of the competent authorities of participating States in combating other drug-related crime,

Reaffirming the crucial role of Member States in developing an effective and comprehensive approach to addressing and countering all aspects of the world drug problem,

Underscoring the important role played by all relevant stakeholders, including law enforcement, judicial and health-care personnel, civil society, the scientific community and academia, as well as the private sector, in supporting the efforts of Member States to implement joint commitments at all levels, and underscoring also the importance of promoting relevant partnerships,

Reaffirming its commitment to a balanced, integrated, comprehensive, multidisciplinary and scientific evidence-based approach to the world drug problem, based on the principle of common and shared responsibility, and recognizing the importance of appropriately mainstreaming a gender and age perspective into drug-related policies and programmes and that appropriate emphasis should be placed on individuals, families, communities and society as a whole, with a particular focus on women, children and youth, with a view to promoting and protecting health, including access to treatment, safety and the well-being of all humanity,

Expressing concerns about the serious challenges to the States of Central Asia posed by illicit trafficking in drugs, including opiates and synthetic drugs, in particular methamphetamine,

Recognizing that transit States continue to face multifaceted challenges, and reaffirming the continuing need for cooperation and support, including the provision of technical assistance to, inter alia, enhance their capacities to effectively address and counter the world drug problem, in conformity with the 1988 Convention,

[152] Resolution 217 A (III).

[153] Resolution 70/1.

Concerned about the persistent and emerging challenges posed by the links between drug trafficking and other forms of organized crime, including money-laundering, trafficking in firearms and corruption and, in some cases, terrorism, including money-laundering in connection with the financing of terrorism,

Noting the existence of the ongoing cooperation processes among the States of Central Asia to counter the illicit trafficking in narcotic drugs, psychotropic substances and their precursor chemicals and related illicit financial flows, and their commitment to addressing the regional drug-related challenges through a balanced, integrated, comprehensive, multidisciplinary and scientific evidence-based approach, in line with the principle of common and shared responsibility,

Recognizing the indispensable role of quality, timely, relevant, disaggregated, including geographically disaggregated, and reliable data in driving scientific evidence-based policies to better understand persistent, new and emerging trends, patterns and dynamics, and the commitment to sharing data, in particular through the United Nations Office on Drugs and Crime annual report questionnaire and other tools of the Office, the International Narcotics Control Board and the World Health Organization, as appropriate and achievable,

Recognizing also the importance of benefiting from technological innovation and know-how to address persistent, new and emerging trends and challenges, and acknowledging the need for increased international cooperation aimed at addressing and overcoming effectively challenges, obstacles and impediments at all levels to leverage these advancements for joint efforts, as well as the importance of addressing existing technological gaps and the need to strengthen the capabilities of Member States through specialized, targeted, effective and sustainable technical assistance to Member States, upon their request,

Reaffirming the need to address the key causes and consequences of the world drug problem, including those in the health, social, human rights, economic, justice, public security and law enforcement fields, in line with the principle of common and shared responsibility, and recognizing the value of comprehensive and balanced policy interventions, including those in the field of promotion of sustainable and viable livelihoods,

Recognizing that misperceptions of drug-related risks, along with other behavioural and socioeconomic factors, in societies can lead to increased or more harmful illicit drug use and require more scientific evidence-based evaluation and further systematic and sustainable preventive approaches to protect people, in particular children and youth, from illicit drug use,

1. *Acknowledges* the efforts of the States of Central Asia to actively promote a society free of drug abuse by considering the development, implementation and evaluation of comprehensive, balanced, scientific evidence-based and multidisciplinary strategies aligned with the obligations under applicable international law, including the three international drug control conventions, and the international drug policy commitments, and also acknowledges the ongoing joint efforts in the region to implement specific practical measures in this direction, while stressing the importance of respecting, protecting and promoting all human rights, fundamental freedoms and the inherent dignity of all individuals and the rule of law in the development and implementation of drug policies;

2. *Also acknowledges* the commitment of Central Asian States to continuing to fully comply with their obligations, achieve the goals and objectives and implement the provisions of the Single Convention on Narcotic Drugs of 1961 as amended by the 1972 Protocol, the Convention on Psychotropic Substances of 1971 and the United Nations Convention against Illicit Traffic in Narcotic Drugs and Psychotropic Substances of 1988;

3. *Acknowledges* the strong intention of the States of the Central Asian region to improve national and regional cooperation on drug-related matters, including an enhanced integrated border management, and cross-border information exchange, especially along the trade and transit corridors to prevent drug trafficking and related illicit financial flows, the development of unified approaches to scheduling of controlled substances as well as the introduction of a regional electronic database of results of forensic chemical examinations of amphetamine-type stimulants and new psychoactive substances, within the regional networks of interaction between law enforcement and judicial authorities and between them;

4. *Invites* Member States of the Central Asian region to consider enhancing cooperation among public health, education and law enforcement authorities when developing and implementing scientific evidence-based drug use prevention initiatives;

5. *Underscores* the importance of strengthening cooperation in Central Asia by considering and developing strategic initiatives and action plans to counter threats posed by illicit trafficking in opiates and synthetic drugs, including methamphetamine, as well as their precursor chemicals, at the regional and international levels;

6. *Welcomes* the efforts of Central Asian States to promote increased access to and availability of controlled substances for medical and scientific purposes, while preventing their diversion, misuse and trafficking, to achieve the goals and objectives as well as to implement provisions set out in the three international drug control conventions;

7. *Calls upon* the relevant United Nations institutions to assist the countries of the region, upon their request and within respective mandates, in countering the illicit production of and trafficking in narcotic drugs, psychotropic substances and their precursors, and the laundering of proceeds of drug-related crime, in particular within the framework of the programmes of the United Nations Office on Drugs and Crime, as well as sustained activities of the Central Asian Regional Information and Coordination Centre for combating the illicit trafficking of narcotic drugs, psychotropic substances and their precursors, and to support the development of regional strategies and enhance regional cooperation through information-sharing and joint operational activities, using capabilities of regional organizations where feasible, and reinforcing national programmes in Central Asia aimed at providing non-discriminatory and voluntary access to drug-related prevention, treatment, education, care, sustained recovery, rehabilitation, social reintegration and related support services, in particular for people who may face obstacles when accessing those services, including, where relevant, those impacted by social marginalization, while mainstreaming a gender perspective into the development and implementation of those national programmes and services;

8. *Calls upon* the United Nations Office on Drugs and Crime, in collaboration with the World Health Organization and other relevant United Nations entities, to support countries of the region in taking effective and practical scientific evidence-based measures, including interventions related to prevention, treatment, care and recovery support, as well as other public health interventions, to address harm associated with illicit drug use as part of comprehensive, systematic and sustainable demand reduction initiatives, and addressing challenges related to drug use disorders and co-occurring comorbidities;

9. *Encourages* Member States to promote bilateral, regional and international cooperation with and technical assistance to States, including in Central Asia, affected by illicit crop cultivation and illicit production, manufacture, transit, trafficking, distribution and abuse of narcotic drugs and psychotropic substances, including synthetic drugs, in developing and implementing comprehensive and integrated policies, including through intelligence-sharing and cross-border cooperation, and by reinforcing national programmes aimed at education, prevention, early intervention, treatment, care, rehabilitation and social reintegration;

10. *Encourages* Central Asian States, with the support of the United Nations Office on Drugs and Crime and other relevant international and regional organizations and the donor community, subject to the availability of funds, to enhance data collection, research, the sharing of information and the scaling-up of studies on the impact of illicit drug trafficking and distribution on those affected by and vulnerable to illicit drug use, including youth and women, in support of the comprehensive scientific evidence-based and balanced decision-making and drug policies;

11. *Welcomes* the establishment of the United Nations Office on Drugs and Crime Information Centre for researching and analysing transnational threats in the region related to drugs and crime with a view to enhancing data collection and understanding of the drug-related trends and driving scientific evidence-based policies;

12. *Encourages* the Central Asian States to establish partnerships, with the support of the United Nations Office on Drugs and Crime and other relevant United Nations entities, regional and international organizations, within their respective mandates, including the Information Centre for researching and analysing transnational threats in the region related to drugs and crime, as appropriate, other Member States and relevant stakeholders, including law enforcement, judicial and health-care personnel, by voluntarily establishing and strengthening partnerships or cooperation with civil society, academia and private sector entities, where relevant and in accordance with domestic laws, to conduct research and surveys to address drug-related public health and public security challenges related to the illicit production of and trafficking in drugs and all other aspects of the regional drug problem in Central Asia;

13. *Also encourages* Central Asian States to consider, including in the context of comprehensive and balanced drug demand reduction efforts, relevant interventions that prevent the transmission of HIV, viral hepatitis and other blood-borne diseases associated with drug use, as well as consider ensuring access to such interventions, including in treatment and outreach services, prisons and other custodial settings, and promoting in that regard the use, as appropriate, of the technical guide for countries to set targets for universal access to HIV prevention, treatment and

care for injecting drug users, issued by the World Health Organization, the United Nations Office on Drugs and Crime and the Joint United Nations Programme on HIV/AIDS;

14. *Further calls for* strengthening common efforts of Central Asian countries on promoting the use of new technologies and means to counter illicit trafficking of narcotic drugs and psychotropic substances and their precursor chemicals, including through the darknet, surface web and social networks as well as on preventing the use of electronic payment systems and virtual assets, including those provided by virtual asset service providers, and non-cash assets, for these purposes, in particular, through continued development and implementation of measures aimed at mitigating risks, associated with these assets, and preventing their misuse and abuse for illicit drug-related purposes;

15. *Invites* Member States, relevant United Nations entities, international financial institutions and other relevant stakeholders to enhance the provision of tailored, targeted, effective and sustainable technical assistance to the States of Central Asia, upon request, in the form of training, capacity-building, provision of equipment, sharing of knowledge, and transfer of technology on a voluntary and mutually agreed basis, through the United Nations Office on Drugs and Crime and other relevant specialized agencies and bodies of the United Nations system, within their respective mandates and existing resources, and international and regional mechanisms, to implement the provisions of the present resolution in Central Asia.

RESOLUTION 78/285

Adopted at the 88th plenary meeting, on 7 June 2024, without a vote, on the basis of draft resolution A/78/L.73, submitted by the President of the General Assembly

78/285. Review of the implementation of General Assembly resolution 75/290 A on the strengthening of the Economic and Social Council and resolution 75/290 B on the high-level political forum on sustainable development and the follow-up and review of the 2030 Agenda for Sustainable Development at the global level

The General Assembly,

Recalling its resolutions 75/290 A and 75/290 B of 25 June 2021,

1. *Decides* that the thematic focus of the Economic and Social Council and the high-level political forum on sustainable development for their 2025, 2026 and 2027 sessions shall be:

(a) For 2025: Advancing sustainable, inclusive, science- and evidence-based solutions for the 2030 Agenda for Sustainable Development and its Sustainable Development Goals for leaving no one behind;

(b) For 2026: Transformative, equitable, innovative and coordinated actions for the 2030 Agenda for Sustainable Development and its Sustainable Development Goals for a sustainable future for all;

(c) For 2027: Scaling up just transitions to achieving sustainable development, poverty eradication and the full implementation of the 2030 Agenda for Sustainable Development and its Sustainable Development Goals;

2. *Decides also* that, for the 2025, 2026 and 2027 sessions of the high-level political forum convened under the auspices of the Economic and Social Council, without prejudice to the integrated, indivisible and interlinked nature of the Sustainable Development Goals, the sets of Sustainable Development Goals to be reviewed in depth shall be:

(a) For 2025: Goals 3, 5, 8, 14 and 17;

(b) For 2026: Goals 6, 7, 9, 11 and 17;

(c) For 2027: Goals 4, 10, 12, 15 and 17;

3. *Agrees* to fully review at its eightieth session the arrangements contained in resolutions 75/290 A and 75/290 B and their annexes, in conjunction with each other, in order to benefit from lessons learned from the previous cycles of the high-level political forum as well as from relevant processes under the General Assembly and the Economic and Social Council related to the follow-up and review of the 2030 Agenda;

4. *Decides* that all provisions contained in resolutions 75/290 A and 75/290 B and their annexes and all previous resolutions on strengthening the Economic and Social Council and on the high-level political forum on

sustainable development and the follow-up and review of the 2030 Agenda for Sustainable Development at the global level shall remain in effect unless updated or replaced in the present resolution or subsequent resolutions of the General Assembly.

RESOLUTION 78/286

Adopted at the 88th plenary meeting, on 7 June 2024, without a vote, on the basis of draft resolution A/78/L.75, sponsored by: Afghanistan, Algeria, Armenia, Azerbaijan, Bahrain, Bangladesh, Belarus, Bolivia (Plurinational State of), Brunei Darussalam, Burkina Faso, Burundi, Cambodia, Cameroon, Central African Republic, Chad, China, Cuba, Cyprus, Democratic People's Republic of Korea, Djibouti, Dominica, Ecuador, Egypt, Equatorial Guinea, Eritrea, Ethiopia, Gambia, Greece, Hungary, Indonesia, Iran (Islamic Republic of), Iraq, Kazakhstan, Kenya, Kiribati, Kuwait, Kyrgyzstan, Lao People's Democratic Republic, Lebanon, Liberia, Libya, Malaysia, Maldives, Mali, Mauritius, Morocco, Mozambique, Namibia, Nicaragua, Niger, Pakistan, Peru, Philippines, Qatar, Russian Federation, Rwanda, Saudi Arabia, Serbia, Seychelles, Sierra Leone, Solomon Islands, Somalia, South Africa, South Sudan, Sri Lanka, Sudan, Suriname, Syrian Arab Republic, Tajikistan, Thailand, Timor-Leste, Togo, Trinidad and Tobago, Tunisia, Türkiye, Turkmenistan, Uganda, United Arab Emirates, United Republic of Tanzania, Uzbekistan, Venezuela (Bolivarian Republic of), Viet Nam, Zimbabwe

78/286. International Day for Dialogue among Civilizations

The General Assembly,

Reaffirming the purposes and principles of the Charter of the United Nations, the Universal Declaration of Human Rights,[154] in which it is proclaimed that everyone is entitled to all the rights and freedoms set forth therein, without distinction of any kind, and States' obligations under international human rights law,

Recalling previous resolutions of the General Assembly on promoting understanding, development and exchange among civilizations and cultures, in particular its resolution 53/22 of 4 November 1998, by which the Assembly proclaimed the year 2001 as the United Nations Year of Dialogue among Civilizations, and its resolution 56/6 of 9 November 2001 on the Global Agenda for Dialogue among Civilizations and the Programme of Action and its objectives, principles and participants, contained therein,

Noting that globalization brings greater interrelatedness among people and increased interaction among cultures and civilizations, and encouraged by the fact that the proclamation and celebration of the United Nations Year of Dialogue among Civilizations in 2001 and the implementation of the Global Agenda for Dialogue among Civilizations invite us to embrace the interdependence of humankind and its rich cultural diversity,

Recalling its resolutions 53/199 of 15 December 1998 and 61/185 of 20 December 2006 on the proclamation of international years and Economic and Social Council resolution 1980/67 of 25 July 1980 on international years and anniversaries,

Recalling also previous relevant resolutions of the General Assembly, including its resolution 51/95 of 12 December 1996, by which the Assembly proclaimed 16 November as the International Day for Tolerance, its resolution 72/130 of 8 December 2017, by which it declared 16 May as the International Day of Living Together in Peace, its resolution 75/200 of 21 December 2020, by which it proclaimed 4 February as the International Day of Human Fraternity, and its resolution 75/309 of 21 July 2021, by which it proclaimed 18 June as the International Day for Countering Hate Speech,

Bearing in mind the valuable contribution that dialogue among civilizations can make to an improved awareness and understanding of the universal values, enshrined in the Charter of the United Nations and the Universal Declaration of Human Rights, and reaffirming that civilizational achievements constitute the collective heritage of humankind,

Convinced that dialogue contributes to combining the efforts of the international community in consolidating the traditions of peaceful and trust-based coexistence among the peoples of the world,

[154] Resolution 217 A (III).

Emphasizing that participation in dialogue among civilizations should be global in scope and open to all and should contribute to gender equality and the empowerment of women and girls from different backgrounds and cultures,

Recognizing with deep concern the overall rise in instances of discrimination, intolerance and violence, regardless of the actors, directed against members of many religious and other communities in various parts of the world,

Recognizing that all cultures and civilizations contribute to the enrichment of humankind, and encouraging tolerance, peaceful coexistence, respect, dialogue and cooperation among different cultures, civilizations and peoples in order to promote international peace and security, human welfare, freedom and progress everywhere,

Recalling the United Nations Millennium Declaration of 8 September 2000,[155] in which Member States consider, inter alia, that tolerance is one of the fundamental values essential to international relations in the twenty-first century and should include the active promotion of a culture of peace and dialogue among civilizations, with human beings respecting one another, in all their diversity of belief, culture and language, neither fearing nor repressing differences within and between societies but cherishing them as a precious asset of humanity,

Recalling also the 2005 World Summit Outcome,[156] in which the Heads of State and Government reaffirmed the Global Agenda for Dialogue among Civilizations and its Programme of Action and the value of different initiatives on dialogue among cultures and civilizations, welcomed the United Nations Alliance of Civilizations initiative announced by the Secretary-General on 14 July 2005 and committed to promoting a culture of peace and dialogue at the local, national, regional and international levels,

Underlining that all civilizations celebrate the unity and diversity of humankind and are enriched and have evolved through dialogue with others, respect for human rights as well as the need to acknowledge and respect the richness of all civilizations and to seek common ground among civilizations in order to address comprehensively challenges facing humanity,

Convinced that the full enjoyment of human rights by all persons, the promotion of cultural pluralism and tolerance towards and dialogue among various cultures and civilizations would contribute to the efforts of all peoples and nations to enrich their cultures and traditions by engaging in a mutually beneficial exchange of knowledge and intellectual, moral and material achievements,

Aware that positive and mutually beneficial interaction among civilizations has continued throughout human history despite impediments arising from intolerance, disputes and wars,

Recognizing that civilizations and cultures take diverse forms across time and space and flourish in contact with others and therefore shall be preserved, enhanced and handed on for the benefit of current and future generations as a record of human experience and aspirations, and recognizing also that the defence of cultural diversity implies a commitment to human rights and fundamental freedoms,

Noting with appreciation the valuable role played by the United Nations Educational, Scientific and Cultural Organization and the other relevant entities of the United Nations, within their mandates, in implementing relevant resolutions and agendas,

Noting with appreciation also the valuable role of the United Nations Alliance of Civilizations and its High Representative in promoting greater understanding and respect among civilizations, cultures, religions and beliefs,

Noting with appreciation further the United Nations Alliance of Civilizations Global Forum as a global platform for dialogue among various stakeholders, including civil society organizations, religious leaders, youth, media and academia, as well as artists and athletes, and noting the efforts of relevant stakeholders to promote cross-cultural dialogue and mutual understanding among different civilizations, cultures, religions and beliefs,

---

[155] Resolution 55/2.

[156] Resolution 60/1.

Noting the various initiatives at the local, national, regional and international levels for enhancing dialogue, understanding and cooperation among civilizations, as well as declarations and statements from various meetings in this regard,

Recognizing the role of national parliaments and their active contribution at the national, regional and international levels for the dialogue among civilizations,

1. *Decides* to declare 10 June the International Day for Dialogue among Civilizations, in order to raise awareness of the value of the diversity of civilizations and promote dialogue, mutual respect, tolerance and global solidarity in this regard;

2. *Invites* all Member States and organizations of the United Nations system, within existing resources, as well as other international and regional organizations and other relevant stakeholders, including civil society, the private sector, academia and the media, to commemorate the International Day in an appropriate manner, including through educational and public awareness-raising activities, and to share best practices in this regard;

3. *Invites* the United Nations Educational, Scientific and Cultural Organization and the United Nations Alliance of Civilizations with other relevant entities of the United Nations to facilitate the observance of the International Day;

4. *Stresses* that the cost of all activities that may arise from the implementation of the present resolution should be met from voluntary contributions;

5. *Invites* all relevant stakeholders to contribute to and support the International Day.

RESOLUTION 78/287

Adopted at the 88th plenary meeting, on 7 June 2024, without a vote, on the basis of draft resolution A/78/L.70, sponsored by: Algeria, Angola, Argentina, Armenia, Austria, Bahamas, Belarus, Botswana, Cabo Verde, China, Congo, Côte d'Ivoire, Croatia, Cuba, Czechia, Djibouti, Egypt, Equatorial Guinea, Estonia, Ethiopia, Fiji, Finland, Gabon, Georgia, Germany, Ghana, Guatemala, Guinea, Hungary, India, Indonesia, Israel, Italy, Kenya, Kyrgyzstan, Lebanon, Liberia, Luxembourg, Malaysia, Mali, Malta, Mauritius, Mexico, Morocco, New Zealand, Pakistan, Peru, Portugal, Republic of Korea, Republic of Moldova, Rwanda, Saint Vincent and the Grenadines, Senegal, Serbia, Slovenia, South Africa, South Sudan, Spain, Sri Lanka, Suriname, Thailand, Tunisia, Turkmenistan, Uganda, Ukraine, United Arab Emirates, United Republic of Tanzania, United States of America, Uruguay, Viet Nam

78/287. International Year of Quantum Science and Technology, 2025

The General Assembly,

Recalling its resolutions 53/199 of 15 December 1998 and 61/185 of 20 December 2006 on the proclamation of international years, and Economic and Social Council resolution 1980/67 of 25 July 1980 on international years and anniversaries,

Stressing that increased global cooperation, awareness and education in quantum science and technology could help to address the challenges of achieving sustainable development and the Sustainable Development Goals and improving the quality of life in countries around the world,

Recalling the need to mobilize and scale up the means of implementation, including financing, for science, technology and innovation, including the field of quantum science and technology, especially in developing countries, in support of the Sustainable Development Goals,

Emphasizing that quantum science and technology is vital for economic advancement and that its potential applications could address basic needs such as food, health, sustainable cities and communities, communications, clean water and energy, and support climate action,

Acknowledging the need to collectively address the challenges posed by quantum science and technology,

Recognizing that the year 2025 coincides with the 100th anniversary of the development of the methods of quantum mechanics that have led to its prominence in both science and technology today,

Stressing that the celebration of scientific discoveries provides an opportunity to promote science, technology, engineering and mathematics education and research for all, including youth, girls and women, especially in developing countries, in emerging technologies, and to encourage their greater participation in science, including opportunities for career development, and recognizing the achievements of women in science,

Emphasizing that, at the heart of the International Decade of Sciences for Sustainable Development, 2024–2033, lies the advancement of basic sciences and recognizing that quantum science offers unparalleled insights into the behaviour of matter and energy at the atomic and subatomic levels,

Acknowledging the recommendation made by the General Conference of the United Nations Educational, Scientific and Cultural Organization at its forty-second session for the United Nations General Assembly to proclaim 2025 the International Year of Quantum Science and Technology,[157]

1. *Decides* to proclaim 2025 as the International Year of Quantum Science and Technology;

2. *Invites* the United Nations Educational, Scientific and Cultural Organization to act as the lead agency and focal point for the International Year of Quantum Science and Technology, and invites all Member States of the United Nations, members of the specialized agencies, observers of the General Assembly, as well as organizations within the United Nations system and other international and regional organizations, academia, civil society, the private sector and other relevant stakeholders to observe 2025 as the International Year of Quantum Science and Technology;

3. *Recommends* that the International Year of Quantum Science and Technology should be observed through activities at all levels aimed at increasing public awareness of the importance of quantum science and applications; enhancing international, multilateral and interdisciplinary scientific cooperation among research institutions, researchers and innovators in quantum science and technology; and ensuring a focus on the application of quantum science and technology for sustainable development;

4. *Welcomes* initiatives aimed at harnessing quantum science and technology for sustainable development;

5. *Stresses* that the costs of all activities that may arise from the implementation of the present resolution should be met from voluntary contributions;

6. *Requests* the Secretary-General to bring the present resolution to the attention of all Member States, organizations of the United Nations system and other relevant stakeholders, including intergovernmental and non-governmental organizations, to promote the observance of 2025 as the International Year of Quantum Science and Technology.

RESOLUTION 78/288

Adopted at the 88th plenary meeting, on 7 June 2024, without a vote, on the basis of draft resolution A/78/L.69, sponsored by the Dominican Republic

78/288. Twenty-fifth anniversary of the International Day for the Elimination of Violence against Women

The General Assembly,

Recalling its resolution 54/134 of 17 December 1999, by which it designated 25 November as the International Day for the Elimination of Violence against Women,

Reaffirming the Universal Declaration of Human Rights[158] and other relevant international human rights instruments, including the Convention on the Elimination of All Forms of Discrimination against Women,[159]

[157] United Nations Educational, Scientific and Cultural Organization, *Records of the General Conference, Forty-second Session, Paris, 7–22 November 2023*, vol. 1, *Resolutions*, resolution 23.

[158] Resolution 217 A (III).

[159] United Nations, *Treaty Series*, vol. 1249, No. 20378.

Reaffirming also the Vienna Declaration and Programme of Action[160] as well as the Beijing Declaration and Platform for Action,[161] the Cairo Programme of Action of the International Conference on Population and Development[162] and the outcomes of their review conferences,

Reaffirming further the Declaration on the Elimination of Violence against Women, adopted on 20 December 1993,[163] and its provisions, including article 1, in which violence against women was defined as any act of gender-based violence that results in, or is likely to result in, physical, sexual or psychological harm or suffering to women, including threats of such acts, coercion or arbitrary deprivation of liberty, whether occurring in public or in private life, and noting the economic and social harm caused by such violence,

Reaffirming the obligation of all States to promote and protect all human rights and fundamental freedoms, and recognizing that violence against women and girls is a major impediment to the achievement of gender equality and the empowerment of all women and girls and that it violates and impairs or nullifies the full enjoyment of all their human rights and fundamental freedoms,

Recognizing the efforts to eliminate all forms of violence against women and girls and the high number of activities undertaken by the United Nations bodies, entities, funds and programmes and the specialized agencies,

Welcoming the commitment to achieve gender equality and the empowerment of all women and girls contained in the 2030 Agenda for Sustainable Development,[164] and stressing that preventing and eliminating all forms of violence against all women and girls in the public and private spheres is essential to achieving gender equality and empowering all women and girls and to promoting women's full, equal and meaningful participation and leadership in all spheres of society, including in economic and political life,

Strongly condemning all forms of violence against women and girls, many of which are rooted in historical and structural inequalities and unequal power relations, and recognizing that, while progress has been made, violence against women remains pervasive and is enabled through discriminatory norms that reinforce stereotypes and gender inequality and the corresponding impunity and lack of accountability,

Expressing concern that current global challenges may exacerbate violence against women and girls and therefore threaten to reverse much of the development progress made in recent decades and pose a challenge to the implementation of the 2030 Agenda for Sustainable Development, and concerned about the challenges of new and emerging forms of violence against women and girls that occur through or are amplified by the use of technologies and in digital contexts, especially against women in public and political life,

Recognizing that the International Day for the Elimination of Violence against Women was established in the light of the killing of the three Mirabal sisters from the Dominican Republic,

1. *Welcomes* the twenty-fifth anniversary of the International Day for the Elimination of Violence against Women, to be observed on 25 November 2024;

2. *Acknowledges* the progress made towards the elimination of all forms of violence against women and girls and the remaining challenges that need to be addressed at all levels;

3. *Recognizes* the importance of the International Day for the Elimination of Violence against Women for raising awareness, educating and engaging communities, advocacy and mobilization of decision makers, policymakers and the whole of society to step up efforts to prevent and eliminate all forms of violence against women and girls;

4. *Invites* all Member States, the United Nations system and other global, regional and subregional organizations, as well as other relevant stakeholders, including civil society, the private sector, academia and individuals, to commemorate the twenty-fifth anniversary of the International Day for the Elimination of Violence

[160] A/CONF.157/24 (Part I), chap. III.

[161] *Report of the Fourth World Conference on Women, Beijing, 4–15 September 1995* (United Nations publication, Sales No. E.96.IV.13), chap. I, resolution 1, annexes I and II.

[162] *Report of the International Conference on Population and Development, Cairo, 5–13 September 1994* (United Nations publication, Sales No. E.95.XIII.18), chap. I, resolution 1, annex.

[163] Resolution 48/104.

[164] Resolution 70/1.

against Women in order to increase awareness on the prevention of all forms of violence against women and girls and achieve gender equality and a culture of peace, non-violent behaviour and respectful relationships;

5. *Requests* the President of the General Assembly to convene a full-day high-level meeting, within existing resources, to mark the twenty-fifth anniversary of the International Day for the Elimination of Violence against Women, with a focus on highlighting achievements, sharing best practices and identifying gaps and challenges to eliminating all forms of violence against women and girls, and to galvanize accelerated efforts on the prevention and elimination of all forms of violence against women and girls in line with the Beijing Declaration and Platform for Action as the thirtieth anniversary of their adoption approaches in 2025.

RESOLUTION 78/289

Adopted at the 91st plenary meeting, on 19 June 2024, without a vote, on the basis of draft resolution A/78/L.71, sponsored by: Albania, Angola, Armenia, Austria, Bangladesh, Belarus, Bhutan, Bolivia (Plurinational State of), Botswana, Burundi, Cabo Verde, Chile, China, Colombia, Congo, Costa Rica, Cuba, Dominican Republic, Gambia, Germany, Guatemala, Haiti, Honduras, Hungary, Indonesia, Israel, Japan, Kazakhstan, Kenya, Kyrgyzstan, Lao People's Democratic Republic, Lesotho, Luxembourg, Malaysia, Maldives, Mongolia, Morocco, Myanmar, Namibia, Nepal, Nicaragua, Pakistan, Paraguay, Philippines, Poland, Portugal, Qatar, Russian Federation, Rwanda, Senegal, Slovenia, South Africa, Sri Lanka, Suriname, Tajikistan, Thailand, Tunisia, Türkiye, Uganda, United Republic of Tanzania, United States of America, Uzbekistan, Viet Nam, Zambia

78/289. International Year of Cooperatives 2025

The General Assembly,

Reaffirming its resolution 70/1 of 25 September 2015, entitled "Transforming our world: the 2030 Agenda for Sustainable Development", in which it adopted a comprehensive, far-reaching and people-centred set of universal and transformative Sustainable Development Goals and targets,

Reaffirming also the Addis Ababa Action Agenda of the Third International Conference on Financing for Development,[165] in which the role of cooperatives in the implementation of the 2030 Agenda for Sustainable Development and in relation to financing for development was acknowledged,

Reaffirming further its resolutions 53/199 of 15 December 1998 and 61/185 of 20 December 2006 on the proclamation of international years, and Economic and Social Council resolution 1980/67 of 25 July 1980 on international years and anniversaries, in particular paragraphs 1 to 10 of the annex thereto on the agreed criteria for the proclamation of international years, as well as paragraphs 13 and 14, in which it is stated that an international day or year should not be proclaimed before the basic arrangements for its organization and financing have been made,

Recognizing that cooperatives, in their various forms, promote the fullest possible participation in the economic and social development of local communities and all people, including women, young people, older persons, persons with disabilities and Indigenous Peoples, whose inclusion strengthens economic and social development, and contribute to the eradication of poverty and hunger,

Recalling its resolutions 64/136 of 18 December 2009 and 65/184 of 21 December 2010, by which it proclaimed the year 2012 the International Year of Cooperatives,

Recalling also its resolution 78/175 of 19 December 2023, in which it noted with appreciation the celebration of the International Year of Cooperatives, in 2012, called for the proclamation of another International Year of Cooperatives in 2025, and encouraged all Member States, as well as the United Nations and all other relevant stakeholders, to take advantage of the International Year as a way of promoting cooperatives and raising awareness of their contribution to the implementation of the Sustainable Development Goals and to overall social and economic development,

1. *Proclaims* 2025 the International Year of Cooperatives;

2. *Invites* all Member States to consider taking action towards establishing national mechanisms, where appropriate, such as national committees, to prepare for, observe and follow up on the International Year of

[165] Resolution 69/313, annex.

Cooperatives, in particular for the purpose of planning, stimulating and harmonizing the activities of the governmental and non-governmental agencies and organizations concerned with the preparations for and observance of the International Year;

3. *Invites* the Department of Economic and Social Affairs of the Secretariat, in cooperation with the relevant international organizations, the specialized agencies and local, national and international cooperative organizations, and all other relevant stakeholders, including the Committee for the Promotion and Advancement of Cooperatives, to facilitate the implementation of the International Year of Cooperatives as a way of promoting cooperatives and raising awareness of their contribution to social and economic development, and support Member States in planning and coordinating activities for observing the International Year;

4. *Stresses* that the costs of all the activities that may arise from the implementation of the present resolution should be met through voluntary contributions, including from the private sector;

5. *Requests* the Secretary-General to bring the present resolution to the attention of all Member States, the organizations of the United Nations system and other relevant stakeholders, including civil society, the private sector and academia, for appropriate observance.

RESOLUTION 78/290

Adopted at the 92nd plenary meeting, on 24 June 2024, without a vote, on the basis of draft resolution A/78/L.78, sponsored by: Andorra, Angola, Antigua and Barbuda, Bahrain, Belarus, Belgium, Botswana, Brazil, Bulgaria, Cabo Verde, Cambodia, Cameroon, Colombia, Congo, Croatia, Cyprus, Czechia, Denmark, Dominican Republic, Egypt, El Salvador, Equatorial Guinea, Estonia, Finland, France, Germany, Greece, Guatemala, Guinea-Bissau, Hungary, Indonesia, Italy, Latvia, Luxembourg, Malaysia, Maldives, Malta, Monaco, Morocco, Paraguay, Philippines, Poland, Portugal, Republic of Moldova, Russian Federation, San Marino, Senegal, Slovakia, Slovenia, Spain, Suriname, Tajikistan, Thailand, Trinidad and Tobago, Türkiye, Turkmenistan, Uruguay, Viet Nam

78/290. Improving global road safety

The General Assembly,

Recalling its resolutions 57/309 of 22 May 2003, 58/9 of 5 November 2003, 58/289 of 14 April 2004, 60/5 of 26 October 2005, 62/244 of 31 March 2008, 64/255 of 2 March 2010, 66/260 of 19 April 2012, 68/269 of 10 April 2014, 70/260 of 15 April 2016, 72/271 of 12 April 2018 and 74/299 of 31 August 2020, on improving global road safety, and the recommendations contained therein,

Reaffirming its resolution 70/1 of 25 September 2015, entitled "Transforming our world: the 2030 Agenda for Sustainable Development", in which it adopted a comprehensive, far-reaching and people-centred set of universal and transformative Sustainable Development Goals and targets, its commitment to working tirelessly for the full implementation of the Agenda by 2030 ensuring that no one is left behind, its recognition that eradicating poverty in all its forms and dimensions, including extreme poverty, is the greatest global challenge and an indispensable requirement for sustainable development, its commitment to achieving sustainable development in its three dimensions – economic, social and environmental – in a balanced and integrated manner, and to building upon the achievements of the Millennium Development Goals and seeking to address their unfinished business,

Reaffirming also its resolution 69/313 of 27 July 2015 on the Addis Ababa Action Agenda of the Third International Conference on Financing for Development, which is an integral part of the 2030 Agenda for Sustainable Development, supports and complements it, helps to contextualize its means of implementation targets with concrete policies and actions, and reaffirms the strong political commitment to address the challenge of financing and creating an enabling environment at all levels for sustainable development in the spirit of global partnership and solidarity,

Recalling the New Urban Agenda adopted at the United Nations Conference on Housing and Sustainable Urban Development (Habitat III),[166] which, taking into account that the majority of road traffic deaths and serious injuries take place in urban areas, gives appropriate consideration to road safety and access to safe, affordable, accessible and sustainable public transport and non-motorized modes of transport,

[166] Resolution 71/256, annex.

Recalling also the Global Plan for the Decade of Action for Road Safety 2021-2030, which provides a set of options and strategies for use by Governments and other relevant stakeholders to guide policies and actions to improve road safety,

Reaffirming its commitment to the political declaration of the high-level meeting on improving global road safety of 30 June 2022,[167] in which road safety was recognized as a major public health concern and an urgent development challenge that requires commitment at all levels of government,

Recalling its resolution 78/148, entitled "Strengthening the links between all modes of transport to achieve the Sustainable Development Goals", adopted on 19 December 2023, by which it proclaimed the United Nations Decade of Sustainable Transport, beginning in 2026,

Acknowledging the importance of the Moscow Declaration adopted at the first Global Ministerial Conference on Road Safety in 2009,[168] the Brasilia Declaration adopted at the second Global High-level Conference on Road Safety in 2015 and the Stockholm Declaration adopted at the third Global Ministerial Conference on Road Safety in 2020,

Reaffirming the importance of continued action through 2030 on all road safety-related targets of the 2030 Agenda, such as targets 3.6 and 11.2, and recognizing their importance in enabling the achievement of Sustainable Development Goals 3 and 11 and in catalysing action on other Goals, including on poverty eradication, gender equality, climate change, decent jobs, innovation and transport,

Acknowledging the fifth *Global Status Report on Road Safety*, released by the World Health Organization in December 2023, which provided an assessment of progress made by Member States during the Decade of Action for Road Safety 2011-2020,

Noting that, while globally there has been a reduction of 5 per cent in the number of deaths between 2010 and 2021, the overall target of a 50 per cent reduction of global deaths and injuries from road traffic accidents, as included in Sustainable Development Goal target 3.6, was not achieved by 2020,

Acknowledging that, despite the slow progress between 2010 and 2021, 35 Member States achieved reductions of 30 to 49 per cent in the number of deaths due to road traffic crashes and 10 Member States[169] commendably reached the 50 per cent target reduction in road traffic deaths during that period,

Noting with concern that, despite the strong evidence demonstrating the effectiveness of legislation, only 7 countries have legislation related to road safety that align with best practice criteria for all five key risk factors as defined by the World Health Organization (drink driving, speeding, non-use of motorcycle helmets, non-use of seat belts, and non-use of child-restraint systems) and only 16 have acceded to all seven of the core road safety-related United Nations legal instruments,

Recognizing the tremendous global burden that road traffic crashes continue to place on society in terms of both human suffering, with nearly 1.2 million preventable deaths and an estimated 50 million injuries each year, and average costs to countries of 3 to 5 per cent of their gross domestic product, which makes road safety an urgent public health and development priority,

Expressing concern that road safety remains severely underfunded through both public and private financing, and that, despite the existence of a national strategy for road safety in a majority of Member States, most of these are unfunded and are not implemented,

Taking into account the evolving nature of transport, and noting with concern the challenges brought about by these changes, including an increasing number of deaths among riders of powered two- and three-wheelers, electric bicycles and micromobility devices,

---

[167] Resolution 76/294, annex.

[168] A/64/540, annex.

[169] Belarus, Brunei Darussalam, Denmark, Japan, Lithuania, Norway, Russian Federation, Trinidad and Tobago, United Arab Emirates and Venezuela (Bolivarian Republic of).

Taking into account also the needs of non-motorized transport, while recognizing the impact of road traffic crashes on children and youth, and emphasizing the importance of taking into account their needs and those of road users who are in vulnerable situations, including older persons and persons with disabilities,

Taking into account further the emerging safety challenges and increased demands put on existing transport infrastructure by the growth of Internet-based transport services, including ride share companies and delivery platforms,

Recognizing the important role that national and local government authorities play in ensuring the implementation of the safe system approach to road safety, particularly in land-use planning and enforcement,

Emphasizing the importance of road policing and the enforcement of traffic laws, particularly in low- and middle-income countries, where almost 90 per cent of global road casualties occur, by means of strengthening global and regional road policing cooperation initiatives, to leverage the capacities of traffic police by information exchange on training, capacity-building and enforcement activities,

Emphasizing also the need for multisectoral approaches and engagement of diverse actors, including businesses and industries, which can make important contributions to improving road safety globally by managing road safety throughout their value chain,

Commending the World Health Organization for its leadership role in preventing road traffic injury and for its role in implementing the mandate conferred upon it by the General Assembly to act, in close cooperation with the United Nations regional commissions, as a coordinator on road safety issues within the United Nations system,

Welcoming the efforts of the Special Envoy of the Secretary-General for Road Safety, with secretariat support from the Economic Commission for Europe, in effectively mobilizing sustained high-level commitment to road safety by advocating adherence to and raising awareness of the United Nations legal instruments on road safety, sharing good practices, including through participation in global and regional conferences, and advocating for increased funds for global road safety,

Commending the United Nations regional commissions for their work in increasing road safety activities and advocating increased political commitment to road safety, and in working towards setting regional and national road traffic casualty reduction targets, in particular the work of the Economic Commission for Europe in elaborating global road safety-related legal instruments, including international conventions and agreements, technical standards, resolutions and good practice recommendations, as well as in servicing 59 global and regional legal instruments that provide a commonly accepted legal and technical framework for the development of international road, rail, inland water and combined transport,

Noting with approval the road safety performance review projects of the Economic Commission for Europe, carried out in collaboration with the Economic and Social Commission for Asia and the Pacific and the Economic Commission for Latin America and the Caribbean under the United Nations Development Account and with the Economic Commission for Africa with support from the Special Envoy of the Secretary-General for Road Safety, as well as the work of the Economic and Social Commission for Western Asia on prioritizing road safety to strengthen the national road safety management capacity of selected countries, and commending the development and implementation of road traffic safety management systems for different types of organizations, such as the extensive work of the International Organization for Standardization in developing the requirements for road traffic safety management systems,

Recalling the midterm milestone of the Decade of Action for Road Safety 2021-2030 in 2026 and the timeline to achieve the 2030 target of a 50 per cent reduction in deaths and injuries,

1. *Urges* Member States and relevant actors to accelerate and scale up efforts to implement the Global Plan for the Decade of Action for Road Safety 2021–2030, making road safety a political priority and ensuring its relevance in the broader sustainable development agenda;

2. *Welcomes* the offer of the Kingdom of Morocco to host the Fourth Global Ministerial Conference on Road Safety, to be held from 18 to 20 February 2025 in Marrakech, which will serve to facilitate the scale-up of effective measures to address road safety, identify emerging challenges and opportunities in the coming years, and to strengthen the links with other development challenges in order to realize co-benefits and achieve greater efficiency;

3. *Encourages* Member States to establish mechanisms for interministerial coordination, notably among the health, transport, education, infrastructure, interior and environment ministries, in order to address cross-cutting issues that have an impact on all the sectors involved in matters addressing road safety;

4. *Also encourages* Member States to take steps to ensure that safety features are built in at the stages of design, manufacture, usage, operation and maintenance of both motorized and non-motorized vehicles in line with international standards and practices in order to minimize adverse safety and environmental effects of vehicle operation on road users, including pedestrians and bicyclists, and infrastructure;

5. *Calls upon* Member States to implement a safe system approach through policies that foster safe urban and rural road infrastructure design and engineering; set safe adequate speed limits supported by appropriate speed management measures; enable multimodal transport and active mobility; establish, where possible, an optimal mix of motorized and non-motorized transport, with particular emphasis on public transport, walking and cycling, including bike-sharing services, safe pedestrian infrastructure and level crossings, especially in urban areas;

6. *Invites* Member States and relevant stakeholders to leverage the recently proclaimed United Nations Decade of Sustainable Transport that will begin in 2026 as an opportunity to embed road safety as an integral part of the agenda for sustainable transport, especially beyond the current Sustainable Development Goals deadline of 2030;

7. *Invites* Member States that have not already done so to consider adopting comprehensive legislation on key risk factors, including the non-use of seat belts, child restraints and helmets, the drinking of alcohol and driving, and speeding, and to consider implementing appropriate, effective and evidence- and/or science-based legislation on other risk factors related to distracted or impaired driving;

8. *Encourages* Member States that have not yet done so to consider becoming contracting parties to the United Nations legal instruments on road safety and, beyond accession, applying, implementing and promoting their provisions or safety regulations;

9. *Invites* Member States and relevant stakeholders, in particular civil society, to engage with local governments and authorities to implement context-specific interventions and prevention strategies that include massive awareness campaigns on road safety, safe habits and behaviours, aimed at all road stakeholders, that respond to the road safety needs and challenges of communities;

10. *Encourages* businesses and industries to monitor and report on the road safety impact, or footprint, of operations throughout their value chain;

11. *Calls upon* international bodies to develop guidelines for impact investments for road safety as a means of stimulating large-scale financing for road safety, in particular among private investors and donors;

12. *Encourages* Member States and relevant stakeholders to support the United Nations Road Safety Fund, for which a pledging conference will be held alongside the Fourth Global Ministerial Conference on Road Safety, in 2025, and the replenishment, as appropriate, of the World Bank Global Road Safety Facility;

13. *Acknowledges* the importance of adequate, predictable, sustainable and timely international financing without conditionalities in complementing the efforts of countries in mobilizing resources domestically, especially in low- and middle-income countries; and encourages support for the demands of financing in developing countries by leveraging the United Nations Road Safety Fund and other dedicated mechanisms, as appropriate, for promoting safe road transport infrastructure and for supporting the implementation of measures required to meet the voluntary global performance targets, including by supporting the voluntary replenishment of all United Nations system road safety funds and mechanisms;

14. *Encourages* the promotion of capacity-building, knowledge-sharing, technical support and technology transfer programmes and initiatives on mutually agreed terms in the area of road safety, especially in developing countries, which confront unique challenges and, where possible, the integration of such programmes and initiatives into sustainable development assistance programmes through North-South, South-South and triangular cooperation formats, as well as public-private collaboration;

15. *Welcomes* the initiative of the World Health Organization to establish a global network of national road safety agencies, and encourages Member States to actively participate in knowledge exchange and peer mentorship through informal and formal modalities;

16. *Calls upon* relevant actors and United Nations entities to monitor and conduct research on the impact of evolving technologies, including artificial intelligence, on land transport and road safety in order to inform the development of guidelines and recommendations to address the opportunities and challenges presented by these issues;

17. *Calls upon* Member States to strengthen the collection, reporting and use of data related to road safety as a means of generating real-time feedback to inform the implementation of the Global Plan for the Decade of Action for Road Safety 2021-2030;

18. *Requests* the Secretary-General to provide, in consultation with the World Health Organization and other relevant agencies, a progress report during the eightieth session of the General Assembly, as mandated in the political declaration of 2022, which will serve to inform the high-level meeting to be convened by the Assembly in 2026.

RESOLUTION 78/310

Adopted at the 97th plenary meeting, on 1 July 2024, without a vote, on the basis of draft resolution A/78/L.85, sponsored by: Albania, Andorra, Antigua and Barbuda, Argentina, Azerbaijan, Bahrain, Belarus, Belgium, Bolivia (Plurinational State of), Brunei Darussalam, Bulgaria, Burundi, Cabo Verde, Cambodia, Central African Republic, Chad, Chile, China, Colombia, Congo, Costa Rica, Croatia, Cuba, Djibouti, Dominica, Dominican Republic, Ecuador, El Salvador, Equatorial Guinea, Gabon, Gambia, Georgia, Germany, Guatemala, Guinea-Bissau, Hungary, Indonesia, Ireland, Israel, Italy, Kazakhstan, Kenya, Kiribati, Kuwait, Kyrgyzstan, Lao People's Democratic Republic, Lebanon, Libya, Luxembourg, Malaysia, Maldives, Malta, Marshall Islands, Monaco, Mongolia, Montenegro, Morocco, Mozambique, Myanmar, Namibia, Nepal, Netherlands (Kingdom of the), Oman, Pakistan, Philippines, Portugal, Qatar, Republic of Korea, Republic of Moldova, Romania, San Marino, Saudi Arabia, Senegal, Serbia, Seychelles, Singapore, Slovakia, Slovenia, Somalia, South Africa, Sri Lanka, Suriname, Tajikistan, Thailand, Togo, Türkiye, Turkmenistan, United Arab Emirates, United Republic of Tanzania, United States of America, Uzbekistan, Viet Nam, Zambia

78/310. World Fair Play Day

The General Assembly,

Reaffirming its resolution 70/1 of 25 September 2015, entitled "Transforming our world: the 2030 Agenda for Sustainable Development", in which it adopted a comprehensive, far-reaching and people-centred set of universal and transformative Sustainable Development Goals and targets, its commitment to working tirelessly for the full implementation of the Agenda by 2030, its recognition that eradicating poverty in all its forms and dimensions, including extreme poverty, is the greatest global challenge and an indispensable requirement for sustainable development, its commitment to achieving sustainable development in its three dimensions – economic, social and environmental – in a balanced and integrated manner, and to building upon the achievements of the Millennium Development Goals and seeking to address their unfinished business,

Reaffirming also its resolutions 53/199 of 15 December 1998 and 61/185 of 20 December 2006 on the proclamation of international years, and Economic and Social Council resolution 1980/67 of 25 July 1980 on international years and anniversaries,

Recalling its resolution 77/27 of 1 December 2022, in which it reaffirmed that sport is an important enabler of sustainable development, and recognized the growing contribution of sport to the realization of development and peace in its promotion of tolerance and respect and the contributions it makes to the empowerment of women and girls and of young people, individuals and communities, and persons with disabilities, as well as to physical and mental health, education and social inclusion objectives,

Recalling its resolutions 58/5 of 3 November 2003 and 59/10 of 27 October 2004, its decision to proclaim 2005 the International Year for Sport and Physical Education to strengthen sport as a means to promote education, health, development and peace, and its resolutions 60/1 of 16 September 2005, 60/9 of 3 November 2005, 61/10 of 3 November 2006, 62/271 of 23 July 2008, 63/135 of 11 December 2008, 65/4 of 18 October 2010, 67/17 of 28 November 2012, 69/6 of 31 October 2014, 71/160 of 16 December 2016, 73/24 of 3 December 2018, 75/18 of 1 December 2020 and 77/27,

Recalling also its resolution 78/10 of 21 November 2023 on building a peaceful and better world through sport and the Olympic ideal, and all its previous resolutions on this matter,

Recalling further its resolution 67/296 of 23 August 2013, in which it proclaimed 6 April the International Day of Sport for Development and Peace,

Recognizing that sports, the arts and physical activity have the power to change perceptions, prejudices and behaviours, as well as to inspire people, break down racial and political barriers, combat discrimination and defuse conflict, as reflected in the political declaration adopted at the Nelson Mandela Peace Summit in 2018,[170]

Recognizing also that the spirit of fair play is deeply rooted in the Olympic ideal,

Welcoming the work carried out by the International Fair Play Committee, and noting its aim to preserve and promote respect for the spirit of fair play and the values it represents in elite sport and in sport for all, as well as in daily life, in particular the observance of rules, respect for the opponent and combating violence and doping,

1. *Decides* to proclaim 19 May as World Fair Play Day;

2. *Invites* all Member States, the United Nations system and, in particular, the Division for Inclusive Social Development of the Department of Economic and Social Affairs of the Secretariat and the United Nations Educational, Scientific and Cultural Organization, relevant international organizations and international, regional and national sports organizations, civil society, including non-governmental organizations and the private sector, and all other relevant stakeholders to cooperate, observe and raise awareness of World Fair Play Day to promote the practice of sport with a spirit of friendship, solidarity, tolerance and inclusion and without discrimination;

3. *Commends* countries that have hosted and will host significant international sporting events, and encourages them to ensure that these events leave a lasting legacy for global peace, sportsmanship and fair play;

4. *Stresses* that sport, including sport for persons with disabilities, has an important role to play in the promotion of peace and development, community cohesion, respect for human rights, gender equality and the empowerment of all women and girls, given its universal popularity;

5. *Reaffirms* the independence and autonomy of sport as well as the mission of the International Olympic Committee in leading the Olympic movement and of the International Paralympic Committee in leading the Paralympic movement;

6. *Stresses* that the cost of all activities that may arise from the implementation of the present resolution should be met from voluntary contributions;

7. *Requests* the Secretary-General to bring the present resolution to the attention of all Member States, the organizations of the United Nations system and other relevant stakeholders for appropriate observance.

RESOLUTION 78/311

Adopted at the 97th plenary meeting, on 1 July 2024, without a vote, on the basis of draft resolution A/78/L.86, sponsored by: Afghanistan, Albania, Algeria, Angola, Antigua and Barbuda, Armenia, Australia, Austria, Azerbaijan, Bahrain, Bangladesh, Barbados, Belarus, Belgium, Bolivia (Plurinational State of), Brazil, Brunei Darussalam, Bulgaria, Burkina Faso, Burundi, Cabo Verde, Cambodia, Canada, Central African Republic, Chad, Chile, China, Colombia, Comoros, Congo, Côte d'Ivoire, Croatia, Cuba, Cyprus, Czechia, Democratic Republic of the Congo, Denmark, Djibouti, Dominica, Dominican Republic, Ecuador, Egypt, Equatorial Guinea, Eritrea, Estonia, Ethiopia, Finland, France, Gabon, Gambia, Georgia, Germany, Ghana, Greece, Guinea-Bissau, Guyana, Hungary, Iceland, Indonesia, Iran (Islamic Republic of), Iraq, Ireland, Israel, Italy, Japan, Jordan, Kazakhstan, Kenya, Kiribati, Kuwait, Kyrgyzstan, Lao People's Democratic Republic, Latvia, Lebanon, Liberia, Liechtenstein, Luxembourg, Madagascar, Malaysia, Maldives, Mali, Malta, Mauritania, Monaco, Montenegro, Morocco, Myanmar, Nepal, Netherlands (Kingdom of the), New Zealand, Nicaragua, Niger, Nigeria, Norway, Oman, Pakistan, Panama, Papua New Guinea, Peru, Poland, Portugal, Qatar, Republic of Korea, Republic of Moldova, Romania, Russian Federation, Rwanda, Saudi Arabia, Serbia, Sierra Leone, Singapore, Slovakia, Slovenia, South Africa, South Sudan, Spain, Sri Lanka, Sudan, Suriname, Sweden, Switzerland, Syrian Arab Republic, Tajikistan, Thailand, Timor-Leste, Togo, Trinidad and Tobago, Tunisia, Türkiye, Turkmenistan, Uganda, Ukraine, United Arab Emirates, United Kingdom of Great Britain and Northern Ireland, United Republic of Tanzania, United States of America, Uruguay, Uzbekistan, Venezuela (Bolivarian Republic of), Viet Nam, Yemen, Zambia, Zimbabwe

[170] Resolution 73/1.

78/311. Enhancing international cooperation on capacity-building of artificial intelligence

The General Assembly,

Reaffirming international law, in particular the Charter of the United Nations, and recalling the Universal Declaration of Human Rights,[171]

Reaffirming also its resolution 70/1 of 25 September 2015, entitled "Transforming our world: the 2030 Agenda for Sustainable Development", its resolution 69/313 of 27 July 2015 on the Addis Ababa Action Agenda of the Third International Conference on Financing for Development, the political declaration adopted at the high-level political forum on sustainable development convened under the auspices of the General Assembly contained in the annex to its resolution 78/1 of 29 September 2023, and its resolution 70/125 of 16 December 2015, entitled "Outcome document of the high-level meeting of the General Assembly on the overall review of the implementation of the outcomes of the World Summit on the Information Society",

Reaffirming its resolutions 78/265 of 21 March 2024, entitled "Seizing the opportunities of safe, secure and trustworthy artificial intelligence systems for sustainable development", 77/320 of 25 July 2023, entitled "Impact of rapid technological change on the achievement of the Sustainable Development Goals and targets", 78/132 of 19 December 2023, entitled "Information and communications technologies for sustainable development", and 78/213 of 19 December 2023, entitled "Promotion and protection of human rights in the context of digital technologies",

Recognizing that rapid technological change, including the rapid advancement of artificial intelligence has the potential to bring new opportunities for socioeconomic development and accelerate the progress and achievement of the Sustainable Development Goals and sustainable development in its three dimensions – economic, social and environmental – in a balanced and integrated manner, while recognizing also that the improper or malicious design, development, deployment and use of artificial intelligence systems, such as without adequate safeguards or in a manner inconsistent with international law, could pose potential risks and challenges,

Recognizing that eradicating poverty in all its forms and dimensions, including extreme poverty, is the greatest global challenge for sustainable development and an indispensable requirement for sustainable development,

Stressing that artificial intelligence systems should be safe, secure and trustworthy – whose life cycle includes the stages: pre-design, design, development, evaluation, testing, deployment, use, sale, procurement, operation and decommissioning, are such that they are human-centric, reliable, explainable, ethical, inclusive, in full respect, promotion and protection of human rights and international law – in line with the principle of artificial intelligence for good for all, with the vision of a people-centred, inclusive and development-oriented information society, bearing in mind that this resolution focuses on international cooperation on artificial intelligence capacity-building in the non-military domain and does not touch the development or use of artificial intelligence for military purposes,

Emphasizing that Member States should enjoy equal opportunities in the design, development, deployment, decommissioning and use of artificial intelligence, while respecting intellectual property rights and promoting innovation,

Noting with concern that artificial intelligence and other digital divides between and within countries continue to widen, and developing countries face unique challenges in keeping pace with the rapid acceleration of artificial intelligence development, in particular in terms of the design, development, deployment and use of artificial intelligence, thus stressing the need and urgency to narrow the disparities and assist developing countries in artificial intelligence capacity-building so that they will not be further left behind,

Noting also with concern that actions inconsistent with international law and the Charter of the United Nations could hinder the development and innovation of artificial intelligence and global cooperation,

Noting both the positive benefits of open-source software, open models and open data, among other methods and business models, in spreading the benefits of artificial intelligence, as well as the potential risks, and recognizing the importance of the participation of developing countries in relevant global cooperation,

[171] Resolution 217 A (III).

Recognizing that the lack of digital infrastructure connectivity and skills, including education, expertise and human capacity, remains a fundamental challenge in many developing countries, in particular the least developed countries, which can contribute to artificial intelligence and other digital divides, including different levels of readiness to make use of and benefit from artificial intelligence,

Stressing the need and urgency to bridge artificial intelligence and other digital divides between and within countries, and emphasizing the quality of access to the benefits of artificial intelligence, therefore stressing the importance of providing adequate public and private financing, mobilizing action-oriented means of implementation, such as knowledge sharing activities and the transfer of technology on mutually agreed terms, and capacity-building assistance for developing countries in line with their national needs, policies and priorities,

Noting the important role that international, regional and subregional organizations and international financial institutions, the private sector, companies, civil society, the media, academia and research institutions and technical communities and individuals, and other relevant stakeholders could play in enhancing artificial intelligence capacity-building and promoting safe, secure and trustworthy artificial intelligence systems for sustainable development,

Stressing the importance of enhancing coordination and cooperation among and within countries and increasing investment in artificial intelligence capacity-building, with specific consideration of the needs, priorities and conditions of developing countries, and encouraging developed countries and developing countries in a position to do so, as well as international organizations and all relevant stakeholders, to take active measures,

Recognizing that the United Nations system has an important role to play in artificial intelligence capacity-building, and emphasizing that it is important to enhance international cooperation and multi-stakeholder collaboration on capacity-building and support developing countries' effective, equitable and meaningful participation and representation in international processes and forums on the governance of artificial intelligence systems,

1. *Resolves* to bridge the artificial intelligence and other digital divides between and within countries, and to enhance international cooperation on capacity-building in developing countries, including through North-South, South-South and triangular cooperation, with full consideration of the needs, policies and priorities of developing countries, with the aim of harnessing the benefits of artificial intelligence, minimizing its risks, and accelerating innovation and progress toward the achievement of all 17 Sustainable Development Goals;

2. *Encourages* Member States, where appropriate and in line with their national circumstances and priorities, to incorporate capacity-building and the design, development, deployment and use of artificial intelligence into their national development plans and strategies, in full respect, promotion and protection of human rights and international law, and make necessary investments in this regard, and also encourages the international community, as well as relevant stakeholders, to increase financing and technical assistance to developing countries in the field of capacity-building, including by drawing on voluntary cooperative initiatives;

3. *Calls upon* the international community to foster an enabling environment for international cooperation on artificial intelligence capacity-building, and emphasizes that international law, in particular the Charter of the United Nations, as well as human rights and fundamental freedoms, must be respected;

4. *Calls upon* Member States to strengthen cooperation and partnerships that bring benefits for all to address major structural impediments and lift obstacles, including through expansion of access to infrastructure, knowledge and skills, with a view to promoting universal and meaningful digital connectivity, which can help lay the foundation for digital transformation and equitable and inclusive access to the benefits of digital and artificial intelligence development and innovations;

5. *Encourages* Member States, in particular developed countries and those developing countries in a position to do so, to increase capacity-building cooperation, including policy exchanges, knowledge sharing activities and the transfer of technology on mutually agreed terms, technical assistance, lifelong learning, personnel training, skilling of workforce, international research cooperation, voluntary joint international research laboratories and artificial intelligence capacity-building centres, with full consideration of developing countries' national needs, policies and priorities, and to hold training courses, seminars and workshops, among others for sharing experiences and best practices;

6. *Calls upon* the international community to provide and promote a fair, open, inclusive and non-discriminatory business environment across the life cycle of safe, secure and trustworthy artificial intelligence systems;

7. *Encourages* Member States to consider the benefits and risks when scaling up the responsible use of digital solutions, such as open-source artificial intelligence and digital public infrastructure, among other methods and business models; to promote, protect and preserve linguistic and cultural diversity, taking into account multilingualism in their training data, particularly for the large language models; to adopt proactive measures to counteract racism, discrimination and other forms of algorithmic bias; and to enable fair competition in the artificial intelligence market place, promote an innovation environment and the use of digital public goods to harness the potential of safe, secure and trustworthy artificial intelligence systems;

8. *Encourages* Governments, the private sector, international, regional and subregional organizations, civil society, the media, academia and research institutions and technical communities and individuals, to strengthen international cooperation on artificial intelligence capacity-building and take necessary and positive steps, as appropriate, to eliminate barriers faced by all people, women and girls, persons with disabilities, Indigenous Peoples, local communities, children and youth, those living in poverty and in rural and remote areas, and those in vulnerable situations, and to ensure the full enjoyment of artificial intelligence benefits for all, improve digital inclusion and realize gender equality and the empowerment of women and girls, through investment, education, training, technological innovation, use and application;

9. *Calls upon* specialized agencies, funds, programmes, other entities, bodies and offices, and related organizations of the United Nations system, within their respective mandates and resources, to leverage the opportunities and address the challenges in enhancing international cooperation on artificial intelligence capacity-building, including through using appropriate inter-agency mechanisms, conducting research, mapping and analysis, reporting on progress and challenges in this field, and leveraging their resources and expertise to provide tailored assistance;

10. *Calls upon* other international, regional and subregional organizations and international financial institutions and all relevant stakeholders, within their respective mandates and resources, to strengthen artificial intelligence capacity-building in developing countries, and to carry out relevant cooperation and coordination, fully utilizing the existing international and regional mechanisms and platforms;

11. *Encourages* Member States, in particular developing countries, to make use of capacity-building resources relating to artificial intelligence in the United Nations system and other international, regional and subregional organizations, to enhance capacity-building, including support for the preparation of national digital and artificial intelligence strategies in line with their national needs, policies and priorities, ensuring that those investments lead to long-term and sustainable results;

12. *Supports* the United Nations in playing a central and coordinating role in international development cooperation;

13. *Calls upon* the United Nations system to enhance action-oriented international cooperation on artificial intelligence capacity-building, including through voluntary and transparent cooperation frameworks or initiatives, which also promotes the meaningful participation of developing countries in artificial intelligence processes;

14. *Looks forward* to the final report of the High-level Advisory Body on Artificial Intelligence, and the discussions on capacity-building related to artificial intelligence in the context of the Global Digital Compact, the Pact for the Future, and relevant follow-up processes in the United Nations as appropriate;

15. *Requests* the Secretary-General to report to the General Assembly at its eightieth session, within existing resources, processes and documents, on unique challenges faced by developing countries in artificial intelligence capacity-building, with recommendations that address those challenges.

RESOLUTION 78/312

Adopted at the 97th plenary meeting, on 1 July 2024, without a vote, on the basis of draft resolution A/78/L.83, sponsored by: Algeria, Andorra, Angola, Austria, Belgium, Benin, Botswana, Bulgaria, Burkina Faso, Burundi, Cabo Verde, Cameroon, Canada, Central African Republic, Chad, China, Comoros, Congo, Côte d'Ivoire, Croatia, Cyprus, Czechia, Democratic Republic of the Congo, Denmark, Djibouti, Egypt, Equatorial Guinea, Eritrea, Estonia, Eswatini, Ethiopia, Gabon, Gambia, Germany, Ghana, Greece, Guatemala, Guinea, Guinea-Bissau, Hungary, Iceland, Indonesia, Ireland, Israel, Italy, Kenya, Kiribati, Kyrgyzstan, Latvia, Lesotho, Liberia, Libya, Luxembourg, Madagascar, Malawi, Maldives, Mali, Mauritania, Mauritius, Morocco, Mozambique, Namibia, Niger, Nigeria, Oman, Peru, Philippines, Poland, Portugal, Qatar, Rwanda, Sao Tome and

Principe, Saudi Arabia, Senegal, Serbia, Seychelles, Sierra Leone, Slovenia, Somalia, South Africa, South Sudan, Spain, Sudan, Suriname, Sweden, Thailand, Togo, Tunisia, Uganda, United Republic of Tanzania, Uzbekistan, Zambia, Zimbabwe

78/312. World Kiswahili Language Day

The General Assembly,

Reaffirming its resolution 70/1 of 25 September 2015, entitled "Transforming our world: the 2030 Agenda for Sustainable Development", in which it adopted a comprehensive, far-reaching and people-centred set of universal and transformative Sustainable Development Goals and targets, its commitment to working tirelessly for the full implementation of the Agenda by 2030, its recognition that eradicating poverty in all its forms and dimensions, including extreme poverty, is the greatest global challenge and an indispensable requirement for sustainable development, its commitment to achieving sustainable development in its three dimensions – economic, social and environmental – in a balanced and integrated manner, and to building upon the achievements of the Millennium Development Goals and seeking to address their unfinished business,

Recognizing that multilingualism, as a core value of the Organization, contributes to the achievement of the goals of the United Nations, as set out in Article 1 of the Charter of the United Nations,

Recognizing also that the United Nations pursues multilingualism as a means of promoting, protecting and preserving diversity of languages and cultures globally,

Reaffirming its resolutions 53/199 of 15 December 1998 and 61/185 of 20 December 2006 on the proclamation of international years, and Economic and Social Council resolution 1980/67 of 25 July 1980 on international years and anniversaries, in particular paragraphs 1 to 10 of the annex thereto on the agreed criteria for the proclamation of international years, as well as paragraphs 13 and 14, in which it is stated that an international year should not be proclaimed before the basic arrangements for its organization and financing have been made,

Reaffirming also its resolution 76/268 of 10 June 2022 on multilingualism, in which it encouraged the Secretary-General to enhance support for non-official languages spoken throughout the world, in a cost-neutral manner, with the aim of informing and raising awareness of the history, culture and use of those languages,

Recalling resolution 41C/53 adopted by the General Conference of the United Nations Educational, Scientific and Cultural Organization on 23 November 2021, in which it proclaimed 7 July of each year as World Kiswahili Language Day,[172]

Noting that Kiswahili is among the 10 most widely spoken languages in the world, with more than 200 million speakers, being the lingua franca in many countries within East, Central and Southern Africa as well as the Middle East, and recognizing the role it plays in promoting peace, unity and cultural diversity, creating awareness and fostering dialogues among peoples,

Taking note of the approval and adoption of Kiswahili as an official and working language of the African Union, the Southern African Development Community and the East African Community as an important tool in fostering regional integration,

Recognizing the need to raise awareness of the multiple economic and cultural values of the Kiswahili language and its contribution as a catalyst for peace, unity and socioeconomic development, with a view to implementing the 2030 Agenda for Sustainable Development,

1. *Decides* to proclaim 7 July of each year as World Kiswahili Language Day, to be observed each year beginning in 2024;

2. *Invites* all Member States, organizations and agencies of the United Nations system, other international and regional organizations and other relevant stakeholders, including civil society organizations, non-governmental organizations, academic institutions, the private sector and individuals, to observe World Kiswahili Language Day, as appropriate, in order to raise awareness of the history, culture and use of the language;

---

[172] United Nations Educational, Scientific and Cultural Organization, *Records of the General Conference, Forty-first Session, Paris, 9–24 November 2021*, vol. 1, *Resolutions*, sect. VIII, resolution 53.

3. *Invites* the United Nations Educational, Scientific and Cultural Organization and the Department of Global Communications of the Secretariat to facilitate the observance of World Kiswahili Language Day, in collaboration with other relevant organizations of the United Nations system, mindful of the provisions contained in the annex to Economic and Social Council resolution 1980/67;

4. *Stresses* that the costs of all the activities that may arise from the implementation of the present resolution should be met through voluntary contributions, including from the private sector, and invites all relevant stakeholders to contribute to and support the observance of World Kiswahili Language Day;

5. *Requests* the Secretary-General to bring the present resolution to the attention of all Member States, the organizations of the United Nations system and other relevant stakeholders, including civil society, the private sector and academia, for appropriate observance.

RESOLUTION 78/313

Adopted at the 97th plenary meeting, on 1 July 2024, without a vote, on the basis of draft resolution A/78/L.72, sponsored by: Algeria, Angola, Antigua and Barbuda, Argentina, Azerbaijan, Bahrain, Bangladesh, Belarus, Burkina Faso, Burundi, Chad, Chile, China, Colombia, Comoros, Congo, Cuba, Djibouti, Dominican Republic, Egypt, Equatorial Guinea, Eritrea, Gambia, Guinea-Bissau, Guyana, Hungary, Indonesia, Iraq, Japan, Jordan, Kazakhstan, Kenya, Kiribati, Kyrgyzstan, Kuwait, Latvia, Lebanon, Libya, Malaysia, Maldives, Marshal Islands, Mauritania, Morocco, Namibia, Nepal, Nigeria, Oman, Pakistan, Palau, Peru, Philippines, Qatar, Russian Federation, Saint Vincent and the Grenadines, Saudi Arabia, Senegal, Serbia, Singapore, South Africa, Suriname, Syrian Arab Republic, Tajikistan, Thailand, Tunisia, Turkmenistan, Uganda, United Arab Emirates, United Republic of Tanzania, Yemen, Zambia

78/313. World Conjoined Twins Day

The General Assembly,

Reaffirming its resolution 70/1 of 25 September 2015, entitled "Transforming our world: the 2030 Agenda for Sustainable Development", in which it adopted a wide, far-reaching and people-centred set of universal and transformative Sustainable Development Goals and targets, and its commitment to working tirelessly for the full implementation of the Agenda by 2030,

Reaffirming also its resolutions 53/199 of 15 December 1998 and 61/185 of 20 December 2006 on the proclamation of international years, and Economic and Social Council resolution 1980/67 of 25 July 1980 on international years and anniversaries, in particular paragraphs 1 to 10 of the annex thereto on the agreed criteria for the proclamation of international years, as well as paragraphs 13 and 14, in which it is stated that an international day or year should not be proclaimed before the basic arrangements for its organization and financing have been made,

Reaffirming further the commitment to ensure healthy lives and promote well-being for all at all ages, including by strengthening health systems and achieving universal health coverage and all other health-related targets and leaving no one behind,

Reaffirming the right of every human being, without distinction of any kind, to the enjoyment of the highest attainable standard of physical and mental health,

Stressing the need to ensure that no one is left behind, with an endeavour to reach the furthest behind first, and address the physical and mental health needs of all, while respecting and promoting human rights and the dignity of the person and the principles of equality and non-discrimination,

Reaffirming the need to scale up efforts to build and strengthen quality, people-centred, sustainable and resilient health systems, and to promote strong global partnerships with all relevant stakeholders to collaboratively support the efforts of Member States, as appropriate, to achieve universal health coverage and other health-related targets of the Sustainable Development Goals,

Reaffirming also the need to strengthen regional and international cooperation, multilateralism, global solidarity, coordination and health governance, towards the progressive realization of the right to the enjoyment of the highest attainable standard of physical and mental health for all, without distinction of any kind,

Recognizing that the case of conjoined twins is a rare condition where the estimated incidence can be 1 in 50,000 births, and that the rate of stillbirth is high and is estimated to be around 60 per cent, while noting the lack of quality, timely and reliable data in this regard,

Emphasizing the need to address the condition of conjoined twins, by raising awareness of their cases at all levels and through a life-course approach, in cooperation with relevant United Nations agencies and other stakeholders, as well as by advocating for their well-being and social inclusion, while taking into account relevant agreed international standards, norms and principles,

1. *Decides* to proclaim 24 November as World Conjoined Twins Day, to be observed each year beginning in 2024;

2. *Invites* all Member States, relevant organizations of the United Nations system, other international organizations and civil society, including non-governmental organizations and the private sector, to observe World Conjoined Twins Day, in an appropriate manner, in order to raise awareness of the condition of conjoined twins, and to promote their human rights, as well as their well-being and social inclusion;

3. *Requests* the Secretary-General to bring the present resolution to the attention of all Member States and organizations of the United Nations system;

4. *Stresses* that the cost of all activities that may arise from the implementation of the present resolution should be met from voluntary contributions and that such activities would be subject to the availability and provision of voluntary contributions.

RESOLUTION 78/314

Adopted at the 98th plenary meeting, on 10 July 2024, without a vote, on the basis of draft resolution A/78/L.88, sponsored by: Belarus, Kyrgyzstan, Uganda (on behalf of the States Members of the United Nations that are members of the Group of 77 and China), Uzbekistan

78/314. United Nations Decade on Combating Sand and Dust Storms (2025–2034)

The General Assembly,

Recalling its resolutions 70/195 of 22 December 2015, 71/219 of 21 December 2016, 72/225 of 20 December 2017, 73/237 of 20 December 2018, 74/226 of 19 December 2019, 75/222 of 21 December 2020, 76/211 of 17 December 2021, 77/171 of 14 December 2022 and 78/158 of 19 December 2023 on combating sand and dust storms,

Reaffirming its resolution 70/1 of 25 September 2015, entitled "Transforming our world: the 2030 Agenda for Sustainable Development", in which it adopted a comprehensive, far-reaching and people-centred set of universal and transformative Sustainable Development Goals and targets, its commitment to working tirelessly for the full implementation of the Agenda by 2030, its recognition that eradicating poverty in all its forms and dimensions, including extreme poverty, is the greatest global challenge and an indispensable requirement for sustainable development, its commitment to achieving sustainable development in its three dimensions – economic, social and environmental – in a balanced and integrated manner, and to building upon the achievements of the Millennium Development Goals and seeking to address their unfinished business,

Reaffirming also its resolution 69/313 of 27 July 2015 on the Addis Ababa Action Agenda of the Third International Conference on Financing for Development, which is an integral part of the 2030 Agenda for Sustainable Development, supports and complements it, helps to contextualize its means of implementation targets with concrete policies and actions, and reaffirms the strong political commitment to address the challenge of financing and creating an enabling environment at all levels for sustainable development in the spirit of global partnership and solidarity,

Recalling its resolution 77/294 of 8 June 2023, in which 12 July of each year was proclaimed as International Day of Combating Sand and Dust Storms, to further raise international awareness of sand and dust storms, and stressing the need for global and regional cooperation to manage and mitigate their effects,

Recalling also its resolutions 53/199 of 15 December 1998 and 61/185 of 20 December 2006 on the proclamation of international years, and Economic and Social Council resolutions 1980/67 of 25 July 1980 on international years and anniversaries and 1989/84 of 24 May 1989 on guidelines for international decades in economic and social fields,

Recognizing that sand and dust storms are an issue of international concern, the costs of which are measured in economic, social and environmental terms, and that sand and dust storms continue to grow and negatively affect the achievement of 11 of the 17 Sustainable Development Goals and their means of implementation,

Acknowledging the work done by the secretariat of the United Nations Convention to Combat Desertification in Those Countries Experiencing Serious Drought and/or Desertification, Particularly in Africa,[173] towards mitigating sand and dust storm issues at source, and acknowledging also the continuing support of the Food and Agriculture Organization of the United Nations for countries affected by sand and dust storms through the promotion of sustainable land use management, agroforestry, shelter belts, afforestation/reforestation and land restoration programmes, which all contribute to sand and dust storm source mitigation,

Noting that sand and dust storms are a challenge with impacts on, among others, infrastructure, transport, communication, agriculture, ecosystems and human health and transboundary impacts that require institutional, technical and scientific responses, and that the global frequency and intensity of sand and dust storms have increased in the last decade and pose a great challenge to the sustainable development of affected countries,

Recognizing that sand and dust storms cause numerous human health problems in different regions around the world, especially in arid, semi-arid and dry subhumid regions, and that there is a need to reinforce protective strategies to reduce the negative impacts of sand and dust storms on human health and well-being,

Stressing the need for cooperation at the global and regional levels with a view to managing and mitigating the effects of sand and dust storms through the enhancement of early warning systems and the sharing of climate and weather information to forecast sand and dust storms, and affirming that resilient action to combat and prevent sand and dust storms requires a better understanding of the severe multidimensional impacts of sand and dust storms, including the deterioration of the health, well-being and livelihood of people, increased desertification and land degradation, deforestation, loss of biodiversity and land productivity, and their impact on sustainable economic growth,

Reaffirming that climate change is one of the greatest challenges of our time and, among other factors, is a serious challenge to the sustainable development of all countries, including those affected by sand and dust storms, and emphasizing that, among other factors, climate change is an important potential contributor to future wind erosion and the risk of sand and dust storms, especially the occurrence of more extreme wind events and the movement towards drier climates, although reverse effects are possible,

1. *Decides* to proclaim 2025–2034 the United Nations Decade on Combating Sand and Dust Storms, within existing structures and available resources, with the aim of enhancing international and regional cooperation and supporting and scaling up efforts to prevent, halt and mitigate the negative effects of sand and dust storms, especially on the affected countries;

2. *Stresses* that combating sand and dust storms contributes to the implementation of the 2030 Agenda for Sustainable Development;[174]

3. *Recalls* the United Nations Framework Convention on Climate Change[175] and the Paris Agreement,[176] the Convention on Biological Diversity[177] and the Kunming-Montreal Global Biodiversity Framework adopted at the fifteenth meeting of the Conference of the Parties to the Convention, and the United Nations Convention to Combat Desertification in Those Countries Experiencing Serious Drought and/or Desertification, particularly in Africa, including the Land Degradation Neutrality Target Setting Programme, as well as the outcomes of the high-level political forum on sustainable development;

[173] United Nations, *Treaty Series*, vol. 1954, No. 33480.

[174] Resolution 70/1.

[175] United Nations, *Treaty Series*, vol. 1771, No. 30822

[176] Adopted under the UNFCCC in FCCC/CP/2015/10/Add.1, decision 1/CP.21.

[177] United Nations, *Treaty Series*, vol. 1760, No. 30619.

4. *Emphasizes* the need for further steps to accelerate and sustain action towards the mobilization of means of implementation and for the stepping up of international cooperation and collaboration in science, research and innovation for combating sand and dust storms at the local, national and regional levels, including through public-private and multi-stakeholder partnerships, and on the basis of common interest and mutual benefit;

5. *Invites* the Secretary-General, with the support of the United Nations Coalition on Combating Sand and Dust Storms, to take appropriate steps to plan and organize the activities of the Decade at the global, regional and country levels;

6. *Invites* all States Members of the United Nations, members of the specialized agencies and observers of the General Assembly, as well as organizations of the United Nations system, other international and regional organizations, civil society, the private sector and academia, and other relevant stakeholders, to contribute to the United Nations Decade on Combating Sand and Dust Storms;

7. *Stresses* that the cost of all activities that may arise from the implementation of the present resolution should be met from voluntary contributions, including from the private sector;

8. *Decides*, in accordance with Economic and Social Council resolution 1989/84, to review the implementation of the Decade at its eighty-fourth session, and requests, in this regard, the Secretary-General to report to the General Assembly at its eighty-fourth session on the status of the implementation of the Decade, including its contribution to the implementation of the Sustainable Development Goals.

RESOLUTION 78/315

Adopted at the 98th plenary meeting, on 10 July 2024, without a vote, on the basis of draft resolution A/78/L.87, sponsored by: Armenia, Bulgaria, Croatia, Cyprus, Czechia, Denmark, Estonia, Finland, Germany, Greece, Italy, Kazakhstan, Kyrgyzstan, Latvia, Luxembourg, Netherlands (Kingdom of the), North Macedonia, Poland, Portugal, Republic of Moldova, Romania, Slovenia, Sweden, Uganda (on behalf of the States Members of the United Nations that are members of the Group of 77 and China)

78/315. Further modalities of the third United Nations Conference on Landlocked Developing Countries

The General Assembly,

Recalling its resolutions 76/217 of 17 December 2021, 77/246 of 30 December 2022 and 77/329 of 25 August 2023, in which the Assembly decided to convene the third United Nations Conference on Landlocked Developing Countries from 18 to 21 June 2024 in Kigali at the highest possible level, including Heads of State and Government,

Recalling also its decision 78/550 of 7 May 2024, by which it decided that the third United Nations Conference on Landlocked Developing Countries should be postponed to a later date,

1. *Welcomes and accepts with appreciation* the generous offer of the Government of Botswana to host the third United Nations Conference on Landlocked Developing Countries, and decides that the Conference will be held in Gaborone for a duration of four days, from 10 to 13 December 2024, at the highest possible level, including Heads of State and Government, on the theme "Driving progress through partnerships";

2. *Strongly encourages* Governments, intergovernmental and non-governmental organizations, major groups and other donors to contribute in a timely manner to the trust fund in support of activities undertaken by the Office of the High Representative for the Least Developed Countries, Landlocked Developing Countries and Small Island Developing States to support the preparations for the third United Nations Conference on Landlocked Developing Countries and the participation of landlocked developing countries in the Conference.

RESOLUTION 78/316

Adopted at the 99th plenary meeting, on 11 July 2024, by a recorded vote of 99 to 9, with 60 abstentions,* on the basis of draft resolution A/78/L.90, sponsored by: Albania, Andorra, Argentina, Australia, Austria, Belgium, Belize, Bosnia and Herzegovina, Bulgaria, Cabo Verde, Canada, Costa Rica, Croatia, Cyprus, Czechia, Denmark, Estonia, Fiji, Finland, France, Georgia, Germany, Greece, Hungary, Iceland, Ireland, Italy, Japan, Latvia, Liberia, Liechtenstein, Lithuania, Luxembourg, Malta, Marshall Islands, Micronesia (Federated States of), Monaco, Montenegro, Myanmar, Netherlands (Kingdom of the), New Zealand, North Macedonia, Norway, Palau, Poland, Portugal, Republic of Moldova, Romania, San Marino, Singapore,

Slovakia, Slovenia, Spain, Sweden, Switzerland, Tonga, Ukraine, United Kingdom of Great Britain and Northern Ireland, United States of America, Vanuatu

* *In favour:* Albania, Andorra, Antigua and Barbuda, Argentina, Australia, Austria, Bahamas, Barbados, Belgium, Belize, Benin, Bosnia and Herzegovina, Botswana, Bulgaria, Cabo Verde, Canada, Chile, Comoros, Costa Rica, Côte d'Ivoire, Croatia, Cyprus, Czechia, Democratic Republic of the Congo, Denmark, Dominican Republic, Ecuador, Estonia, Fiji, Finland, France, Gambia, Georgia, Germany, Ghana, Greece, Guatemala, Guyana, Hungary, Iceland, Ireland, Israel, Italy, Jamaica, Japan, Kenya, Latvia, Liechtenstein, Lithuania, Luxembourg, Malawi, Maldives, Malta, Marshall Islands, Mauritius, Micronesia (Federated States of), Monaco, Montenegro, Myanmar, Netherlands (Kingdom of the), New Zealand, North Macedonia, Norway, Palau, Panama, Papua New Guinea, Paraguay, Peru, Philippines, Poland, Portugal, Qatar, Republic of Korea, Republic of Moldova, Romania, Saint Kitts and Nevis, Samoa, San Marino, Sao Tome and Principe, Serbia, Seychelles, Sierra Leone, Singapore, Slovakia, Slovenia, Spain, Suriname, Sweden, Switzerland, Timor-Leste, Tonga, Trinidad and Tobago, Türkiye, Ukraine, United Kingdom of Great Britain and Northern Ireland, United States of America, Uruguay, Vanuatu, Zambia

Against: Belarus, Burundi, Cuba, Democratic People's Republic of Korea, Eritrea, Mali, Nicaragua, Russian Federation, Syrian Arab Republic

Abstaining: Algeria, Angola, Armenia, Bahrain, Bangladesh, Bhutan, Bolivia (Plurinational State of), Brazil, Brunei Darussalam, Cambodia, Central African Republic, China, Colombia, Congo, Egypt, El Salvador, Equatorial Guinea, Ethiopia, Gabon, Guinea, Guinea-Bissau, Haiti, India, Indonesia, Iran (Islamic Republic of), Iraq, Jordan, Kazakhstan, Kuwait, Kyrgyzstan, Lao People's Democratic Republic, Lebanon, Libya, Madagascar, Malaysia, Mauritania, Mexico, Mongolia, Mozambique, Namibia, Nepal, Nigeria, Oman, Pakistan, Saudi Arabia, Senegal, South Africa, Sri Lanka, Sudan, Tajikistan, Thailand, Togo, Tunisia, Uganda, United Arab Emirates, United Republic of Tanzania, Uzbekistan, Viet Nam, Yemen, Zimbabwe

78/316. Safety and security of nuclear facilities of Ukraine, including the Zaporizhzhia nuclear power plant

The General Assembly,

Recalling the purposes and principles enshrined in the Charter of the United Nations,

Recalling also the obligation of all States under Article 2 of the Charter of the United Nations to refrain in their international relations from the threat or use of force against the territorial integrity or political independence of any State, or in any other manner inconsistent with the purposes of the United Nations, and to settle their international disputes by peaceful means, and reaffirming that no territorial acquisition resulting from the threat or use of force shall be recognized as legal,

Recalling further the order of provisional measures of the International Court of Justice of 16 March 2022,[178]

Recalling its relevant resolutions adopted at its eleventh emergency special session[179] as well as its resolutions 68/262 of 27 March 2014, 78/8 of 8 November 2023 and 78/221 of 19 December 2023,

Condemning in the strongest terms the aggression by the Russian Federation against Ukraine in violation of Article 2 (4) of the Charter, including the ongoing temporary control or occupation by the Russian Federation of part of the territory of Ukraine, including the Autonomous Republic of Crimea and the city of Sevastopol, and certain areas of the Kherson, Zaporizhzhia, Donetsk and Luhansk regions, and reaffirming that the attempted illegal annexation of these regions has no validity under international law and does not form the basis for any alteration of the status of these regions of Ukraine,

Recalling that attacks must not be directed against civilians or civilian objects, and recalling also article 56 (1) of Additional Protocol I of 1977 to the Geneva Conventions of 12 August 1949,[180] to which Ukraine and the Russian Federation are parties, which includes the provision that works or installations containing dangerous forces, namely dams, dykes and nuclear electrical generating stations, shall not be made the object of attack, even where these objects are military objectives, if such attack may cause the release of dangerous forces and consequent severe losses among the civilian population,

Taking note of decision GC(53)/DEC/13 of 18 September 2009 of the General Conference of the International Atomic Energy Agency, entitled "Prohibition of armed attack or threat of attack against nuclear installations, during operation or under construction", as well as relevant resolutions of the General Conference of the Agency,

---

[178] See *Official Records of the General Assembly, Seventy-seventh Session, Supplement No. 4* (A/77/4), paras. 189–197.

[179] Resolutions ES-11/1, ES-11/2, ES-11/4 and ES-11/6.

[180] United Nations, *Treaty Series*, vol. 1125, No. 17512.

Taking note also of resolution GC(67)/RES/16 of 28 September 2023, entitled "Nuclear safety, security and safeguards in Ukraine", of the General Conference of the International Atomic Energy Agency, as well as resolutions GOV/2022/17 of 3 March 2022, GOV/2022/58 of 15 September 2022 and GOV/2022/71 of 17 November 2022, entitled "The safety, security and safeguards implications of the situation in Ukraine", and GOV/2024/18 of 7 March 2024, entitled "Nuclear safety, security and safeguards in Ukraine", of the Board of Governors of the Agency,

Condemning the attacks by the Russian Federation against critical energy infrastructure of Ukraine, which increases the risk of a nuclear accident or incident at all nuclear facilities of Ukraine,

Condemning also the illegal and unprecedented forceful seizure of the Zaporizhzhia nuclear power plant of Ukraine, and stressing that it has been more than two years that Russian military and other unauthorized personnel have remained at the plant, and recalling that direct threats to the safety and security of the site and its civilian personnel significantly raise the risk of a nuclear accident or incident, which endangers the population of Ukraine, neighbouring States and the international community,

Expressing grave concern over the precarious nuclear safety and security situation at the Zaporizhzhia nuclear power plant, and that all of the "seven indispensable pillars for ensuring nuclear safety and security during an armed conflict" of the Director General of the International Atomic Energy Agency have been "compromised either fully or partially" at the site, including the denial of access to Ukrainian operating personnel, gaps in routine maintenance activities, the lack of reliable supply chains, the vulnerable status of water and off-site power supply due to attacks on critical energy infrastructure, the planting of anti-personnel mines in a buffer zone between the facility's internal and external fences, and other actions by Russian military and other unauthorized personnel present at the site,

Emphasizing the importance of the International Atomic Energy Agency Director General's "seven indispensable pillars for ensuring nuclear safety and security during an armed conflict", derived from Agency safety standards and nuclear security guidance, and the five concrete principles to help to ensure nuclear safety and security at the Zaporizhzhia nuclear power plant, and stressing that the implementation of Agency safety standards and security guidance must be carried out in full respect of the sovereignty and territorial integrity of Ukraine,

Taking note of the Summit on Peace in Ukraine, held on 15 and 16 June 2024, at which it was, inter alia, emphasized that any use of nuclear energy and nuclear installations must be safe, secured, safeguarded and environmentally sound, and that Ukrainian nuclear power plants and installations, including the Zaporizhzhia nuclear power plant, must remain under full sovereign control of Ukraine in line with International Atomic Energy Agency principles,

1. *Reaffirms its commitment* to the sovereignty, independence, unity and territorial integrity of Ukraine within its internationally recognized borders, extending to its territorial waters;

2. *Demands* that the Russian Federation immediately cease its aggression against Ukraine and unconditionally withdraw all of its military forces from the territory of Ukraine within its internationally recognized borders;

3. *Also demands* that the Russian Federation urgently withdraw its military and other unauthorized personnel from the Zaporizhzhia nuclear power plant and immediately return the plant to the full control of the sovereign and competent authorities of Ukraine to ensure its safety and security and in order for the International Atomic Energy Agency to conduct safe, efficient and effective safeguards implementation in accordance with the comprehensive safeguards agreement and additional protocol of Ukraine, consistent with the repeated calls by the General Conference and the Board of Governors of the Agency;

4. *Condemns* the failure of the Russian Federation to implement relevant resolutions of the General Assembly and the General Conference and the Board of Governors of the International Atomic Energy Agency;

5. *Calls for* immediate cessation of the attacks by the Russian Federation against critical energy infrastructure of Ukraine, which increase the risk of a nuclear accident or incident at all nuclear facilities of Ukraine;

6. *Welcomes* and *encourages* the continued efforts of the Director General of the International Atomic Energy Agency to address the risks to nuclear safety and security, as well as to safeguards implementation at the Zaporizhzhia nuclear power plant, caused by the aggression by the Russian Federation against Ukraine, including through the continued and reinforced physical presence of the International Atomic Energy Agency Support and Assistance Mission to Zaporizhzhia;

7. *Calls upon* the Russian Federation, until it returns the Zaporizhzhia nuclear power plant of Ukraine to the full control of the sovereign and competent authorities of Ukraine, to provide the International Atomic Energy Agency Support and Assistance Mission to Zaporizhzhia with timely and full access to all areas at the plant that are important for nuclear safety and security in order to allow the Agency to report fully on the nuclear safety and security situation at the site;

8. *Calls upon* all parties to the armed conflict to respect international humanitarian law in all circumstances;

9. *Also calls upon* all parties to the armed conflict to implement fully the "seven indispensable pillars for ensuring nuclear safety and security during an armed conflict" and the five concrete principles of the Director General of the International Atomic Energy Agency to help to ensure nuclear safety and security at the Zaporizhzhia nuclear power plant;

10. *Urges* the Russian Federation to immediately remove all anti-personnel mines placed along the perimeter of the Zaporizhzhia nuclear power plant;

11. *Calls upon* Member States to continue to support the efforts of the Director General of the International Atomic Energy Agency to uphold nuclear safety, security and safeguards implementation at all nuclear facilities in Ukraine;

12. *Requests* the Secretary-General to provide his good offices in close cooperation with the Director General of the International Atomic Energy Agency;

13. *Decides* to continue its consideration of the matter at its seventy-ninth session under the agenda item entitled "The situation in the temporarily occupied territories of Ukraine".

RESOLUTION 78/317

Adopted at the 100th plenary meeting, on 16 July 2024, without a vote, on the basis of draft resolution A/78/L.80, submitted by the President of the General Assembly

78/317. The Antigua and Barbuda Agenda for Small Island Developing States: A Renewed Declaration for Resilient Prosperity

The General Assembly,

Recalling its resolution 76/203 of 17 December 2021, in which it decided to organize, in 2024, the fourth International Conference on Small Island Developing States at the highest possible level, as well as its resolutions 77/245 of 30 December 2022 and 77/328 of 25 August 2023,

1. *Expresses its profound gratitude* to the Government and the people of Antigua and Barbuda for hosting the fourth International Conference on Small Island Developing States in Antigua and Barbuda from 27 to 30 May 2024 and for providing all the necessary support;

2. *Endorses* the outcome document of the Conference, entitled "The Antigua and Barbuda Agenda for Small Island Developing States: A Renewed Declaration for Resilient Prosperity", which is annexed to the present resolution.

Annex

The Antigua and Barbuda Agenda for Small Island Developing States: A Renewed Declaration for Resilient Prosperity

I. The small island developing States story

1. In 1992, at the United Nations Conference on Environment and Development, we, the international community, formally declared small island developing States a special case both for environment and development and committed to assist them in meeting their sustainable development objectives. This was further promulgated in the first decennial United Nations conference on small island developing States in Barbados in 1994 and was subsequently reiterated at the second conference in Mauritius in 2005 and the third conference in Samoa in 2014.

2. After three decades and three programmes of action, small island developing States remain a special case for sustainable development, given their unique vulnerabilities. We note the remarkable successes and progress that they have made over the years, and welcome in this regard the ownership, leadership and considerable efforts that have been demonstrated by small island developing States, along with the support provided by the international community.

3. During this period, small island developing States have and continue to provide stable and democratic governance for their citizenry and have strived to provide productive economies and safe societies throughout unrelenting turbulent global times. Small island developing States were heavily affected by two "once-in-a-generation" crises that struck in 2008 and 2020, while grappling with even more intense and frequent disasters and natural hazards. In addition, they have assumed leadership roles in areas such as finance, climate change and plastics, and are stewards of the ocean, including managing 19.1 per cent of the world's exclusive economic zones and the resources they hold. Small island developing States have paved the way for many of the most progressive movements in these areas in policy development and the establishment of concrete actions in the multilateral arena.

4. We remain concerned that small island developing States are facing the unrelenting and compounding impacts of climate change, biodiversity loss, pollution, disasters and natural hazards, health and other social-related challenges and economic vulnerabilities, as well as the progressive deterioration in their ability to withstand external shocks and enhance their resilience. Successive global crises, along with the coronavirus disease (COVID-19) pandemic, have further exacerbated and negatively compounded the sustainable development of small island developing States.

5. Small island developing States are inherently and uniquely vulnerable to exogenous shocks owing to, inter alia, their small size, geographical remoteness, highly dispersed populations, the limited scale and undiversified nature of their economies, high dependence on external markets, and extreme exposure to disasters and natural hazards and the effects of climate change. Recognizing vulnerability does not mean that small island developing States exhibit weakness or lack potential for development. Rather, it means recognizing that they are disproportionately impacted in terms of physical destruction and non-economic and economic losses to a far greater scale than elsewhere.

6. Small island developing States are particularly vulnerable to adverse impacts of climate change, including, inter alia, erratic precipitation, increasingly frequent and extreme weather phenomena, more frequent and severe tropical cyclones, floods and drought, diminishing freshwater resources, desertification, coastal erosion, land degradation and sea level rise, which represent the gravest of threats to the survival and viability of their people, natural ecosystems and overall sustainable development. We take note of the concerns expressed by small island developing States that the impacts of climate change could have possible implications on small island developing States, including humanitarian, economic, social, cultural, ecological and, as exacerbated by other factors, security consequences.

7. In order for small island developing States to achieve sustainable development and resilient prosperity, we must assist small island developing States to diversify their economies and strengthen State and productive capacities. At the same time, the international financial architecture should go further to fully address the unique development circumstances of small island developing States and make accessing concessional finance easier for them, which could mitigate their fiscal constraints and reduce the risk of indebtedness, especially for highly indebted small island developing States, and prevent the reversal of hard-earned development gains. Therefore, the special case of small island developing States must continue to be recognized by the international community and must take into account these new and emerging challenges.

8. We recognize small island developing States' need for access to affordable, reliable, sustainable and modern energy, particularly renewable energy. Small island developing States are facing significant barriers related to accessing finance, cost of capital, market readiness and upskilling and reskilling workforces needed for just, inclusive and resilient energy transitions.

9. We reaffirm the importance of freedom, peace and security, respect for all human rights, including the right to development and the right to an adequate standard of living, including the right to food, the rule of law, gender equality, women's empowerment, reducing inequalities and the overall commitment to just and democratic societies for development.

10. We recognize that gender equality and women's empowerment and the full realization of human rights for women and girls have a transformative and multiplier effect on sustainable development and are a driver of economic growth in small island developing States. Women can be powerful agents of change.

11. Small island developing States aspire to a resilient form of prosperity that is reflected in sustainable development for all in their countries, where economic growth and well-being are sustained and their economies are robust,

diversified, adaptable and able to withstand shocks, ensuring social equity and promoting environmental sustainability.

12. The next 10 years are critical for small island developing States. A new context is emerging wherein the economic, social and environmental as well as geopolitical threats to the development of small island developing States are so great that they can only be ameliorated by a reinvigorated enabling environment that gives meaningful effect to their sustainable development. Without the full support of the international community, small island developing States will endure potentially far-reaching consequences.

13. We reaffirm the continued applicability of the Programme of Action for the Sustainable Development of Small Island Developing States (Barbados Programme of Action)[181] adopted in 1994, the Mauritius Strategy for the Further Implementation of the Programme of Action for the Sustainable Development of Small Island Developing States (Mauritius Strategy)[182] of 2005 and the SIDS Accelerated Modalities of Action (SAMOA) Pathway[183] of 2014 as blueprints setting out the sustainable development priorities of small island developing States.

14. We recommit to the full and timely implementation of the 2030 Agenda for Sustainable Development,[184] the Addis Ababa Action Agenda of the Third International Conference on Financing for Development[185] and the United Nations Framework Convention on Climate Change[186] and the Paris Agreement,[187] as well as the Sendai Framework for Disaster Risk Reduction 2015–2030,[188] the New Urban Agenda,[189] the Kunming-Montreal Global Biodiversity Framework and other relevant intergovernmentally agreed development outcomes, frameworks and instruments.

15. We reaffirm all the principles of the Rio Declaration on Environment and Development,[190] including, inter alia, the principle of common but differentiated responsibilities, as set out in principle 7 thereof.

16. We, the Heads of State and Government and high-level representatives, having met in St. John's from 27 to 30 May 2024, at the fourth International Conference on Small Island Developing States, with the participation of civil society, the private sector, youth, academia and other relevant stakeholders, firmly reaffirm our commitment to support small island developing States on their pathway to achieving sustainable development and resilient prosperity, where the progress of today does not compromise the possibilities of tomorrow. Through targeted, results-focused interventions and investments, we will support small island developing States as they exercise full ownership of their new agenda and seek to establish partnerships as equals, upholding values of equity, national ownership, mutual trust, transparency and accountability, and cooperation and promoting benefits across priority areas in their new 10-year agenda.

II. What do small island developing States want?

A. Build resilient economies

17. Enhancing inter-island connectivity and linking economies of small island developing States to regional markets and global supply chains, including by integrating them into existing and emerging maritime and multimodal transport and economic corridors, and encouraging sustainable transport initiatives to support small island developing States remains key.

---

[181] *Report of the Global Conference on the Sustainable Development of Small Island Developing States, Bridgetown, Barbados, 25 April–6 May 1994* (United Nations publication, Sales No. E.94.I.18 and corrigenda), chap. I, resolution 1, annex II.

[182] *Report of the International Meeting to Review the Implementation of the Programme of Action for the Sustainable Development of Small Island Developing States, Port Louis, Mauritius, 10–14 January 2005* (United Nations publication, Sales No. E.05.II.A.4 and corrigendum), chap. I, resolution 1, annex II.

[183] Resolution 69/15, annex.

[184] Resolution 70/1.

[185] Resolution 69/313, annex.

[186] United Nations, *Treaty Series*, vol. 1771, No. 30822.

[187] Adopted under the UNFCCC in FCCC/CP/2015/10/Add.1, decision 1/CP.21.

[188] Resolution 69/283, annex II.

[189] Resolution 71/256, annex.

[190] *Report of the United Nations Conference on Environment and Development, Rio de Janeiro, 3–14 June 1992*, vol. I, *Resolutions Adopted by the Conference* (United Nations publication, Sales No. E.93.I.8 and corrigendum), resolution 1, annex I.

18. We underscore that small island developing States face substantial structural challenges in building the necessary ecosystem, institutions and capacity for promoting and using science, technology, innovation and digitalization to drive economic growth and sustainable development.

19. Small island developing States face significant challenges in data collection, analysis, technical and institutional capacity, which hinders evidence-informed policymaking, monitoring progress and accessing development financing, and we emphasize that capacity-building for stronger data governance and management will allow small island developing States to support better data collection, protection, transparency and data sharing.

20. We welcome and call for support for the efforts of small island developing States in establishing a Small Island Developing States Centre of Excellence in Antigua and Barbuda that will be launched at the fourth International Conference on Small Island Developing States, which will include, inter alia, a small island developing States data hub, a technology and innovation mechanism and an Island Investment Forum.

21. Acknowledging that small island developing States are highly dependent on imports, with limited export capacity, and face current account deficits and limited fiscal space, compounded by limited access to concessional financing, small island developing States seek the support of the international community to:

(a) Develop and expand their productive capacity by:

(i) Undertaking national productive capacities gap assessments;

(ii) Implementing holistic productive capacities development programmes;

(iii) Investing in higher productivity sectors, including in advanced technologies and digital economy to provide better paying jobs for people in small island developing States and reduce brain drain and labour mobility;

(b) Increase trade and investment by:

(i) Designing prioritized trade and investment strategies to consolidate market opportunities in existing sectors and markets and identify opportunities for economic diversification to reduce vulnerability;

(ii) Enabling market access in goods and services for small island developing States by considering trade rules, as appropriate, that take into account the special circumstances of small island developing States, and encouraging the full utilization of preferential market access by improving the application of trade rules and their transparency for small island developing States, in compliance with World Trade Organization commitments;

(iii) Strengthening local, national and regional institutions as well as the regulatory and domestic policy environment and trade facilitation bodies;

(iv) Enabling business environments for private sector investment, entrepreneurship, especially micro-, small and medium-sized enterprises, cooperatives and enterprise development;

(v) Strengthening capacity for resource mobilization, investment flows monitoring, and firm-level data collection, analysis and use;

(vi) Supporting the establishment of the biennial Island Investment Forum in the Small Island Developing States Centre of Excellence as a dedicated platform for promoting sustainable economic development in small island developing States by promoting investment opportunities, knowledge exchange and collaborative initiatives, addressing the unique challenges faced by small island developing States and contributing to their long-term resilience and prosperity;

(vii) Reviewing and reforming old-generation investment treaties that are in force for small island developing States, where desired, with the aim of safeguarding policy space to pursue sustainable development objectives;

(c) Promote resilient and sustainable tourism by:

(i) Minimizing pollution and waste, enhancing environmental awareness, conserving and protecting the environment, respecting wildlife, biodiversity, ecosystems and cultural diversity;

(ii) De-risking investments, strengthening cross-sector collaboration between tourism and other sectors, and modernizing the sector and related up- and downstream services;

(iii) Raising awareness of the importance of resilient and sustainable tourism, including through Global Tourism Resilience Day;[191]

(iv) Developing creative and innovative employment solutions, including for informal workers, to provide resilience to the workforce, taking into account national circumstances;

(v) Enhancing entrepreneurship, education and training in cultural and heritage management and preservation, and in specific domains of the creative industries;

(vi) Promoting and investing in the resilience of cultural heritage, traditions and customs, assets and infrastructure;

(d) Promote sustainable ocean-based economies by:

(i) Assisting in the pursuit of opportunities in sustainable fisheries, aquaculture, mariculture, marine and coastal tourism, ocean-based renewable energy, and mineral and other related resources, sustainable shipping and maritime transport and ports;

(ii) Establishing public-private sector partnerships and appropriate capital market instruments and providing technical assistance to stock exchanges and security market regulators to enhance bankability and feasibility of projects;

(iii) Creating and supporting an enabling policy environment to maximize diaspora remittances, investment, skills and experience for research, innovation, economic development and diversification to shift towards environmentally sustainable practices and technologies.

B. Foster safe, healthy and prosperous societies

22. We underline the need to promote peaceful, prosperous, inclusive societies and safe communities for achieving sustainable development, and to build effective, accountable and inclusive institutions at all levels. Good governance, rule of law, human rights, fundamental freedoms, equal access to fair justice systems, and measures to combat corruption and curb illicit financial flows will be integral to our efforts.

23. We remain concerned that poverty, including extreme poverty, unemployment, inequality and exclusion continue to disproportionately affect people in vulnerable situations, particularly women, children, youth, persons with disabilities and older persons, and reduces the potential productive capacities in small island developing States. These challenges are compounded by youth unemployment, loss of skilled and semi-skilled labour, through labour mobility, and gender inequality, including unpaid care and domestic work.

24. The inadequacy of the health and social protection systems of small island developing States and the prevalence of communicable and non-communicable diseases in small island developing States pose a threat to sustainable development and economic productivity, disproportionately affecting the poorest and those in vulnerable situations.

25. Acknowledging the efforts of small island developing States to improve health and social protection systems, boost State capacity in the public sector, and reduce poverty, unemployment, inequality and exclusion, small island developing States seek the support of the international community to:

(a) Strengthen health systems by:

(i) Promoting and ensuring equitable and timely access to affordable and quality health-care services in order to achieve universal health coverage, leaving no one behind, noting that any external financing should be aligned with national and regional priorities;

(ii) Developing nationally appropriate, inclusive social protection systems, including through the One Health approach and other holistic approaches as well as the integration of climate and health policies;

(iii) Enhancing prevention, preparedness and response to better cope with health emergencies, epidemics, pandemics and climate change-related health impacts through capacity-building, upgrading of surveillance and

[191] See resolution 77/269.

early warning systems and adapting sustainable infrastructure and equipment so that it is climate-resilient, low greenhouse gas emission and sustainable;

(iv) Integrating essential non-communicable diseases and mental health services into primary health care and universal health coverage;

(v) Enhancing health literacy to promote healthy lifestyles and preventive measures to address risk factors for non-communicable diseases, including obesity, unhealthy diets, physical inactivity, harmful use of alcohol, tobacco use and exposure to air pollution and addressing the linkages between the environment and nutrition;

(vi) Establishing an integrated and whole-of-government approach to address the growing challenges of vision impairment, particularly myopia and other preventable conditions, including integrating comprehensive eye care services as part of primary health care and universal health coverage;

(vii) Building and retaining a trained, skilled, efficient and motivated health workforce that is equipped to meet the health needs of the population at all levels;

(b) Build strong institutions by:

(i) Increasing public participation and consultation, promoting civic education and engaging civil society organizations to actively and meaningfully participate in policy and budget decisions, including by establishing citizen participation mechanisms and creating spaces for inclusive dialogue;

(ii) Strengthening coordination and collaboration among government institutions and working beyond traditional boundaries to unify capabilities across agencies, sectors and society;

(iii) Strengthening the synergy between public policy planning and financing through integrated national financing frameworks to increase the expenditure efficiency of public resources, as a complement to resource mobilization from all sources;

(iv) Investing in continuous education and training and professional development programmes for public servants, and building public sector skill sets for the future, including in improving the agility of public service delivery and public procurement;

(v) Designing systems for government institutions to generate effective policies and investment decisions;

(vi) Boosting State capacity to effectively implement policies through the strengthening of public sector reforms, building effective, accountable and inclusive institutions at all levels and improving transparency and accountability;

(vii) Incorporating and strengthening e-government and digital solutions as a means of overcoming accessibility, scale and dispersion of population, bridging the digital divides and supporting the institutional capacity of local and national government institutions;

(viii) Assisting national and regional institutions to combat transnational crime and violence, including drug trafficking and the illicit trade in small arms and light weapons, taking into account the national circumstances of small island developing States;

(c) Achieve gender equality, empower youth and leave no one behind by:

(i) Promoting and protecting the full realization of the human rights of all women and girls and eliminating all forms of discrimination and of violence against all women and girls, including, inter alia, by developing and implementing gender-responsive action plans;

(ii) Increasing women's leadership and promoting their full, equal and meaningful participation and representation at all stages and levels of decision-making processes;

(iii) Investing in policies and programmes in productive capacities, education and skills that would also address emerging issues among children, young people, particularly boys and young men, taking into account national circumstances;

(iv) Meaningfully involving youth in decision-making processes as appropriate, including through youth councils and advisory committees, supporting youth-led initiatives and creating opportunities for engaging youth in sustainable development;

(v) Promoting and protecting the full realization of the human rights of persons with disabilities, and enabling their full, equal, meaningful and effective participation, representation and leadership in decision-making, addressing stigma and discrimination, eliminating violence and increasing their access to economic opportunities, education and health care;

(vi) Strengthening adaptive social protection systems and expanding coverage of national social protection programmes through comprehensive risk management strategies, to promote the realization of equity and equality, particularly for those in vulnerable situations, including women, children, youth, persons with disabilities and older persons;

(vii) Investing in developing the skills of and fostering opportunities to pursue alternative livelihoods for communities displaced by disasters, many of which are exacerbated by climate change, while recognizing the importance of safeguarding and passing on tangible and intangible cultural heritage from generation to generation and ensuring their financial, economic and social inclusion so that they can leverage their talent and ideas to contribute to, and benefit from, their new communities;

(viii) Supporting the advancement of sports as an important enabler of sustainable development, including for its growing contribution to the realization of development and peace in its promotion of tolerance and respect and the contributions it makes to the empowerment of women, young people, children, in particular girls, individuals and communities as well as to health, education and social inclusion objectives.

C. A secure future

26. Recognizing that various anthropogenic pressures and adverse impacts of climate change as well as global shocks continue to impede water availability and food and energy security, and further recognizing the importance of access to affordable, reliable, sustainable and modern energy, and connectivity, small island developing States seek the support of the international community to:

(a) Foster sustainable energy transitions and energy efficiency and ensure access to affordable, reliable, sustainable and modern energy, based on all energy sources, in particular renewable energy sources, by:

(i) Urgently enhancing support, investment and partnerships for just, inclusive, equitable and resilient energy transitions and energy efficiency, including clean and renewable energy infrastructure, technology and training, with a view to fulfilling small island developing States' bold and ambitious renewable energy targets for the next decade;

(ii) Addressing the underlying barriers in accessing and mobilizing finance to deploy renewable energy, including enabling environments and policy, legal and regulatory frameworks;

(iii) Developing small island developing States-specific technologies and applications for renewable energy deployment, and integration into the power system, and promoting efforts to reduce the cost of capital for renewables;

(iv) Providing support to overcome the structural barriers that hinder just, inclusive, resilient energy transitions, including institutional capacity, particularly skills gaps, and grid stabilization and upgrading;

(b) Develop integrated water resources management by:

(i) Developing policies, legislative frameworks, institutional and human capacities for effective, inclusive, sustainable and integrated water resources management and facilitate the expansion of wastewater treatment, recycling and reuse;

(ii) Significantly reducing the impact of climate change on water scarcity through enhancing climate resilience to water-related hazards and supporting a climate- and disaster-resilient water supply and sanitation, and access to safe and affordable potable water and sanitation, and hygiene for all;

(iii) Providing appropriate gender-sensitive and disability-inclusive facilities and infrastructure for safe drinking water, sanitation and hygiene, and waste management systems;

(c) Enhance food security by:

(i) Developing and implementing adaptation and mitigation strategies that take into account the linkages between food, water and energy, such as integrating climate-resilient infrastructure and promoting sustainable agricultural practices and the deployment of agricultural technologies that are resilient to the adverse impacts of climate change;

(ii) Increasing sustainable agriculture and fisheries, food security and nutrition and livelihoods in small island developing States in a manner that helps with climate adaptation, mitigates emissions and promotes sustainable use of biodiversity, including through incubation, diversification, local value addition, climate-resilient best practices and promoting, scaling up and replicating locally grown ideas, to accelerate the achievement of sustainable agriculture and fisheries, food security and good and improved nutrition, as well as improved overall health and well-being;

(iii) Developing sustainable food and agricultural production that is resilient to the impacts of climate change, addresses water availability and efficiently uses water resources, improving supply and distribution of food, including the reduction of food loss and waste, and enhancing resilience to potential excessive food price volatility and food crises;

(d) Build resilient infrastructure by:

(i) Scaling up planning, development and management of quality, reliable, sustainable and resilient infrastructure and energy-efficient land, marine and air transportation systems;

(ii) Applying the Principles for Resilient Infrastructure in small island developing States to create risk-informed policy, investment decisions and systems in sectors including transportation, energy, communications, water, health and education, with a view to nurturing a culture of maintenance for resilient societies;

(e) Enhance transportation and connectivity to link economies of small island developing States to regional markets and global supply chains by:

(i) Investing in sound, safe, sustainable, climate-resilient and affordable land, air, maritime and inter-island transportation infrastructure, including traditional and sustainable modes, that is inclusive for all, with a focus on community engagement and empowerment;

(ii) Developing and implementing climate- and disaster-resilient, safe, affordable, accessible and well-maintained sustainable transportation infrastructure in small island developing States, in line with the Principles for Resilient Infrastructure, including for remote and underserved communities, taking into account the local impacts of climate change, to ensure the longevity of transport infrastructure;

(iii) Establishing integrated and sustainable maritime and air transportation systems to foster regional economic and value chain integration, improving inter-island connectivity, modernizing transport fleets and equipment;

(iv) Developing coordinated regional transportation, fostering connectivity between small island developing States and neighbouring regions to strengthen economic ties and facilitate the movement of goods and people.

D. Environmental protection and planetary sustainability

27. We acknowledge that the widespread, rapid and adverse impacts of climate change continue to pose increasing risks to small island developing States and their efforts to achieve sustainable development, while representing the greatest threats to the survival and viability of their people and natural ecosystems. Even with limiting global warming to 1.5 degrees Celsius above pre-industrial levels, small island developing States will continue to incur severe loss and damage.

28. Small island developing States are gravely concerned that global emissions are not in line with modelled global mitigation pathways consistent with the temperature goal of the Paris Agreement, and that there is a rapidly narrowing window out to 2030 to raise ambition and implement existing commitments in order to keep warming to 1.5 degrees Celsius above pre-industrial levels within reach, which is crucial to the sustainable development of small island developing States.

29. Small island developing States have extraordinary marine and terrestrial biodiversity that, in many cases, is fundamental to their livelihoods, culture and identity, but their vulnerabilities are drastically limiting the resources and means by which they can protect their ecosystems and the natural environment. The ocean and its resources are under considerable stress from anthropogenic sources, impacting small island developing States, which are especially dependent on their maritime resources for their food security and livelihoods.

30. Small island developing States seek the support of the international community to:

(a) Urgently take action on climate change by:

(i) Accelerated actions on the effective implementation of the United Nations Framework Convention on Climate Change and the Paris Agreement, guided by science and agreed principles;

(ii) Supporting the recruitment and development of technical expertise to facilitate the development of loss and damage response plans and actions, including risk assessment, loss modelling, governance, management, disbursement, monitoring, evaluation and reporting on loss and damage solutions and impacts;

(iii) Recognizing the important role of forests in climate mitigation and adaptation, including through promoting the adoption and implementation of reducing emissions from deforestation and forest degradation, on the role of conservation and sustainable management of forests in developing countries, as well as other alternative policy approaches in small island developing States, including those with high forest low deforestation (HFLD) regions, as per article 5.2 of the Paris Agreement, on national or, an interim basis, subnational jurisdictional scales, can foster information exchange, expertise-sharing and collective problem-solving, fostering a united effort in addressing climate mitigation and adaptation goals, and also noting it is essential for those small island developing States that have maintained forest cover and other ecosystems such as mangroves, seagrass, peatlands, old-growth forests, and marshes, over decades of sustainable management and use to pursue opportunities to mobilize financing in this regard;

(b) Conserve and sustainably use the ocean and its resources by:

(i) Ensuring the conservation and sustainable use of marine resources, including through sustainable management of aquaculture, mariculture, tourism and fisheries, such as through the implementation of measures to end illegal, unreported and unregulated fishing for mutually reinforcing economic and environmental benefits;

(ii) Addressing biodiversity loss caused by harmful human activities, including inadequate waste management and unsustainable production and consumption, including of plastics; overfishing; illegal, unreported and unregulated fishing; introduction of alien invasive species; noise and light pollution; coral bleaching, ocean acidification, eutrophication and harmful algal blooms; and coastal erosion, including through measures such as, inter alia, satellite monitoring, and the establishment and strengthened management of area-based management tools, including marine protected areas and integrated coastal zone management; and other effective area-based conservation measures and locally managed marine areas;

(iii) Strengthening partnerships at the subregional, regional and international levels to prevent and reduce plastic pollution in the marine environment and support investment in modern integrated solid waste management systems;

(c) Conserve, restore and sustainably use biodiversity by:

(i) Developing, enhancing and applying environmental statistics frameworks in their national statistical systems, such as natural capital accounting framework, including ecosystems services valuation, to assess the contribution of natural ecosystems to economies and inform policy decisions and development;

(ii) Supporting small island developing States to identify financing and capacity gaps in meeting biodiversity objectives and develop partnerships, particularly with the private sector, to develop innovative strategies to bridge these gaps;

(iii) Updating the programme of work on island biodiversity adopted under the Convention on Biological Diversity,[192] particularly in the context of the ongoing process to identify scientific and technical needs of small island developing States;

(iv) Developing an island biodiversity capacity-building and development action plan, on the basis of the review of the capacity and technology absorption and sustaining abilities of small island developing States and in line with the programme of work on island biodiversity;

(v) Acknowledging the important roles and contributions of Indigenous Peoples and local communities as custodians of biodiversity and as partners in its conservation, restoration and sustainable use; and ensuring the rights, knowledge, including traditional knowledge associated with biodiversity, innovations, worldviews, values and practices of Indigenous Peoples and local communities are respected, and documented and preserved with their free, prior and informed consent, including through their full and effective participation in decision-making, in accordance with relevant national legislation, international instruments, including the United Nations Declaration on the Rights of Indigenous Peoples,[193] and human rights law;

(d) Mainstream disaster risk reduction by:

(i) Increasing local, national and regional capacity, particularly among key national agencies, to improve coordination with international, regional and humanitarian partners and donor Governments, as appropriate, to prevent and reduce disaster risk and to respond to intensifying disasters;

(ii) Building more robust multi-hazard risk governance, including the development of national legislative frameworks for disaster risk reduction and strengthened local authorities and community-based disaster risk management approaches that can capture whole-of-government and whole-of-society actions that are also gender-responsive and disability-inclusive;

(iii) Strengthening disaster preparedness, including multi-hazard early warning systems and capacity to take early action, through initiatives such as Early Warnings for All and Climate Risk and Early Warning Systems, timely evacuation planning, planning for relocation of communities, and developing post-disaster needs assessments;

(iv) Implementing creative arrangements and risk reduction mechanisms that allow small island developing States to access low and concessional financing rates, including government guarantees and insurance schemes, as appropriate;

(v) Reducing disaster risks, including by building protective infrastructure and enhancing resilience of freshwater and other water systems, and using the recovery, rehabilitation and reconstruction phases after a disaster to increase resilience, and developing systems for managing evacuations and the distribution of basic relief support.

III. How do small island developing States get there?

31. While acknowledging the primary responsibility of small island developing States for their own sustainable development, we recognize that the persistent development challenges of the small island developing States require enhanced global partnership for development, adequate provision and mobilization of all means of implementation and continued international support to achieve internationally agreed goals.

32. Therefore, to realize the Antigua and Barbuda Agenda for Small Island Developing States by 2034, we, the international community, commit to the following actions:

A. Build economic resilience

(a) Reform the international financial architecture and address gaps and shortfalls, and facilitate easier access to affordable and concessional finance by:

(i) Considering how best multidimensional vulnerability could be incorporated into existing practices and policies for debt sustainability and development support, including access to concessional finance, looking forward

[192] United Nations, *Treaty Series*, vol. 1760, No. 30619.

[193] Resolution 61/295, annex.

to the intergovernmental process to consider the recommendations presented in the final report of the High-level Panel on the Development of a Multidimensional Vulnerability Index for Small Island Developing States, which can also provide a basis for moving forward in this direction;

(ii) Expanding multilateral lending to small island developing States, while maintaining financial sustainability of multilateral development institutions, and taking note of the identification by the Heads of Multilateral Development Banks Group of capital adequacy measures which could potentially yield additional lending headroom in the order of up to 400 billion United States dollars over the next decade, with a view to strengthening support for small island developing States in achieving resilient prosperity;

(iii) Ensuring representation and participation of small island developing States, as well as other developing countries, in decision-making in global economic and international financial institutions in order to deliver more effective, credible, accountable and legitimate institutions, giving due consideration to priorities, needs and perspectives of small island developing States in the process;

(b) Increase effectiveness of development finance by:

(i) Improving donors' aid effectiveness, development cooperation and donor coordination in line with national and regional priorities and needs of small island developing States, including through the small island developing States principles for development effectiveness, as appropriate;

(ii) Promoting a risk-informed approach to investment and financing in small island developing States so that all development finance strengthens resilience and accelerates the development aspirations of small island developing States;

(c) Support the sustainable management of debt by:

(i) Considering the establishment of a dedicated small island developing States debt sustainability support service to enable sound debt management and devise effective solutions for small island developing States in relation to debt vulnerability in the immediate term and debt sustainability in the long term, building on and avoiding duplication with relevant dedicated initiatives;

(ii) Considering the use of state-contingent instruments to strengthen borrower resilience and increase the ability of small island developing States to withstand economic shocks;

(d) Increase investments in small island developing States by strengthening capacity for resource mobilization, investment flows monitoring, firm-level data collection and analysis, as well as trade-related support to strengthen investment promotion agencies in small island developing States to attract stable and development-conducive foreign direct investment and other private capital flows, in accordance with national circumstances, priorities and legislation;

(e) Enable youth economic participation by:

(i) Harnessing the demographic dividend by equipping youth with education and skills, including through capacity-building and training initiatives to pursue opportunities in traditional, emerging and innovative economies;

(ii) Supporting youth-driven startups, providing financial backing, mentorship and resources to cultivate a new generation of entrepreneurs and steer small island developing States towards economic resilience and diversification through innovation;

B. Scale up climate action and support, including climate finance, in line with existing commitments and obligations under the United Nations Framework Convention on Climate Change and the Paris Agreement

(a) Accelerated actions towards full and effective implementation of the United Nations Framework Convention on Climate Change and the Paris Agreement by:

(i) Taking urgent actions to hold the increase in the global average temperature to well below 2 degrees Celsius above pre-industrial levels and pursue efforts to limit the temperature increase to 1.5 degrees Celsius above pre-industrial levels and to accelerate action in this critical decade on the basis of the best available science, reflecting equity and the principle of common but differentiated responsibilities and respective capabilities in the light of different national circumstances and in the context of sustainable development and efforts to eradicate poverty;

(ii) Implementing the decisions adopted at sessions of the Conference of the Parties to the United Nations Framework Convention on Climate Change and the Conference of the Parties serving as the Meeting of the Parties to the Paris Agreement;

(iii) Timely support for action on adaptation through, inter alia, the operationalization and implementation of the United Arab Emirates Framework for Global Climate Resilience to guide the achievement of the global goal on adaptation and the review of overall progress in achieving it with a view to reducing the increasing adverse impacts, risks and vulnerabilities associated with climate change, as well as to enhance adaptation action and support;

(iv) Phasing out inefficient fossil fuel subsidies that do not address energy poverty or just transitions, as soon as possible in a nationally determined manner, taking into account the Paris Agreement different national circumstances, pathways and approaches;

(v) Accelerating and substantially reducing non-carbon dioxide emissions globally, including in particular methane emissions by 2030, in a nationally determined manner, taking into account the Paris Agreement, different national circumstances, pathways and approaches, while providing targeted support to enable small island developing States to address non-carbon dioxide emissions;

(vi) Providing climate finance by developed countries to small island developing States in line with existing obligations and commitments under the United Nations Framework Convention on Climate Change and the Paris Agreement;

(vii) Strengthening, and mobilizing and providing financial resources to, existing multilateral climate funds, including the Green Climate Fund, the Global Environment Facility and its Special Climate Change Fund, and the Adaptation Fund;

(viii) Harmonizing, as appropriate, and simplifying the application requirements, as well as access and approval procedures for climate financing instruments, and continuing to advocate for dedicated financing and programmes for small island developing States, including advocating for minimum allocation funding criteria for small island developing States, as appropriate to address, inter alia, the current high barriers and transaction costs, especially for financing small-sized projects for small island developing States;

(ix) Providing technical support for small island developing States for the development of carbon markets in accordance with article 6 of the Paris Agreement, as well as the further development of private financial products such as green and blue bonds;

(x) Providing resources, recognizing the urgent and immediate need for new, additional, predictable and adequate financial resources to assist developing countries that are particularly vulnerable to the adverse impacts of climate change in responding to economic and non-economic loss and damage associated with the adverse effects of climate change with special consideration for small island developing States;

(xi) Urgently operationalizing and further capitalizing the new fund for responding to loss and damage, ensuring that priorities and needs of small island developing States are also considered in the context of access and resource allocation and the development of programmatic, nationally led approaches, with due regard for the governing instrument of the fund and special consideration for small island developing States;

(xii) Addressing the significant challenges small island developing States face in accessing climate finance for implementing their national adaptation plans;

(xiii) Activating private sector finance for climate mitigation and adaptation, with a view to strengthening financial support for small island developing States in achieving resilient prosperity;

C. Scale up biodiversity action

(a) Accelerated and urgent actions to halt and reverse biodiversity loss by:

(i) Advancing, by parties to the Convention on Biological Diversity, the full and effective implementation of the decisions of the Conference of the Parties to the Convention, including the Kunming-Montreal Global Biodiversity Framework;

(ii) Ensuring adequate financial and technical support for small island developing States and timely operationalization and capitalization of the Global Biodiversity Framework Fund;

D. Conserve and sustainably use the ocean and its resources

(a) Support ocean-based action by:

(i) Building the capacity of small island developing States in understanding their rights, obligations and responsibilities under the United Nations Convention on the Law of the Sea,[194] including to enable their effective participation in activities under the Convention;

(ii) Building the capacity of small island developing States to ratify and implement the provisions of the Agreement under the United Nations Convention on the Law of the Sea on the Conservation and Sustainable Use of Marine Biological Diversity in Areas Beyond National Jurisdiction;[195]

(iii) Exploring, developing and promoting innovative financing solutions to drive the transformation to sustainable ocean-based economies, and the scaling up of nature-based solutions, ecosystem-based approaches to support the resilience, restoration and conservation of coastal ecosystems, including through public-private sector partnerships and capital market instruments, provide technical assistance to enhance the bankability and feasibility of projects, as well as mainstream the values of marine natural capital into decision-making and address barriers to accessing financing, recognizing that further support is needed from developed countries, especially regarding capacity-building, financing and technology transfer;

(iv) Pursuing opportunities for research and innovation in ocean-related industries that explore new technologies, sustainable practices and innovative solutions;

(v) Assisting small island developing States in planning and implementing area-based management tools, including effectively and equitably managed, ecologically representative and well-connected marine protected areas, and other effective area-based conservation measures, integrated coastal zone management and marine spatial planning, in small island developing States, in accordance with national legislation and international law;

(vi) Encouraging the increase of funding to the trust funds[196] for the efficient and effective operation of the Commission on the Limits of the Continental Shelf;

E. Mainstream disaster risk reduction

(a) Build resilience to disasters by:

(i) Providing financial and technical assistance, and capacity-building for disaster risk reduction and more robust multi-hazard risk governance;

(ii) Assisting small island developing States to respond to disasters by supporting them, through the international financial institutions, to build and design risk-resilient infrastructure and improving the speed of post-disaster support;

(iii) Allocating ex-ante financing to enable the systemic reduction of disaster risk and resilience-building, including the disclosure of disaster risk;

(iv) Continuing to support the development of vehicles and instruments aimed at providing support to small island developing States, including through emergency liquidity as required, and funding reconstruction after disasters;

---

[194] United Nations, *Treaty Series*, vol. 1833, No. 31363.

[195] A/CONF.232/2023/4.

[196] The voluntary trust fund for the purpose of defraying the cost of participation of the members of the Commission on the Limits of the Continental Shelf from developing States in the meetings of the Commission and the voluntary trust fund for the purpose of facilitating the preparation of submissions to the Commission for developing States, in particular the least developed countries and small island developing States, and compliance with article 76 of the United Nations Convention on the Law of the Sea.

(v) Increasing support, including financing, to improve small island developing States' data collection, governance, management, analysis and assessment of hazards, disaster events and their impacts, including losses and damages in small island developing States;

F. Safe and healthy societies

(a) Strengthen health systems by:

(i) Increasing access to assistance for health systems, including financing, aligned with national and regional priorities;

(ii) Providing financial and technical assistance and capacity-building support to prevent and address the impact of non-communicable diseases and mental health conditions, including in support of the Bridgetown Declaration on Non-communicable Diseases and Mental Health, as appropriate;

G. Data collection, analysis and use

(a) Strengthen data collection, storage and analysis by:

(i) Investing in building human and institutional capacity in small island developing States to collect quality, accessible, timely and reliable, disaggregated data, according to their national contexts, to measure progress and to ensure that no one is left behind;

(ii) Strengthening and modernizing national data infrastructure and systems in small island developing States to better integrate data into development planning, and enhancing the capacity of statistical offices in small island developing States;

(iii) Enhancing science-based and innovative approaches, including sustainable development-oriented, inclusive and responsible use of artificial intelligence, in the non-military domain, in full respect, promotion and protection of human rights and international law, for the collection, storage, analysis, disaggregation, dissemination and use of demographic data in small island developing States, including use of geospatial technologies;

(iv) Enhancing partnerships and the sharing of best practice, expertise, digital public goods and data in order to facilitate small island developing States peer-to-peer learning, including through the Small Island Developing States Centre of Excellence and existing statistical initiatives, including through regional organizations;

(v) Providing high-quality spatial data for small island developing States and working to downscale global datasets to provide accurate information for small island developing States;

H. Science, technology, innovation and digitalization

(a) Harness the potential of science, technology and innovation and advance the benefits of digitalization in small island developing States by:

(i) Providing small island developing States with the necessary means of implementation to strengthen their scientific and technological capacities;

(ii) Taking action to harness digital technologies to achieve sustainable development in small island developing States by strengthening digital cooperation, developing digital infrastructure, bridging digital divides and ensuring an open and inclusive digital future for all;

(iii) Assisting small island developing States in developing national road maps for digitalization, science, technology and innovation and to support small island developing States to build up national capacities for developing and utilizing state-of-the-art technologies, including renewable energy technologies, marine technologies for the ocean-based economy and other areas significant to sustainable development, including digital technologies;

(iv) Assisting the development of policies and legislation to create an enabling environment to boost digital transformation, innovation, enhance digital infrastructure and connectivity, bridge digital divides, enhance digital skills, support government digital services and digital public infrastructure, and leverage science and technology, including new and emerging technology and artificial intelligence, taking into account the unique needs of small island developing States;

(v) Supporting the Small Island Developing States Centre of Excellence through its innovation and technology mechanism to provide learning opportunities, exchange experiences and support innovation, so as to enhance capacity-building and narrow the digital divides;

(vi) Creating and supporting inclusive digital societies, and implementing initiatives at all levels to develop human resources in science and technology, engineering, the arts and mathematics, especially to promote the interest of children, including girls, youth, women, persons with disabilities and other people in vulnerable situations, and to strengthen the quality of education and reskilling in these fields by modernizing school curricula;

(vii) Developing digital solutions to expand commerce to support efforts to overcome the adverse impacts of remoteness and other structural constraints in small island developing States;

(viii) Supporting the building of capacity among populations of small island developing States to access new and emerging technological innovations, improving digital and financial literacy and skills, to ensure that everyone, especially the most vulnerable, has access to services, both offline and online, and benefits from economic opportunities;

I. Productive populations

(a) Increase prosperity and productive capacities, employment, equality and inclusivity in small island developing States by:

(i) Empowering small island developing States to capture the benefits of digital technologies and resources for inclusive, equitable and quality education and lifelong learning opportunities, including through distance learning;

(ii) Promoting, protecting and improving the health and nutrition of populations through multisectoral action and strengthening health systems to support educational attainment, a growing and productive workforce, poverty reduction and resilience to shocks;

(iii) Providing quality education opportunities for children and youth at risk and developing strategies to address underperformance, especially of boys in school, to ensure they are educated with skill sets to enable them to successfully enter the labour market, taking into account national circumstances;

(iv) Developing policies, strategies and norms to promote employment and reduce unemployment and underemployment, by promoting skills development and productivity, technology transfer on mutually agreed terms and experience-sharing that respond to evolving job markets and reducing barriers to employment, especially for youth and women;

(v) Increasing investment in the quality of education, reskilling and lifelong learning opportunities, especially for children, youth, women, Indigenous Peoples, local communities, persons with disabilities, migrants and displaced persons and other people in vulnerable situations;

J. Partnerships

(a) New, innovative and bold approaches to partnership based on mutual collaboration and ownership, trust, alignment, harmonization, respect, results orientation, accountability, transparency, including with relevant stakeholders, and cooperation that leverages a whole-of-government and whole-of-society approach, by:

(i) Expanding and diversifying partnerships with local authorities, civil society and non-governmental organizations, foundations, the private sector, academia and international financial institutions to implement the Antigua and Barbuda Agenda for Small Island Developing States;

(ii) Supporting SIDS-SIDS cooperation, capacity-building and knowledge exchange, particularly among institutions of small island developing States, including the SIDS-SIDS Green-Blue Economy Knowledge Transfer Hub at the University of the West Indies Cave Hill campus in Barbados;

(iii) Leveraging North-South, triangular and South-South cooperation, including SIDS-to-SIDS, to mobilize human, financial, technical and technological resources, while recalling that South-South cooperation is not a substitute for, but rather a complement to, North-South cooperation.

IV. A more effective United Nations in support of small island developing States

33. We value the role of the United Nations system in supporting small island developing States to achieve their sustainable development objectives and request all United Nations development system entities to contribute to the implementation of, and to integrate, the Antigua and Barbuda Agenda for Small Island Developing States into their strategic and work plans, in accordance with their mandates.

34. We underline the need to give due consideration to the issues and concerns of small island developing States in all relevant major United Nations conferences and processes and the relevant work of the United Nations development system.

35. We call upon the United Nations system to ensure country and multi-country offices of all United Nations entities operating in small island developing States are well resourced, with staff with the appropriate skills, experience, country context and capacities to operate effectively, and to avoid vacancies at the country level, particularly in resident coordinator offices.

36. We request the Secretary-General, in his annual report to the General Assembly at its eightieth session on the implementation of the Antigua and Barbuda Agenda for Small Island Developing States, to present proposals to ensure a coordinated, coherent and effective United Nations system-wide capacity-development approach to small island developing States and to enhance the implementation, monitoring and evaluation of the Agenda, including a potential single SIDS-dedicated entity at the Secretariat.

37. We also request the Secretary-General, in consultation with States, including through the Steering Committee on Partnerships for Small Island Developing States, to present recommendations for the strengthening of the Small Island Developing States Partnership Framework and the Small Island Developing States Global Business Network and its Forum.

V. Monitoring and evaluation

38. We commit to engaging in systematic monitoring and evaluation of the Antigua and Barbuda Agenda for Small Island Developing States over the next 10 years. We request the Secretary-General to convene an inter-agency task force to develop a monitoring and evaluation framework, with clear targets and indicators, to be completed by no later than the second quarter of 2025. The framework should build on the monitoring and evaluation framework for the Samoa Pathway, in line with the targets and indicators of the Sustainable Development Goals, and use data from existing reporting mechanisms where possible and should not be overly burdensome or create new processes or requirements for small island developing States.

39. We call upon the Department of Economic and Social Affairs and the Office of the High Representative for the Least Developed Countries, Landlocked Developing Countries and Small Island Developing States to conduct workshops to familiarize small island developing States with the application of the framework and build capacity to collect and submit their data.

40. We call for the annual small island developing States segment of the high-level political forum on sustainable development convened under the auspices of the Economic and Social Council to be repurposed to review annually progress against commitments in the Antigua and Barbuda Agenda for Small Island Developing States that are aligned with the Sustainable Development Goals under review. To support this, we request the Secretary-General to prepare an annual report on progress in implementing the Agenda, drawing on data from the monitoring and evaluation framework.

41. Beginning in 2026, we call upon the Economic Commission for Latin America and the Caribbean, the Economic and Social Commission for Asia and the Pacific and the Economic Commission for Africa to conduct a comprehensive biennial review of progress in each small island developing State in their respective regions, which should inform the report of the Secretary-General on follow-up to the Antigua and Barbuda Agenda for Small Island Developing States. In this regard, we note the call for the establishment of a regional coordination mechanism for the Atlantic, Indian Ocean and South China Sea small island developing States to support implementation of the Agenda

and contribute to its monitoring and review. We request the Economic and Social Commission for Asia and the Pacific and the Economic Commission for Africa to establish small island developing States divisions, within existing resources, to coordinate monitoring, evaluation and reporting for the Atlantic, Indian Ocean and South China Sea small island developing States.

42. We call for the General Assembly to undertake a comprehensive midterm review of the Antigua and Barbuda Agenda for Small Island Developing States, informed by regional preparatory meetings, to highlight solutions to address the gaps and challenges in the implementation of the Agenda and identify priorities for the final five years of its implementation.

RESOLUTION 78/318

Adopted at the 101st plenary meeting, on 16 July 2024, without a vote, on the basis of draft resolution A/78/L.93, submitted by the President of the General Assembly

78/318. Modalities of the "World Social Summit" under the title "the Second World Summit for Social Development"

The General Assembly,

Recalling the World Summit for Social Development, held in Copenhagen from 6 to 12 March 1995, and the twenty-fourth special session of the General Assembly, entitled "World Summit for Social Development and beyond: achieving social development for all in a globalizing world", held in Geneva from 26 June to 1 July 2000,

Reaffirming that the Copenhagen Declaration on Social Development and the Programme of Action of the World Summit for Social Development[197] and the further initiatives for social development adopted by the General Assembly at its twenty-fourth special session,[198] as well as a continued global dialogue on social development issues, constitute the basic framework for the promotion of social development for all at the national and international levels,

Reaffirming also all previous resolutions on the implementation of the outcome of the World Summit for Social Development and of the twenty-fourth special session of the General Assembly, including resolution 78/174 of 19 December 2023,

Reaffirming further its resolution 78/261 of 26 February 2024, entitled "World Social Summit" under the title "Second World Summit for Social Development", by which it decided to convene the "World Social Summit" in 2025, under the title "the Second World Summit for Social Development", to address the gaps and recommit to the Copenhagen Declaration on Social Development and the Programme of Action and its implementation and give momentum towards the implementation of the 2030 Agenda for Sustainable Development,[199]

Welcoming the progress made towards the full implementation of the Copenhagen Declaration and the Programme of Action through concerted action at the national, regional and international levels, and expressing its deep concern that, more than 25 years after the convening of the World Summit for Social Development, progress has been slow and uneven, and major gaps remain,

Recognizing that the three core themes of social development, namely, poverty eradication, full and productive employment and decent work for all and social integration, are interrelated and mutually reinforcing, and that an enabling environment therefore needs to be created so that all three objectives can be pursued simultaneously,

Sharing the conviction that social development and social justice are indispensable for the achievement and maintenance of peace and security within and among nations, and that, in turn, social development and social justice cannot be attained in the absence of peace and security or in the absence of respect for all human rights and fundamental freedoms,

---

[197] *Report of the World Summit for Social Development, Copenhagen, 6–12 March 1995* (United Nations publication, Sales No. E.96.IV.8), chap. I, resolution 1, annexes I and II.

[198] Resolution S-24/2, annex.

[199] Resolution 70/1.

Reaffirming that the Commission for Social Development continues to have the primary responsibility for the follow-up to and review of the World Summit for Social Development and the outcome of the twenty-fourth special session of the General Assembly, and that it serves as the main United Nations forum for an intensified global dialogue on social development issues,

Recognizing the role and positive contributions of the International Labour Organization and its constituents, namely Governments, employers and workers, to promote social justice and decent work for all,

Recalling General Assembly resolution 70/1 of 25 September 2015, entitled "Transforming our world: the 2030 Agenda for Sustainable Development", in which the Assembly adopted a comprehensive, far-reaching and people-centred set of universal and transformative Sustainable Development Goals and targets and affirmed its commitment to working tirelessly for the full implementation of the Agenda by 2030 with a view to leaving no one behind and reaching the furthest behind first, and its recognition that eradicating poverty in all its forms and dimensions, including extreme poverty, is the greatest global challenge and an indispensable requirement for sustainable development,

Recalling also its resolution 76/6 of 15 November 2021, entitled "Follow-up to the report of the Secretary-General entitled 'Our Common Agenda'",[200] and noting the proposal contained in that report to convene a world social summit in 2025, to be discussed and agreed upon by Member States, including its modalities, title, objectives, scope and possible outcomes, and emphasizing that the possible summit's outcome should have a social development approach including the need to place people at the centre of development and the pledge to make poverty eradication, full employment and social integration the overriding development objectives, and give momentum towards the implementation of the 2030 Agenda,

1. *Decides* that the "World Social Summit" under the title "the Second World Summit for Social Development" will be held at the level of Heads of State or Government in Qatar from 4 to 6 November 2025, and welcomes the offer by the Government of Qatar to host the "World Social Summit" under the title "the Second World Summit on Social Development" in 2025;

2. *Also decides* that the Summit will adopt a concise, action-oriented political declaration, agreed in advance by consensus through intergovernmental negotiations in New York, that should have a social development approach and give momentum towards the implementation of the 2030 Agenda for Sustainable Development;

3. *Further decides* that the Summit, subject to the rules of procedure of the General Assembly, will consist of:

(a) Plenary meetings from 9 a.m. to 1 p.m. and from 3 to 6 p.m.;

(b) An opening segment on the first day from 9 to 10.30 a.m., which will include the adoption of the political declaration followed by statements from the President of the General Assembly, the Secretary-General and the President of the Economic and Social Council;

(c) A closing segment on the third day from 5 to 6 p.m., which will feature a statement from the President of the General Assembly;

4. *Decides* that the Summit will have two high-level round tables, each to be co-chaired by two Heads of State or Government, one from a developed country and one from a developing country, to be appointed by the President of the General Assembly after consultations with the Member States, ensuring geographical balance, on the following themes:

Round table 1: Strengthening the three pillars of social development: poverty eradication, full and productive employment and decent work for all, and social inclusion

Round table 2: Assessing progress and addressing gaps and challenges in the implementation of the commitments of the Copenhagen Declaration on Social Development and its Programme of Action and giving momentum towards the implementation of the 2030 Agenda for Sustainable Development;

[200] A/75/982.

5. *Encourages* Member States, members of the United Nations specialized agencies and observers of the General Assembly to be represented at the level of Head of State or Government or at the highest possible level to make statements in plenary of up to five minutes;

6. *Invites* the United Nations system, including the funds, programmes, specialized agencies and regional commissions, as well as the international financial institutions, to participate in the Summit and make contributions, within their respective mandates, to the preparation of the Summit;

7. *Invites* representatives of non-governmental organizations that are in consultative status with the Economic and Social Council to participate in the Summit in accordance with relevant rules and procedures of the General Assembly;

8. *Encourages* Member States and members of the United Nations specialized agencies to include in their delegations to the Summit, as appropriate, representatives of relevant stakeholders, such as parliamentarians, representatives of civil society, including non-governmental organizations, Indigenous Peoples, people with disabilities, people of African descent, youth representatives, youth-led organizations, community organizations and faith-based organizations, academic institutions, representatives of workers and employers and the private sector, with due regard to gender balance;

9. *Requests* the President of the General Assembly to draw up a list of representatives of other relevant non-governmental organizations, civil society organizations, academic institutions and the private sector who may participate in the Summit, taking into account the principles of transparency and equitable geographical representation, with due regard for gender parity, to submit the proposed list to Member States for their consideration on a non-objection basis[201] and to bring the list to the attention of the Assembly for a final decision by the Assembly on participation in the Summit;

10. *Decides* that preparations should be carried out in a most effective, well-structured and broad participatory manner and that, for this purpose, the Department of Economic and Social Affairs of the Secretariat, and the relevant organizations of the United Nations system, including the regional commissions, within their respective mandates and available resources, should provide the necessary support to the Summit and its preparatory process;

11. *Requests* the Secretary-General to provide the necessary assistance and support for the organization of the Summit and its preparation;

12. *Encourages* States and international donors, as well as the private sector, financial institutions, foundations and other donors in a position to do so, to support the preparations for the Summit through voluntary contributions to a trust fund in support of preparations for the Summit and to support the participation of representatives of developing countries in the Summit, priority being given to representatives of the least developed countries and small island developing States, including coverage of economy-class air tickets, daily subsistence allowances and terminal expenses, in the meetings of the Summit.

RESOLUTION 78/319

Adopted at the 102nd plenary meeting, on 1 August 2024, without a vote, on the basis of draft resolution A/78/L.100, submitted by the President of the General Assembly

78/319. Scope, modalities, format and organization of the high-level plenary meeting on addressing the existential threats posed by sea level rise

The General Assembly,

Recalling its decision 78/544 of 16 January 2024, in which it decided to hold a high-level plenary meeting of the General Assembly on addressing the existential threats posed by sea level rise, in New York on 25 September 2024, during the high-level week of the seventy-ninth session of the Assembly,

[201] The list will include proposed as well as final names. The general basis of any objections, if requested by one or more States Members of the United Nations or States members of the specialized agencies, will be made known to the Office of the President of the General Assembly and the requester.

Recalling also the outcome document of the United Nations Conference on Sustainable Development, held in Rio de Janeiro, Brazil, from 20 to 22 June 2012, entitled "The future we want",[202]

Reaffirming its resolution 70/1 of 25 September 2015, entitled "Transforming our world: the 2030 Agenda for Sustainable Development", in which it adopted a comprehensive, far-reaching and people-centred set of universal and transformative Sustainable Development Goals and targets, and its commitment to working tirelessly for the full implementation of the Agenda by 2030,

Recalling its resolution 78/153 of 19 December 2023 on the protection of global climate for present and future generations of humankind,

Recalling also its resolution 78/69 of 5 December 2023 on oceans and the law of the sea,

Recalling further its resolution 78/155 of 19 December 2023 on the implementation of the Convention on Biological Diversity and its contribution to sustainable development,

Acknowledging the ongoing work of the open-ended Study Group of the International Law Commission on the topic "Sea-level rise in relation to international law",[203] and encouraging States to share their views on the various aspects of this topic with that Commission,

Taking note with concern of the findings contained in the recent reports of the Intergovernmental Panel on Climate Change, including the synthesis report of the Sixth Assessment Report and the special reports entitled *Global Warming of 1.5°C*, *Climate Change and Land*, and *The Ocean and Cryosphere in a Changing Climate*, and also noting, among other things, that increasing warming amplifies the exposure of small islands, low-lying coastal areas and deltas to the risks associated with sea level rise and extreme sea level events,

Taking note of the recent global and regional reports of the World Meteorological Organization on the state of the climate, that find, among other things, that global mean sea level reached a record high, including the finding that the rate of sea level rise in the past 10 years (2014–2023) has more than doubled since the first decade of the satellite record (1993–2002),

Recognizing the importance of improving understanding of the impacts of climate change on oceans and seas, and recalling that, in "The future we want", States noted that sea level rise and coastal erosion are serious threats for many coastal regions and islands, particularly in developing countries, and in this regard called upon the international community to enhance its efforts to address these challenges, and noting the attention paid to the themes of "The effects of climate change on oceans" and "Sea level rise and its impacts" at the eighteenth and twenty-first meetings, respectively, of the United Nations Open-ended Informal Consultative Process on Oceans and the Law of the Sea, in 2017 and 2021, which, inter alia, highlighted the urgency of sea level rise for small island developing States and coastal States, including low-lying coastal areas,

Recalling the endorsement of the Pacific Islands Forum leaders on 6 August 2021 at the fifty-first Pacific Islands Forum of a declaration on preserving maritime zones in the face of climate change-related sea level rise, and of the Heads of State and Government of the Alliance of Small Island States on 22 September 2021 of the Leaders' Declaration addressing, inter alia, the relationship between climate change-related sea level rise and Forum and Alliance members' maritime zones in response to long-standing concerns in the face of climate change-related sea level rise,

Recalling also the endorsement of the Pacific Islands Forum leaders on 9 November 2023 at the fifty-second Pacific Islands Forum of a declaration on the continuity of statehood and the protection of persons in the face of climate change-related sea level rise addressing, inter alia, the relationship between climate change-related sea level rise and Forum members' statehood, sovereignty and protection of persons,

Taking note of the ocean and climate change dialogue, first established at the twenty-fifth session of the Conference of the Parties to the United Nations Framework Convention on Climate Change,

---

[202] Resolution 66/288, annex.

[203] See *Official Records of the General Assembly, Seventy-fourth Session, Supplement No. 10* (A/74/10); ibid., *Seventy-sixth Session, Supplement No. 10* (A/76/10); ibid., *Seventy-seventh Session, Supplement No. 10* (A/77/10); and ibid., *Seventy-eighth Session, Supplement No. 10* (A/78/10).

Acknowledging the important role of the United Nations Decade of Ocean Science for Sustainable Development (2021–2030) in supporting the efforts and commitments necessary for delivering the science we need, for the ocean we want,

Recognizing the importance of enhanced international cooperation and collective action to address sea level rise, and determined to strengthen the global response and support to developing countries, especially those that are particularly vulnerable to the adverse effects of climate change, and coastal communities, to build resilience and adapt to its consequences,

1. *Decides* that the overall theme of the high-level plenary meeting of the General Assembly to be held on 25 September 2024 will be "Addressing the threats posed by sea level rise";

2. *Also decides* that the high-level meeting will focus on building common understanding, mobilizing political leadership and promoting multisectoral and multi-stakeholder collaboration and international cooperation towards the objective of addressing the threats posed by sea level rise;

3. *Further decides* that the organizational arrangements for the high-level meeting should be as follows;

(a) The high-level meeting will comprise an opening segment, a plenary segment, four multi-stakeholder thematic panel discussions and a brief closing segment;

(b) The opening segment, to be held from 10 to 10.20 a.m., will feature statements by the President of the General Assembly at its seventy-ninth session, the Secretary-General, the President of the General Assembly at its seventy-eighth session and a representative of a Member State affected by the adverse effects of sea level rise;

(c) The plenary segment, to be held from 10.20 a.m. to 1 p.m. and from 3 to 5.40 p.m., will comprise statements by Member States and observers of the General Assembly and members of the United Nations specialized agencies; a list of speakers will be established in accordance with the rules of procedure and established practices of the Assembly and the time limits for these statements will be three minutes for individual delegations and five minutes for statements made on behalf of a group of States;

(d) The closing segment, to be held from 5.40 to 6 p.m., will comprise summaries of the multi-stakeholder thematic panel discussions presented by the Co-Chairs of the panels and concluding remarks by the President of the General Assembly at its seventy-ninth session;

4. *Decides* that the organizational arrangements for the four multi-stakeholder thematic panel discussions will be as follows:

(a) Two multi-stakeholder panels will be held consecutively from 10.30 to 11.45 a.m. and from 11.45 a.m. to 1 p.m. and two multi-stakeholder panels will be held consecutively from 3 to 4.15 p.m. and from 4.15 to 5.30 p.m., in parallel with the plenary meeting;

(b) Each of the four multi-stakeholder panel discussions will be co-chaired by two representatives, one from a developing country and one from a developed country, to be appointed by the President of the General Assembly from among the representatives attending the high-level meeting, in consultation with Member States, taking into account gender balance and geographical representation;

(c) The discussions in and summaries of the Co-Chairs of the four multi-stakeholder panels will be without prejudice to existing processes and the panels will be entitled:

(i) "Knowledge, data and science to inform sea level rise risk assessments and decision-making";

(ii) "Adaptation, finance and resilience in relation to sea level rise";

(iii) "Livelihoods, socioeconomic challenges and culture and heritage in relation to sea level rise";

(iv) "Sea level rise and its legal dimensions";

(d) The President of the General Assembly should consider inviting the heads or senior representatives of Member States, parliamentarians or local governments of Member States, relevant United Nations entities, development partners, civil society, regional and subregional organizations, non-governmental organizations, representatives of Indigenous Peoples, representatives of local communities, the private sector, philanthropic organizations, academia, the science community, youth-led organizations and community organizations to serve as speakers in the panel discussions, taking into account their relevant expertise, as well as gender balance, level of development and geographical representation;

5. *Requests* the Secretary-General to prepare a concise summary of the high-level meeting;

6. *Encourages* all Member States and observers of the General Assembly and members of the United Nations specialized agencies to be represented at the level of Head of State or Government or at the highest possible level;

7. *Invites* the United Nations system, including funds, programmes, specialized agencies and regional commissions, to participate in the high-level meeting and to support the meeting, including its preparations, particularly with regard to sharing evidence and good practices, challenges and lessons learned, and to demonstrate ambition to accelerate action on the overall theme of the meeting;

8. *Invites* representatives of non-governmental organizations that are in consultative status with the Economic and Social Council to participate in the high-level meeting in accordance with relevant rules and procedures of the General Assembly;

9. *Requests* the President of the General Assembly to draw up a list of representatives of other relevant non-governmental organizations, civil society organizations, academic institutions and the private sector who may participate in the high-level meeting, including its panel discussions, taking into account the principles of transparency and equitable geographical representation, with due regard for gender parity, to submit the proposed list to Member States for their consideration on a non-objection basis[204] and to bring the list to the attention of the Assembly for a final decision by the Assembly on participation in the high-level meeting;

10. *Invites* representatives mentioned in paragraphs 6, 7, 8 and 9 above to participate in the multi-stakeholder thematic panel discussions;

11. *Encourages* all Member States and observers of the General Assembly and members of the United Nations specialized agencies to facilitate the participation of youth in the high-level meeting;

12. *Encourages* all representatives invited in paragraphs 7, 8 and 9 above to facilitate the participation of youth, of Indigenous Peoples and of local communities in the high-level meeting;

13. *Requests* the President of the General Assembly and the Secretary-General to provide adequate support to the organization and preparation of the high-level meeting;

14. *Recalls* rule 52 of the rules of procedure of the General Assembly, reaffirms multilingualism as a core and fundamental value of the Organization, re-emphasizes the paramount importance of the equality of the six official languages of the United Nations, and requests the Secretary-General to provide interpretation into the six official languages of the United Nations for the high-level meeting;

15. *Encourages* States and international donors, as well as the private sector, financial institutions, foundations and other donors, to support the participation of representatives of developing countries in the high-level meeting;

16. *Decides* that the proceedings of the high-level meeting will be webcast, and encourages the President of the General Assembly and the Secretary-General to give the highest visibility to the high-level meeting, including its preparations, through all relevant media platforms and information and communications technologies.

RESOLUTION 78/320

Adopted at the 103rd plenary meeting, on 13 August 2024, without a vote, on the basis of draft resolution A/78/L.95, sponsored by: Albania, Algeria, Andorra, Angola, Antigua and Barbuda, Armenia, Austria, Azerbaijan, Bahrain, Bangladesh, Belarus, Belgium, Bhutan, Bolivia (Plurinational State of), Bosnia and Herzegovina, Bulgaria, Burundi, Cabo Verde, Chad, China, Colombia, Congo, Costa Rica, Côte d'Ivoire, Croatia, Cyprus, Czechia, Democratic Republic of the Congo, Denmark, Djibouti, Dominica, Dominican Republic, Eritrea, Estonia, Finland, France, Gambia, Georgia, Germany, Greece, Guatemala, Guinea-Bissau, Guyana, Honduras, Hungary, Iceland, Indonesia, Ireland, Italy, Jamaica, Jordan, Kazakhstan, Kenya, Kiribati,

[204] The list will include proposed as well as final names. The general basis of any objections, if requested by one or more States Members of the United Nations or States members of the specialized agencies, will be made known to the Office of the President of the General Assembly and the requester.

Kyrgyzstan, Latvia, Lebanon, Lesotho, Luxembourg, Mauritius, Monaco, Mongolia, Montenegro, Morocco, Namibia, Nepal, Netherlands (Kingdom of the), Nicaragua, North Macedonia, Oman, Pakistan, Paraguay, Peru, Philippines, Poland, Portugal, Qatar, Republic of Korea, Republic of Moldova, Russian Federation, Saint Kitts and Nevis, Saint Vincent and the Grenadines, San Marino, Saudi Arabia, Senegal, Serbia, Seychelles, Slovakia, Slovenia, Sri Lanka, Suriname, Syrian Arab Republic, Tajikistan, Timor-Leste, Togo, Tunisia, Türkiye, Turkmenistan, United Arab Emirates, United Republic of Tanzania, Uzbekistan, Zimbabwe

78/320. Fostering sustainable forest management, including afforestation and reforestation, in degraded lands, including drylands, as an effective solution to environmental challenges

The General Assembly,

Reaffirming its resolution 70/1 of 25 September 2015, entitled "Transforming our world: the 2030 Agenda for Sustainable Development", in which it adopted a comprehensive, far-reaching and people-centred set of universal and transformative Sustainable Development Goals and targets, its commitment to working tirelessly for the full implementation of the Agenda by 2030, its recognition that eradicating poverty in all its forms and dimensions, including extreme poverty, is the greatest global challenge and an indispensable requirement for sustainable development, its commitment to achieving sustainable development in its three dimensions – economic, social and environmental – in a balanced and integrated manner, and to building upon the achievements of the Millennium Development Goals and seeking to address their unfinished business,

Recalling the United Nations Framework Convention on Climate Change[205] and the Paris Agreement,[206] the Convention on Biological Diversity[207] and the Kunming-Montreal Global Biodiversity Framework adopted at the fifteenth meeting of the Conference of the Parties to the Convention, and the United Nations Convention to Combat Desertification in Those Countries Experiencing Serious Drought and/or Desertification, Particularly in Africa,[208] including the Land Degradation Neutrality Target Setting Programme, as well as the outcomes of the high-level political forum on sustainable development,

Welcoming the Kunming-Montreal Global Biodiversity Framework adopted in decision 15/4 of 19 December 2022[209] at the fifteenth meeting of the Conference of the Parties to the Convention on Biological Diversity, and its goals and targets,

Recalling the United Nations strategic plan for forests 2017–2030[210] and its global forest goals, as well as the midterm review of the effectiveness of the international arrangement on forests in achieving its objectives, and the declaration of the high-level segment of the nineteenth session of the United Nations Forum on Forests,

Stressing that the sustainable management of forests and trees outside forests is vital to the integrated implementation of the 2030 Agenda for Sustainable Development, including achieving the Sustainable Development Goals, especially Goal 15,

Emphasizing the continuous need to increase the visibility of the social, economic and environmental benefits of forests and sustainable forest management and place them as an important component of responses to global challenges, and in this regard noting recent forest-related declarations, pledges and developments, including but not limited to the forest-relevant contributions of the Glasgow Leaders' Declaration on Forests and Land Use and the United Nations Decade on Ecosystem Restoration (2021–2030),

Recognizing that forests provide essential ecosystem services, such as timber, food, fuel, fodder, non-wood products and shelter, as well as contribute to soil and water conservation and clean air, prevent land degradation and desertification and reduce the risk of floods, landslides, avalanches, droughts, dust storms, sandstorms and other natural disasters, and contribute substantially to climate change mitigation and adaptation and to the conservation of biodiversity,

---

205 United Nations, *Treaty Series*, vol. 1771, No. 30822.

206 Adopted under the UNFCCC in FCCC/CP/2015/10/Add.1, decision 1/CP.21.

207 United Nations, *Treaty Series*, vol. 1760, No. 30619.

208 Ibid., vol. 1954, No. 33480.

209 United Nations Environment Programme, document CBD/COP/DEC/15/4, annex.

210 See resolution 71/285.

Recognizing also the valuable contributions of Indigenous Peoples as well as local communities, where applicable, in sustainable forest management, including afforestation and reforestation, in degraded lands, including drylands, and therefore further recognizing the need to promote their full and meaningful participation in forest-related decision-making, contributing to better conserving and managing forests,

Recognizing further the vital role that women play in the conservation and sustainable use of biological diversity, and reaffirming the need for their full, equal, effective and meaningful participation at all levels of policymaking and implementation for the conservation and sustainable use of biological diversity, as well as ecosystem restoration,

Recognizing the Global Initiative on Reducing Land Degradation and Enhancing Conservation of Terrestrial Habitats to prevent, halt and reverse land degradation adopted by the leaders of the Group of 20 in Riyadh in 2020, as well as the Riyadh Leader's Declaration,

Welcoming the convening of the twenty-first session of the Committee for the Review of the Implementation of the United Nations Convention to Combat Desertification in Samarkand, Uzbekistan, from 13 to 17 November 2023,

Looking forward to the sixteenth session of the Conference of the Parties to the United Nations Convention to Combat Desertification in Those Countries Experiencing Serious Drought and/or Desertification, Particularly in Africa, in Riyadh, Saudi Arabia, from 2 to 13 December 2024,

Looking forward also to the sixteenth meeting of the Conference of the Parties to the Convention on Biological Diversity in Cali, Colombia, from 21 October to 1 November 2024,

1. *Emphasizes* that sustainable forest management, including afforestation and reforestation through tree planting, seeding and regeneration in degraded lands, including drylands, can have economic, social and environmental benefits inter alia by increasing biodiversity, providing habitat for diverse plant and animal species, protecting against natural hazards and disasters, contributing substantially to climate change mitigation and adaptation, particularly by absorbing and storing carbon dioxide from the atmosphere, as well as providing opportunities for agroforestry and ecotourism;

2. *Also emphasizes* the need to ensure that afforestation and reforestation activities are carried out in line with sustainable forest management and that they do not lead to the degradation of non-forested natural ecosystems;

3. *Strives* to strengthen the provision and mobilization of and access to new and additional resources from all sources, given the importance of predictability for the conservation, restoration and sustainable management of forests, in particular developing countries, including through innovative mechanisms, as well as strives to promote investment, innovative financing mechanisms, and scientific, technological and capacity-building support for efforts towards halting and reversing deforestation and forest degradation by 2030 in the context of sustainable development and poverty eradication and to leave no one behind, including through results-based payments, positive incentives for the conservation, restoration and sustainable management of forests, and alternative policy approaches, and make this support accessible and attractive to stakeholders involved in sustainable forest management and use, including forest owners, smallholders, Indigenous Peoples, local communities, women and youth;

4. *Invites* Member States to implement, participate in and support, as appropriate, sustainable forest management, including protection, restoration, afforestation and reforestation projects and initiatives incorporating tree planting, seeding or regeneration in degraded lands, including drylands, as appropriate, taking into account their national circumstances, policies, priorities, capacities, levels of development and forest conditions;

5. *Emphasizes* the importance of strengthening international cooperation, including North-South, South-South and triangular cooperation, as well as public-private partnerships and cross-sectoral cooperation at all levels, to promote sustainable forest management;

6. *Reaffirms* the contribution of nature-based solutions, ecosystem-based approaches and other sustainable management and conservation approaches, in line with United Nations Environment Assembly resolution 5/5 of 2 March 2022,[211] for combating desertification, reversing land degradation and halting and reversing biodiversity loss;

[211] UNEP/EA.5/Res.5.

7. *Emphasizes* the role of forests and trees outside forests in mitigating the effects of air, water and soil pollution, as well as their role as natural barriers against wind, sand and dust storms, preventing soil erosion and further desertification;

8. *Recognizes* the value of afforestation and reforestation, including tree planting, seeding and regeneration programmes, through careful planning and consideration of the local environment and ecosystem, using non-invasive, drought-resistant and productive plant species, adapted to the local climate, soil conditions and environmental conditions in the respective areas;

9. *Also recognizes* the significant contributions of forests and trees outside forests in achieving Sustainable Development Goals, in particular in relation to poverty eradication and food security;

10. *Notes* the importance of appropriate species selection and ensuring long-term maintenance, care and monitoring of trees planted, seeded or regenerated in degraded lands, including drylands, through the development of sustainable and effective maintenance strategies;

11. *Recognizes* the need to work collaboratively to protect, conserve, sustainably manage and restore forests and forest ecosystems in line with the global forest goals and all relevant multilateral agreements and related processes, including through meaningful engagement with and supporting the contributions of partners and stakeholders, including forest owners, Indigenous Peoples, local communities, local authorities, the private sector, non-governmental organizations, women, children, youth, and scientific, academic and philanthropic organizations at all levels;

12. *Emphasizes* the importance of education and awareness-raising programmes to inform the public on the benefits of sustainable forest management, including forest protection, restoration, afforestation and reforestation;

13. *Encourages* relevant United Nations entities, within their respective mandates, to integrate sustainable forest management, including afforestation and reforestation, into their programmes and reporting, as appropriate, when providing support to countries affected by desertification and land degradation, to accelerate the achievement of the 2030 Agenda for Sustainable Development.[212]

RESOLUTION 78/321

Adopted at the 103rd plenary meeting, on 13 August 2024, without a vote, on the basis of draft resolution A/78/L.99, sponsored by: Afghanistan, Albania, Andorra, Angola, Armenia, Austria, Bahrain, Belarus, Belgium, Belize, Bolivia (Plurinational State of), Bosnia and Herzegovina, Bulgaria, Cabo Verde, China, Colombia, Comoros, Congo, Croatia, Cyprus, Czechia, Djibouti, Dominican Republic, Estonia, France, Gabon, Georgia, Germany, Greece, Guyana, Honduras, India, Ireland, Italy, Kazakhstan, Kyrgyzstan, Latvia, Lebanon, Luxembourg, Malaysia, Malta, Monaco, Montenegro, Morocco, Nepal, Netherlands (Kingdom of the), North Macedonia, Pakistan, Peru, Philippines, Poland, Portugal, Republic of Korea, Russian Federation, Senegal, Serbia, Seychelles, Singapore, Slovakia, Spain, Sri Lanka, Switzerland, Tajikistan, Tunisia, Turkmenistan, Ukraine, United Arab Emirates, United Kingdom of Great Britain and Northern Ireland, United Republic of Tanzania, Uruguay, Uzbekistan, Viet Nam, Zimbabwe

78/321. Decade of Action for Cryospheric Sciences, 2025–2034

The General Assembly,

Recalling its resolution 77/158 of 14 December 2022, in which it decided to declare 2025 the International Year of Glaciers' Preservation and to proclaim 21 March of each year the World Day for Glaciers, to be observed starting in 2025,

Recalling also its resolution 77/326 of 25 August 2023 on the International Decade of Sciences for Sustainable Development, 2024–2033,

Recalling further its resolution 77/172 of 14 December 2022 on sustainable mountain development, in which it proclaimed the period 2023–2027 as Five Years of Action for the Development of Mountain Regions,

[212] Resolution 70/1.

Recalling its resolution 72/73 of 5 December 2017, in which it proclaimed the United Nations Decade of Ocean Science for Sustainable Development,

Recognizing that the need for a worldwide inventory of existing perennial ice and snow masses was first considered during the International Hydrological Decade, declared by the United Nations Educational, Scientific and Cultural Organization for the period 1965–1974,

Noting that glaciers and ice sheets are a critical component of the hydrological cycle and that the current accelerated melting and retreat of glaciers and melting of ice sheets have severe impacts on the climate, global sea level, the environment, the maintenance of human well-being and health and sustainable development,

Recognizing the important role of the cryosphere, including glaciers, snow, ice and permafrost, in maintaining ecosystems that provide essential services, which are critical foundations for sustainable development and human well-being, especially for the most vulnerable populations,

Recognizing also the importance of initiatives related to the Earth's cryosphere for the achievement of the Sustainable Development Goals[213] and for the implementation of the International Decade for Action, "Water for Sustainable Development", 2018–2028,

Noting with concern the findings contained in the Sixth Assessment Report of the Intergovernmental Panel on Climate Change and its special reports entitled *Global Warming of 1.5°C* and *The Ocean and Cryosphere in a Changing Climate*,

Noting with concern also the findings of the 2022 report of the United Nations Educational, Scientific and Cultural Organization and the International Union for Conservation of Nature entitled *World Heritage Glaciers: Sentinels of Climate Change* regarding the accelerated melting of glaciers in world heritage sites, with glaciers in a third of those sites projected to disappear by 2050,

Noting with concern further the findings of the report of the World Meteorological Organization entitled *State of the Global Climate 2023* regarding the profound changes seen in the cryosphere, illustrating the global scale of climate change,

Recalling that many United Nations Educational, Scientific and Cultural Organization world heritage sites, biosphere reserves and global geoparks include glaciers, and being aware of the need to assess how these sites designated by the Organization, including local communities, face the loss of glaciers and biodiversity, and how scientific data and local knowledge can contribute to a better understanding of climate change impact on mountain glaciers and ecosystems,

Acknowledging the efforts of the United Nations Educational, Scientific and Cultural Organization and the World Meteorological Organization in facilitating the implementation of the International Year of Glaciers' Preservation and coordinating relevant activities,

Taking note of the invitation, expressed in its resolution 77/158, to Governments, intergovernmental and non-governmental organizations, major groups, other relevant stakeholders and donors to voluntarily contribute to the trust fund in support of activities for glaciers' preservation to be coordinated by the Secretary-General, in partnership with relevant agencies of the United Nations system, including the United Nations Educational, Scientific and Cultural Organization and the World Meteorological Organization, to support countries in addressing issues related to accelerated melting of glaciers and its consequences,

Welcoming the initiative of Tajikistan to convene an international conference dedicated to glaciers' preservation in Tajikistan in 2025 and to assume the costs of the conference, and acknowledging its contribution towards the advancement of the Decade of Action for Cryospheric Sciences,

Looking forward to the 2026 United Nations Water Conference to Accelerate the Implementation of Sustainable Development Goal 6: Ensure availability and sustainable management of water and sanitation for all, to be co-hosted by Senegal and the United Arab Emirates, and the 2028 United Nations Conference on the Final Comprehensive

[213] See resolution 70/1.

Review of the Implementation of the Objectives of the International Decade for Action, "Water for Sustainable Development", 2018–2028, to be hosted by Tajikistan in Dushanbe,

Recognizing that the observance of the Decade of Action for Cryospheric Sciences by the international community would contribute significantly to raising awareness on these issues,

1. *Decides* to proclaim the period from 2025 to 2034 as the Decade of Action for Cryospheric Sciences, within existing structures, available resources and voluntary contributions, to address the challenges associated with melting glaciers and changes to the cryosphere by advancing related scientific research and monitoring, under the overarching goal of advancing global scientific cooperation and sustainable development efforts as articulated in the International Decade of Sciences for Sustainable Development, 2024–2033;

2. *Invites* all States Members of the United Nations, all relevant organizations of the United Nations system, other global, regional and subregional organizations and Indigenous Peoples, as well as other relevant stakeholders, including academia, civil society organizations, the private sector and individuals, to observe the Decade of Action as appropriate, at all levels, by promoting activities aimed at raising awareness of the Decade and the importance of glaciers, snow and ice in the climate system and the hydrological cycle, and the economic, social and environmental impacts of the impending changes in the Earth's cryosphere, and to share best practices and knowledge in this regard, including on building resilience to related risks;

3. *Invites* the United Nations Educational, Scientific and Cultural Organization to lead the implementation of the Decade of Action, in collaboration with other relevant organizations of the United Nations system as well as other stakeholders, including those involved in the International Year of Glaciers' Preservation, 2025, identifying and developing activities and programmes within their mandates and using voluntary contributions.

RESOLUTION 78/322

Adopted at the 103rd plenary meeting, on 13 August 2024, without a vote, on the basis of draft resolution A/78/L.98, submitted by the President of the General; Assembly

78/322. Multidimensional vulnerability index

The General Assembly,

Recalling its resolutions 75/215 of 21 December 2020, 76/203 of 17 December 2021, 77/245 of 30 December 2022 and 78/232 of 22 December 2023,

Recognizing that sustainable development is multidimensional and affected by multiple, intersecting, exogenous and endogenous factors, and that vulnerability to adverse exogenous shocks and stressors poses risks for sustainable development,

Recognizing also that income-based measures may not fully reflect all development realities, vulnerabilities and challenges,

Highlighting the need to strengthen the capacity of national statistical systems and provide financial and technical support to improve data collection and statistical analysis in developing countries,

Noting the lack of a universally accepted, international quantitative benchmark to measure exogenous structural vulnerability and lack of resilience to exogenous shocks across multiple dimensions of sustainable development at the national level that can be used to complement gross national income per capita,

Recognizing that the Panel and its report were guided by the report of the Secretary-General,[214] including on multidimensionality, universality, exogeneity, availability and readability,

Recalling paragraph 10 of resolution 77/245, in which it, inter alia, supported the proposed definitions for structural vulnerability and resilience and the two-level structure outlined in the interim report of the High-level Panel on the Development of a Multidimensional Vulnerability Index for Small Island Developing States as the basis for the Panel's continued work, guiding the selection of appropriate indicators to inform vulnerability across all sectors

[214] A/76/211 and A/76/211/Corr.1.

of sustainable development, the proposed governance structure and the development of the country vulnerability-resilience profiles,

Noting that the multidimensional vulnerability index, developed by the High-level Panel, has a two-tiered structure, comprising a universal-level quantitative assessment of structural vulnerability, understood as exposure to adverse external shocks and stressors and lack of resilience, and vulnerability-resilience country profiles, which can provide a more detailed, tailored and individualized characterization of a country's structural and non-structural vulnerability and resilience,

Recognizing that the multidimensional vulnerability index does not address endogenous factors,

Noting the importance of upholding data ownership, integrity, reliability, accuracy and simplicity in the multidimensional vulnerability index,

Noting also the Panel's finding of a weak correlation between income level and both vulnerability and lack of resilience, and that even for some countries that have sufficient resources to invest in resilience-building and may reach high-income status, their vulnerability remains a threat to their sustainable development, and the importance of measuring and addressing vulnerability even within developing countries with a relatively high national income,

Noting further the Panel's finding that it is difficult to establish any vulnerability threshold or cutoff analogous to income cutoffs,

Noting that the multidimensional vulnerability index provides an assessment of vulnerability by measuring the risk of harm from exposure to adverse external (exogenous) shocks and stressors, was designed to reflect structural challenges, and is not a general measure of development or policy performance,

Acknowledging the various indices produced by the United Nations, including those developed by the Committee for Development Policy, the United Nations Development Programme and the United Nations Conference on Trade and Development,

Acknowledging also that the multidimensional vulnerability index is a living tool that is a complement to, and not a substitute for, existing indices and metrics, and that it can contribute to a more comprehensive understanding of development realities,

Recognizing the potential to further improve the multidimensional vulnerability index, inter alia, by considering additional indicators to be included in future iterations of the index as well as indicators for potential refinement or removal, to effectively capture the vulnerabilities of all developing countries,

Recognizing also that the multidimensional vulnerability index may inform future initiatives that go beyond gross domestic product,

Final report

1. *Welcomes* the work of the "High-level Panel on the Development of a Multidimensional Vulnerability Index for Small Island Developing States", takes note of its final report, and decides to advance the multidimensional vulnerability index;

Scope

2. *Notes* that, although initially proposed by small island developing States, the multidimensional vulnerability index aims to capture exogenous vulnerabilities and lack of resilience to exogenous shocks of all developing countries, so as to ensure credibility and comparability, under the guidance provided in the report of the Secretary-General;

Applicability

3. *Stresses* that the use of the multidimensional vulnerability index is voluntary, guided by the specific needs of the end user and informed by national contexts;

4. *Also stresses* that the multidimensional vulnerability index should not be used directly or indirectly as a criterion to limit or hinder the ability of any developing country to access development cooperation, including through existing arrangements and practices;

5. *Requests* the entities of the United Nations development system, within their respective mandates and where applicable, to consider using the multidimensional vulnerability index, including the vulnerability-resilience country profiles, in their relevant programmes of work and reporting, focusing on the countries interested in its use, as a complement to existing measures;

6. *Encourages* the entities of the United Nations development system to gather data and lessons learned on early implementation of the multidimensional vulnerability index and to share this information, with a view to improving the index;

7. *Notes* the work of the international financial institutions, international organizations and multilateral development banks to consider structural vulnerability, and invites them to consider using the multidimensional vulnerability index, as appropriate, as a complement to their existing practices and policies, in line with their respective mandates;

8. *Invites* development partners to explore using the multidimensional vulnerability index, as a complement to existing policies, to inform their development cooperation policies and practices, taking into account the priorities of those countries interested in its use;

Custodianship and governance

9. *Decides* that the multidimensional vulnerability index will be maintained by:

(a) A relevant existing United Nations entity, which will act as the secretariat of the multidimensional vulnerability index, and which will compute the index on a periodic basis, and fulfil other duties and responsibilities necessary and appropriate for the upkeep, maintenance, improvement of and reporting on the index, including the provision of capacity-building support to Member States;

(b) An Independent Expert Advisory Panel, which will prepare recommendations on future technical updates to the multidimensional vulnerability index to reflect new and emerging concepts of structural vulnerability and lack of structural resilience and their associated indicators, as well as new data;

(c) The Statistical Commission, which will provide technical reviews of future technical improvements to the multidimensional vulnerability index;

10. *Also decides* that the secretariat of the multidimensional vulnerability index will present a triennial report to the General Assembly, commencing at its eightieth session, under the relevant agenda sub-item, on future improvements to the index, informed by timely technical input and recommendations from the Independent Expert Advisory Panel and the Statistical Commission, respectively;

11. *Further decides* that the relevant existing United Nations entity, which will act as the secretariat of the multidimensional vulnerability index, and the members of the Independent Expert Advisory Panel will be appointed by the Secretary-General, in consultation with Member States, by no later than the end of the seventy-ninth session of the General Assembly;

12. *Decides* that the Independent Expert Advisory Panel will:

(a) Comprise 15 independent experts, including a minimum of 5 from Member States, who will serve in their personal capacity, without remuneration, with a good mix of expertise, who are to be drawn from the fields of economic development, social development and environmental protection, in order to avoid the need to engage the assistance of consultants and so as to reflect an adequate geographical and gender balance;

(b) Conduct its work virtually, as appropriate;

(c) Comprise members who are appointed for a four-year term and are eligible for reappointment;

13. *Also decides* that the Department of Economic and Social Affairs and the Office of the High Representative for the Least Developed Countries, Landlocked Developing Countries and Small Island Developing States of the Secretariat, within their respective mandates, should continue to act as interim secretariat for the multidimensional vulnerability index, until a relevant existing United Nations entity is appointed to act as the secretariat of the multidimensional vulnerability index by the Secretary-General;

14. *Requests* the Secretary-General to ensure that adequate resources are available to support the work on the multidimensional vulnerability index, including its periodic review, in particular for travel for the members of the Independent Expert Advisory Panel who are from developing countries, especially from least developed countries, landlocked developing countries and small island developing States, when in-person meetings are needed;

15. *Requests* all entities involved with the multidimensional vulnerability index to ensure consistency and complementarity with existing intergovernmentally agreed arrangements for data, indicators, indices and metrics, and, as appropriate, those related to the 2030 Agenda for Sustainable Development;[215]

Ways to further improve the multidimensional vulnerability index

16. *Requests* the Independent Expert Advisory Panel to recommend future improvements to the multidimensional vulnerability index triennially to ensure continued relevance, robustness and accessibility, and ensure that indicators for potential addition or removal adhere to the criteria for data sources recommended in the report of the High-level Panel to ensure the continued relevance and effectiveness of the index;

17. *Requests* the Statistical Commission to advance technical reviews on the future improvements to the multidimensional vulnerability index, including on the potential addition or removal of indicators, and to present recommendations triennially as needed;

18. *Requests* the Independent Expert Advisory Panel to also consider the data and lessons learned from the utilization of the vulnerability-resilience country profiles, as well as the initial application of the multidimensional vulnerability index within the United Nations system;

19. *Invites* the United Nations system to promote improved understanding of vulnerability and share data and lessons learned from the implementation of the multidimensional vulnerability index among stakeholders, encompassing the international financial institutions, including multilateral development banks, international organizations, research institutions, think tanks, civil society and the private sector, through specialized events, workshops, training sessions and online presentations;

20. *Also invites* the United Nations system to scale up capacity-building programmes for developing countries to improve their national statistical systems, including the ability to collect quality, accessible, timely, reliable, comparable data, including disaggregated data;

Vulnerability-resilience country profiles

21. *Stresses* that the vulnerability-resilience country profiles should be country-led and strictly voluntary;

22. *Also stresses* that the vulnerability-resilience country profiles may be taken into account to enhance, inform and contribute to national development plans and processes, including the development of United Nations Sustainable Development Cooperation Frameworks, as appropriate;

23. *Requests* the Secretary-General:

(a) To develop an electronic handbook with guidance for developing vulnerability-resilience country profiles, based on the principles set out in the report of the High-level Panel, including a standard structure for the profiles to ensure consistency and comparability between them;

(b) To pilot test the vulnerability-resilience country profiles in at least four interested developing countries from different regions with different contexts and features;

(c) To conduct online workshops to familiarize developing countries with the development of vulnerability-resilience country profiles;

Multidimensional vulnerability index reporting

24. *Decides* to include in the provisional agenda of its eightieth session, under the item entitled "Sustainable development", a sub-item entitled "Multidimensional vulnerability index", which will be considered triennially.

---

[215] Resolution 70/1.

RESOLUTION 78/323

Adopted at the 103rd plenary meeting, on 13 August 2024, without a vote, on the basis of draft resolution A/78/L.96, as orally amended, sponsored by: Albania, Angola, Antigua and Barbuda, Austria, Barbados, Belgium, Bolivia (Plurinational State of), Bosnia and Herzegovina, Brazil, Bulgaria, Burundi, Cabo Verde, Chad, Chile, Colombia, Costa Rica, Croatia, Cyprus, Czechia, Denmark, Dominican Republic, Ecuador, Equatorial Guinea, Eritrea, Estonia, Germany, Ghana, Greece, Guatemala, Guyana, Honduras, Hungary, Indonesia, Ireland, Italy, Jamaica, Kyrgyzstan, Latvia, Luxembourg, Malta, Marshall Islands, Mexico, Namibia, Netherlands (Kingdom of the), Niger, North Macedonia, Pakistan, Paraguay, Peru, Philippines, Poland, Portugal, Saint Kitts and Nevis, Senegal, Serbia, Seychelles, Slovakia, Slovenia, Spain, Suriname, Sweden, Togo, Ukraine, United Kingdom of Great Britain and Northern Ireland, United States of America, Uruguay, Uzbekistan, Venezuela (Bolivarian Republic of)

78/323. International Day of Women and Girls of African Descent

The General Assembly,

Reaffirming the purposes and principles of the Charter of the United Nations,

Recalling the Universal Declaration of Human Rights,[216] the International Covenant on Civil and Political Rights[217] and the International Covenant on Economic, Social and Cultural Rights,[218] the Convention on the Elimination of All Forms of Discrimination against Women,[219] which condemns any discrimination against women in all its forms, in particular relevant articles thereof, the International Convention on the Elimination of All Forms of Racial Discrimination,[220] the Convention on the Rights of the Child,[221] the Convention on the Rights of Persons with Disabilities[222] and other international instruments related to the rights of women and girls, and the importance of promoting actions to prevent and eliminate all forms of discrimination and violence against women,

Recalling also its resolutions 53/199 of 15 December 1998 and 61/185 of 20 December 2006 on the proclamation of international years, and Economic and Social Council resolution 1980/67 of 25 July 1980 on international years and anniversaries,

Observing the mutually reinforcing relationship between achieving gender equality and the empowerment of all women and girls and the full realization of all their human rights and fundamental freedoms and the implementation of the 2030 Agenda for Sustainable Development,[223] and noting in this regard Sustainable Development Goals 5 and 10, which seek, respectively, to achieve gender equality and empower all women and girls and to reduce inequality within and among countries, including through specific measures to address racial discrimination,

Reaffirming the Vienna Declaration and Programme of Action,[224] as well as the Beijing Declaration and Platform for Action,[225] the Programme of Action of the International Conference on Population and Development[226] and the outcomes of their review conferences,

---

[216] Resolution 217 A (III).

[217] See resolution 2200 A (XXI), annex.

[218] Ibid.

[219] United Nations, *Treaty Series*, vol. 1249, No. 20378.

[220] Ibid., vol. 660, No. 9464.

[221] Ibid., vol. 1577, No. 27531.

[222] Ibid., vol. 2515, No. 44910.

[223] Resolution 70/1.

[224] A/CONF.157/24 (Part I), chap. III.

[225] *Report of the Fourth World Conference on Women, Beijing, 4–15 September 1995* (United Nations publication, Sales No. E.96.IV.13), chap. I, resolution 1, annexes I and II.

[226] *Report of the International Conference on Population and Development, Cairo, 5–13 September 1994* (United Nations publication, Sales No. E.95.XIII.18), chap. I, resolution 1, annex.

Noting the general recommendations of the Committee on the Elimination of Racial Discrimination, especially general recommendation No. 25 (2000) on gender-related dimensions of racial discrimination[227] and general recommendation No. 34 (2011) on racial discrimination against people of African descent,[228]

Recalling its resolution 68/237 of 23 December 2013, in which it proclaimed the International Decade for People of African Descent, commencing on 1 January 2015 and ending on 31 December 2024, with the theme "People of African descent: recognition, justice and development", and in this regard contributing to the implementation of the Durban Declaration and Programme of Action,

Recognizing the significant contribution of all women and girls of African descent to the development of societies and the importance of ensuring the full, equal and meaningful participation and decision-making of women of African descent in all aspects of society,

1. *Decides* to proclaim 25 July as the International Day of Women and Girls of African Descent, in order to highlight the importance of this day as a moment to commemorate the global fight against slavery and racism and the commitment to achieve gender equality, as well as the significant contribution of all women and girls of African descent to the development of societies;

2. *Invites* all Member States, organizations of the United Nations system, international and regional organizations and other relevant stakeholders, including civil society, the private sector, academia and the media, to commemorate the International Day in an appropriate manner, promoting events and activities that highlight the history, culture and struggles of women and girls of African descent around the world;

3. *Encourages* all Member States and the United Nations system to take concrete measures to address and prevent racial and gender-based discrimination, as well as to eliminate all forms of violence against all women and girls of African descent, and to ensure the full enjoyment of human rights by women and girls of African descent;

4. *Emphasizes* that the cost of all activities that may result from the implementation of the present resolution should be covered by voluntary contributions, including from the private sector;

5. *Requests* the Secretary-General to bring the present resolution to the attention of all States Members of the United Nations, members of the specialized agencies and observers of the General Assembly, as well as the organizations of the United Nations system and other relevant stakeholders, for appropriate observance of the International Day of Women and Girls of African descent.

RESOLUTION 78/324

Adopted at the 103rd plenary meeting, on 13 August 2024, without a vote, on the basis of draft resolution A/78/L.104/Rev.1, as orally revised, sponsored by: Albania, Argentina, Austria, Bosnia and Herzegovina, Brazil, Bulgaria, Cabo Verde, Canada, Chile, Colombia, Dominican Republic, Ecuador, El Salvador, Estonia, Georgia, Germany, Guatemala, Honduras, Latvia, Luxembourg, Malta, Myanmar, North Macedonia, Paraguay, Peru, Philippines, Portugal, Saint Kitts and Nevis, Slovakia, Slovenia, Türkiye, Ukraine, United Kingdom of Great Britain and Northern Ireland, United States of America, Uruguay

78/324. Consideration of decision 14/1 of the Open-ended Working Group on Ageing, entitled "Recommendations regarding the identification of possible gaps in the protection of the human rights of older persons and how best to address them"

The General Assembly,

Recalling its resolution 65/182 of 21 December 2010, in which it established an open-ended working group, open to all States Members of the United Nations, for the purpose of strengthening the protection of the human rights of older persons by considering the existing international framework of the human rights of older persons and identifying possible gaps and how best to address them, including by considering, as appropriate, the feasibility of further instruments and measures, as well as all its subsequent resolutions on the follow-up to the Second World Assembly on Ageing, including resolution 78/177 of 19 December 2023,

[227] *Official Records of the General Assembly, Fifty-fifth Session, Supplement No. 18* (A/55/18), annex V, sect. A.

[228] Ibid., *Sixty-sixth Session, Supplement No. 18* (A/66/18), annex IX.

Taking note of decision 13/1 of the Open-ended Working Group on Ageing,[229]

Taking note also of decision 14/1 of the Open-ended Working Group on Ageing, entitled "Recommendations regarding the identification of possible gaps in the protection of the human rights of older persons and how best to address them",[230]

Taking note with appreciation of the work of the Open-ended Working Group on Ageing, and recognizing the positive contributions of Member States, as well as relevant bodies and organizations of the United Nations system, including relevant human rights mandate holders and treaty bodies and the regional commissions, as well as national human rights institutions, intergovernmental and relevant non-governmental organizations with an interest in the matter and invited panellists, during its past 14 sessions,

1. *Decides* that the Open-ended Working Group on Ageing has completed its work, in view of the adoption of decision 14/1 by the Open-ended Working Group on Ageing in line with its mandate outlined in the resolution 65/182 and all subsequent resolutions on the follow-up to the Second World Assembly on Ageing, including 78/177 of 19 December 2023, and to conclude the mandate of the Open-ended Working Group on Ageing, under agenda item "Social development: social development, including questions relating to the world social situation and to youth, ageing, persons with disabilities and the family" of the Third Committee;

2. *Urges* relevant United Nations bodies, respecting the relevant mandate, to further consider the recommendations as adopted by the Open-ended Working Group on Ageing in its decision 14/1;

3. *Requests* the President of the General Assembly to hold a high-level meeting at its seventy-ninth session to exchange views and share experiences on the recommendations included in decision 14/1 of the Open-ended Working Group on Ageing, in an equitable and non-exclusive manner, and to define next steps on the challenges and opportunities regarding the rights and well-being of older persons.

RESOLUTION 78/325

Adopted at the 107th plenary meeting, on 6 September 2024, without a vote, on the basis of draft resolution A/78/L.107, sponsored by: Albania, Angola, Armenia, Bahrain, Bangladesh, Belarus, Bolivia (Plurinational State of), Brunei Darussalam, Burundi, Cabo Verde, Cambodia, Central African Republic, China, Colombia, Comoros, Congo, Cuba, Cyprus, Democratic Republic of the Congo, Djibouti, Dominica, Dominican Republic, Egypt, El Salvador, Equatorial Guinea, Gabon, Georgia, Germany, Guatemala, Guinea-Bissau, Guyana, Hungary, India, Indonesia, Iraq, Jordan, Kazakhstan, Kenya, Kyrgyzstan, Lao People's Democratic Republic, Latvia, Liberia, Libya, Malaysia, Mali, Mauritania, Montenegro, Morocco, Myanmar, Namibia, Nepal, Nicaragua, Nigeria, Oman, Pakistan, Peru, Philippines, Portugal, Qatar, Republic of Moldova, Russian Federation, Rwanda, Saint Kitts and Nevis, Senegal, Serbia, Seychelles, Singapore, Slovenia, Solomon Islands, South Sudan, Sri Lanka, Sudan, Suriname, Syrian Arab Republic, Tajikistan, Timor-Leste, Tunisia, Türkiye, Turkmenistan, Tuvalu, Uganda, United Republic of Tanzania, Uzbekistan, Venezuela (Bolivarian Republic of), Viet Nam, Zambia, Zimbabwe

78/325. United Nations Games

The General Assembly,

Recalling its resolutions 58/5 of 3 November 2003 and 59/10 of 27 October 2004, its decision to proclaim 2005 the International Year for Sport and Physical Education to strengthen sport as a means to promote education, health, development and peace, and its resolutions 60/1 of 16 September 2005, 60/9 of 3 November 2005, 61/10 of 3 November 2006, 62/271 of 23 July 2008, 63/135 of 11 December 2008, 65/4 of 18 October 2010, 67/17 of 28 November 2012, 69/6 of 31 October 2014, 71/160 of 16 December 2016, 73/24 of 3 December 2018, 75/18 of 1 December 2020 and 77/27 of 1 December 2022,

Recognizing that sports, the arts and physical activity have the power to change perceptions, prejudices and behaviours, as well as to inspire people, break down racial and political barriers, combat discrimination and defuse conflict as reflected in the political declaration adopted at the Nelson Mandela Peace Summit in 2018,[231]

---

[229] A/AC.278/2023/2, para. 30.

[230] A/AC.278/2024/2, para. 28.

[231] Resolution 73/1.

Recognizing also the valuable contribution of sport in promoting education, sustainable development, peace, cooperation, solidarity, fairness, social inclusion and health at the local, regional and international levels, and noting that, as declared in the 2005 World Summit Outcome,[232] sports can contribute to an atmosphere of tolerance and understanding among peoples and nations,

Recognizing further that sport, including sport for persons with disabilities and persons living with rare diseases, has an important role to play in the promotion of peace and development, physical and mental health, gender equality, the empowerment of women and girls, respect for human rights, and the fight against racism and racial discrimination,

Recognizing the importance of international, continental and regional sport events, such as the World Artistic Gymnastics Championships, the Special Olympics World Games, the Deaflympics, the World Indigenous Games, the European Games, the Games of La Francophonie, the Pan American Games and the Parapan American Games, the All-Africa Games, the Asian Games, the Pacific Games, the Asian Indoor and Martial Arts Games, the World Nomad Games, the Commonwealth Games and the World University Games, for promoting education, health, development, peace and solidarity among nations,

Welcoming the designation of 6 April as the International Day of Sport for Development and Peace,

Acknowledging the success of the inaugural United Nations New York-based Missions Games (United Nations Games), held in New York from 11 April to 8 May 2024 at the initiative of Turkmenistan within the framework of the General Assembly Sustainability Week, and devoted to the International Day of Sport for Development and Peace,

Welcoming the positive impact of the United Nations Games on fostering camaraderie, collaboration and dialogue among the staff of the permanent missions accredited to the United Nations and the Secretariat of the United Nations,

1. *Commends* the efforts and contribution of Australia, El Salvador, India, Kazakhstan, Qatar and Turkmenistan in organizing the inaugural United Nations Games;

2. *Recognizes* the potential of the United Nations Games to serve as a sports diplomacy platform for cultivating sport culture and promoting sport as a tool for development and peace;

3. *Calls for* the convening of the United Nations Games annually, in venues accessible to representatives of all Member States of the United Nations, members of the specialized agencies and observers of the General Assembly, and of the Second United Nations Games in New York in April 2025, and encourages all delegations to support the organization of these Games, in collaboration with the Department of Economic and Social Affairs of the Secretariat;

4. *Invites* the five regional groups to nominate their candidates, one from each regional group, for the organizing committee of the Second United Nations Games in a timely fashion, so that they can participate in the first meeting of the committee on an informal basis in New York in January 2025;

5. *Invites* all relevant stakeholders to make voluntary contributions to a trust fund dedicated to the United Nations Games and to provide other forms of support for their observance;

6. *Stresses* that the costs of all the activities that may arise from the implementation of the present resolution should be met through voluntary contributions to the trust fund of the United Nations Games, including from the private sector;

7. *Requests* the organizing committee of the Second United Nations Games, in collaboration with the Department of Economic and Social Affairs of the Secretariat, to collect feedback from all Member States of the United Nations, members of the specialized agencies and observers of the General Assembly on the inaugural United Nations Games in the form of an informal summary to incorporate lessons learned into the planning of future Games;

8. *Requests* the Secretary-General to bring the present resolution to the attention of all Member States and organizations of the United Nations system and other relevant stakeholders.

[232] Resolution 60/1.

RESOLUTION 78/326

Adopted at the 107th plenary meeting, on 6 September 2024, without a vote, on the basis of draft resolution A/78/L.84/Rev.2, as amended in A/78/L.92/Rev.1, sponsored by: Algeria, Angola, Antigua and Barbuda, Armenia, Bangladesh, Belarus, Bhutan, Cabo Verde, Cambodia, China, Colombia, Dominican Republic, El Salvador, Ghana, India, Indonesia, Kazakhstan, Kyrgyzstan, Lao People's Democratic Republic, Lebanon, Liberia, Malaysia, Mauritania, Mongolia, Myanmar, Nepal, Nigeria, Pakistan, Peru, Philippines, Qatar, Russian Federation, Saint Kitts and Nevis, Senegal, Singapore, Sri Lanka, Tajikistan, Thailand, Türkiye, Turkmenistan, United Republic of Tanzania, Uzbekistan, Viet Nam

78/326. World Rural Development Day

The General Assembly,

Reaffirming its resolution 70/1 of 25 September 2015, entitled "Transforming our world: the 2030 Agenda for Sustainable Development", in which it adopted a comprehensive, far-reaching and people-centred set of universal and transformative Sustainable Development Goals and targets, its commitment to working tirelessly for the full implementation of the Agenda by 2030, its recognition that eradicating poverty in all its forms and dimensions, including extreme poverty, is the greatest global challenge and an indispensable requirement for sustainable development, its commitment to achieving sustainable development in its three dimensions – economic, social and environmental – in a balanced and integrated manner, and to building upon the achievements of the Millennium Development Goals and seeking to address their unfinished business,

Reaffirming also its resolutions 53/199 of 15 December 1998 and 61/185 of 20 December 2006 on the proclamation of international years, and Economic and Social Council resolution 1980/67 of 25 July 1980 on international years and anniversaries, in particular paragraphs 1 to 10 of the annex thereto on the agreed criteria for the proclamation of international years, as well as paragraphs 13 and 14, in which it is stated that an international year should not be proclaimed before the basic arrangements for its organization and financing have been made,

Reaffirming further the Addis Ababa Action Agenda of the Third International Conference on Financing for Development of 2015,[233]

Reaffirming the Universal Declaration of Human Rights,[234]

Noting its resolution 73/165 of 17 December 2018, by which it adopted the United Nations Declaration on the Rights of Peasants and Other People Working in Rural Areas,

Noting the Declaration on the Right to Development,[235]

Noting with concern that rural poor and other people working in rural areas, including Indigenous Peoples and local communities, suffer disproportionately from poverty, hunger and malnutrition,

Recognizing the interlinkages and integrated nature of the Sustainable Development Goals, and reiterating that the eradication of rural poverty and hunger is crucial for the achievement of the Sustainable Development Goals, and that rural development should be pursued through an integrated approach that encompasses economic, social and environmental dimensions,

Recognizing also the critical role and contribution of rural women, including smallholders and women farmers, fishers, Indigenous women and their traditional knowledge and women in local communities, in enhancing agricultural and rural development, improving food security and nutrition and eradicating rural poverty, and therefore highlighting the importance of promoting their economic empowerment, their full access to land ownership and decent work and economic opportunities and their participation in decision-making,

Underscoring that investing in key facilities and services in rural areas will be an effective approach to address rural poverty and hunger, create productive employment and enterprises, and promote digital financial inclusion for rural communities and rural institutions such as community-based organizations and cooperatives, particularly for rural youth and women, including through regional and national initiatives,

---

[233] Resolution 69/313, annex.

[234] Resolution 217 A (III).

[235] Resolution 41/128, annex.

Recognizing the importance of sharing locally driven development approaches and pathways to promote rural development and accelerate the implementation of the 2030 Agenda,

Noting the efforts of regional organizations, including the Centre on Integrated Rural Development for Asia and the Pacific (CIRDAP), in assisting national action and promoting regional cooperation relating to integrated rural development,

Trusting that the observance of an international day will create a comprehensive platform to assess the challenges and opportunities of rural development,

1. *Decides* to declare 6 July World Rural Development Day, to highlight the critical importance of rural development and transformation for the achievement of the Sustainable Development Goals;[236]

2. *Invites* all Member States, organizations of the United Nations system and other international and regional organizations, as well as non-governmental organizations, individuals and other relevant stakeholders, including civil society, farmers' organizations, Indigenous Peoples, local communities, the private sector and academia, as well as schools, to observe World Rural Development Day by presenting and promoting, as appropriate in national and regional contexts, concrete activities with regard to the sustainable development of rural areas and communities;

3. *Invites* the Department of Economic and Social Affairs of the Secretariat, in cooperation with Governments, relevant international and regional organizations, the specialized agencies and all other stakeholders, and mindful of the provisions contained in the annex to Economic and Social Council resolution 1980/67, to facilitate the organization and implementation of World Rural Development Day as a way of promoting rural development, raising awareness of the contribution of rural development in achieving the Sustainable Development Goals and supporting Member States in planning and coordinating activities for observing the Day;

4. *Stresses* that the cost of all activities that may arise from the implementation of the present resolution should be met from voluntary contributions;

5. *Invites* all relevant stakeholders to contribute to and support World Rural Development Day;

6. *Requests* the Secretary-General to bring the present resolution to the attention of all Member States, the organizations of the United Nations system and other relevant stakeholders, including civil society, farmers' organizations, Indigenous Peoples, local communities, the private sector and academia, for appropriate observance.

RESOLUTION 78/327

Adopted at the 107th plenary meeting, on 6 September 2024, without a vote, on the basis of draft resolution A/78/L.110, sponsored by: Albania, Angola, Antigua and Barbuda, Austria, Bahrain, Belgium, Bulgaria, Burkina Faso, Cabo Verde, Cambodia, Cameroon, Central African Republic, Chad, Comoros, Congo, Côte d'Ivoire, Croatia, Cyprus, Czechia, Denmark, Dominican Republic, Egypt, Equatorial Guinea, Estonia, Eswatini, Finland, France, Gabon, Germany, Ghana, Greece, Guinea, Guinea-Bissau, Guyana, Hungary, Indonesia, Iraq, Ireland, Israel, Italy, Jordan, Kazakhstan, Kenya, Kuwait, Kyrgyzstan, Latvia, Lesotho, Libya, Lithuania, Luxembourg, Mali, Malta, Mauritania, Mauritius, Monaco, Morocco, Nepal, Netherlands (Kingdom of the), Niger, Nigeria, Oman, Philippines, Poland, Portugal, Qatar, Republic of Moldova, Romania, Rwanda, Saint Kitts and Nevis, Saint Vincent and the Grenadines, Saudi Arabia, Sierra Leone, Singapore, Slovakia, Slovenia, Solomon Islands, Spain, Sweden, Switzerland, Syrian Arab Republic, Tajikistan, Timor-Leste, Tunisia, Ukraine, Senegal, United Arab Emirates, United Republic of Tanzania, Uzbekistan, Viet Nam, Yemen

78/327. Modalities of the 2026 United Nations Water Conference to Accelerate the Implementation of Sustainable Development Goal 6: Ensure availability and sustainable management of water and sanitation for all

The General Assembly,

Reaffirming its resolution 70/1 of 25 September 2015, entitled "Transforming our world: the 2030 Agenda for Sustainable Development", in which it adopted a comprehensive, far-reaching and people-centred set of universal and transformative Sustainable Development Goals and targets, its commitment to working tirelessly for the full implementation of the Agenda by 2030, its recognition that eradicating poverty in all its forms and dimensions,

[236] See resolution 70/1.

including extreme poverty, is the greatest global challenge and an indispensable requirement for sustainable development, its commitment to achieving sustainable development in its three dimensions – economic, social and environmental – in a balanced and integrated manner, and to building upon the achievements of the Millennium Development Goals and seeking to address their unfinished business,

Reaffirming also its resolution 69/313 of 27 July 2015 on the Addis Ababa Action Agenda of the Third International Conference on Financing for Development, which is an integral part of the 2030 Agenda for Sustainable Development, supports and complements it, helps to contextualize its means of implementation targets with concrete policies and actions, and reaffirms the strong political commitment to address the challenge of financing and creating an enabling environment at all levels for sustainable development in the spirit of global partnership and solidarity,

Recalling its resolution 77/334 of 1 September 2023, in which it decided to convene the 2026 United Nations Water Conference to Accelerate the Implementation of Sustainable Development Goal 6: Ensure availability and sustainable management of water and sanitation for all,

Recalling also its resolution 64/292 of 28 July 2010 on the human right to water and sanitation, as well as its resolutions 74/141 of 18 December 2019 and 76/153 of 19 December 2021 on the human rights to safe drinking water and sanitation,

Emphasizing that water is critical for sustainable development and the eradication of poverty and hunger, that water, ecosystems, energy, food security and nutrition are linked and that water is indispensable for health, well-being and human development, including the empowerment of women, and a vital element of achieving the Sustainable Development Goals and other relevant goals in the social, environmental and economic fields,

Noting with concern that the world is not on track to achieve water-related Sustainable Development Goals and targets at the global level by 2030 at the current rate of progress, which has a tremendous impact on human well-being and on the three dimensions of sustainable development,

Noting with concern also that climate change is one of the factors that can exacerbate the global water stress and the need for climate adaptation strategies to address water issues, and acknowledging that disasters, many of which are exacerbated by climate change and are increasing in frequency and intensity, significantly impede progress towards sustainable development,

Stressing the importance of the ecosystem approach for the integrated management of land, water and living resources and the need to increase efforts to tackle desertification, land degradation, drought, water scarcity, biodiversity loss and pollution,

Noting the importance of water ecosystems and water quality for mitigating the risk of health challenges in accordance with the One Health approach and other holistic approaches that deliver multiple benefits to the health and well-being of people, animals, plants and ecosystems,

Recognizing that water-related issues, including the relevant Sustainable Development Goals and targets, need to be better reflected in the agendas of the General Assembly and the Economic and Social Council,

Recognizing also synergies between the 2030 Agenda, the Addis Ababa Action Agenda, the Paris Agreement[237] and the Sendai Framework for Disaster Risk Reduction 2015–2030,[238]

Emphasizing that the achievement of the water-related goals and targets would contribute to the successful implementation of the New Urban Agenda,[239] the United Nations Framework Convention on Climate Change[240] and the Paris Agreement, the Convention on Biological Diversity[241] and the Kunming-Montreal Global Biodiversity Framework adopted at the fifteenth meeting of the Conference of the Parties to the Convention, the United Nations Convention to Combat Desertification in Those Countries Experiencing Serious Drought and/or Desertification,

---

[237] Adopted under the UNFCCC in FCCC/CP/2015/10/Add.1, decision 1/CP.21, annex.

[238] Resolution 69/283, annex II.

[239] Resolution 71/256, annex.

[240] United Nations, *Treaty Series*, vol. 1771, No. 30822.

[241] Ibid., vol. 1760, No. 30619.

Particularly in Africa,[242] the Sendai Framework for Disaster Risk Reduction 2015–2030, the Doha Programme of Action for the Least Developed Countries,[243] the outcome document of the fourth International Conference on Small Island Developing States, entitled "The Antigua and Barbuda Agenda for Small Island Developing States: A Renewed Declaration for Resilient Prosperity",[244] and the decisions adopted at the twenty-eighth session of the Conference of the Parties to the United Nations Framework Convention on Climate Change, the eighteenth session of the Conference of the Parties serving as the Meeting of the Parties to the Kyoto Protocol and the fifth session of the Conference of the Parties serving as the Meeting of the Parties to the Paris Agreement, held in Dubai, United Arab Emirates, including the decisions adopted under the United Arab Emirates consensus,

Recognizing that international cooperation, including at the global, regional and subregional levels, is needed to strengthen the complementarity of actions and programmes dedicated to achieving water- and sanitation-related goals and targets, including those contained in the 2030 Agenda, especially in developing countries,

Recalling the political declaration adopted by the high-level political forum on sustainable development convened under the auspices of the General Assembly (Sustainable Development Goals Summit), held in New York on 18 and 19 September 2023,[245] in which leaders committed to addressing water scarcity and stressing and driving transformation from a global water crisis to a world where water is a sustainable resource, ensuring the availability and sustainable management of water and sanitation for all,

Welcoming the convening of the United Nations Conference on the Midterm Comprehensive Review of the Implementation of the Objectives of the International Decade for Action, "Water for Sustainable Development," 2018–2028, from 22 to 24 March 2023, which generated significant momentum towards enhancing water action and political commitment at all levels to address water-related challenges,

Welcoming also the decision to convene, in 2028, the United Nations Conference on the Final Comprehensive Review of the Implementation of the Objectives of the International Decade for Action, "Water for Sustainable Development", 2018–2028, which will be held in Dushanbe, and looking forward to the third Ocean Conference, co-hosted by Costa Rica and France, to be held in Nice, France, in 2025, and the Fourth International Conference on Financing for Development, to be held in Spain in 2025,

Taking note of the *United Nations World Water Development Report 2024*, the outcome document of the High-level Panel on Water, entitled "Making every drop count: an agenda for water action", the outcomes of the review by the high-level political forum on sustainable development of Sustainable Development Goal 6, *Blueprint for Acceleration: Sustainable Development Goal 6 Synthesis Report on Water and Sanitation 2023*, the outcomes of the tenth World Water Forum, held in Bali, Indonesia, from 18 to 25 May 2024, the final declaration of the Third High-level International Conference on the International Decade for Action "Water for Sustainable Development", 2018–2028, held in Dushanbe from 10 to 13 June 2024,[246] the outcomes of the United Nations special thematic sessions on water and disasters and the Sustainable Development Goal 6 Global Acceleration Framework,

Recalling the importance of enhancing the provision and mobilization of financing from public and private sources and international and domestic sources to close the water financing gap to bolster progress on the implementation of Sustainable Development Goal 6 and water-related goals and targets,

1. *Decides* that the 2026 United Nations Water Conference to Accelerate the Implementation of Sustainable Development Goal 6: Ensure availability and sustainable management of water and sanitation for all, co-hosted by Senegal and the United Arab Emirates, will be held in the United Arab Emirates from 2 to 4 December 2026, to support the implementation of Sustainable Development Goal 6;

2. *Also decides* that all costs relating to the Conference and its preparation shall be financed through extrabudgetary resources;

[242] Ibid., vol. 1954, No. 33480.

[243] Resolution 76/258, annex.

[244] Resolution 78/317, annex.

[245] Resolution 78/1, annex.

[246] A/78/955, annex.

3. *Further decides* that the Conference will result in a summary of the proceedings of the Conference, to be prepared by the Presidents of the Conference, to reflect the diversity of Member States' perspectives and present a balanced approach, as its outcome document, focusing on areas of accelerated and collective action to support the implementation of Sustainable Development Goal 6;

4. *Decides* that the Conference shall:

(a) Focus on actions to accelerate the achievement of Sustainable Development Goal 6: Ensure availability and sustainable management of water and sanitation for all, while reaffirming the internationally agreed water-related goals and targets, including those contained in the 2030 Agenda for Sustainable Development;[247]

(b) Identify possible challenges and obstacles related to the achievement of Sustainable Development Goal 6, as well as opportunities and innovative ways and means to support its implementation and the acceleration of progress, in order to help to achieve the internationally agreed water-related goals and targets, including those contained in the 2030 Agenda;

(c) Exchange views and develop actions and initiatives needed for accelerating progress towards the achievement of Sustainable Development Goal 6;

(d) Support further concrete action and initiatives to enhance means of implementation and partnerships, as well as cooperation at all relevant levels, including international cooperation, to accelerate the achievement of Sustainable Development Goal 6, including the Sustainable Development Goal 6 Global Acceleration Framework;

(e) Share ongoing efforts, best practices and experience gained in the acceleration of the implementation of Sustainable Development Goal 6, such as the voluntary commitments of the Water Action Agenda;

(f) Invite Member States and relevant stakeholders to announce voluntary commitments contributing to the objectives of the Conference;

(g) Involve all relevant stakeholders, bringing together Governments, the United Nations system, intergovernmental organizations, international financial institutions, other interested international bodies, non-governmental organizations, civil society organizations, academic institutions, the scientific community, Indigenous Peoples and local communities, the private sector, philanthropic organizations and other actors to assess challenges and opportunities relating to, as well as support further action to accelerate the implementation of, Sustainable Development Goal 6 and the water-related goals and targets of the 2030 Agenda;

(h) Contribute to the mainstreaming of a gender perspective in ensuring safe drinking water and sanitation for all, including through the empowerment of women and girls, as their full, equal and meaningful participation is key to achieving Sustainable Development Goal 6;

(i) Also contribute to the follow-up and review process of the 2030 Agenda for Sustainable Development by providing an input to the high-level political forum on sustainable development, in accordance with resolutions 67/290 of 9 July 2013, 70/1, 70/299 of 29 July 2016 and 75/290 B of 25 June 2021;

5. *Also decides* that the Conference shall elect from among the representatives of participating States two Presidents, one from Senegal and one from the United Arab Emirates, 13 Vice-Presidents,[248] one of whom shall be designated as Rapporteur-General, and two ex officio Vice-Presidents from the host countries;

6. *Further decides* that the Conference shall comprise an opening and a closing segment, seven plenary meetings and six interactive dialogues in accordance with annex II to the present resolution;

7. *Decides* that interactive dialogues will be held in parallel with the plenary meetings in accordance with annex II to the present resolution;

8. *Requests* the Secretary-General to appoint a Secretary-General of the Conference to serve as focal point within the Secretariat for providing support to the Conference;

---

[247] Resolution 70/1.

[248] Three from each of the following groups: African States; Asia-Pacific States; Eastern European States; Latin American and Caribbean States; and Western European and other States. The election of the Presidents will, however, have the effect of reducing by one the number of Vice-Presidents allocated to the regions from which each of the Presidents is elected.

9. *Decides* that, in order to accelerate the implementation of Sustainable Development Goal 6 and as outlined in the Sustainable Development Goal 6 Global Acceleration Framework, the organizational arrangements for the interactive dialogues will be as follows:

(a) Proposals for themes of the interactive dialogues will be prepared in a background note by the Secretary-General of the Conference, in consultation with Member States, with the support of UN-Water and relevant United Nations entities;

(b) The interactive dialogues shall be collaborative and multi-stakeholder in nature, with due regard for gender and geographical balance;

(c) Each interactive dialogue will be presided over by two Co-Chairs, one from a developing country and one from a developed country, to be appointed by the two Presidents of the Conference and identified by the two host countries of the Conference at least six months in advance of the Conference;

(d) The two host countries of the Conference, in coordination with the Secretary-General of the Conference, will designate a moderator and up to four panellists for each interactive dialogue, taking into account gender balance and equitable geographical representation in the appointment of Co-Chairs, moderators and panellists;

(e) The Secretary-General of the Conference will prepare concept papers on each of the themes of the interactive dialogues;

(f) The interactive dialogues, facilitated by the moderator, will be followed by an interactive discussion among States and other relevant stakeholders;

(g) Summaries of the interactive dialogues shall be presented to the Conference at its closing meeting;

10. *Encourages* participation in the Conference at the highest possible level;

11. *Recommends* the provisional agenda set forth in annex I to the present resolution for adoption by the Conference;

12. *Decides* that the Conference shall be organized in accordance with the organization of work set forth in annex II to the present resolution;

13. *Recommends* the provisional rules of procedure set forth in annex III to the present resolution, which are based on the established practice of the General Assembly and its conferences, for adoption by the Conference;

14. *Decides* that the Conference will be preceded by regional and global preparatory meetings, as appropriate, and that all costs relating to the Conference and its preparation will be financed through voluntary contributions, and in this connection requests the Secretary-General to coordinate the preparatory process and to invite all relevant organizations of the United Nations system, including the regional commissions and other relevant organizations, within their respective mandates, to provide support to the review process and the Conference;

15. *Also decides* that a one-day organizational session will be held in New York in 2025 to make updated recommendations to the General Assembly on the themes of the interactive dialogues, with a view to adopting them at a later date during a one-day meeting to be convened by the President of the General Assembly, to promote the achievement of Sustainable Development Goal 6 and to agree on the themes of the interactive dialogues;

16. *Notes* that the Conference will build upon the discussions held during the interactive dialogues of the United Nations Conference on the Midterm Comprehensive Review of the Implementation of the Objectives of the International Decade for Action, "Water for Sustainable Development", 2018–2028;

17. *Welcomes* the generous offer of the Government of Senegal to convene a high-level international meeting in Dakar in 2025 to support an effective preparation for the Conference and review the progress and the gaps in the implementation of Sustainable Development Goal 6, and explore ideas to accelerate the achievement of the internationally agreed water-related goals and targets, including those contained in the 2030 Agenda for Sustainable Development;

18. *Considers* the contribution from other existing water-related meetings that may serve to provide input for the preparatory process of the Conference, and of Member States in organizing meetings intended to feed into the 2026 Conference;

19. *Encourages* Member States, relevant United Nations bodies, the specialized agencies, the regional commissions and other organizations of the United Nations system, as well as other relevant partners, including the private sector, to continue to contribute to the achievement of Sustainable Development Goal 6, including through capacity-building, in order to support the implementation of the 2030 Agenda;

20. *Takes note* of the United Nations System-wide Strategy for Water and Sanitation, which aims to enhance the coordination and delivery of water priorities across the United Nations system and to place particular emphasis on the water-related needs of the developing countries, including those related to finance, technology transfer and capacity-building;

21. *Decides* that the Conference and its preparatory process shall be open to all States Members of the United Nations and members of the specialized agencies;

22. *Invites* other relevant stakeholders, including organizations and bodies of the United Nations, intergovernmental organizations, international financial institutions, other interested international bodies and non-governmental organizations, civil society organizations, academic institutions, the scientific community, Indigenous Peoples and local communities, persons with disabilities, the private sector and philanthropic organizations, whose work is relevant to the Conference, accredited in accordance with the provisions set forth in annex II to the present resolution, to participate as observers in the Conference and its preparatory meeting;

23. *Decides* that accreditation to the Conference and the preparatory meeting shall be in accordance with the provisions set forth in annex II to the present resolution;

24. *Requests* the Secretary-General to provide appropriate support from all relevant parts of the Secretariat, and in cooperation with other relevant parts of the United Nations system, to the work of the Conference and to facilitate inter-agency cooperation to that end, as well as to ensure the efficient use of resources, so that the objectives of the Conference can be achieved;

25. *Encourages* States and international donors, as well as the private sector, financial institutions, foundations and other donors in a position to do so, to support the preparations for the Conference through voluntary contributions to a trust fund in support of preparations for the Conference and to support the participation of representatives of developing countries, priority being given to representatives of the least developed countries and small island developing States, including coverage of economy-class air tickets, daily subsistence allowances and terminal expenses, in the meetings of the Conference and its preparatory meeting.

Annex I

Provisional agenda of the 2026 United Nations Water Conference to Accelerate the Implementation of Sustainable Development Goal 6: Ensure availability and sustainable management of water and sanitation for all

United Arab Emirates, 2 to 4 December 2026

1. Opening of the Conference.
2. Election of the two Presidents.
3. Adoption of the rules of procedure.
4. Adoption of the agenda of the Conference.
5. Election of officers other than the Presidents.
6. Organization of work, including the establishment of subsidiary organs, and other organizational matters.
7. Credentials of representatives to the Conference:
   (a) Appointment of the members of the Credentials Committee;
   (b) Report of the Credentials Committee.
8. General debate.
9. Interactive dialogues.
10. Outcome of the Conference.

11. Adoption of the report of the Conference.

12. Closure of the Conference.

Annex II

Proposed organization of work of the 2026 United Nations Water Conference to Accelerate the Implementation of Sustainable Development Goal 6: Ensure availability and sustainable management of water and sanitation for all

United Arab Emirates, 2 to 4 December 2026

1. The 2026 United Nations Water Conference to Accelerate the Implementation of Sustainable Development Goal 6: Ensure availability and sustainable management of water and sanitation for all will be held in the United Arab Emirates, from 2 to 4 December 2026.

I. Organization of work

A. Plenary meetings

2. The Conference will consist of a total of seven plenary meetings, to be held as follows:

Wednesday, 2 December: from 9 to 10 a.m., from 10 a.m. to 1 p.m. and from 3 to 6 p.m.

Thursday, 3 December: from 10 a.m. to 1 p.m. and from 3 to 6 p.m.

Friday, 4 December: from 10 a.m. to 1 p.m. and from 3 to 6 p.m.

3. The plenary meetings will be devoted to statements.

4. The list of speakers for the plenary meetings will be established on a first-come first-served basis, with the customary protocol that ensures that Heads of State or Government speak first, followed by other heads of delegation. The European Union will be included in the list of speakers. Detailed arrangements will be communicated in a timely manner through a note by the Secretariat.

5. At the opening of the Conference, to take place during the first plenary meeting, to be held on Wednesday, 2 December, from 9 to 10 a.m., consideration will be given to all procedural and organizational matters, including the adoption of the rules of procedure and the agenda, the election of the two Presidents of the Conference, the election of officers, the establishment of subsidiary organs, as appropriate, the appointment of the members of the Credentials Committee, arrangements for the preparation of the report of the Conference and other matters. At the first plenary meeting, statements will be made by the Presidents of the Conference, the Secretary-General of the United Nations, the President of the General Assembly, the President of the Economic and Social Council, the Secretary-General of the Conference and the Chair of UN-Water.

6. The plenary meetings will also hear statements, in accordance with the practices of the General Assembly, from representatives of intergovernmental organizations, international financial institutions, international bodies, the specialized agencies, funds and programmes, as well as major groups and other stakeholders accredited to the Conference as observers in accordance with the present annex.

7. The final plenary meeting, to be held on the afternoon of Friday, 4 December, is expected to conclude with, inter alia, reporting on the interactive dialogues, to be followed by the adoption of the report of the Conference.

8. The plenary meetings will run in parallel with the interactive dialogues, unless otherwise specified in the present resolution.

B. Interactive dialogues

9. The Conference will include six interactive dialogues, to be held in parallel with the plenary meetings, as follows:

Wednesday, 2 December: from 10 a.m. to 1 p.m. and from 3 to 6 p.m.

Thursday, 3 December: from 10 a.m. to 1 p.m. and from 3 to 6 p.m.

Friday, 4 December: from 10 a.m. to 1 p.m. and from 3 to 5 p.m.

10. Summaries of the interactive dialogues should be presented to the Conference at its closing plenary meeting, followed by a written submission for the final report of the Conference.

C. Main Committee

11. The Main Committee, established in accordance with the rules of procedure of the Conference, will meet, if necessary, in parallel with plenary meetings, except during the opening and closing of the Conference, and will be responsible for finalizing any outstanding matters.

II. Credentials of representatives to the Conference: appointment of the members of the Credentials Committee

12. The Credentials Committee will be appointed according to the rules of procedure of the Conference.

III. Accreditation: international organizations and other entities

13. Relevant intergovernmental organizations, international financial institutions and international bodies with a standing invitation to participate in the work of the General Assembly as observers or that were accredited to the World Summit on Sustainable Development, the United Nations Conference on the Midterm Comprehensive Review of the Implementation of the Objectives of the International Decade for Action, "Water for Sustainable Development", 2018–2028, the United Nations Conference on Sustainable Development, the intergovernmental conference on an international legally binding instrument under the United Nations Convention on the Law of the Sea on the conservation and sustainable use of marine biological diversity of areas beyond national jurisdiction, the United Nations Conference on Straddling Fish Stocks and Highly Migratory Fish Stocks, the Review Conference on the Agreement for the Implementation of the Provisions of the United Nations Convention on the Law of the Sea of 10 December 1982 relating to the Conservation and Management of Straddling Fish Stocks and Highly Migratory Fish Stocks, the international meeting entitled "Stockholm+50: a healthy planet for the prosperity of all – our responsibility, our opportunity", the 2017 and 2022 United Nations Conferences to Support the Implementation of Sustainable Development Goal 14: Conserve and sustainably use the oceans, seas and marine resources for sustainable development and to the United Nations conferences on the sustainable development of small island developing States, held in Barbados, Mauritius, Samoa and Antigua and Barbuda, may participate in the deliberations of the Conference and its preparatory meeting, as appropriate, in accordance with the rules of procedure of the Conference.

14. Interested intergovernmental organizations that were not accredited to the conferences and summits listed in paragraph 13 above may apply to the General Assembly for accreditation following the established accreditation procedure.

IV. Accreditation: non-governmental organizations and all relevant stakeholders

15. The non-governmental organizations and major groups as identified in Agenda 21,[249] in consultative status with the Economic and Social Council, as well as those that were accredited to the conferences and summits listed in paragraph 13 above, shall register in order to participate.

16. The President of the General Assembly shall also draw up lists of other relevant non-governmental organizations, including civil society organizations, academic institutions, the scientific community, the private sector and philanthropic organizations whose work is relevant to the Conference, which may participate in the Conference and the preparatory meeting as observers, taking into account the principles of transparency and of equitable geographical representation, and shall submit the proposed lists to Member States for their consideration on a

[249] *Report of the United Nations Conference on Environment and Development, Rio de Janeiro, 3–14 June 1992,* vol. I, *Resolutions Adopted by the Conference* (United Nations publication, Sales No. E.93.I.8 and corrigendum), resolution 1, annex II.

non-objection basis. The President of the General Assembly shall bring a list to the attention of the General Assembly before the preparatory meeting and, in any case, no later than six months before the Conference.[250]

17. The provisions of paragraph 15 of General Assembly resolution 67/290 of 9 July 2013 shall apply mutatis mutandis to the Conference and its preparatory process.

V. Secretariat

18. The Secretary-General of the Conference will serve as focal point within the Secretariat for providing support to the organization of the Conference, in cooperation with the representatives of the two Presidents.

VI. Documentation

19. In accordance with the practice followed at previous United Nations conferences, the official documentation of the Conference will include documents issued before, during and after the Conference.

20. In accordance with the practice followed at previous United Nations conferences, it is recommended that the Conference adopt a report consisting of the decisions of the Conference, a brief account of the proceedings and a reportorial account of the work of the Conference and the action taken at the plenary meetings.

21. Summaries of the plenary meetings and interactive dialogues of the Conference and a list of voluntary commitments announced at the Conference should also be included in the report of the Conference.

VII. Organization of parallel meetings and other events of the Conference

22. Parallel meetings and other events, including those of major groups and other stakeholders, will be held during the same hours as the plenary meetings and interactive dialogues, space permitting. Interpretation services will be provided for such meetings, as available.

VIII. Side events

23. Side events, including briefings, seminars, workshops and panel discussions on issues related to the implementation of Sustainable Development Goal 6 will be organized by participants in the Conference. Guidelines for organizing such events and the calendar of those events will be made available on the Conference website.

IX. Media coverage

24. Press materials will be prepared by the Department of Global Communications of the Secretariat for journalists covering the Conference. In addition, regular press releases will be issued on the results of plenary meetings, interactive dialogues and other events. All relevant documentation will be made available on the Conference website.

25. The plenary meetings, the interactive dialogues and the press conferences will be broadcast live to the media area. A programme of special media briefings and press conferences will be announced.

Annex III
Provisional rules of procedure of the 2026 United Nations Water Conference to Accelerate the Implementation of Sustainable Development Goal 6: Ensure availability and sustainable management of water and sanitation for all

I. Representation and credentials

Rule 1
Composition of delegations

The delegation of each State participating in the Conference and that of the European Union shall consist of a head of delegation and such other representatives, alternate representatives and advisers as may be required.

[250] The lists will include proposed as well as final names. The general basis of any objections, if requested by one or more States Members of the United Nations or States members of the specialized agencies, will be made known to the Office of the President of the General Assembly and the requester.

Rule 2
Alternates and advisers

The head of delegation may designate an alternate representative or an adviser to act as a representative.

Rule 3
Submission of credentials

The credentials of representatives and the names of alternate representatives and advisers shall be submitted to the Secretary-General of the United Nations, if possible, not less than one week before the date fixed for the opening of the Conference. The credentials shall be issued either by the Head of the State or Government or by the Minister for Foreign Affairs or, in the case of the European Union, by the President of the European Commission.

Rule 4
Credentials Committee

A Credentials Committee of nine members shall be appointed at the beginning of the Conference. Its composition shall be based on that of the Credentials Committee of the General Assembly at its eighty-first session. It shall examine the credentials of representatives and report to the Conference without delay.

Rule 5
Provisional participation in the Conference

Pending a decision of the Conference on their credentials, representatives shall be entitled to participate provisionally in the Conference.

II. Officers

Rule 6
Elections

The Conference shall elect from among the representatives of participating States the following officers: two Presidents, one from Senegal and one from the United Arab Emirates, each of whom shall preside separately. The Conference shall also elect 13 Vice-Presidents,[251] one of whom shall be designated as Rapporteur-General, two ex officio Vice-Presidents from the host countries, as well as a Chair for the Main Committee established in accordance with rule 46. The officers shall be elected with a view to ensuring the representative character of the General Committee. The Conference may also elect such other officers as it deems necessary for the performance of its functions.

Rule 7
General powers of the presiding President

1. The Presidents shall take turns in presiding at the plenary meetings of the Conference. In addition to exercising the powers conferred upon her or him elsewhere by these rules, the presiding President shall declare the opening and closing of each meeting, put questions to the vote and announce decisions. The presiding President shall rule on points of order and, subject to those rules, shall have complete control over the proceedings and the maintenance of order thereat. The presiding President may propose to the Conference the closure of the list of speakers, a limitation on the time to be allowed to speakers and on the number of times each representative may speak on a question, the adjournment or closure of the debate and the suspension or adjournment of a meeting.

2. The presiding President remains, in the exercise of her or his functions, under the authority of the Conference.

[251] Three from each of the following groups: African States; Asia-Pacific States; Eastern European States; Latin American and Caribbean States; and Western European and other States. The election of the two Presidents will, however, have the effect of reducing by one the number of Vice-Presidents allocated to the regions from which each of the Presidents is elected.

Rule 8
Acting President

1. If both Presidents are to be absent from a meeting or any part thereof, they may designate one of the Vice-Presidents to preside.

2. A Vice-President acting as President shall have the same powers and duties as the President.

Rule 9
Replacement of a President or the Presidents

If either of the Presidents is unable to perform her or his functions, a new President shall be elected. If both Presidents are unable to perform their functions, new Presidents shall be elected.

Rule 10
Voting rights of the presiding President

The presiding President, or a Vice-President acting as the presiding President, shall not vote in the Conference, but may appoint another member of her or his delegation to vote in her or his place.

III. General Committee

Rule 11
Composition

The two Presidents, the Vice-Presidents, the Rapporteur-General and the Chair of the Main Committee shall constitute the General Committee. One of the two Presidents, as agreed between them, or, in their absence, one of the Vice-Presidents designated by them, shall serve as Chair of the General Committee. The Chair of the Credentials Committee and other committees established by the Conference in accordance with rule 48 may participate, without the right to vote, in the General Committee.

Rule 12
Substitute members

If a President or a Vice-President of the Conference is to be absent during a meeting of the General Committee, she or he may designate a member of her or his delegation to sit and vote in the Committee. In case of absence, the Chair of the Main Committee shall designate the Vice-Chair of that Committee as her or his substitute. When serving on the General Committee, a Vice-Chair of the Main Committee shall not have the right to vote if she or he is a member of the same delegation as another member of the General Committee.

Rule 13
Functions

The General Committee shall assist both Presidents in the general conduct of the business of the Conference and, subject to the decisions of the Conference, shall ensure the coordination of the work of the Conference.

IV. Secretariat of the Conference

Rule 14
Duties of the Secretary-General of the United Nations

1. The Secretary-General of the United Nations or a designated representative shall act in that capacity in all meetings of the Conference and its subsidiary organs.

2. The Secretary-General of the United Nations or a designated representative shall direct the staff required by the Conference.

Rule 15
Duties of the secretariat of the Conference

The secretariat of the Conference shall, in accordance with the present rules:

(a) Provide simultaneous interpretation of speeches made at meetings;

(b) Receive, translate, reproduce and circulate the documents of the Conference;

(c) Publish and circulate the official documents of the Conference;

(d) Prepare and circulate records of public meetings;

(e) Make and arrange for the keeping of sound recordings of meetings;

(f) Arrange for the custody and preservation of the documents of the Conference in the archives of the United Nations;

(g) Generally perform all other work that the Conference may require.

Rule 16
Statements by the Secretariat

The Secretary-General of the United Nations, or any member of the Secretariat designated for that purpose, may, at any time, make either oral or written statements concerning any question under consideration.

V. Opening of the Conference

Rule 17
Temporary President

The Secretary-General of the United Nations or, in his absence, any member of the Secretariat designated by him for that purpose, shall open the first meeting of the Conference and preside until the Conference has elected its Presidents.

Rule 18
Decisions concerning organization

The Conference shall, at its first meeting:

(a) Adopt its rules of procedure;

(b) Elect its officers and constitute its subsidiary organs;

(c) Adopt its agenda, the draft of which shall, until such adoption, be the provisional agenda of the Conference;

(d) Decide on the organization of its work.

VI. Conduct of business

Rule 19
Quorum

The presiding President may declare a meeting open and permit the debate to proceed when at least one third of the States participating in the Conference are present. The presence of a majority of the States so participating shall be required for any decision to be taken.

Rule 20
Speeches

1. No representative may address the Conference without having previously obtained the permission of the presiding President. Subject to rules 21, 22 and 25 to 27, the presiding President shall call upon speakers in the order in which they indicate their desire to speak. The secretariat shall be in charge of drawing up a list of speakers.

2. Debate shall be confined to the question before the Conference and the presiding President may call a speaker to order if her or his remarks are not relevant to the subject under discussion.

3. The Conference may limit the time allowed to each speaker and the number of times each participant may speak on any question. Permission to speak on a motion to set such limits shall be accorded to only two representatives in favour of and to two opposing such limits, after which the motion shall be immediately put to the vote. In any event, with the consent of the Conference, the presiding President shall limit each intervention on procedural matters to five minutes. When the debate is limited and a speaker exceeds the allotted time, the presiding President shall call her or him to order without delay.

Rule 21
Points of order

During the discussion of any matter, a representative may at any time raise a point of order, which shall be immediately decided by the presiding President in accordance with the present rules. A representative may appeal against the ruling of the presiding President. The appeal shall be immediately put to the vote, and the presiding President's ruling shall stand unless overruled by a majority of the States present and voting. A representative may not, in raising a point of order, speak on the substance of the matter under discussion.

Rule 22
Precedence

The Chair or the Rapporteur of the Main Committee, or of other subsidiary organs, may be accorded precedence for the purpose of explaining the conclusions arrived at by the body concerned.

Rule 23
Closing of the list of speakers

During the course of a debate, the presiding President may announce the list of speakers and, with the consent of the Conference, declare the list closed.

Rule 24
Right of reply

1. Notwithstanding rule 23, the presiding President shall accord the right of reply to a representative of any State participating in the Conference or of the European Union who requests it. Any other representative of a State may be granted the opportunity to make a reply.

2. The statements made under the present rule shall normally be made at the end of the last meeting of the day, or at the conclusion of the consideration of the relevant item if that is sooner.

3. Representatives of a State or of the European Union may make no more than two statements under the present rule at a given meeting on any item. The first shall be limited to five minutes and the second to three minutes. Representatives shall, in any event, attempt to be as brief as possible.

Rule 25
Adjournment of debate

A representative of any State participating in the Conference may at any time move the adjournment of the debate on the question under discussion. In addition to the proposer of the motion, permission to speak on the motion shall be accorded to only two representatives in favour and to two opposing the adjournment, after which the motion shall, subject to rule 28, be immediately put to the vote.

Rule 26
Closure of debate

A representative of any State participating in the Conference may at any time move the closure of the debate on the question under discussion, whether or not any other representative has signified her or his wish to speak.

Permission to speak on the motion shall be accorded to only two representatives opposing the closure, after which the motion shall, subject to rule 28, be immediately put to the vote.

Rule 27
Suspension or adjournment of the meeting

Subject to rule 38, a representative of any State participating in the Conference may at any time move the suspension or the adjournment of the meeting. No discussion on such motions shall be permitted and they shall, subject to rule 28, be immediately put to the vote.

Rule 28
Order of motions

The motions indicated below shall have precedence in the following order over all proposals or other motions before the meeting:

(a) To suspend the meeting;

(b) To adjourn the meeting;

(c) To adjourn the debate on the question under discussion;

(d) To close the debate on the question under discussion.

Rule 29
Submission of proposals and substantive amendments

Proposals and substantive amendments shall normally be submitted in writing to the Secretary-General or her or his designated representative, who shall circulate copies to all delegations in the languages of the Conference. Unless the Conference decides otherwise, substantive proposals shall not be discussed or put to a decision unless copies have been circulated to all delegations not later than the day preceding the meeting. The presiding President may, however, permit the discussion and consideration of amendments, even though those amendments have not been circulated or have been circulated only the same day.

Rule 30
Withdrawal of proposals and motions

A proposal or a motion may be withdrawn by its sponsor at any time before a decision on it has been taken, provided that it has not been amended. A proposal or a motion thus withdrawn may be reintroduced by any representative.

Rule 31
Decisions on competence

Subject to rule 28, any motion calling for a decision on the competence of the Conference to adopt a proposal submitted to it shall be put to the vote before a decision is taken on the proposal in question.

Rule 32
Reconsideration of proposals

When a proposal has been adopted or rejected, it may not be reconsidered unless the Conference, by a two-thirds majority of the States present and voting, so decides. Permission to speak on a motion to reconsider shall be accorded to only two speakers opposing reconsideration, after which the motion shall be immediately put to the vote.

VII. Decision-making

Rule 33
General agreement

The Conference shall make its best endeavour to ensure that the work of the Conference is accomplished by consensus.

Rule 34
Voting rights

Each State participating in the Conference shall have one vote.

Rule 35
Majority required

1. Subject to rule 33, decisions of the Conference on all matters of substance shall be taken by a two-thirds majority of the States present and voting.

2. Except as otherwise provided in the present rules, decisions of the Conference on all matters of procedure shall be taken by a majority of the States present and voting.

3. If the question arises whether a matter is one of procedure or of substance, the presiding President of the Conference shall rule on the question. An appeal against that ruling shall be immediately put to the vote, and the presiding President's ruling shall stand unless overruled by a majority of the States present and voting.

4. If a vote is equally divided, the proposal or motion shall be regarded as rejected.

Rule 36
Meaning of the phrase "States present and voting"

For the purpose of the present rules, the phrase "States present and voting" means States casting an affirmative or negative vote. States which abstain from voting shall be regarded as not voting.

Rule 37
Method of voting

1. Except as provided in rule 44, the Conference may vote by show of hands, except that a representative may request a roll call, which shall then be taken in the English alphabetical order of the names of the States participating in the Conference, beginning with the delegation whose name is drawn by lot by the presiding President. The name of each State shall be called in all roll calls, and its representative shall reply "yes", "no" or "abstention".

2. When the Conference votes by mechanical means, a non-recorded vote shall replace a vote by show of hands and a recorded vote shall replace a roll call. A representative may request a recorded vote, which shall, unless a representative requests otherwise, be taken without calling out the names of the States participating in the Conference.

3. The vote of each State participating in a roll call or a recorded vote shall be inserted in any record of or report on the meeting.

Rule 38
Conduct during voting

After the presiding President has announced the commencement of voting, no representative shall interrupt the voting, except on a point of order in connection with the actual conduct of the voting.

Rule 39
Explanation of vote

1. Representatives may make brief statements, consisting solely of explanations of vote, before the voting has commenced or after the voting has been completed. The presiding President may limit the time to be allowed for such explanations. The representative of a State sponsoring a proposal or motion shall not speak in explanation of vote thereon, except if it has been amended.

2. When the same matter is considered successively in several organs of the Conference, a State should, as far as possible, explain its vote only in one such organ, unless its vote in one organ is different from that in another organ.

Rule 40
Division of proposals

A representative may move that parts of a proposal be decided on separately. If a representative objects, the motion for division shall be voted upon. Permission to speak on the motion shall be accorded to only two representatives in favour of and to two opposing the division. If the motion is carried, those parts of the proposal that are subsequently approved shall be put to the Conference for decision as a whole. If all operative parts of the proposal have been rejected, the proposal shall be considered to have been rejected as a whole.

Rule 41
Amendments

A proposal is considered an amendment to another proposal if it merely adds to, deletes from or revises part of that proposal. Unless specified otherwise, the word "proposal" in these rules shall be regarded as including amendments.

Rule 42
Order of voting on amendments

When an amendment is moved to a proposal, the amendment shall be voted on first. When two or more amendments are moved to a proposal, the Conference shall vote first on the amendment furthest removed in substance from the original proposal and then on the amendment next furthest removed therefrom, and so on, until all the amendments have been put to the vote. Where, however, the adoption of one amendment necessarily implies the rejection of another amendment, the latter shall not be put to the vote. If one or more amendments are adopted, the amended proposal shall then be voted upon.

Rule 43
Order of voting on proposals

1. If two or more proposals, other than amendments, relate to the same question, they shall, unless the Conference decides otherwise, be voted on in the order in which they were submitted. The Conference may, after each vote on a proposal, decide whether to vote on the next proposal.

2. Revised proposals shall be voted on in the order in which the original proposals were submitted, unless the revision substantially departs from the original proposal. In that case, the original proposal shall be regarded as withdrawn and the revised proposal shall be treated as a new proposal.

3. A motion requiring that no decision be taken on a proposal shall be put to the vote before a decision is taken on the proposal in question.

Rule 44
Elections

All elections shall be held by secret ballot unless, in the absence of any objection, the Conference decides to proceed without taking a ballot when there is an agreed candidate or slate of candidates.

Rule 45
Balloting

1. When one or more elective places are to be filled at one time under the same conditions, those candidates, in a number not exceeding the number of such places, obtaining in the first ballot a majority of the votes cast and the largest number of votes shall be elected.

2. If the number of candidates obtaining such majority is less than the number of places to be filled, additional ballots shall be held to fill the remaining places, the voting being restricted to the candidates obtaining the largest number of votes in the previous ballot, to a number not more than twice the places remaining to be filled.

VIII. Subsidiary organs

Rule 46
Main Committee

The Conference may establish a Main Committee.

Rule 47
Representation on the Main Committee

Each State participating in the Conference and the European Union may be represented by one representative on the Main Committee. They may assign to the Committee such alternate representatives and advisers as may be required.

Rule 48
Other committees and working groups

1. In addition to the Main Committee referred to above, the Conference may establish such committees and working groups as it deems necessary for the performance of its functions.

2. Subject to the decision of the plenary of the Conference, the committees may set up subcommittees and working groups.

Rule 49
Members of committees, subcommittees and working groups

1. The members of the committees and working groups of the Conference, referred to in rule 48, paragraph 1, shall be appointed by the two Presidents, subject to the approval of the Conference, unless the Conference decides otherwise.

2. Members of the subcommittees and working groups of committees shall be appointed by the Chair of the committee in question, subject to the approval of that committee, unless the committee decides otherwise.

Rule 50
Officers

Except as otherwise provided in rule 6, each committee, subcommittee and working group shall elect its own officers.

Rule 51
Quorum

1. The Chair of the Main Committee may declare a meeting open and permit the debate to proceed when at least one quarter of the States participating in the Conference are present. The presence of a majority of the States so participating shall be required for any decision to be taken.

2. A majority of the members of the General Committee or the Credentials Committee or of any committee, subcommittee or working group shall constitute a quorum.

Rule 52
Officers, conduct of business and voting

The rules contained in sections II, VI (except rule 19) and VII above shall be applicable, mutatis mutandis, to the proceedings of committees, subcommittees and working groups, except that:

(a) The Chairs of the General Committee and the Credentials Committee and the Chairs of the committees, subcommittees and working groups may exercise the right to vote, provided that they are representatives of participating States;

(b) Decisions of committees, subcommittees and working groups shall be taken by a majority of the members present and voting, except that the reconsideration of a proposal or an amendment shall require the majority established by rule 32.

IX. Languages and records

Rule 53
Languages of the Conference

Arabic, Chinese, English, French, Russian and Spanish shall be the languages of the Conference.

Rule 54
Interpretation

1. Speeches made in a language of the Conference shall be interpreted into the other five languages.

2. A representative may speak in a language other than a language of the Conference if the delegation concerned provides for interpretation into one of the languages of the Conference.

Rule 55
Languages of official documents

Official documents of the Conference shall be made available in the languages of the Conference.

Rule 56
Sound recordings of meetings

Sound recordings of the plenary meetings of the Conference, the interactive dialogues and of the meetings of the Main Committee shall be made and kept in accordance with the practice of the United Nations. Unless otherwise decided by the Conference or the Main Committee, no such recordings shall be made of any of the other meetings held during the Conference.

X. Public and private meetings

General principles

Rule 57

The plenary meetings of the Conference and the meetings of any committee shall be held in public unless the body concerned decides otherwise. All decisions taken by the plenary of the Conference at a private meeting shall be announced at an early public meeting of the plenary.

Rule 58

As a general rule, meetings of the General Committee, the Credentials Committee, subcommittees or working groups shall be held in private.

Rule 59
Communiqués on private meetings

At the close of a private meeting, the presiding officer of the organ concerned may issue a communiqué through the Secretary-General of the United Nations or a designated representative.

XI. Other participants and observers

Rule 60
Intergovernmental organizations and other entities[252] having received a standing invitation to participate as observers in the sessions and work of the General Assembly

Representatives designated by intergovernmental organizations and other entities having received a standing invitation to participate as observers in the sessions and work of the General Assembly have the right to participate as observers, without the right to vote, in the deliberations of the Conference, the Main Committee and, as appropriate, any other committee or working group.

Rule 61
Associate members of regional commissions[253]

Representatives designated by the associate members of regional commissions listed in the footnote below may participate as observers, without the right to vote, in the deliberations of the Conference, the Main Committee and, as appropriate, any other committee or working group.

Rule 62
Representatives of the specialized agencies and related organizations[254]

Representatives designated by the specialized agencies and related organizations may participate as observers, without the right to vote, in the deliberations of the Conference, the Main Committee and, as appropriate, any other committee or working group on questions within the scope of their activities.

Rule 63
Representatives of other intergovernmental organizations and other international bodies

Save where otherwise specifically provided with respect to the European Union in these rules of procedure, representatives designated by other intergovernmental organizations and other international bodies invited to the Conference may participate as observers, without the right to vote, in the deliberations of the Conference, the Main Committee and, as appropriate, any other committee or working group on questions within the scope of their activities.

Rule 64
Representatives of interested United Nations organs

Representatives designated by interested organs of the United Nations may participate as observers, without the right to vote, in the deliberations of the Conference, the Main Committee and, as appropriate, any other committee or working group on questions within the scope of their activities.

---

[252] For the purpose of the present rules, the term "other entities" includes the International Committee of the Red Cross, the International Federation of Red Cross and Red Crescent Societies, the International Olympic Committee, the Inter-Parliamentary Union and the Sovereign Order of Malta.

[253] American Samoa, Anguilla, Aruba, Bermuda, the British Virgin Islands, the Cayman Islands, the Commonwealth of the Northern Mariana Islands, Curaçao, French Polynesia, Guam, Montserrat, New Caledonia, Puerto Rico, Sint Maarten, the Turks and Caicos Islands and the United States Virgin Islands.

[254] For the purpose of the present rules, the term "related organizations" includes the International Atomic Energy Agency, the International Criminal Court, the International Organization for Migration, the International Seabed Authority, the International Tribunal for the Law of the Sea, the Organisation for the Prohibition of Chemical Weapons, the Preparatory Commission for the Comprehensive Nuclear-Test-Ban Treaty Organization and the World Trade Organization.

Rule 65
Representatives of non-governmental organizations[255]

1. Non-governmental organizations accredited to participate in the Conference may designate representatives to attend public meetings of the Conference and the Main Committee as observers.

2. Upon the invitation of the presiding officer of the Conference and subject to the approval of the Conference, such observers may make oral statements on questions in which they have special competence. If the number of requests to speak is too large, the non-governmental organizations shall be requested to form themselves into constituencies, such constituencies to speak through spokespersons.

Rule 66
Written statements

Written statements submitted by the designated representatives referred to in rules 60 to 65 shall be circulated by the secretariat to all delegations in the quantities and the languages in which the statements are made available to it at the site of the Conference, provided that a statement submitted on behalf of a non-governmental organization must be related to the work of the Conference and be on a subject in which the organization has a special competence. Written statements shall not be made available at United Nations expense and shall not be issued as official documents.

XII. Suspension and amendment of the rules of procedure

Rule 67
Method of suspension

Any of these rules may be suspended by the Conference provided that 24 hours' notice of the proposal for the suspension has been given, which may be waived if no representative objects. Any such suspension shall be limited to a specific and stated purpose and to a period required to achieve that purpose.

Rule 68
Method of amendment

These rules of procedure may be amended by a decision of the Conference taken by a two-thirds majority of the States present and voting, after the General Committee has reported on the proposed amendment.

RESOLUTION 78/328

Adopted at the 107th plenary meeting, on 6 September 2024, without a vote, on the basis of draft resolution A/78/L.106, submitted by the President of the General Assembly

78/328. Enhancing the participation of Indigenous Peoples' representatives and institutions in meetings of relevant United Nations bodies on issues affecting them

The General Assembly,

Reaffirming the purposes and principles contained in the Charter of the United Nations,

Reaffirming also the United Nations Declaration on the Rights of Indigenous Peoples[256] and the solemn commitment to respect, promote and advance and in no way diminish the rights of Indigenous Peoples and to uphold the principles of the Declaration, including the right to participate in decision-making in matters which would affect their rights, through representatives chosen by themselves in accordance with their own procedures,

---

[255] Paragraph 23.3 of Agenda 21 provides that "Any policies, definitions or rules affecting access to and participation by non-governmental organizations in the work of United Nations institutions or agencies associated with the implementation of Agenda 21 must apply equally to all major groups". Agenda 21 defines major groups as comprising women, children and youth, indigenous people, non-governmental organizations, local authorities, workers and their trade unions, business and industry, the scientific and technological community and farmers. Therefore, based on Agenda 21, rule 65 shall apply equally to non-governmental organizations and other major groups.

[256] Resolution 61/295, annex.

Reaffirming further the outcome document of the high-level plenary meeting of the General Assembly known as the World Conference on Indigenous Peoples,[257] and recalling the commitment by Member States to consider ways to enable the participation of Indigenous Peoples' representatives and institutions in meetings of relevant United Nations bodies on issues affecting them,

Recalling its resolution 70/232 of 23 December 2015, whereby it requested the President of the General Assembly to conduct timely, inclusive, representative and transparent consultations with Member States, Indigenous Peoples' representatives and institutions from all regions of the world, and existing relevant mechanisms of the United Nations, on the possible measures necessary, including procedural and institutional steps and accreditation criteria, to enable the participation of Indigenous Peoples' representatives and institutions in meetings of relevant United Nations bodies on issues affecting them,

Recalling also its resolution 71/321 of 8 September 2017, in which Member States acknowledged the need to find ways and means of promoting the participation of Indigenous Peoples' representatives and institutions within the United Nations system on issues affecting them, and recalling further its resolution 77/203 of 15 December 2022, whereby it decided to continue the consideration of possible further measures necessary to enhance the participation of Indigenous Peoples' representatives and institutions in relevant United Nations meetings on issues affecting them at the seventy-eighth session, as originally requested in resolution 71/321, and its resolution 78/189 of 19 December 2023,

1. *Decides* to continue its consideration of possible further measures necessary to enhance the participation of Indigenous Peoples' representatives and institutions in relevant United Nations meetings on issues affecting them at its eightieth session, taking into account the achievements in that regard of other bodies and organizations throughout the United Nations system, with the aim of adopting procedural and institutional steps;

2. *Requests* the President of the General Assembly to appoint, at the beginning of the eightieth session, two co-facilitators from Member States and two advisers from Indigenous Peoples in relation to the above-mentioned process, which shall include consultations with Indigenous Peoples' representatives and institutions from all regions of the world as an input to the intergovernmental process;

3. *Continues to encourage* further efforts to facilitate the participation of Indigenous Peoples' representatives and institutions in meetings of relevant United Nations bodies on issues affecting them, in accordance with their respective rules of procedure, inter alia, through the inclusion of Indigenous Peoples' representatives and institutions in the modalities for relevant conferences, summits and other meetings convened by the United Nations on issues affecting them, in accordance with the relevant decisions established by the appropriate body or organization responsible for those meetings;

4. *Urges* Governments and intergovernmental and non-governmental organizations to continue to contribute to the United Nations Voluntary Fund for Indigenous Peoples in order to assist Indigenous Peoples' representatives and institutions to participate in the consultation process on the procedural and institutional steps to enable the participation of Indigenous Peoples' representatives and institutions in meetings of relevant United Nations bodies on issues affecting them, and invites the United Nations Voluntary Fund for Indigenous Peoples, within the rules and established procedures of the Fund, to facilitate the participation of Indigenous Peoples' representatives and institutions in such meetings, promoting balanced regional, gender and intergenerational representation.

RESOLUTION 78/329

Adopted at the 107th plenary meeting, on 6 September 2024, without a vote, on the basis of draft resolution A/78/L.105, sponsored by: Algeria, Angola, Belarus, Bolivia (Plurinational State of), Burkina Faso, China, Congo, Cuba, Democratic People's Republic of Korea, Equatorial Guinea, Eritrea, Iran (Islamic Republic of), Lao People's Democratic Republic, Mali, Nicaragua, Russian Federation, Saint Vincent and the Grenadines, Senegal, Syrian Arab Republic, Venezuela (Bolivarian Republic of), Zimbabwe

[257] Resolution 69/2.

78/329. Biennialization of the agenda item entitled "Elimination of unilateral extraterritorial coercive economic measures as a means of political and economic compulsion"

The General Assembly,

Recalling its resolution 58/316 of 1 July 2004 on further measures for the revitalization of the work of the General Assembly,

Decides:

(a) To include in the provisional agenda of its seventy-ninth session for consideration in the plenary of the General Assembly the agenda item entitled "Elimination of unilateral extraterritorial coercive economic measures as a means of political and economic compulsion";

(b) To biennialize the consideration of the agenda item in the plenary of the General Assembly as of its seventy-ninth session.

RESOLUTION 78/330

Adopted at the 107th plenary meeting, on 6 September 2024, without a vote, on the basis of draft resolution A/78/L.108, sponsored by: Albania, Andorra, Angola, Argentina, Armenia, Austria, Bahamas, Bangladesh, Belgium, Benin, Bolivia (Plurinational State of), Bosnia and Herzegovina, Brazil, Bulgaria, Burkina Faso, Burundi, Cabo Verde, Cambodia, Cameroon, Canada, Central African Republic, Chile, Colombia, Comoros, Congo, Costa Rica, Côte d'Ivoire, Croatia, Cyprus, Democratic Republic of the Congo, Denmark, Djibouti, Dominican Republic, Ecuador, Egypt, El Salvador, Equatorial Guinea, Eswatini, Finland, France, Gabon, Georgia, Ghana, Greece, Guatemala, Guinea-Bissau, Haiti, Honduras, Hungary, Iceland, India, Indonesia, Ireland, Jordan, Kazakhstan, Kenya, Kyrgyzstan, Latvia, Lebanon, Liberia, Libya, Liechtenstein, Lithuania, Luxembourg, Madagascar, Mali, Mauritania, Mexico, Monaco, Montenegro, Morocco, Mozambique, Myanmar, Nepal, Oman, Pakistan, Panama, Paraguay, Peru, Philippines, Portugal, Qatar, Republic of Moldova, Romania, Russian Federation, Rwanda, San Marino, Senegal, Serbia, Sierra Leone, Slovenia, Spain, Suriname, Switzerland, Tajikistan, Timor-Leste, Togo, Tunisia, Turkmenistan, Uganda, United Republic of Tanzania, Uruguay, Uzbekistan, Zambia

78/330. Multilingualism

The General Assembly,

Recognizing that multilingualism, as a core value of the Organization, contributes to the achievement of the goals of the United Nations, as set out in Article 1 of the Charter of the United Nations,

Bearing in mind that multilingualism is an enabler of multilateral diplomacy and that it contributes to the promotion of the values of the United Nations, as well as the faith of our peoples in the purposes and principles enshrined in its Charter,

Recognizing that the United Nations pursues multilingualism as a means of promoting, protecting and preserving diversity of languages and cultures globally, as well as of improving the efficiency, performance and transparency of the Organization,

Recognizing also, in this regard, that multilingualism promotes unity in diversity and international understanding, tolerance and dialogue, and recognizing the importance of the capacity to communicate to the peoples of the world in their own languages, including in formats accessible to persons with disabilities, by contributing to the ownership and sustainability of the actions of the United Nations,

Recalling that Arabic, Chinese, English, French, Russian and Spanish are both the official and the working languages of the General Assembly, including its committees and subcommittees,[258] and of the Security Council,[259] that Arabic, Chinese, English, French, Russian and Spanish are the official languages and English, French and Spanish

[258] Rule 51 of the rules of procedure of the General Assembly.

[259] Rule 41 of the provisional rules of procedure of the Security Council.

the working languages of the Economic and Social Council[260] and that English and French are the working languages of the Secretariat,[261]

Recognizing the efforts of the United Nations to use non-official languages, in addition to the six official languages, where appropriate, for communications with specific local target audiences,

Stressing the need for strict observance of the resolutions and rules establishing language arrangements for the different bodies and organs of the United Nations,

Emphasizing the importance of multilingualism in the activities of the United Nations,

Recognizing the contribution of multilingualism in promoting international peace and security, development and human rights, through the work of the United Nations departments and offices,

Emphasizing that multilingualism, as a core value, should be fully respected, in the preparation, holding and follow-up of multilateral conferences and processes,

Recalling that the International Court of Justice, in accordance with Article 39 of its Statute, also authorizes languages other than French or English to be used by any party upon request,

Recognizing the growing demand for the use of other languages in the International Court of Justice, including Spanish,

Reaffirming its resolution 70/1 of 25 September 2015, entitled "Transforming our world: the 2030 Agenda for Sustainable Development", and reaffirming its unwavering commitment to achieving the 2030 Agenda and utilizing it to transform our world for the better by 2030,

Recalling its resolution 47/135 of 18 December 1992, by which it adopted the Declaration on the Rights of Persons Belonging to National or Ethnic, Religious and Linguistic Minorities, and the International Covenant on Civil and Political Rights,[262] in particular article 27 thereof, concerning the rights of persons belonging to ethnic, religious or linguistic minorities,

Recalling also its resolution 74/135 of 18 December 2019 proclaiming 2022–2032 as the International Decade of Indigenous Languages (IDIL) as mentioned in the Los Pinos Declaration of 27–28 February 2020 in Mexico City, to draw attention to the critical loss of indigenous languages and the urgent need for their preservation, revitalization and promotion,

Recalling further the decision taken by the General Conference of the United Nations Educational, Scientific and Cultural Organization on 17 November 1999 that 21 February should be proclaimed International Mother Language Day,

Recalling its resolutions 2 (I) of 1 February 1946, 2480 B (XXIII) of 21 December 1968, 42/207 C of 11 December 1987 and 50/11 of 2 November 1995 and other subsequent resolutions relating to multilingualism, including resolutions 56/262 of 15 February 2002, 71/288 of 24 May 2017, 71/328 of 11 September 2017, 72/90 A and B of 7 December 2017, 72/161 of 19 December 2017, 72/304 of 13 July 2018, 72/313 of 17 September 2018, 73/102 A and B of 7 December 2018, 73/270 of 22 December 2018, 73/341 of 12 September 2019, 74/252 of 27 December 2019, 74/303 of 4 September 2020, 75/101 A and B of 10 December 2020, 75/325 of 10 September 2021, 76/84 A and B of 9 December 2021, 76/237 of 24 December 2021, 76/268 of 10 June 2022, 77/128 A and B of 12 December 2022, 77/255 of 30 December 2022, 77/335 of 1 September 2023, 78/80 A and B of 7 December 2023 and 78/245 of 22 December 2023,

1. *Takes note* of the report of the Secretary-General;[263]

2. *Supports* the approach presented by the Secretary-General to integrate multilingualism, as a core value of the Organization, into the activities of the Secretariat, on an equitable basis;

---

[260] Rule 32 of the rules of procedure of the Economic and Social Council.

[261] See resolution 2 (I), annex.

[262] See resolution 2200 A (XXI), annex.

[263] A/78/790.

3. *Emphasizes* the paramount importance of the equality of the six official languages of the United Nations;

I
Multilingualism in general and the role of the Secretariat

4. *Notes with appreciation* the publication of the United Nations Strategic Framework on Multilingualism on 27 March 2024, in the six official languages, the first of its kind within the Secretariat and system-wide;

5. *Notes with concern* the impact of the measures taken by the Secretary-General in response to the current liquidity situation and the residual impact of the coronavirus disease (COVID-19) on the provision of language services and the management of meetings, including the recruitment of new staff to fill vacant posts in the six official language services, and requests the Secretary-General to continue to make efforts to ensure that multilingualism, as a fundamental value of the Organization, is not undermined;

6. *Requests* the Secretary-General to ensure adequate human oversight and appropriate quality control in the provision of multilingual online content through translation tools in order to effectively leverage the benefits that they might offer, while taking into account the communication and reputational risks of the errors inherent to unedited machine translation;

7. *Requests* the Secretariat to continue to provide procedural notes, statements and remarks for the Presidents of the main organs, the Chairs of the Main Committees of the General Assembly, the Chairs of their subsidiary bodies and for representatives of the Secretariat, in the United Nations official language spoken by the presiding officer of the meeting;

8. *Requests* the Secretary-General to ensure that further updates of the Procurement Manual are reflected in all six official language versions in an appropriate time frame, and welcomes the procurement business seminars conducted to date in various languages;

9. *Notes* that a high proportion of calls for bids are published in English, and therefore requests the Secretariat to make use of existing multilingualism policies to facilitate the participation of local vendors in the United Nations procurement bidding process;

10. *Also notes* that United Nations Development Business (Department of Global Communications) published 30,425 procurement notices in Arabic, English, French, Portuguese, Russian and Spanish in 2021 and 2022, and requests United Nations Development Business to update the information in the next report of the Secretary-General on multilingualism on how to ensure the publication of procurement notices in the six official languages of the United Nations, notes that SAP Ariba Sourcing will support multiple languages, and further encourages the testing of the new tool in the six official languages of the United Nations in a timely manner;

11. *Recalls with appreciation* the appointment by the Secretary-General of the Coordinator for Multilingualism, who is responsible for the overall coordination of multilingualism Secretariat-wide and facilitates implementation thereof, and calls upon all departments and offices within the Secretariat to fully support the work of the Coordinator in the implementation of the relevant mandates on multilingualism;

12. *Welcomes* the designation of the Coordinator for Multilingualism as lead entity on multilingualism at the United Nations System Chief Executives Board for Coordination level, as well as the joint efforts of the Coordinator and the secretariat of the Chief Executives Board towards a more coordinated approach to multilingualism across member organizations of the Board, with a view to sharing information on innovative solutions to common challenges;

13. *Requests* the Secretary-General to implement the United Nations Strategic Framework on Multilingualism;

14. *Recognizes* the need to strengthen the human resources capacity of the Office of the Coordinator for Multilingualism in order to facilitate successful implementation of the United Nations Strategic Framework on Multilingualism across the Secretariat in a timely manner, and requests the Secretary-General to submit a proposal in this regard, including on the revised estimates for 2025 and the proposed programme budget for 2026 and thereafter, in accordance within existing procedures, in particular rule 153 of the rules of procedure of the General Assembly;

15. *Welcomes* the ongoing development of the network of focal points that supports the Coordinator for Multilingualism in effectively and consistently implementing relevant resolutions throughout all Secretariat entities

and the United Nations system, notes with satisfaction that the Coordinator invited all entities to establish objectives for their designated focal points in 2023 with a view to establishing an operational action plan in favour of multilingualism, and encourages the Coordinator to follow up on the establishment of objectives for all designated focal points;

16. *Requests* the Secretary-General to issue the relevant administrative and operational guidelines for the implementation of the United Nations Strategic Framework on Multilingualism;

17. *Emphasizes* the importance of the strategic vision for multilingualism and the areas of action presented in the United Nations Strategic Framework on Multilingualism, and requests the Coordinator for Multilingualism and all Secretariat entities to contribute to the implementation of the Framework;

18. *Notes* the difficulties reported by Secretariat entities in compiling accurate and comprehensive data for the report of the Secretary-General, owing, inter alia, to the lack of disaggregated data by language, and welcomes efforts by the Coordinator for Multilingualism to address the problem among Secretariat entities;

19. *Welcomes* the efforts of the Coordinator for Multilingualism to encourage all Secretariat entities to promote the celebration of a day dedicated to each of the official languages of the United Nations, in order to inform and raise awareness of their history, culture and use, encourages the Secretary-General to provide communication about each language day in the six official languages and further strengthen this approach, if needed through the participation of partner organizations, including Member States and institutions such as the United Nations Educational, Scientific and Cultural Organization, and also encourages the Secretary-General to consider extending this important initiative to other non-official languages spoken throughout the world, in a cost-neutral manner;

20. *Welcomes with appreciation* that in 2022 the United Nations Secretary-General Award in the category of multilingualism, aimed at honouring a staff member or team for their best practices and innovative approaches to fostering multilingualism at the United Nations, was received by the United Nations News team;

21. *Welcomes* the efforts made by international organizations based on a shared language to increase their cooperation with the United Nations regarding multilingualism;[264]

22. *Calls upon* Member States and the Secretariat to promote the preservation and protection of all languages used by peoples of the world, including by observing International Mother Language Day on 21 February with due solemnity;

23. *Welcomes* the activities of the United Nations Educational, Scientific and Cultural Organization, Member States, entities of the United Nations system, other international organizations and all other participating bodies aimed at fostering respect for and the promotion and protection of all languages, in particular endangered ones, linguistic diversity and multilingualism;

24. *Reaffirms* that linguistic diversity is an important element of cultural diversity, stresses the importance of the full and effective implementation of the Convention on the Protection and Promotion of the Diversity of Cultural Expressions,[265] which entered into force on 18 March 2007, and recalls the Recommendation concerning the Promotion and Use of Multilingualism and Universal Access to Cyberspace of 15 October 2003;[266]

25. *Recalls* paragraph 9 of its resolution 76/242 of 24 December 2021, and welcomes with appreciation the continued measures taken by the Secretary-General to implement multilingualism within the system of administration of justice;

II
Role of the Department of Global Communications in multilingualism

26. *Reaffirms* that the primary mission of the Department of Global Communications of the Secretariat is to provide, through its outreach activities, accurate, impartial, comprehensive, balanced, timely, relevant and

[264] See, for example, resolution 77/331 on cooperation between the United Nations and the International Organization of la Francophonie and resolution 77/14 on cooperation between the United Nations and the Community of Portuguese-speaking Countries.

[265] United Nations, *Treaty Series*, vol. 2440, No. 43977.

[266] United Nations Educational, Scientific and Cultural Organization, *Records of the General Conference, Thirty-second Session, Paris, 29 September–17 October 2003*, vol. 1, *Resolutions*, sect. IV, resolution 41, annex.

multilingual information to the public on the tasks and responsibilities of the United Nations in order to strengthen international support for the activities of the Organization with the greatest transparency;

27. *Requests* the Secretary-General to intensify his efforts to ensure the full implementation of existing mandates in the area of multilingualism as they relate to information and communication, and in this regard requests the Secretariat to explore the opportunities offered by the new information and communications technologies;

28. *Also requests* the Secretary-General to ensure that any decisions made by the Department of Global Communications, including those justified by budget limitations or reductions, do not undermine the principles of multilingualism;

29. *Recalls* paragraphs 51 and 52 of its resolution 76/237, and regrets the delays in the elimination of the disparity between the use of English and the use of the five other official languages in the archiving of official meetings webcasts by the Department of Global Communications;

30. *Emphasizes* the importance of making use of all the official languages of the United Nations, ensuring their full and equitable treatment in all the activities of the Department of Global Communications, with the aim of eliminating the disparity between the use of English and the use of the five other official languages, and in this regard reaffirms its request that the Secretary-General ensure that the Department has the necessary staffing capacity in all the official languages to undertake all its activities;

31. *Welcomes* the ongoing efforts of the Department of Global Communications to enhance multilingualism in all its activities, and stresses the importance of ensuring that the texts of all new public United Nations documents in all official languages, information materials and all older United Nations documents are made available through the United Nations websites and are accessible to Member States without delay;

32. *Regrets* that to date the meetings coverage and daily press releases are issued only in English and French, and highlights the importance of these to be issued in all official languages, in full respect of the principle of parity of all six official languages;

33. *Also regrets* that to date Security Council press statements are issued only in English and French and highlights the importance of these being issued in all official languages, in full respect of the principle of parity, and requests the Secretary-General to study the feasibility of issuing the press statements in all official languages and to report thereon in the context of the upcoming review of the Department of Global Communications;

34. *Encourages* the Department of Global Communications to continue to use other languages in addition to the official languages, when appropriate, according to the targeted audiences, without preferences and in line with the relevant General Assembly resolutions, with a view to reaching the widest possible spectrum of audiences and extending the United Nations message to all corners of the world in order to strengthen international support for the activities of the Organization;

35. *Notes with appreciation* that, following the launch in 2021 of the English version of the new United Nations Web TV website, the Department of Global Communications launched the versions in the other five official languages in early 2023, thereby resulting in live multilingual streaming coverage of United Nations meetings and events;

36. *Welcomes* the work done by the network of United Nations information centres, including the United Nations Regional Information Centre, in favour of the publication of United Nations information materials and the translation of important documents into languages other than the official languages of the United Nations, encourages the information centres to continue their important multilingual activities in the interactive and proactive aspects of their work and to develop web pages and social media accounts in local languages, and the Department of Global Communications to provide the necessary resources and technical facilities, with a view to reaching the widest possible spectrum of audiences and extending the United Nations message to all corners of the world in order to strengthen international support for the activities of the Organization, and encourages the continuation of efforts in this regard;

37. *Encourages* the Department of Global Communications to continue to disseminate through its flagship social media accounts original content in all six official languages as well as in Hindi, Kiswahili and Portuguese, and in this regard requests the Department to continue its efforts to mobilize adequate resources, including by exploring

innovative financing options as well as voluntary contributions to include more languages outside the six official languages of the United Nations;

38. *Emphasizes* the importance of the network of United Nations information centres in enhancing the public image of the United Nations, in disseminating messages on the United Nations to local populations, especially in developing countries, bearing in mind that information in local languages has the strongest impact on local populations, and in mobilizing support for the work of the United Nations at the local level;

39. *Welcomes* the sustained effort to disseminate information globally by using traditional means of communication in official languages and, in addition to them, non-official languages, and in this regard expresses its particular appreciation for the work currently being carried out by United Nations Radio;

40. *Recalls* paragraph 111 of its resolution 78/80 B, and requests the Secretary-General to continue to support those efforts;

41. *Notes with interest* the cost-neutral initiatives of the Secretariat to produce publications in official and non-official languages, to increase the volume of translated publications and to encourage a multilingual acquisition policy for the libraries of the United Nations, and requests the Secretariat to continue those initiatives;

42. *Acknowledges* the role of the libraries of the United Nations in the promotion of multilingualism;

43. *Notes with appreciation* the efforts of the Department of Global Communications to work at the local level with other organizations and bodies of the United Nations system to enhance the coordination of their communications activities, and urges the Department to encourage the United Nations Communications Group to promote multilingualism in its work;

44. *Expresses appreciation* for the efforts of the Department of Global Communications in highlighting some recent important communications and messages of the Secretary-General in non-official languages, such as Bangla, Hindi, Kiswahili, Persian, Portuguese and Urdu, in addition to official languages, in order to promote multilingualism, and encourages the Department to disseminate them in all six official languages, as well as in non-official languages whenever appropriate and in line with relevant General Assembly resolutions;

45. *Recalls* paragraph 116 of its resolution 78/80 B, and encourages the Department of Global Communications to prioritize the development of collaborative arrangements for the digitization of the audiovisual archives of the United Nations while preserving their multilingual character;

46. *Welcomes* the Department of Global Communications partnerships with universities for translation services on a pro bono basis, and requests the Secretary-General to grow the number of such partnerships;

47. *Requests* the Secretary-General to continue to exert all efforts to ensure that publications and other information services of the Secretariat, including the United Nations website, social media platforms and the United Nations News Service, contain comprehensive, balanced, objective and equitable information in all official languages about the issues before the Organization and that they maintain editorial independence, impartiality, accuracy and full consistency with resolutions and decisions of the General Assembly;

48. *Reaffirms* the crucial role of the Department of Global Communications in addressing the spread of misinformation, disinformation and information manipulation, and in supporting the efforts of the United Nations system to eradicate hate speech, and requests the Secretary-General to ensure that multilingualism is integrated into efforts taken in that regard and report thereon in the context of the upcoming review of the Department of Global Communications;

III
Websites, social media and other web-based communication tools

49. *Reaffirms* that the United Nations website and social media are an essential tool for Member States, the media, non-governmental organizations, educational institutions and the general public;

50. *Stresses* the need to treat the six official languages on the websites, social media and other web-based communication tools equally, and decides to limit the practice of granting waivers from the Department of Global Communications to Secretariat entities when establishing and maintaining websites on the un.org domain to a

maximum period of six months and stresses the importance of including in the next report of the Secretary-General the number of waivers granted and follow-up on the websites after the waiver has expired;

51. *Welcomes* the renewed efforts of the Secretary-General to conduct a comprehensive review of the United Nations websites, including content discrepancies among the official languages, and notes with appreciation the innovative ideas, potential synergies and other measures proposed in the report of the Secretary-General on multilingualism to achieve full parity among the six official languages;

52. *Also welcomes* the renewed efforts of the Secretary-General to conduct a comprehensive review of the United Nations websites, presenting the status of content in non-official languages, and notes with appreciation the innovative ideas, potential synergies and other cost-neutral measures proposed in the report of the Secretary-General on multilingualism to reinforce the broader multilingual development and enrichment of the United Nations websites, as appropriate;

53. *Recalls* paragraph 49 of its resolution 76/268, notes with concern the disparity between the English and the non-English languages on the websites maintained by the Secretariat, urges the Secretary-General to lead the efforts of all offices and departments of the Secretariat to take concrete action to address such uneven development, and in this regard calls upon all stakeholders, including the Department of Global Communications, content-providing Secretariat entities and the Office of Information and Communications Technology of the Secretariat, to continue their collaboration, within their respective mandates, so as to achieve full parity among the six official languages on all United Nations websites developed and maintained by all Secretariat entities, in full conformance with the principles of multilingualism and in compliance with the relevant resolutions addressing multilingualism and accessibility for persons with disabilities, by making every effort to translate materials currently available only in English and by providing offices and departments with technological solutions that comply with the principle of parity;

54. *Reaffirms its request* that the Secretary-General ensure, while maintaining an up-to-date and accurate website and social media, the equitable distribution of financial and human resources within the Department of Global Communications allocated to the United Nations website and social media among all six official languages, to ensure engagement, with full respect for the needs and specificities of all six languages;

55. *Notes with concern* that the multilingual development and enrichment of the United Nations website and social media accounts in certain official languages has improved at a much slower rate than expected, and in this regard requests the Department of Global Communications, in coordination with content-providing offices, to advance actions to achieve full parity among the six official languages on the United Nations website, in particular by expediting the filling of vacant posts in some sections;

56. *Requests* the Department of Global Communications, in cooperation with the Office of Information and Communications Technology, to continue its efforts to ensure that technological infrastructures and supportive applications fully support Latin, non-Latin and bidirectional scripts in order to enhance the equality of all official languages on the United Nations website;

57. *Recognizes* the language landing page of the domain un.org as one solution to enabling multilingualism in United Nations websites, and encourages the Secretary-General to continue to explore innovative solutions to enhance multilingual capabilities for Secretariat websites;

58. *Emphasizes* the importance for the Secretary-General to ensure that the Department of Global Communications guidelines on minimum standards for multilingualism, which serve as a guide for website developers and managers, ensure the full and equitable use of all the official languages of the United Nations in websites regardless of the domain;

59. *Welcomes* the mention of the language skills of the members of the senior leadership in some of the appointment notices issued by the Secretary-General under un.org, and encourages the Secretary-General to include them in those notices;

60. *Also welcomes* the cooperative arrangements undertaken by the Department of Global Communications with academic institutions to increase the number of web pages available in official and non-official languages, and requests the Secretary-General, in coordination with content-providing offices, to extend such cooperative arrangements to all the official languages of the United Nations, bearing in mind the necessity of adherence to United Nations standards and guidelines;

61. *Underlines* the importance, in the implementation of new communication tools, such as social networks, of taking into account the linguistic dimension in order to assure full parity among the official languages of the Organization;

62. *Acknowledges* the increasing importance of social media in order to reach the widest possible audience, and as such welcomes the growing popularity of the United Nations official social media accounts across all languages, and encourages the Department of Global Communications to strengthen multilingual diversity in social media activity;

IV
Documentation and conference services

63. *Reiterates its request* that the Secretary-General complete the task of uploading all important older United Nations documents to the United Nations website in all six official languages on a priority basis so that those archives are also made available to Member States through that medium;

64. *Requests* the Secretary-General to continue to ensure, through the provision of documentation services and meetings and publishing services under conference management, including high-quality translation and interpretation, effective multilingual communication equally in all the official languages of the United Nations among representatives of Member States in intergovernmental organs and among members of United Nations expert bodies;

65. *Notes* the use of innovative online language tools and translation technologies such as eLUNa that assist in making human translation more efficient and consistent, and the United Nations Terminology Database (UNTERM), and encourages the Secretariat to explore additional technologies for use by United Nations entities with appropriate quality controls;

66. *Underlines* that all the initiatives on leveraging technology, where applicable, including those introduced on a trial basis, shall comply with the principle of parity among the official languages of the Organization, with a view to preserving and enhancing the quality and scope of the services provided by the Secretariat, and encourages the Secretary-General to continue these efforts as a practical contribution to the achievement of the goals of multilingualism;

67. *Reiterates with concern its request* that the Secretary-General ensure that the rules concerning the simultaneous distribution of documents in all six official languages are strictly respected as regards both the distribution of printed copies and the posting of parliamentary documentation on the Official Document System and the United Nations website, in accordance with section III, paragraph 5, of its resolution 55/222 of 23 December 2000;

68. *Acknowledges* the implementation and observance of rule 55 of the rules of procedure of the General Assembly, which provides that, during the sessions of the Assembly, the *Journal of the United Nations* shall be published in the languages of the Assembly;

69. *Underlines* that all the initiatives on the evolution of the working methods, including those introduced on a trial basis, shall comply with the principle of parity among the official languages of the Organization, with a view to preserving or enhancing the quality and scope of the services provided by the Secretariat;

70. *Reiterates* that the satisfaction of Member States is a key performance indicator in conference management and conference services;

V
Human resources management and staff training

71. *Recalls* its resolution 77/278 of 18 April 2023, in particular paragraph 34 thereof, in which it reaffirmed the need to respect the equality of the two working languages of the Secretariat, reaffirmed the use of additional working languages in specific duty stations as mandated, and in that regard requested the Secretary-General to ensure that job openings specified the need for either of the working languages of the Secretariat, unless the functions of the post required a specific working language;

72. *Notes with satisfaction* the willingness of the Secretariat to encourage staff members, in meetings with interpretation services, to use any of the six official languages of which they have a command;

73. *Encourages* United Nations staff members to continue to actively use existing training facilities to acquire and enhance their proficiency in one or more of the official languages of the United Nations;

74. *Requests* the Secretary-General to continue the efforts to ensure that training opportunities in the six official languages are equally available to all staff and to continue the efforts to expand professional development opportunities provided to staff, including language training and training in the six official languages, to meet the workforce capacity needs of the Secretariat;

75. *Recalls* paragraph 11 of its resolution 71/263 of 23 December 2016, in which it acknowledged that the interaction of the United Nations with the local population in the field was essential and that language skills constituted an important element of the selection and training processes and therefore affirmed that a good command of the official language(s) spoken in the country of residence should be taken into account as an additional asset during those processes;

76. *Welcomes* the inclusion by the Secretary-General of a managerial indicator related to multilingualism in all his compacts with senior managers, including senior managers in the field, requiring that all workplans and, where applicable, mission plans and budgets integrate multilingualism and/or language considerations and that all parliamentary documentation be submitted by authoring entities for multilingual processing on time and within the established word limit;

77. *Stresses* that the employment of staff shall continue to be carried out in strict accordance with Article 101 of the Charter of the United Nations and in line with the relevant provisions of General Assembly resolutions;

78. *Notes with concern* that a number of recruitment handbooks developed by the Office of Human Resources of the Department of Management Strategy, Policy and Compliance of the Secretariat are available only in English, and encourages the Secretary-General to ensure that upcoming reviews and updates, in particular those of the applicant's manual, are published simultaneously in the working languages;

79. *Welcomes* the efforts of the Coordinator for Multilingualism to support the Office of Human Resources of the Department of Management Strategy, Policy and Compliance and the Human Resources Services Division of the Department of Operational Support of the Secretariat in reviewing how language skills are assessed in staff selection;

80. *Invites* the Secretary-General to take the appropriate measures to consider the linguistic specificities mentioned in job openings during the composition of interview panels for the employment of United Nations staff, notes the difficulty of constituting panels whose members are proficient in the additional language, and in that regard invites the Secretary-General to consider the possibility of addressing this issue in the medium term;

81. *Welcomes* the finalization of the United Nations Language Framework and its publication in the Secretary-General's bulletin entitled "United Nations Language Framework and levels of language competence",[267] which ensures greater consistency in language learning, teaching and assessment across the entire Secretariat and across all six United Nations official languages, and requests the Secretary-General to apply it accordingly;

82. *Recognizes* the key contribution of the Language and Communications Training Unit to promoting multilingualism within the United Nations, supporting the language needs of the Organization at Headquarters and in the field, in collaboration with other Secretariat entities, requests the Secretary-General to ensure full implementation of the existing mandate on linguistic training to continue the delivery of an offer adapted to the need of the United Nations, and also requests the Secretary-General to provide further information in this regard at the eightieth session of the General Assembly;

VI
Language services staff

83. *Recalls* its resolution 66/233 of 24 December 2011, in particular paragraph 7 of section III thereof, reiterates its request that the Secretary-General ensure that all language services are given equal treatment and are provided with equally favourable working conditions and resources, with a view to achieving maximum quality of

[267] ST/SGB/2023/2.

services, with full respect for the specificities of the six official languages, and in that regard recalls section D, paragraph 11, of its resolution 54/248 of 23 December 1999;

84. *Acknowledges* the measures taken by the Secretary-General, in accordance with its resolutions, to address the issue of the replacement of retiring staff in the language services, and requests the Secretary-General to maintain and to intensify those efforts, including through the strengthening of cooperation with institutions that train language specialists to meet the needs in the six official languages of the United Nations;

VII
Multilingualism across the three pillars of the United Nations

85. *Notes* the work of the Secretary-General in making available multilingual information, technical assistance and training materials related to the implementation of the 2030 Agenda for Sustainable Development,[268] and encourages the Secretary-General to continue his efforts in this regard;

86. *Stresses* the importance of proposing United Nations information, technical assistance and training materials, whenever possible, in the local languages of the beneficiary countries, including through locally based United Nations websites;

87. *Takes note* of the recommendations related to multilingualism contained in the report of the High-level Independent Panel on Peace Operations,[269] the subsequent report of the Secretary-General[270] and the report of the Advisory Group of Experts on the Review of the Peacebuilding Architecture;[271]

88. *Recalls* its resolution 75/281 of 24 May 2021, in which it endorsed the proposals, recommendations and conclusions of the Special Committee on Peacekeeping Operations;[272]

89. *Takes note* of the ongoing initiatives outlined in the report of the Secretary-General related to field operations, requests the Secretary-General to continue his ongoing efforts in this regard, and recalls its resolution 66/297 of 17 September 2012 without prejudice to Article 101 of the Charter;

90. *Urges* the Secretariat to translate all peacekeeping training documents into the six official languages of the United Nations, from within existing resources, to enable and facilitate their use by all Member States, troop-contributing countries and police-contributing countries, in particular, and by other involved institutions;

91. *Requests* the Secretary-General to submit to the General Assembly at its eightieth session a comprehensive report on the full implementation of its resolutions on multilingualism, including on the implementation of the United Nations Strategic Framework on Multilingualism and further follow-up on the topics of the current report of the Secretary-General;

92. *Decides* to include in the provisional agenda of its eightieth session the item entitled "Multilingualism".

RESOLUTION 78/331

Adopted at the 108th plenary meeting, on 6 September 2024, without a vote, on the basis of draft resolution A/78/L.109, sponsored by: Bangladesh, Brazil, Egypt, El Salvador, Guatemala, Indonesia, Malaysia, Morocco, Philippines, Thailand, Uruguay, Venezuela (Bolivarian Republic of)

78/331. United Nations action on sexual exploitation and abuse

The General Assembly,

Recalling the purposes and principles of the Charter of the United Nations and international law,

[268] Resolution 70/1.

[269] See A/70/95-S/2015/446.

[270] A/70/357-S/2015/682.

[271] See A/69/968-S/2015/490.

[272] *Official Records of the General Assembly, Seventy-fifth Session, Supplement No. 19* (A/75/19), chap. V.

Recalling also its resolutions 71/278 of 10 March 2017, 72/312 of 13 September 2018, 73/302 of 20 June 2019, 75/321 of 2 September 2021, 76/303 of 2 September 2022 and 77/333 of 25 August 2023 on United Nations action on sexual exploitation and abuse, 72/304 of 13 July 2018, 73/293 of 20 May 2019, 74/277 of 18 June 2020, 75/281 of 24 May 2021, 76/263 of 10 May 2022, 77/302 of 29 June 2023 and 78/291 of 28 June 2024 on the comprehensive review of the whole question of peacekeeping operations in all their aspects, resolution 71/297 of 30 June 2017 and section IV of resolution 76/274 of 29 June 2022 on special measures for protection from sexual exploitation and abuse and resolutions 72/112 of 7 December 2017, 73/196 of 20 December 2018, 74/181 of 18 December 2019, 75/132 of 15 December 2020, 76/106 of 9 December 2021, 77/98 of 7 December 2022 and 78/102 of 7 December 2023 on criminal accountability of United Nations officials and experts on mission, and taking note of Security Council resolutions 2242 (2015) of 13 October 2015 and 2272 (2016) of 11 March 2016,

Strongly condemning, and expressing deep concern about, sexual exploitation and abuse by United Nations personnel throughout the system, as well as by non-United Nations personnel serving under a mandate of the Security Council, and underscoring the commitment of Member States to strengthening measures to address sexual exploitation and abuse,

Acknowledging the work of all United Nations personnel throughout the United Nations system, including peacekeepers, who serve the purposes and principles of the Charter, and stressing that the actions of a few will not be allowed to tarnish the achievements of all,

Noting with concern that the coronavirus disease (COVID-19) pandemic exacerbated risks of sexual exploitation and abuse and affected the capacity to address and investigate allegations and provide victims with assistance, and further stressing that everyone should remain safe from sexual exploitation and abuse, including while receiving any kind of aid, assistance, protection or services from the United Nations system and its implementing partners, and noting the importance of ensuring that confidential reporting channels and support services are expeditious and accessible,

Welcoming the commitment by the United Nations to eradicate sexual exploitation and abuse,

1. *Reaffirms its commitment* to the zero-tolerance policy on sexual exploitation and abuse throughout the United Nations system, including the agencies, funds and programmes, and takes note of the report of the Secretary-General;[273]

2. *Notes with concern* that the COVID-19 pandemic exposed those in vulnerable situations to increased risks of sexual exploitation and abuse and limited the capacity of the Organization to provide victims and relevant Member States with assistance and to investigate allegations, urges the Secretary-General to continue to prioritize preventative action across the United Nations system, and calls upon the Secretary-General to remain actively engaged and, in collaboration with Member States, to scale up efforts to create a harmonized approach to preventing sexual exploitation and abuse throughout the United Nations system, including by enhancing the alignment of the policies and practices of the Organization;

3. *Reaffirms* that all categories of United Nations personnel must be held to the same standard of conduct so as to keep people safe from harm, while also preserving the credibility, impartiality, integrity and reputation of the United Nations, and remains committed to further consideration of ways of ensuring managerial, command and individual accountability;

4. *Stresses* the importance of Member States holding accountable those responsible for sexual exploitation and abuse, in a timely and appropriate manner, and that prevention and accountability are critical for the United Nations and its Member States to demonstrate their collective commitment to the zero-tolerance policy and for maintaining the trust of the international community and providing justice for victims, in this regard emphasizes that accountability rests on the cooperation of the Member States, and also emphasizes the need to enhance international cooperation in this regard;

5. *Reaffirms its support* to the United Nations for its efforts to implement the zero-tolerance policy, in particular to strengthen the Organization's prevention, reporting, enforcement and remedial actions in order to

[273] A/78/774.

promote greater accountability, and in this regard requests the Secretary-General to continue to work in close consultation with Member States for the effective implementation of the policy;

6. *Stresses* that enhanced accountability and transparency at all levels, including at the senior leadership level, both at Headquarters and in the field, contribute positively to combating sexual exploitation and abuse;

7. *Recognizes* that a culture of impunity could result in an increase in sexual exploitation and abuse, and in this regard underlines the necessity of immediate, safe and appropriate measures, including through investigations and prosecution where appropriate, and of reporting to the United Nations promptly on action taken;

8. *Underscores* that predeployment and in-mission training on the prevention of sexual exploitation and abuse plays an effective role in raising awareness about the United Nations zero-tolerance policy on such acts, and encourages relevant stakeholders, including Member States and the Secretariat, in accordance with their different responsibilities, to continue to collaborate to ensure that mandatory, effective, monitored and targeted training on sexual exploitation and abuse is implemented;

9. *Also underscores* that troop-contributing countries bear the responsibility for investigating, and troop- and police-contributing countries bear the responsibility for holding their personnel accountable for perpetrating, acts of sexual exploitation and abuse in accordance with their national laws, in this regard takes note of Security Council resolution 2272 (2016), and requests the Secretary-General to consult with Member States, as appropriate, in particular troop- and police-contributing countries, regarding the implementation of the Operational Guidance for the Implementation of Security Council Resolution 2272 (2016);

10. *Stresses* the importance of further improving the collaboration between the Secretary-General, United Nations system entities and Member States, including troop- and police-contributing countries, regarding preventing and responding to sexual exploitation and abuse to improve accountability and transparency and support for victims, and emphasizes the need to maintain a frequent exchange of information on all aspects related to sexual exploitation and abuse;

11. *Requests* the Secretary-General and all relevant entities to continue to immediately inform the Member States concerned about allegations of sexual exploitation and abuse by United Nations personnel system-wide, as well as by non-United Nations personnel serving under a Security Council mandate, of which United Nations entities may become aware, and requests the Secretary-General to ensure that the Member States concerned receive all available information to allow for appropriate follow-up by their national authorities;

12. *Pays tribute* to all peacekeepers who risk their lives while serving in United Nations peacekeeping operations, underscores that acts of sexual exploitation and abuse damage the credibility, effectiveness and reputation of the United Nations, in this regard commends the troop- and police-contributing countries that have taken effective steps to prevent and investigate acts of sexual exploitation and abuse, and combat impunity and hold accountable those individuals responsible for such acts, and highlights the importance of establishing best practices within the United Nations system;

13. *Calls upon* Member States deploying non-United Nations forces authorized under a Security Council mandate to take appropriate steps to investigate allegations of sexual exploitation and abuse and to hold perpetrators accountable, and urges all non-United Nations forces authorized under a Security Council mandate to take adequate measures to prevent, and combat impunity for, sexual exploitation and abuse by their personnel;

14. *Underscores* that victims of sexual exploitation and abuse should be at the core of the United Nations efforts, throughout the United Nations system, in implementing the zero-tolerance policy, in this regard highlights the importance of providing expeditious support to them and welcomes voluntary contributions to the trust fund in support of victims of sexual exploitation and abuse, encourages the Secretary-General to strengthen coordination across United Nations entities in order for victims to safely access immediate basic assistance and support in accordance with their individual needs, and also encourages the relevant authorities of non-United Nations personnel serving under a mandate of the Security Council to provide adequate and immediate assistance and support to victims of sexual exploitation and abuse committed by their personnel;

15. *Takes note* of the pilot mapping of victims' services, capacities and approaches completed in May 2020 by the Office of the Victims' Rights Advocate, through which it was noted in particular that there was no cohesive system-wide tool to track services and assistance received by victims, and requests the Secretary-General to analyse

shortcomings that were identified through the mapping exercise and present possible solutions to support and track victims' access to and utilization of services;

16. *Decides* to include in the provisional agenda of its seventy-ninth session the item entitled "Sexual exploitation and abuse: implementing a zero-tolerance policy", and requests the Secretary-General to continue to submit annual reports, pursuant to resolution 57/306 of 15 April 2003, on special measures for protection from sexual exploitation and abuse, including on progress made in implementing a zero-tolerance policy within the United Nations system, as well as on emerging best practices and lessons learned, for consideration by the General Assembly under the aforementioned item, in line with existing mandates and procedures.

II. Resolutions adopted on the reports of the Special Political and Decolonization Committee (Fourth Committee)

Contents

RESOLUTION 78/291

Adopted at the 95th plenary meeting, on 28 June 2024, without a vote, on the recommendation of the Committee (A/78/422/Add.1, para. 6)[1]

78/291. Comprehensive review of the whole question of peacekeeping operations in all their aspects

The General Assembly,

Recalling its resolution 2006 (XIX) of 18 February 1965 and all other relevant resolutions,

Recalling in particular its resolution 77/302 of 29 June 2023,

Affirming that the efforts of the United Nations in the peaceful settlement of disputes, including through its peacekeeping operations, are indispensable,

Convinced of the need for the United Nations to continue to improve its capabilities in the field of peacekeeping and to enhance the effective and efficient deployment of its peacekeeping operations,

Considering the contribution that all States Members of the United Nations make to peacekeeping,

Noting the widespread interest in contributing to the work of the Special Committee on Peacekeeping Operations expressed by Member States, in particular troop- and police-contributing countries,

Bearing in mind the continuous necessity of preserving the efficiency and strengthening the effectiveness of the work of the Special Committee,

1. *Welcomes* the report of the Special Committee on Peacekeeping Operations;[2]

2. *Endorses* the proposals, recommendations and conclusions of the Special Committee contained in chapter V of its report;

3. *Urges* Member States, the Secretariat and relevant organs of the United Nations to take all steps necessary to implement the proposals, recommendations and conclusions of the Special Committee;

4. *Reiterates* that those Member States that become personnel contributors to the United Nations peacekeeping operations in years to come or that participate in the future in the Special Committee for three consecutive years as observers shall, upon request in writing to the Chair of the Special Committee, become members at the following session of the Special Committee;

5. *Decides* that the Special Committee, in accordance with its mandate, shall continue its efforts for a comprehensive review of the whole question of peacekeeping operations in all their aspects and shall review the implementation of its previous proposals and consider any new proposals so as to enhance the capacity of the United Nations to fulfil its responsibilities in this field;

6. *Requests* the Special Committee to submit a report on its work to the General Assembly at its seventy-ninth session;

7. *Decides* to include in the provisional agenda of its seventy-ninth session the item entitled "Comprehensive review of the whole question of peacekeeping operations in all their aspects".

---

[1] The draft resolution recommended in the report was sponsored in the Committee by: Argentina, Canada, Egypt, Japan, Nigeria and Poland.

[2] *Official Records of the General Assembly, Seventy-eighth Session, Supplement No. 19* (A/78/19).

III. Resolutions adopted on the reports of the Fifth Committee*

Contents

* Unless otherwise stated, the draft resolutions recommended in the reports were submitted by the Chair or another officer of the Bureau of the Committee.

RESOLUTION 78/242 B

Adopted at the 95th plenary meeting, on 28 June 2024, without a vote, on the recommendation of the Committee (A/78/644/Add.1, para. 6)

78/242. Financial reports and audited financial statements, and reports of the Board of Auditors

B[1]

The General Assembly,

Recalling its resolutions 77/253 B of 30 June 2023 and 78/242 A of 22 December 2023,

Having considered the financial report and audited financial statements for the 12-month period from 1 July 2022 to 30 June 2023 and the report of the Board of Auditors on United Nations peacekeeping operations,[2] the report of the Secretary-General on the implementation of the recommendations of the Board of Auditors concerning United Nations peacekeeping operations for the financial period ended 30 June 2023[3] and the related report of the Advisory Committee on Administrative and Budgetary Questions,[4]

1. *Takes note* of the audit opinions and findings, and endorses the recommendations, contained in the report of the Board of Auditors;

2. *Endorses* the conclusions and recommendations contained in the report of the Advisory Committee on Administrative and Budgetary Questions;

3. *Commends* the Board of Auditors for the quality of its report and the streamlined format thereof, reaffirms that the findings presented annually by the Board of Auditors in its audit reports constitute an essential pillar of the Organization's oversight framework, and encourages the Board to continue focusing its efforts to ensure the transparency and accountability of administrative and financial matters in peacekeeping operations;

4. *Takes note* of the report of the Secretary-General on the implementation of the recommendations of the Board of Auditors concerning United Nations peacekeeping operations for the financial period ended 30 June 2023;

5. *Requests* the Secretary-General to ensure the full implementation of the recommendations of the Board of Auditors and the related recommendations of the Advisory Committee in a prompt and timely manner;

6. *Also requests* the Secretary-General to continue to indicate an expected time frame for the implementation of the recommendations of the Board of Auditors and the priorities for their implementation, including the office holders to be held accountable and measures taken in that regard;

7. *Further requests* the Secretary-General to provide, in his next report on the implementation of the recommendations of the Board of Auditors concerning United Nations peacekeeping operations, a full explanation for the delays in the implementation of all outstanding recommendations of the Board, the root causes of the recurring issues and the measures to be taken.

RESOLUTION 78/250 B

Adopted at the 95th plenary meeting, on 28 June 2024, without a vote, on the recommendation of the Committee (A/78/647/Add.1, para. 6)

[1] Resolution 78/242, in section VI of the *Official Records of the General Assembly, Seventy-eighth Session, Supplement No. 49* (A/78/49), vol. I, becomes resolution 78/242 A.

[2] *Official Records of the General Assembly, Seventy-eighth Session, Supplement No. 5*, vol. II (A/78/5 (Vol. II)).

[3] A/78/773.

[4] A/78/804.

78/250. Financing of the United Nations Multidimensional Integrated Stabilization Mission in Mali

B[5]

The General Assembly,

Having considered the reports of the Secretary-General on the financing of the United Nations Multidimensional Integrated Stabilization Mission in Mali[6] and the related reports of the Advisory Committee on Administrative and Budgetary Questions,[7]

Recalling Security Council resolution 2100 (2013) of 25 April 2013, by which the Council established the United Nations Multidimensional Integrated Stabilization Mission in Mali, and the subsequent resolutions by which the Council extended the mandate of the Mission, the latest of which was resolution 2690 (2023) of 30 June 2023, by which the Council decided to terminate as of 30 June 2023 the mandate of the Mission under resolution 2640 (2022) of 29 June 2022,

Recalling also its resolution 67/286 of 28 June 2013 on the financing of the Mission and its subsequent resolutions thereon, the latest of which was resolution 78/250 A of 22 December 2023,

Reaffirming the general principles underlying the financing of United Nations peacekeeping operations, as stated in its resolutions 1874 (S-IV) of 27 June 1963, 3101 (XXVIII) of 11 December 1973 and 55/235 of 23 December 2000,

1. *Takes note* of the status of contributions to the United Nations Multidimensional Integrated Stabilization Mission in Mali as at 30 April 2024, including the contributions outstanding in the amount of 374.9 million United States dollars, representing some 3.3 per cent of the total assessed contributions, notes with concern that only 85 Member States have paid their assessed contributions in full, and urges all other Member States, in particular those in arrears, to ensure payment of their outstanding assessed contributions;

2. *Expresses its appreciation* to those Member States that have paid their assessed contributions in full, and urges all other Member States to make every possible effort to ensure payment of their assessed contributions to the Mission in full;

3. *Expresses concern* at the financial situation with regard to peacekeeping activities, in particular as regards the reimbursements to troop contributors that bear additional burdens owing to overdue payments by Member States of their assessments;

4. *Emphasizes* that all future and existing peacekeeping missions shall be given equal and non-discriminatory treatment in respect of financial and administrative arrangements;

5. *Also emphasizes* that all peacekeeping missions shall be provided with adequate resources for the effective and efficient discharge of their respective mandates;

6. *Requests* the Secretary-General to ensure that proposed peacekeeping budgets are based on the relevant legislative mandates;

7. *Endorses* the conclusions and recommendations contained in the reports of the Advisory Committee on Administrative and Budgetary Questions, subject to the provisions of the present resolution, and requests the Secretary-General to ensure their full implementation;

8. *Recalls* paragraph 15 of the report of the Advisory Committee,[8] and requests the Secretary-General to continue to coordinate with the Transition Government of Mali to ensure that United Nations-owned and contingent-owned equipment and Mission camps are not diverted from their intended recipients;

[5] Resolution 78/250, in section VI of the *Official Records of the General Assembly, Seventy-eighth Session, Supplement No. 49* (A/78/49), vol. I, becomes resolution 78/250 A.

[6] A/78/635, A/78/761 and A/78/763.

[7] A/78/744/Add.11 and A/78/821.

[8] A/78/821.

9. *Stresses* the importance of appropriate disposition of Mission assets during drawdown, withdrawal and liquidation according to the Financial Regulations and Rules of the United Nations;

10. *Recalls* paragraph 23 of the report of the Advisory Committee,[9] recognizes the request of the Transition Government of Mali to complete the liquidation process from Gao and Bamako by 31 December 2024, and requests the Secretary-General to continue to work closely with the host country and, as appropriate, other Governments of the region to work towards withdrawal and liquidation in the field in that time frame;

11. *Also recalls* paragraph 26 of the report of the Advisory Committee,[10] and encourages the Mission to continue to assist national staff in their transition to future professional careers outside the Mission, in full compliance with the staff regulations and rules;

12. *Reaffirms* the importance of clean-up and remediation activities, and requests the Secretary-General to include information on these activities in the context of the next report;

13. *Notes* the collective efforts in implementing the drawdown and withdrawal of the Mission, and requests the Secretary-General to make efforts to ensure the safety and security of the remaining United Nations peacekeepers and personnel;

Budget performance report for the period from 1 July 2022 to 30 June 2023

14. *Takes note* of the report of the Secretary-General on the budget performance of the Mission for the period from 1 July 2022 to 30 June 2023;[11]

Donation of assets of the United Nations Multidimensional Integrated Stabilization Mission in Mali

15. *Takes note* of the report of the Secretary-General on the donation of assets of the Mission;[12]

16. *Approves* the donation of assets of the Mission, with an acquisition cost of 94,735,900 dollars and a net book value of 42,497,800 dollars, to the Transition Government of Mali;

Budget estimates for the period from 1 July 2024 to 30 June 2025

17. *Decides* to appropriate to the special account for the United Nations Multidimensional Integrated Stabilization Mission in Mali the amount of 222,115,500 dollars for the period from 1 July 2024 to 30 June 2025, inclusive of 202,783,500 dollars for the maintenance of the Mission, 14,735,600 dollars for the support account for peacekeeping operations, 2,572,100 dollars for the United Nations Logistics Base at Brindisi, Italy, and 2,024,300 dollars for the Regional Service Centre in Entebbe, Uganda;

Financing of the appropriation for the period from 1 July 2024 to 30 June 2025

18. *Decides* to apportion among Member States the amount of 111,057,800 dollars for the period from 1 July to 31 December 2024 in accordance with the levels updated in its resolution 76/239 of 24 December 2021, taking into account the scale of assessments for 2024, as set out in its resolution 76/238 of 24 December 2021;

19. *Also decides* that, in accordance with the provisions of its resolution 973 (X) of 15 December 1955, there shall be set off against the apportionment among Member States, as provided for in paragraph 18 above, their respective share in the Tax Equalization Fund of 4,719,000 dollars, comprising the estimated staff assessment income of 3,881,400 dollars approved for the Mission, the prorated share of 600,600 dollars of the estimated staff assessment income approved for the support account, the prorated share of 117,300 dollars of the estimated staff assessment income approved for the United Nations Logistics Base and the prorated share of 119,700 dollars of the estimated staff assessment income approved for the Regional Service Centre;

[9] Ibid.

[10] A/78/744/Add.11.

[11] A/78/635.

[12] A/78/763.

20. *Further decides* to apportion among Member States the amount of 111,057,700 dollars for the period from 1 January to 30 June 2025, in accordance with the scale of assessments for 2025 and the updated levels;[13]

21. *Decides* that, in accordance with the provisions of its resolution 973 (X), there shall be set off against the apportionment among Member States, as provided for in paragraph 20 above, their respective share in the Tax Equalization Fund of 4,719,000 dollars, comprising the estimated staff assessment income of 3,881,400 dollars approved for the Mission, the prorated share of 600,600 dollars of the estimated staff assessment income approved for the support account, the prorated share of 117,300 dollars of the estimated staff assessment income approved for the United Nations Logistics Base and the prorated share of 119,700 dollars of the estimated staff assessment income approved for the Regional Service Centre;

22. *Also decides* that, for Member States that have fulfilled their financial obligations to the Mission, there shall be set off against the apportionment, as provided for in paragraphs 18 and 20 above, their respective share of the unencumbered balance and other revenue in the amount of 109,285,600 dollars in respect of the financial period ended 30 June 2023, in accordance with the levels updated in its resolution 76/239, taking into account the scale of assessments for 2023, as set out in its resolution 76/238;

23. *Further decides* that, for Member States that have not fulfilled their financial obligations to the Mission, there shall be set off against their outstanding obligations their respective share of the unencumbered balance and other revenue in the amount of 109,285,600 dollars in respect of the financial period ended 30 June 2023, in accordance with the scheme set out in paragraph 22 above;

24. *Decides* that the decrease of 418,000 dollars in the estimated staff assessment income in respect of the financial period ended 30 June 2023 shall be set off against the credits in the amount of 109,285,600 dollars referred to in paragraphs 22 and 23 above;

25. *Encourages* the Secretary-General to continue to take additional measures to ensure the safety and security of all personnel participating in the Mission under the auspices of the United Nations, bearing in mind paragraphs 5 and 6 of Security Council resolution 1502 (2003) of 26 August 2003;

26. *Invites* voluntary contributions to the Mission in cash and in the form of services and supplies acceptable to the Secretary-General, to be administered, as appropriate, in accordance with the procedure and practices established by the General Assembly;

27. *Decides* to include in the provisional agenda of its seventy-ninth session the item entitled "Financing of the United Nations Multidimensional Integrated Stabilization Mission in Mali".

RESOLUTION 78/273

Adopted at the 73rd plenary meeting, on 24 April 2024, by a recorded vote of 80 to 12, with 37 abstentions,* on the recommendation of the Committee (A/78/662/Add.1, para. 15)[14]

* *In favour:* Albania, Andorra, Argentina, Australia, Austria, Belgium, Bosnia and Herzegovina, Brazil, Bulgaria, Canada, Chile, Colombia, Costa Rica, Côte d'Ivoire, Croatia, Cyprus, Czechia, Denmark, Dominican Republic, El Salvador, Estonia, Finland, France, Georgia, Germany, Greece, Guatemala, Guyana, Haiti, Honduras, Hungary, Iceland, Ireland, Israel, Italy, Jamaica, Japan, Kuwait, Latvia, Liechtenstein, Lithuania, Luxembourg, Malta, Marshall Islands, Mauritius, Mexico, Micronesia (Federated States of), Monaco, Montenegro, Mozambique, Myanmar, Netherlands (Kingdom of the), New Zealand, North Macedonia, Norway, Panama, Papua New Guinea, Paraguay, Peru, Poland, Portugal, Qatar, Republic of Korea, Republic of Moldova, Romania, San Marino, Singapore, Slovakia, Slovenia, Spain, Suriname, Sweden, Switzerland, Thailand, Türkiye, Ukraine, United Kingdom of Great Britain and Northern Ireland, United States of America, Uruguay, Viet Nam

Against: China, Cuba, Democratic People's Republic of Korea, Eritrea, Iran (Islamic Republic of), Lao People's Democratic Republic, Mali, Nicaragua, Russian Federation, Sudan, Syrian Arab Republic, Zimbabwe

Abstaining: Algeria, Angola, Antigua and Barbuda, Bahrain, Bangladesh, Brunei Darussalam, Congo, Egypt, Ghana, Guinea, India, Indonesia, Iraq, Jordan, Kenya, Lesotho, Malaysia, Mongolia, Morocco, Nepal, Nigeria, Oman, Pakistan, Philippines, Saint Kitts and Nevis, Saint Lucia, Saudi Arabia, Senegal, South Africa, South Sudan, Sri Lanka, Togo, Trinidad and Tobago, Tunisia, Uganda, United Arab Emirates, Yemen

[13] To be adopted by the General Assembly.

[14] The draft resolution recommended in the report was sponsored in the Committee by Albania.

78/273. Revised estimates relating to the Independent Institution on Missing Persons in the Syrian Arab Republic

The General Assembly,

Having considered the report of the Secretary-General[15] and the related report of the Advisory Committee on Administrative and Budgetary Questions,[16]

1. *Takes note* of the report of the Secretary-General;

2. *Endorses* the conclusions and recommendations contained in the report of the Advisory Committee on Administrative and Budgetary Questions, subject to the provisions of the present resolution;

3. *Takes note* of paragraph 10 of the report of the Advisory Committee;

4. *Approves* the establishment of 28 posts (1 Assistant Secretary-General, 1 D-1, 3 P-5, 7 P-4, 9 P-3, 4 P-2, 1 General Service (Principal level) and 2 General Service (Other level)) for the Independent Institution on Missing Persons in the Syrian Arab Republic, under section 24, Human rights, of the programme budget for 2024;

5. *Appropriates* an additional amount of 2,991,700 United States dollars, comprising 24,500 dollars under section 2, General Assembly and Economic and Social Council affairs and conference management, and 2,967,200 dollars under section 24, Human rights, of the programme budget for 2024;

6. *Also appropriates* an amount of 278,600 dollars under section 36, Staff assessment, of the programme budget for 2024, to be offset by an equivalent amount under income section 1, Income from staff assessment.

RESOLUTION 78/274

Adopted at the 73rd plenary meeting, on 24 April 2024, without a vote, on the recommendation of the Committee (A/78/662/Add.1, para. 15)

78/274. Revised estimates relating to the programme budget for 2024 under section 3, Political affairs, and section 36, Staff assessment: special political missions – thematic cluster III: regional offices, offices in support of political processes and other missions – United Nations Integrated Transition Assistance Mission in the Sudan

The General Assembly,

Having considered the report of the Secretary-General[17] and the related report of the Advisory Committee on Administrative and Budgetary Questions,[18]

1. *Takes note* of the report of the Secretary-General;

2. *Endorses* the conclusions and recommendations contained in the report of the Advisory Committee on Administrative and Budgetary Questions;

3. *Approves* resources in the amount of 22,162,600 United States dollars for the transition and liquidation of the United Nations Integrated Transition Assistance Mission in the Sudan, which would supersede the commitment authority in the amount of 21,500,000 dollars approved, with assessment, by the General Assembly in section XVII, paragraph 4, of its resolution 78/253 of 22 December 2023 and paragraph 2 of its resolution 78/254 C of 22 December 2023;

4. *Appropriates* an additional amount of 22,162,600 dollars under section 3, Political affairs, of the programme budget for 2024;

---

[15] A/78/706.

[16] A/78/7/Add.43.

[17] A/78/6 (Sect. 3)/Add.8.

[18] A/78/7/Add.44.

5. *Also appropriates* an additional amount of 1,021,400 dollars under section 36, Staff assessment, to be offset by an equivalent amount under income section 1, Income from staff assessment, of the programme budget for 2024.

RESOLUTION 78/275

Adopted at the 73rd plenary meeting, on 24 April 2024, without a vote, on the recommendation of the Committee (A/78/825, para. 7)

78/275. Amendments to the Staff Regulations and Rules

The General Assembly,

Recalling Articles 8, 97 and 100 of the Charter of the United Nations,

Recalling also Article 101 of the Charter, which governs the appointment, employment and recruitment of staff,

Recalling further its resolutions 42/220 A of 21 December 1987, 49/222 A of 23 December 1994, 49/222 B of 20 July 1995, 51/226 of 3 April 1997, 52/219 of 22 December 1997, 53/221 of 7 April 1999, 55/258 of 14 June 2001, 57/305 of 15 April 2003, 59/266 of 23 December 2004, 59/287 of 13 April 2005, 60/1 of 16 September 2005, 60/238 of 23 December 2005, 60/254 of 8 May 2006, 60/260 of 8 May 2006, 61/244 of 22 December 2006, 62/247 of 3 April 2008, 63/250 of 24 December 2008, 65/247 of 24 December 2010, 66/234 of 24 December 2011, 67/255 of 12 April 2013, 68/252 of 27 December 2013, 68/265 of 9 April 2014, 70/244 of 23 December 2015, 71/263 of 23 December 2016 and 77/278 of 18 April 2023 as well as its other relevant resolutions and decisions,

Having considered the report of the Secretary-General[19] and the related report of the Advisory Committee on Administrative and Budgetary Questions,[20]

1. *Reaffirms* that the staff of the United Nations is an invaluable asset of the Organization, and commends its contribution to furthering the purposes and principles of the United Nations;

2. *Pays tribute* to the memory of all staff members who have lost their lives in the service of the Organization;

3. *Endorses* the conclusions and recommendations contained in the report of the Advisory Committee on Administrative and Budgetary Questions;

4. *Recalls* paragraph 15 of the report of the Advisory Committee, and accordingly decides not to approve the proposed amendments to the Staff Regulations and directs that the provisional staff rules be withdrawn in accordance with regulation 12.3;

5. *Directs* that provisional amendments to rule 3.3 be withdrawn;

6. *Reaffirms* that the Fifth Committee is the appropriate Main Committee of the General Assembly entrusted with responsibilities for administrative and budgetary matters, and carrying out a thorough analysis and approving human and financial resources and policies, with a view to ensuring full, effective and efficient implementation of all mandated programmes and activities and the implementation of policies, and also reaffirms that any changes to staff regulations and rules must be presented to the General Assembly for consideration;

7. *Recalls* paragraph 8 of the report of the Advisory Committee, and requests the Secretary-General to ensure that revisions to the Staff Regulations and Rules consistently respect the established hierarchy of norms of the United Nations, whereby the function of the Staff Regulations is to set broad policy and principles established in the Charter of the United Nations and by the General Assembly, while the Staff Rules should be uniform in the degree of detail provided so as to enable the operational provisions of the Regulations.

[19] A/78/177.

[20] A/78/671.

RESOLUTION 78/276

Adopted at the 73rd plenary meeting, on 24 April 2024, without a vote, on the recommendation of the Committee (A/78/826, para. 6)

78/276. Joint Inspection Unit

The General Assembly,

Recalling its previous resolutions on the Joint Inspection Unit, in particular resolutions 31/192 of 22 December 1976, 50/233 of 7 June 1996, 54/16 of 29 October 1999, 56/245 of 24 December 2001, 57/284 A and B of 20 December 2002, 58/286 of 8 April 2004, 59/267 of 23 December 2004, 60/258 of 8 May 2006, 61/238 of 22 December 2006, 61/260 of 4 April 2007, 62/226 of 22 December 2007, 62/246 of 3 April 2008, 63/272 of 7 April 2009, 64/262 of 29 March 2010, 65/270 of 4 April 2011, 66/259 of 9 April 2012, 67/256 of 12 April 2013, 68/266 of 9 April 2014, 69/275 of 2 April 2015, 70/257 of 1 April 2016, 71/281 of 6 April 2017, 72/269 of 4 April 2018, 73/287 of 15 April 2018, 75/270 of 16 April 2021, 76/261 of 13 April 2022 and 77/279 of 18 April 2023,

Reaffirming the statute of the Unit[21] and the unique role of the Unit as the only external and independent system-wide inspection, evaluation and investigation body,

Having considered the report of the Unit for 2023 and programme of work for 2024[22] and the note by the Secretary-General on the report of the Unit for 2023,[23]

1. *Takes note with appreciation* of the report of the Joint Inspection Unit for 2023 and programme of work for 2024;

2. *Takes note* of the note by the Secretary-General on the report of the Unit for 2023;

3. *Stresses* the importance of the oversight functions of the Unit in identifying concrete managerial, administrative and programming questions within the participating organizations and providing the General Assembly and other legislative organs of participating organizations with practical and action-oriented recommendations to improve and strengthen the governance of the United Nations as a whole;

4. *Recognizes* that the effectiveness of the Unit system-wide is a shared responsibility of the Unit, the Member States and the secretariats of the participating organizations;

5. *Also recognizes* the need to continue to enhance the impact of the Unit on the management efficiency and transparency of the participating organizations within the United Nations system;

6. *Welcomes* the coordination of the Unit with the Board of Auditors and the Office of Internal Oversight Services of the Secretariat, and encourages those bodies to continue to share experiences, knowledge, best practices and lessons learned with other United Nations audit and oversight bodies, as well as with the Independent Audit Advisory Committee, with a view to avoiding overlap or duplication and achieving further synergy, cooperation, effectiveness and efficiency, without prejudice to the respective mandates of the audit and oversight bodies;

7. *Underscores* the unique role of the Unit as an external and independent system-wide inspection, evaluation and investigation body, and stresses the important contribution that its recommendations make towards improving the efficient and effective performance of the United Nations system;

8. *Reaffirms* the independence of the Unit as set out in article 7 of its statute, and stresses that budget estimates are to be prepared in a transparent and consistent manner for submission to the General Assembly in accordance with article 20 of the statute of the Unit;

9. *Encourages* the Unit to continue to identify projects which support a more effective United Nations that is capable of providing relevant single and system-wide solutions to current and future challenges, and underscores that all participating organizations should adhere to the commencement and review procedures outlined by the Unit;

---

[21] Resolution 31/192, annex.

[22] *Official Records of the General Assembly, Seventy-eighth Session, Supplement No. 34* (A/78/34).

[23] A/78/731.

10. *Reiterates its request* to the executive heads of the participating organizations to fully comply with the statutory procedures for consideration of the reports of the Unit and, in particular, to submit their comments, including information on what they intend to do regarding the recommendations of the Unit, to distribute reports in time for their consideration by legislative organs and to provide information on the steps to be taken to implement those recommendations accepted by the legislative organs and the executive heads of participating organizations;

11. *Reiterates its request* to the Secretary-General and the other executive heads of the participating organizations to fully assist the Unit with the timely provision of all information requested by it;

12. *Invites* the legislative bodies of participating organizations to effectively and substantially use the reports of the Unit, and to give unselective and due consideration to its recommendations, in accordance with article 11, paragraph 4, of the statute of the Unit, and regularly review the status of acceptance and implementation of the recommendations of the Unit in an effort to make best use of its recommendations;

13. *Recalls* paragraph 15 of its resolution 77/279 and notes with concern the continuation of significantly different rates of acceptance and implementation of recommendations from the Unit by some participating United Nations system organizations, and therefore requests the Unit to continue to examine and improve the status quo without damaging the strength of recommendations;

14. *Also recalls* paragraph 16 of its resolution 77/279 and invites participating organizations within the United Nations system to regularly review the status of acceptance and implementation of the recommendations of the Unit, especially those related to system-wide coordination and coherence, and invites participating organizations to report non-acceptance and non-implementation to the Unit;

15. *Further recalls* paragraph 18 of its resolution 77/279 and reiterates its strong encouragement to the Unit to strengthen the review of long-term effectiveness of its implemented recommendations, and looks forward to the update to the General Assembly thereon during the comprehensive midpoint assessment in 2024 and during its future comprehensive midpoint assessments;

16. *Recognizes* the efforts made by the Unit to strengthen its outreach and improve its communications products with a view to highlighting the work of the Unit and enhance its engagement with participating organizations and Member States, and encourages the Unit to continue such efforts;

17. *Invites* the executive heads of participating United Nations system organizations to implement accepted recommendations of the Unit in a timely manner;

18. *Recalls* paragraph 19 of its resolution 77/279, and looks forward to a further update on the implementation of the accepted recommendations from the Unit's self-assessment, including updates on the action plan, in the context of the next report of the Unit.

RESOLUTION 78/292

Adopted at the 95th plenary meeting, on 28 June 2024, without a vote, on the recommendation of the Committee (A/78/825/Add.1, para. 6)

78/292. Seconded active-duty military and police personnel

The General Assembly,

Recalling its resolutions 67/287 of 28 June 2013, 68/252 of 27 December 2013, 71/263 of 23 December 2016, 74/254 A of 27 December 2019, 74/254 B of 6 August 2020 and 75/292 of 30 June 2021 as well as its decision 78/542 C of 24 April 2024,

Having considered the report of the Secretary-General on seconded active-duty military and police personnel[24] and the related report of the Advisory Committee on Administrative and Budgetary Questions,[25]

[24] A/78/602.

[25] A/78/762.

1. *Takes note* of the report of the Secretary-General;

2. *Endorses* the conclusions and recommendations contained in the report of the Advisory Committee on Administrative and Budgetary Questions, subject to the provisions of the present resolution;

3. *Recognizes* the importance of the roles carried out and the expertise provided by seconded active-duty military and police personnel in fulfilling United Nations mandates, and requests the Secretary-General to continue to actively engage in the efforts to improve their timely onboarding, using the various tools at his disposal to address challenges beyond the control of the selected active-duty military and police personnel and which prevent their timely onboarding;

4. *Requests* the Secretary General to continue his efforts to engage with Member States to identify the best way to address duplication of remuneration or benefits, including through bilateral agreements;

5. *Recognizes* the challenges in the implementation of the staff regulations and rules with respect to seconded active-duty military and police personnel, and invites the Secretary-General to consider options for additional measures to ensure the impartiality and mitigate conflicts of interest of seconded active-duty military and police personnel in accordance with regulation 1.2 (m);

6. *Takes note* of paragraph 32 of the report of the Advisory Committee, and decides to authorize the Secretary-General to extend the exceptional measures regarding seconded active-duty military and police personnel until 1 July 2027, and requests the Secretary-General to report to the General Assembly at its eighty-first session on viable options to resolve the conflict between the Staff Regulations and Rules of the United Nations and the national legislation or practices of some Member States with respect to their active-duty military and police personnel seconded to the Secretariat;

7. *Requests* the Secretary-General to consider placing the selected active-duty military and police personnel who cannot report to duty promptly owing to onboarding challenges beyond their control against similar positions at the same duty station once the challenges are addressed or, on an exceptional and temporary basis and without setting a precedent, at an alternative duty station.

RESOLUTION 78/293

Adopted at the 95th plenary meeting, on 28 June 2024, without a vote, on the recommendation of the Committee (A/78/920, para. 13)

78/293. Support account for peacekeeping operations

The General Assembly,

Recalling its resolutions 45/258 of 3 May 1991, 47/218 A of 23 December 1992, 48/226 A of 23 December 1993, 48/226 C of 29 July 1994, 49/250 of 20 July 1995, 50/221 B of 7 June 1996, section I of its resolution 55/238 of 23 December 2000, its resolutions 55/271 of 14 June 2001, 56/241 of 24 December 2001, 56/293 of 27 June 2002, 57/318 of 18 June 2003, 58/298 of 18 June 2004, 59/301 of 22 June 2005, 60/268 of 30 June 2006, 61/279 of 29 June 2007, 62/250 of 20 June 2008, 63/287 of 30 June 2009, 64/271 of 24 June 2010, 65/290 of 30 June 2011, 66/265 of 21 June 2012, 67/287 of 28 June 2013, 68/283 of 30 June 2014, 69/308 of 25 June 2015, 70/287 of 17 June 2016, 71/295 of 30 June 2017, 72/288 of 5 July 2018, 73/308 of 3 July 2019, 74/280 of 30 June 2020, 75/293 of 30 June 2021, 76/279 of 29 June 2022, 77/304 of 30 June 2023 and its other relevant resolutions, as well as its decisions 49/469 of 23 December 1994, 50/473 of 23 December 1995, 72/558 of 5 July 2018, 73/555 of 3 July 2019 and 74/571 of 3 September 2020,

Having considered the reports of the Secretary-General on the budget performance of the support account for peacekeeping operations for the period from 1 July 2022 to 30 June 2023[26] and on the budget for the support account for peacekeeping operations for the period from 1 July 2024 to 30 June 2025,[27] the report of the Independent Audit Advisory Committee on the proposed budget of the Office of Internal Oversight Services under the support account

[26] A/78/638.

[27] A/78/746.

for peacekeeping operations for the period from 1 July 2024 to 30 June 2025[28] and the related report of the Advisory Committee on Administrative and Budgetary Questions,[29]

Recognizing the importance of the United Nations being able to respond and deploy rapidly to a peacekeeping operation upon the adoption of a relevant resolution of the Security Council, within 30 days for traditional peacekeeping operations and 90 days for complex peacekeeping operations,

Recognizing also the need for adequate support during all phases of peacekeeping operations, including the liquidation and termination phases,

Mindful that the level of the support account should broadly correspond to the mandate, number, size and complexity of peacekeeping missions,

1. *Takes note* of the report of the Secretary-General on the budget for the support account for peacekeeping operations for the period from 1 July 2024 to 30 June 2025 and the report of the Independent Audit Advisory Committee on the proposed budget of the Office of Internal Oversight Services under the support account for peacekeeping operations for the period from 1 July 2024 to 30 June 2025;

2. *Reaffirms* its role in carrying out a thorough analysis and approval of human and financial resources and policies with a view to ensuring the full, effective and efficient implementation of all mandated programmes and activities and the implementation of policies in this regard;

3. *Also reaffirms* that the Fifth Committee is the appropriate Main Committee of the General Assembly entrusted with responsibility for administrative and budgetary matters;

4. *Further reaffirms* rule 153 of its rules of procedure;

5. *Reaffirms* that the support account funds shall be used for the sole purpose of financing human resources and non-human resources requirements for backstopping and supporting peacekeeping operations at Headquarters, and that any changes in this limitation require the prior approval of the General Assembly;

6. *Also reaffirms* the need for adequate funding for the backstopping of peacekeeping operations, as well as the need for full justification for that funding in support account budget submissions;

7. *Further reaffirms* the need for effective and efficient administration and financial management of peacekeeping operations, and urges the Secretary-General to continue to identify measures to increase the productivity and efficiency of the support account;

8. *Requests* the Secretary-General to ensure the full implementation of the relevant provisions of its resolutions 59/296 of 22 June 2005, 60/266 of 30 June 2006, 61/276 of 29 June 2007, 64/269 of 24 June 2010, 65/289 of 30 June 2011, 66/264 of 21 June 2012, 69/307 of 25 June 2015, 70/286 of 17 June 2016 and 76/274 of 29 June 2022, and its other relevant resolutions;

9. *Endorses* the conclusions and recommendations contained in the report of the Advisory Committee on Administrative and Budgetary Questions, and requests the Secretary-General to ensure their full implementation;

10. *Decides* to maintain, for the financial period from 1 July 2024 to 30 June 2025, the funding mechanism for the support account used in the current period, from 1 July 2023 to 30 June 2024, as approved in paragraph 3 of its resolution 50/221 B;

Budget performance report for the period from 1 July 2022 to 30 June 2023

11. *Takes note* of the report of the Secretary-General on the budget performance of the support account for peacekeeping operations for the period from 1 July 2022 to 30 June 2023;

---

[28] A/78/788.

[29] A/78/820.

Budget estimates for the financial period from 1 July 2024 to 30 June 2025

12. *Approves* the support account requirements in the amount of 384,229,600 United States dollars for the financial period from 1 July 2024 to 30 June 2025, inclusive of the amount of 18,318,600 dollars under enterprise resource planning, 518,400 dollars for death and disability claims for closed peacekeeping operations, 868,500 dollars for the efficiency model for management services (previously the global service delivery model project), 3,326,800 dollars for peacekeeping capability readiness, 19,493,600 dollars for Umoja maintenance and support costs and 13,332,200 dollars for after-service health insurance costs, including 1,336 continuing posts and 2 new temporary posts, as well as the abolishment, redeployment, reassignment and reclassification of posts, 75 continuing and 4 new general temporary assistance positions and 52 person-months, as well as related post and non-post requirements;

Financing of the support account for peacekeeping operations for the financial periods from 1 July 2022 to 30 June 2023 and from 1 July 2024 to 30 June 2025

13. *Decides* that the requirements for the support account for peacekeeping operations for the financial period from 1 July 2024 to 30 June 2025 shall be financed as follows:

(a) The unencumbered balance in the amount of 3,234,100 dollars, in respect of the financial period from 1 July 2022 to 30 June 2023, to be applied to the resources required for the financial period from 1 July 2024 to 30 June 2025;

(b) The total amount of 6,117,400 dollars, comprising investment revenue of 4,065,200 dollars, other miscellaneous revenue of 269,000 dollars and cancellation of prior-period obligations of 1,783,200 dollars in respect of the period from 1 July 2022 to 30 June 2023, to be applied to the resources required for the financial period from 1 July 2024 to 30 June 2025;

(c) The amount of 4,839,200 dollars, representing the excess of the authorized level of the Peacekeeping Reserve Fund in respect of the financial period ended 30 June 2023, to be applied to the resources required for the financial period from 1 July 2024 to 30 June 2025;

(d) The balance of 370,038,900 dollars to be prorated among the budgets of the active peacekeeping operations for the financial period from 1 July 2024 to 30 June 2025;

(e) The net estimated staff assessment income of 30,163,300 dollars, comprising the amount of 29,083,900 dollars for the financial period from 1 July 2024 to 30 June 2025 and the increase of 1,079,400 dollars in respect of the financial period ended 30 June 2023, to be offset against the balance referred to in subparagraph (d) above, to be prorated among the budgets of the individual active peacekeeping operations.

RESOLUTION 78/294

Adopted at the 95th plenary meeting, on 28 June 2024, without a vote, on the recommendation of the Committee (A/78/920, para. 13)

78/294. Financing of the Regional Service Centre in Entebbe, Uganda

The General Assembly,

Recalling its resolutions 69/307 of 25 June 2015 concerning the financing of the Regional Service Centre in Entebbe, Uganda, and its subsequent resolutions thereon, the latest of which was resolution 77/306 of 30 June 2023,

Having considered the reports of the Secretary-General on the financing of the Regional Service Centre[30] and the related report of the Advisory Committee on Administrative and Budgetary Questions,[31]

1. *Reaffirms* its resolutions 57/290 B of 18 June 2003, 59/296 of 22 June 2005, 60/266 of 30 June 2006, 61/276 of 29 June 2007, 64/269 of 24 June 2010, 65/289 of 30 June 2011, 66/264 of 21 June 2012, 69/307, 70/286 of

[30] A/78/601 and A/78/722.

[31] A/78/744/Add.6.

17 June 2016 and 76/274 of 29 June 2022, and requests the Secretary-General to ensure the full implementation of their relevant provisions;

2. *Takes note* of the reports of the Secretary-General;

3. *Endorses* the conclusions and recommendations contained in the report of the Advisory Committee on Administrative and Budgetary Questions, subject to the provisions of the present resolution, and requests the Secretary-General to ensure their full implementation;

4. *Acknowledges* the support of the Government of Uganda in facilitating the work of the United Nations at the Regional Service Centre in Entebbe, Uganda;

5. *Decides* to establish two posts of Planning Officer (P-4) earmarked for seconded active-duty military officers for the Department of Peace Operations;

Budget performance report for the period from 1 July 2022 to 30 June 2023

6. *Takes note* of the report of the Secretary-General on the budget performance of the Regional Service Centre for the period from 1 July 2022 to 30 June 2023;[32]

Budget estimates for the period from 1 July 2024 to 30 June 2025

7. *Approves* the amount of 48,004,100 United States dollars for the maintenance of the Regional Service Centre for the period from 1 July 2024 to 30 June 2025;

Financing of the budget estimates for the period from 1 July 2024 to 30 June 2025

8. *Decides* that the requirements for the Regional Service Centre for the period from 1 July 2024 to 30 June 2025 shall be financed as follows:

(a) The unencumbered balance and other revenue in the amount of 1,914,700 dollars in respect of the financial period ended 30 June 2023, to be applied against the resources required for the period from 1 July 2024 to 30 June 2025;

(b) The amount of 43,790,600 dollars, to be prorated among the budgets of the active client peacekeeping operations for the period from 1 July 2024 to 30 June 2025;

(c) The amount of 2,298,800 dollars, with respect to the share of client special political missions, to be funded under section 3, Political affairs, as may be approved by the General Assembly in the context of the proposed programme budget for 2025;

(d) The estimated staff assessment income of 5,179,100 dollars, comprising the amount of 4,823,500 dollars for the period from 1 July 2024 to 30 June 2025 and the increase of 355,600 dollars in respect of the period from 1 July 2022 to 30 June 2023, to be offset against the balance referred to in subparagraph (b) above, to be prorated among the budgets of the individual active client peacekeeping operations;

9. *Also decides* to consider at its seventy-ninth session the question of the financing of the Regional Service Centre.

RESOLUTION 78/295

Adopted at the 95th plenary meeting, on 28 June 2024, without a vote, on the recommendation of the Committee (A/78/920, para. 13)

[32] A/78/601.

78/295. Financing of the United Nations Logistics Base at Brindisi, Italy

The General Assembly,

Recalling section XIV of its resolution 49/233 A of 23 December 1994 and its resolution 62/231 of 22 December 2007,

Recalling also its decision 50/500 of 17 September 1996 on the financing of the United Nations Logistics Base at Brindisi, Italy, and its subsequent resolutions thereon, the latest of which was resolution 77/305 of 30 June 2023,

Recalling further its resolution 56/292 of 27 June 2002 concerning the establishment of the strategic deployment stocks and its subsequent resolutions on the status of the implementation of the strategic deployment stocks, the latest of which was resolution 77/305,

Having considered the reports of the Secretary-General on the financing of the United Nations Logistics Base[33] and the related report of the Advisory Committee on Administrative and Budgetary Questions,[34]

Reiterating the importance of establishing an accurate inventory of assets,

1. *Notes with appreciation* the facilities provided by the Government of Italy to the United Nations Logistics Base at Brindisi, Italy, and by the Government of Spain to the secondary active telecommunications facility in Valencia, Spain;

2. *Endorses* the conclusions and recommendations contained in the report of the Advisory Committee on Administrative and Budgetary Questions, and requests the Secretary-General to ensure their full implementation;

3. *Requests* the Secretary-General to ensure the full implementation of the relevant provisions of its resolutions 59/296 of 22 June 2005, 60/266 of 30 June 2006, 61/276 of 29 June 2007, 64/269 of 24 June 2010, 65/289 of 30 June 2011, 66/264 of 21 June 2012, 69/307 of 25 June 2015, 70/286 of 17 June 2016 and 76/274 of 29 June 2022, as well as other relevant resolutions;

Budget performance report for the period from 1 July 2022 to 30 June 2023

4. *Takes note* of the report of the Secretary-General on the budget performance of the United Nations Logistics Base for the period from 1 July 2022 to 30 June 2023;[35]

Budget estimates for the period from 1 July 2024 to 30 June 2025

5. *Approves* the cost estimates for the United Nations Logistics Base amounting to 67,935,300 United States dollars for the period from 1 July 2024 to 30 June 2025;

Financing of the budget estimates for the period from 1 July 2024 to 30 June 2025

6. *Decides* that the requirements for the United Nations Logistics Base for the period from 1 July 2024 to 30 June 2025 shall be financed as follows:

(a) The unencumbered balance and other revenue in the amount of 3,346,100 dollars in respect of the financial period ended 30 June 2023, to be applied against the resources required for the period from 1 July 2024 to 30 June 2025;

(b) The balance of 64,589,200 dollars, to be prorated among the budgets of the active peacekeeping operations for the period from 1 July 2024 to 30 June 2025;

(c) The estimated staff assessment income of 5,890,000 dollars, comprising the amount of 6,569,300 dollars for the period from 1 July 2024 to 30 June 2025 and the decrease of 679,300 dollars in respect of the period from 1 July 2022 to 30 June 2023, to be offset against the balance referred to in subparagraph (b) above, to be prorated among the budgets of the individual active peacekeeping operations;

---

[33] A/78/613 and A/78/735.

[34] A/78/744/Add.5.

[35] A/78/613.

7. *Also decides* to consider at its seventy-ninth session the question of the financing of the United Nations Logistics Base.

RESOLUTION 78/296

Adopted at the 95th plenary meeting, on 28 June 2024, without a vote, on the recommendation of the Committee (A/78/920, para. 13)

78/296. Closed peacekeeping missions

The General Assembly,

Recalling its resolution 76/280 of 29 June 2022,

Having considered the report of the Secretary-General on the updated financial position of closed peacekeeping missions as at 30 June 2023[36] and the related report of the Advisory Committee on Administrative and Budgetary Questions,[37]

1. *Takes note* of the report of the Secretary-General;

2. *Endorses* the conclusions and recommendations contained in the report of the Advisory Committee on Administrative and Budgetary Questions.

RESOLUTION 78/297

Adopted at the 95th plenary meeting, on 28 June 2024, without a vote, on the recommendation of the Committee (A/78/921, para. 6)

78/297. Financing of the United Nations Interim Security Force for Abyei

The General Assembly,

Having considered the reports of the Secretary-General on the financing of the United Nations Interim Security Force for Abyei[38] and the related report of the Advisory Committee on Administrative and Budgetary Questions,[39]

Recalling Security Council resolution 1990 (2011) of 27 June 2011, by which the Council established the United Nations Interim Security Force for Abyei for a period of six months, and the subsequent resolutions by which the Council extended the mandate of the Force, the latest of which was resolution 2708 (2023) of 14 November 2023, by which the Council extended until 15 November 2024 the mandate of the Force as set out in paragraph 2 of resolution 1990 (2011) and the mandate modification set forth in resolution 2024 (2011) of 14 December 2011 and paragraph 1 of resolution 2075 (2012) of 16 November 2012,

Recalling also its resolution 66/241 A of 24 December 2011 on the financing of the Force and its subsequent resolutions thereon, the latest of which was resolution 77/290 B of 30 June 2023,

Reaffirming the general principles underlying the financing of United Nations peacekeeping operations, as stated in its resolutions 1874 (S-IV) of 27 June 1963, 3101 (XXVIII) of 11 December 1973 and 55/235 of 23 December 2000,

Mindful of the fact that it is essential to provide the Force with the financial resources necessary to enable it to fulfil its responsibilities under the relevant resolutions of the Security Council,

1. *Requests* the Secretary General to entrust the Head of Mission with the task of formulating future budget proposals in full accordance with the provisions of its resolutions 59/296 of 22 June 2005, 60/266 of 30 June 2006,

---

[36] A/78/689 and A/78/689/Corr.1.

[37] A/78/791.

[38] A/78/597 and A/78/737.

[39] A/78/744/Add.4.

61/276 of 29 June 2007, 64/269 of 24 June 2010, 65/289 of 30 June 2011, 66/264 of 21 June 2012, 69/307 of 25 June 2015, 70/286 of 17 June 2016 and 76/274 of 29 June 2022, as well as other relevant resolutions;

2. *Takes note* of the status of contributions to the United Nations Interim Security Force for Abyei as at 30 April 2024, including the contributions outstanding in the amount of 75.1 million United States dollars, representing some 2 per cent of the total assessed contributions, notes with concern that only 105 Member States have paid their assessed contributions in full, and urges all other Member States, in particular those in arrears, to ensure payment of their outstanding assessed contributions;

3. *Expresses its appreciation* to those Member States that have paid their assessed contributions in full, and urges all other Member States to make every possible effort to ensure payment of their assessed contributions to the Force in full;

4. *Expresses concern* at the financial situation with regard to peacekeeping activities, in particular as regards the reimbursements to troop contributors that bear additional burdens owing to overdue payments by Member States of their assessments;

5. *Emphasizes* that all future and existing peacekeeping missions shall be given equal and non-discriminatory treatment in respect of financial and administrative arrangements;

6. *Also emphasizes* that all peacekeeping missions shall be provided with adequate resources for the effective and efficient discharge of their respective mandates;

7. *Requests* the Secretary-General to ensure that proposed peacekeeping budgets are based on the relevant legislative mandates;

8. *Endorses* the conclusions and recommendations contained in the report of the Advisory Committee on Administrative and Budgetary Questions, subject to the provisions of the present resolution, and requests the Secretary-General to ensure their full implementation;

9. *Requests* the Secretary-General to make greater efforts to reduce the environmental footprint of the Force, especially in the context of the accommodation of contingents and the management of waste generated as a result;

10. *Also requests* the Secretary-General to ensure the full implementation of the relevant provisions of its resolutions 59/296, 60/266, 61/276, 64/269, 65/289, 66/264, 69/307, 70/286 and 76/274;

11. *Further requests* the Secretary-General to take all action necessary to ensure that the Force is administered with a maximum of efficiency and economy;

Budget performance report for the period from 1 July 2022 to 30 June 2023

12. *Takes note* of the report of the Secretary-General on the budget performance of the Force for the period from 1 July 2022 to 30 June 2023;[40]

Budget estimates for the period from 1 July 2024 to 30 June 2025

13. *Decides* to appropriate to the special account for the United Nations Interim Security Force for Abyei the amount of 326,164,100 dollars for the period from 1 July 2024 to 30 June 2025, inclusive of 297,776,200 dollars for the maintenance of the Force, 21,638,400 dollars for the support account for peacekeeping operations, 3,776,900 dollars for the United Nations Logistics Base at Brindisi, Italy, and 2,972,600 dollars for the Regional Service Centre in Entebbe, Uganda;

Financing of the appropriation for the period from 1 July 2024 to 30 June 2025

14. *Decides* to apportion among Member States the amount of 122,311,500 dollars for the period from 1 July to 15 November 2024, in accordance with the levels updated in its resolution 76/239 of 24 December 2021, taking into account the scale of assessments for 2024, as set out in its resolution 76/238 of 24 December 2021;

[40] A/78/597.

15. *Also decides* that, in accordance with the provisions of its resolution 973 (X) of 15 December 1955, there shall be set off against the apportionment among Member States, as provided for in paragraph 14 above, their respective share in the Tax Equalization Fund of 2,566,300 dollars, comprising the estimated staff assessment income of 1,643,900 dollars approved for the Force, the prorated share of 661,400 dollars of the estimated staff assessment income approved for the support account, the prorated share of 129,200 dollars of the estimated staff assessment income approved for the United Nations Logistics Base and the prorated share of 131,800 dollars of the estimated staff assessment income approved for the Regional Service Centre;

16. *Further decides* to apportion among Member States the amount of 40,770,500 dollars for the period from 16 November to 31 December 2024, at a monthly rate of 27,180,342 dollars, in accordance with the levels updated in its resolution 76/239, taking into account the scale of assessments for 2024, as set out in its resolution 76/238, subject to a decision of the Security Council to extend the mandate of the Force;

17. *Decides* that, in accordance with the provisions of its resolution 973 (X), there shall be set off against the apportionment among Member States, as provided for in paragraph 16 above, their respective share in the Tax Equalization Fund of 855,400 dollars, comprising the estimated staff assessment income of 547,900 dollars approved for the Force, the prorated share of 220,500 dollars of the estimated staff assessment income approved for the support account, the prorated share of 43,000 dollars of the estimated staff assessment income approved for the United Nations Logistics Base and the prorated share of 44,000 dollars of the estimated staff assessment income approved for the Regional Service Centre;

18. *Also decides* to apportion among Member States the amount of 163,082,100 dollars for the period from 1 January to 30 June 2025, at a monthly rate of 27,180,342 dollars, in accordance with the scale of assessments for 2025 and the updated levels,[41] subject to a decision of the Security Council to extend the mandate of the Force;

19. *Further decides* that, in accordance with the provisions of its resolution 973 (X), there shall be set off against the apportionment among Member States, as provided for in paragraph 18 above, their respective share in the Tax Equalization Fund of 3,421,700 dollars, comprising the estimated staff assessment income of 2,191,800 dollars approved for the Force, the prorated share of 881,900 dollars of the estimated staff assessment income approved for the support account, the prorated share of 172,200 dollars of the estimated staff assessment income approved for the United Nations Logistics Base and the prorated share of 175,800 dollars of the estimated staff assessment income approved for the Regional Service Centre;

20. *Decides* that, for Member States that have fulfilled their financial obligations to the Force, there shall be set off against the apportionment, as provided for in paragraphs 14, 16 and 18 above, their respective share of the unencumbered balance and other revenue in the amount of 6,770,700 dollars in respect of the financial period ended 30 June 2023, in accordance with the levels updated in its resolution 76/239, taking into account the scale of assessments for 2023, as set out in its resolution 76/238;

21. *Also decides* that, for Member States that have not fulfilled their financial obligations to the Force, there shall be set off against their outstanding obligations their respective share of the unencumbered balance and other revenue in the total amount of 6,770,700 dollars in respect of the financial period ended 30 June 2023, in accordance with the scheme set out in paragraph 20 above;

22. *Further decides* that the increase of 365,900 dollars in the estimated staff assessment income in respect of the financial period ended 30 June 2023 shall be added to the credits in the amount of 6,770,700 dollars referred to in paragraphs 20 and 21 above;

23. *Encourages* the Secretary-General to continue to take additional measures to ensure the safety and security of all personnel participating in the Force under the auspices of the United Nations, bearing in mind paragraphs 5 and 6 of Security Council resolution 1502 (2003) of 26 August 2003;

24. *Invites* voluntary contributions to the Force in cash and in the form of services and supplies acceptable to the Secretary-General, to be administered, as appropriate, in accordance with the procedure and practices established by the General Assembly;

[41] To be adopted by the General Assembly.

25. *Decides* to include in the provisional agenda of its seventy-ninth session the item entitled "Financing of the United Nations Interim Security Force for Abyei".

RESOLUTION 78/298

Adopted at the 95th plenary meeting, on 28 June 2024, without a vote, on the recommendation of the Committee (A/78/922, para. 6)

78/298. Financing of the United Nations Multidimensional Integrated Stabilization Mission in the Central African Republic

The General Assembly,

Having considered the reports of the Secretary-General on the financing of the United Nations Multidimensional Integrated Stabilization Mission in the Central African Republic[42] and the related report of the Advisory Committee on Administrative and Budgetary Questions,[43]

Recalling Security Council resolution 2149 (2014) of 10 April 2014, by which the Council established the United Nations Multidimensional Integrated Stabilization Mission in the Central African Republic as from 10 April 2014 for an initial period until 30 April 2015, and the subsequent resolutions by which the Council extended the mandate of the Mission, the latest of which was resolution 2709 (2023) of 14 November 2023, by which the Council extended the mandate of the Mission until 15 November 2024,

Recalling also its resolution 68/299 of 30 June 2014 on the financing of the Mission and its subsequent resolutions thereon, the latest of which was resolution 77/307 of 30 June 2023,

Reaffirming the general principles underlying the financing of United Nations peacekeeping operations, as stated in its resolutions 1874 (S-IV) of 27 June 1963, 3101 (XXVIII) of 11 December 1973 and 55/235 of 23 December 2000,

Mindful of the fact that it is essential to provide the Mission with the financial resources necessary to enable it to fulfil its responsibilities under the relevant resolutions of the Security Council,

1. *Requests* the Secretary-General to entrust the Head of Mission with the task of formulating future budget proposals in full accordance with the provisions of its resolutions 59/296 of 22 June 2005, 60/266 of 30 June 2006, 61/276 of 29 June 2007, 64/269 of 24 June 2010, 65/289 of 30 June 2011, 66/264 of 21 June 2012, 69/307 of 25 June 2015, 70/286 of 17 June 2016 and 76/274 of 29 June 2022, as well as other relevant resolutions;

2. *Takes note* of the status of contributions to the United Nations Multidimensional Integrated Stabilization Mission in the Central African Republic as at 30 April 2024, including the contributions outstanding in the amount of 398.2 million United States dollars, representing some 4.0 per cent of the total assessed contributions, notes with concern that only 104 Member States have paid their assessed contributions in full, and urges all other Member States, in particular those in arrears, to ensure payment of their outstanding assessed contributions;

3. *Expresses its appreciation* to those Member States that have paid their assessed contributions in full, and urges all other Member States to make every possible effort to ensure payment of their assessed contributions to the Mission in full;

4. *Expresses concern* at the financial situation with regard to peacekeeping activities, in particular as regards the reimbursements to troop contributors that bear additional burdens owing to overdue payments by Member States of their assessments;

5. *Emphasizes* that all future and existing peacekeeping missions shall be given equal and non-discriminatory treatment in respect of financial and administrative arrangements;

---

[42] A/78/631 and A/78/760.

[43] A/78/744/Add.10.

6. *Also emphasizes* that all peacekeeping missions shall be provided with adequate resources for the effective and efficient discharge of their respective mandates;

7. *Requests* the Secretary-General to ensure that proposed peacekeeping budgets are based on the relevant legislative mandates;

8. *Endorses* the conclusions and recommendations contained in the report of the Advisory Committee on Administrative and Budgetary Questions, subject to the provisions of the present resolution, and requests the Secretary-General to ensure their full implementation;

9. *Decides* to further reduce the budget by $24,700,000 due to the Mission's inability to use unmanned aerial systems assets;

10. *Notes* the challenges with fuel delivery, which affected operations and led to a significant financial loss, emphasizes the need to improve the management and procurement of fuel, and requests the Secretary-General to report on the measures taken to assess the financial health of vendors in the next report;

11. *Recalls* paragraph 13 of the report of the Advisory Committee, notes the upcoming elections to be held, and requests the Mission to continue to assist the Central African Republic authorities with the preparation for elections and coordinate with the relevant agencies, funds and programmes as well as Headquarters regarding international electoral assistance, within the parameters of its mandate and resources;

12. *Notes* the difference in the number of international and national posts in the Mission, and requests the Secretary-General to consider options for greater nationalization of functions as appropriate when formulating budget submissions, in accordance with relevant General Assembly resolutions and commensurate with mission mandates, and requirements where applicable, and increase outreach activities in order to address the difficulties in onboarding of national staff;

13. *Requests* the Secretary-General to ensure the full implementation of the relevant provisions of its resolutions 59/296, 60/266, 61/276, 64/269, 65/289, 66/264, 69/307, 70/286 and 76/274;

14. *Also requests* the Secretary-General to take all action necessary to ensure that the Mission is administered with a maximum of efficiency and economy;

Budget performance report for the period from 1 July 2022 to 30 June 2023

15. *Takes note* of the report of the Secretary-General on the budget performance of the Mission for the period from 1 July 2022 to 30 June 2023;[44]

Budget estimates for the period from 1 July 2024 to 30 June 2025

16. *Decides* to appropriate to the special account for the United Nations Multidimensional Integrated Stabilization Mission in the Central African Republic the amount of 1,283,314,000 dollars for the period from 1 July 2024 to 30 June 2025, inclusive of 1,171,619,700 dollars for the maintenance of the Mission, 85,137,700 dollars for the support account for peacekeeping operations, 14,860,500 dollars for the United Nations Logistics Base at Brindisi, Italy, and 11,696,100 dollars for the Regional Service Centre in Entebbe, Uganda;

Financing of the appropriation for the period from 1 July 2024 to 30 June 2025

17. *Decides* to apportion among Member States the amount of 481,242,700 dollars for the period from 1 July to 15 November 2024, in accordance with the levels updated in its resolution 76/239 of 24 December 2021, taking into account the scale of assessments for 2024, as set out in its resolution 76/238 of 24 December 2021;

18. *Also decides* that, in accordance with the provisions of its resolution 973 (X) of 15 December 1955, there shall be set off against the apportionment among Member States, as provided for in paragraph 17 above, their respective share in the Tax Equalization Fund of 10,468,400 dollars, comprising the estimated staff assessment income of 6,839,000 dollars approved for the Mission, the prorated share of 2,602,400 dollars of the estimated staff assessment income approved for the support account, the prorated share of 508,200 dollars of the estimated staff assessment

[44] A/78/631.

income approved for the United Nations Logistics Base and the prorated share of 518,800 dollars of the estimated staff assessment income approved for the Regional Service Centre;

19. *Further decides* to apportion among Member States the amount of 160,414,300 dollars for the period from 16 November to 31 December 2024, at a monthly rate of 106,942,800 dollars, in accordance with the levels updated in its resolution 76/239, taking into account the scale of assessments for 2024, as set out in its resolution 76/238, subject to a decision of the Security Council to extend the mandate of the Mission;

20. *Decides* that, in accordance with the provisions of its resolution 973 (X), there shall be set off against the apportionment among Member States, as provided for in paragraph 19 above, their respective share in the Tax Equalization Fund of 3,489,500 dollars, comprising the estimated staff assessment income of 2,279,700 dollars approved for the Mission, the prorated share of 867,500 dollars of the estimated staff assessment income approved for the support account, the prorated share of 169,400 dollars of the estimated staff assessment income approved for the United Nations Logistics Base and the prorated share of 172,900 dollars of the estimated staff assessment income approved for the Regional Service Centre;

21. *Also decides* to apportion among Member States the amount of 641,657,000 dollars for the period from 1 January to 30 June 2025, at a monthly rate of 106,942,800 dollars, in accordance with the scale of assessments for 2025 and the updated levels,[45] subject to a decision of the Security Council to extend the mandate of the Mission;

22. *Further decides* that, in accordance with the provisions of its resolution 973 (X), there shall be set off against the apportionment among Member States, as provided for in paragraph 21 above, their respective share in the Tax Equalization Fund of 13,958,000 dollars, comprising the estimated staff assessment income of 9,118,800 dollars approved for the Mission, the prorated share of 3,470,000 dollars of the estimated staff assessment income approved for the support account, the prorated share of 677,600 dollars of the estimated staff assessment income approved for the United Nations Logistics Base and the prorated share of 691,600 dollars of the estimated staff assessment income approved for the Regional Service Centre;

23. *Decides* that, for Member States that have fulfilled their financial obligations to the Mission, there shall be set off against the apportionment, as provided for in paragraphs 17, 19 and 21 above, their respective share of the unencumbered balance and other revenue in the amount of 35,229,600 dollars in respect of the financial period ended 30 June 2023, in accordance with the levels updated in its resolution 76/239, taking into account the scale of assessments for 2023, as set out in its resolution 76/238;

24. *Also decides* that, for Member States that have not fulfilled their financial obligations to the Mission, there shall be set off against their outstanding obligations their respective share of the unencumbered balance and other revenue in the amount of 35,229,600 dollars, in respect of the financial period ended 30 June 2023, in accordance with the scheme set out in paragraph 23 above;

25. *Further decides* that the increase of 1,597,800 dollars in the estimated staff assessment income in respect of the financial period ended 30 June 2023 shall be added to the credits in the amount of 35,229,600 dollars referred to in paragraphs 23 and 24 above;

26. *Encourages* the Secretary-General to continue to take additional measures to ensure the safety and security of all personnel participating in the Mission under the auspices of the United Nations, bearing in mind paragraphs 5 and 6 of Security Council resolution 1502 (2003) of 26 August 2003;

27. *Invites* voluntary contributions to the Mission in cash and in the form of services and supplies acceptable to the Secretary-General, to be administered, as appropriate, in accordance with the procedure and practices established by the General Assembly;

28. *Decides* to include in the provisional agenda of its seventy-ninth session the item entitled "Financing of the United Nations Multidimensional Integrated Stabilization Mission in the Central African Republic".

[45] To be adopted by the General Assembly.

RESOLUTION 78/299

Adopted at the 95th plenary meeting, on 28 June 2024, without a vote, on the recommendation of the Committee (A/78/923, para. 6)

78/299. Financing of the United Nations Operation in Côte d'Ivoire

The General Assembly,

Having considered the report of the Secretary-General on the final performance of the United Nations Operation in Côte d'Ivoire[46] and the related report of the Advisory Committee on Administrative and Budgetary Questions,[47]

1. *Takes note* of the status of contributions to the United Nations Operation in Côte d'Ivoire as at 30 April 2024, including the contributions outstanding in the amount of 0.4 million United States dollars, representing some 0.01 per cent of the total assessed contributions, notes with concern that only 188 Member States have paid their assessed contributions in full, and urges all other Member States, in particular those in arrears, to ensure payment of their outstanding assessed contributions;

2. *Endorses* the conclusions and recommendations contained in the report of the Advisory Committee on Administrative and Budgetary Questions, subject to the provisions of the present resolution, and requests the Secretary-General to ensure their full implementation;

3. *Takes note* of the report of the Secretary-General on the final performance of the United Nations Operation in Côte d'Ivoire and the updated information on the net cash available in the special account for the United Nations Operation in Côte d'Ivoire in the amount of 6,481,000 dollars as at 30 April 2024;

4. *Takes note* of paragraph 9 of the report of the Advisory Committee;

5. *Decides* that Member States that have fulfilled their financial obligations to the Operation shall be credited with their respective share of the net cash available in the special account for the Operation in the amount of 6,481,000 dollars as at 30 April 2024, in accordance with the levels updated in its resolution 70/246 of 23 December 2015, taking into account the scale of assessments for 2017, as set out in its resolution 70/245 of 23 December 2015;

6. *Encourages* Member States that are owed credits referred to in paragraph 5 above to apply those credits to any accounts where they have outstanding assessed contributions;

7. *Urges* all Member States to make every possible effort to ensure payment of their assessed contributions in full;

8. *Decides* that, for Member States that have not fulfilled their financial obligations to the Operation, their respective share of the net cash available in the special account for the Operation in the amount of 6,481,000 dollars as at 30 April 2024 shall be set off against their outstanding obligations, in accordance with the scheme set out in paragraph 5 above;

9. *Also decides* that updated information on the financial position of the Operation shall be included in the report on the updated position of closed peacekeeping missions, to be considered by the General Assembly at its seventy-ninth session under the agenda item entitled "Administrative and budgetary aspects of the financing of the United Nations peacekeeping operations";

10. *Further decides* to delete from its agenda the item entitled "Financing of the United Nations Operation in Côte d'Ivoire".

RESOLUTION 78/300

Adopted at the 95th plenary meeting, on 28 June 2024, without a vote, on the recommendation of the Committee (A/78/924, para. 6)

[46] A/74/711.

[47] A/74/785.

78/300. Financing of the United Nations Peacekeeping Force in Cyprus

The General Assembly,

Having considered the reports of the Secretary-General on the financing of the United Nations Peacekeeping Force in Cyprus[48] and the related report of the Advisory Committee on Administrative and Budgetary Questions,[49]

Recalling Security Council resolution 186 (1964) of 4 March 1964 regarding the establishment of the United Nations Peacekeeping Force in Cyprus and the subsequent resolutions by which the Council extended the mandate of the Force, the latest of which was resolution 2723 (2024) of 30 January 2024, by which the Council extended the mandate of the Force until 31 January 2025,

Recalling also its resolution 47/236 of 14 September 1993 on the financing of the Force and its subsequent resolutions and decisions thereon, the latest of which was resolution 77/308 of 30 June 2023,

Reaffirming the general principles underlying the financing of United Nations peacekeeping operations, as stated in its resolutions 1874 (S-IV) of 27 June 1963, 3101 (XXVIII) of 11 December 1973 and 55/235 of 23 December 2000,

Noting with appreciation that voluntary contributions have been made to the Force by certain Governments,

Noting that voluntary contributions were insufficient to cover all the costs of the Force, including those incurred by troop-contributing Governments prior to 16 June 1993, and regretting the absence of an adequate response to appeals for voluntary contributions, including that contained in the letter dated 17 May 1994 from the Secretary-General to all Member States,[50]

Mindful of the fact that it is essential to provide the Force with the financial resources necessary to enable it to fulfil its responsibilities under the relevant resolutions of the Security Council,

1. *Requests* the Secretary-General to entrust the Head of Mission with the task of formulating future budget proposals in full accordance with the provisions of its resolutions 59/296 of 22 June 2005, 60/266 of 30 June 2006, 61/276 of 29 June 2007, 64/269 of 24 June 2010, 65/289 of 30 June 2011, 66/264 of 21 June 2012, 69/307 of 25 June 2015, 70/286 of 17 June 2016 and 76/274 of 29 June 2022, as well as other relevant resolutions;

2. *Takes note* of the status of contributions to the United Nations Peacekeeping Force in Cyprus as at 30 April 2024, including the contributions outstanding in the amount of 19 million United States dollars, representing some 2.3 per cent of the total assessed contributions, notes with concern that only 100 Member States have paid their assessed contributions in full, and urges all other Member States, in particular those in arrears, to ensure payment of their outstanding assessed contributions;

3. *Expresses its appreciation* to those Member States that have paid their assessed contributions in full, and urges all other Member States to make every possible effort to ensure payment of their assessed contributions to the Force in full;

4. *Expresses concern* at the financial situation with regard to peacekeeping activities, in particular as regards the reimbursements to troop contributors that bear additional burdens owing to overdue payments by Member States of their assessments;

5. *Emphasizes* that all future and existing peacekeeping missions shall be given equal and non-discriminatory treatment in respect of financial and administrative arrangements;

6. *Also emphasizes* that all peacekeeping missions shall be provided with adequate resources for the effective and efficient discharge of their respective mandates;

7. *Requests* the Secretary-General to ensure that proposed peacekeeping budgets are based on the relevant legislative mandates;

---

[48] A/78/592 and A/78/719.

[49] A/78/744/Add.2.

[50] S/1994/647.

8. *Endorses* the conclusions and recommendations contained in the report of the Advisory Committee on Administrative and Budgetary Questions, and requests the Secretary-General to ensure their full implementation;

9. *Requests* the Secretary-General to ensure the full implementation of the relevant provisions of its resolutions 59/296, 60/266, 61/276, 64/269, 65/289, 66/264, 69/307, 70/286 and 76/274;

10. *Also requests* the Secretary-General to take all action necessary to ensure that the Force is administered with a maximum of efficiency and economy;

Budget performance report for the period from 1 July 2022 to 30 June 2023

11. *Takes note* of the report of the Secretary-General on the budget performance of the Force for the period from 1 July 2022 to 30 June 2023;[51]

Budget estimates for the period from 1 July 2024 to 30 June 2025

12. *Decides* to appropriate to the special account for the United Nations Peacekeeping Force in Cyprus the amount of 61,252,900 dollars for the period from 1 July 2024 to 30 June 2025, inclusive of 56,436,100 dollars for the maintenance of the Force, 4,101,000 dollars for the support account for peacekeeping operations and 715,800 dollars for the United Nations Logistics Base at Brindisi, Italy;

Financing of the appropriation for the period from 1 July 2024 to 30 June 2025

13. *Notes with appreciation* that a one-third share of the net appropriation, equivalent to 19,429,967 dollars, will be funded through voluntary contributions from the Government of Cyprus and the amount of 6.5 million dollars from the Government of Greece;

14. *Decides* to apportion among Member States the amount of 17,661,466 dollars for the period from 1 July to 31 December 2024, in accordance with the levels updated in its resolution 76/239 of 24 December 2021, taking into account the scale of assessments for 2024, as set out in its resolution 76/238 of 24 December 2021;

15. *Also decides* that, in accordance with the provisions of its resolution 973 (X) of 15 December 1955, there shall be set off against the apportionment among Member States, as provided for in paragraph 14 above, their respective share in the Tax Equalization Fund of 1,481,500 dollars, comprising the estimated staff assessment income of 1,281,700 dollars approved for the Force, the prorated share of 167,150 dollars of the estimated staff assessment income approved for the support account and the prorated share of 32,650 dollars of the estimated staff assessment income approved for the United Nations Logistics Base;

16. *Further decides* to apportion among Member States the amount of 2,943,578 dollars for the period from 1 to 31 January 2025, in accordance with the scale of assessments for 2025 and the updated levels;[52]

17. *Decides* that, in accordance with the provisions of its resolution 973 (X) of 15 December 1955, there shall be set off against the apportionment among Member States, as provided for in paragraph 16 above, their respective share in the Tax Equalization Fund of 246,917 dollars, comprising the estimated staff assessment income of 213,617 dollars approved for the Force, the prorated share of 27,858 dollars of the estimated staff assessment income approved for the support account and the prorated share of 5,442 dollars of the estimated staff assessment income approved for the United Nations Logistics Base;

18. *Also decides* to apportion among Member States the amount of 14,717,889 dollars for the period from 1 February to 30 June 2025, at a monthly rate of 2,943,578 dollars, in accordance with the scale of assessments for 2025 and the updated levels, subject to a decision of the Security Council to extend the mandate of the Force;

19. *Further decides* that, in accordance with the provisions of its resolution 973 (X), there shall be set off against the apportionment among Member States, as provided for in paragraph 18 above, their respective share in the Tax Equalization Fund of 1,234,583 dollars, comprising the estimated staff assessment income of 1,068,083 dollars approved for the Force, the prorated share of 139,292 dollars of the estimated staff assessment income approved for

[51] A/78/592.

[52] To be adopted by the General Assembly.

the support account and the prorated share of 27,208 dollars of the estimated staff assessment income approved for the United Nations Logistics Base;

20. *Decides* that, for Member States that have fulfilled their financial obligations to the Force, there shall be set off against the apportionment, as provided for in paragraphs 14, 16 and 18 above, their respective share of the unencumbered balance and other revenue in the amount of 1,259,112 dollars in respect of the financial period ended 30 June 2023, in accordance with the levels updated in its resolution 76/239, taking into account the scale of assessments for 2023, as set out in its resolution 76/238;

21. *Also decides* that, for Member States that have not fulfilled their financial obligations to the Force, there shall be set off against their outstanding obligations, their respective share of the unencumbered balance and other revenue in the amount of 1,259,112 dollars in respect of the financial period ended 30 June 2023, in accordance with the scheme set out in paragraph 20 above;

22. *Further decides* that the decrease of 133,100 dollars in the estimated staff assessment income in respect of the financial period ended 30 June 2023 shall be set off against the credits in the amount of 1,259,112 dollars referred to in paragraphs 20 and 21 above;

23. *Decides*, taking into account its voluntary contribution for the financial period ended 30 June 2023, that one third of the net unencumbered balance and other revenue in the amount of 765,600 dollars in respect of the financial period ended 30 June 2023 shall be returned to the Government of Cyprus;

24. *Also decides*, taking into account its voluntary contribution for the financial period ended 30 June 2023, that the prorated share of the net unencumbered balance and other revenue in the amount of 272,088 dollars in respect of the financial period ended 30 June 2023 shall be returned to the Government of Greece;

25. *Further decides* to continue to maintain as separate the account established for the Force for the period prior to 16 June 1993, invites Member States to make voluntary contributions to that account, and requests the Secretary-General to continue his efforts in appealing for voluntary contributions to the account;

26. *Encourages* the Secretary-General to continue to take additional measures to ensure the safety and security of all personnel participating in the Force under the auspices of the United Nations, bearing in mind paragraphs 5 and 6 of Security Council resolution 1502 (2003) of 26 August 2003;

27. *Invites* voluntary contributions to the Force in cash and in the form of services and supplies acceptable to the Secretary-General, to be administered, as appropriate, in accordance with the procedure and practices established by the General Assembly;

28. *Decides* to include in the provisional agenda of its seventy-ninth session the item entitled "Financing of the United Nations Peacekeeping Force in Cyprus".

RESOLUTION 78/301

Adopted at the 95th plenary meeting, on 28 June 2024, without a vote, on the recommendation of the Committee (A/78/925, para. 6)

78/301. Financing of the United Nations Organization Stabilization Mission in the Democratic Republic of the Congo

The General Assembly,

Having considered the reports of the Secretary-General on the financing of the United Nations Organization Stabilization Mission in the Democratic Republic of the Congo[53] and the related report of the Advisory Committee on Administrative and Budgetary Questions,[54]

Recalling Security Council resolution 1925 (2010) of 28 May 2010, by which the Council decided that, as from 1 July 2010, the United Nations Organization Mission in the Democratic Republic of the Congo would bear the title

[53] A/78/640 and A/78/741.

[54] A/78/744/Add.9.

"United Nations Organization Stabilization Mission in the Democratic Republic of the Congo", and recalling also the subsequent resolutions by which the Council extended the mandate of the Mission, the latest of which was resolution 2717 (2023) of 19 December 2023, by which the Council extended the mandate of the Mission until 20 December 2024,

Recalling also its resolution 54/260 A of 7 April 2000 on the financing of the Mission and its subsequent resolutions thereon, the latest of which was resolution 77/309 of 30 June 2023,

Recalling further its resolution 58/315 of 1 July 2004,

Reaffirming the general principles underlying the financing of United Nations peacekeeping operations, as stated in its resolutions 1874 (S-IV) of 27 June 1963, 3101 (XXVIII) of 11 December 1973 and 55/235 of 23 December 2000,

Noting with appreciation that voluntary contributions have been made to the Mission,

Mindful of the fact that it is essential to provide the Mission with the financial resources necessary to enable it to fulfil its responsibilities under the relevant resolutions of the Security Council,

1. *Requests* the Secretary General to entrust the Head of Mission with the task of formulating future budget proposals in full accordance with the provisions of its resolutions 59/296 of 22 June 2005, 60/266 of 30 June 2006, 61/276 of 29 June 2007, 64/269 of 24 June 2010, 65/289 of 30 June 2011, 66/264 of 21 June 2012, 69/307 of 25 June 2015, 70/286 of 17 June 2016 and 76/274 of 29 June 2022, as well as other relevant resolutions;

2. *Takes note* of the status of contributions to the United Nations Organization Stabilization Mission in the Democratic Republic of the Congo as at 30 April 2024, including the contributions outstanding in the amount of 407.0 million United States dollars, representing some 1.6 per cent of the total assessed contributions, notes with concern that only 101 Member States have paid their assessed contributions in full, and urges all other Member States, in particular those in arrears, to ensure payment of their outstanding assessed contributions;

3. *Expresses its appreciation* to those Member States that have paid their assessed contributions in full, and urges all other Member States to make every possible effort to ensure payment of their assessed contributions to the Mission in full;

4. *Expresses concern* at the financial situation with regard to peacekeeping activities, in particular as regards the reimbursements to troop contributors that bear additional burdens owing to overdue payments by Member States of their assessments;

5. *Emphasizes* that all future and existing peacekeeping missions shall be given equal and non-discriminatory treatment in respect of financial and administrative arrangements;

6. *Also emphasizes* that all peacekeeping missions shall be provided with adequate resources for the effective and efficient discharge of their respective mandates;

7. *Requests* the Secretary-General to ensure that proposed peacekeeping budgets are based on the relevant legislative mandates;

8. *Endorses* the conclusions and recommendations contained in the report of the Advisory Committee on Administrative and Budgetary Questions, subject to the provisions of the present resolution, and requests the Secretary-General to ensure their full implementation;

9. *Notes* the extensive mandate of the Mission for the protection of civilians, and requests the Secretary-General to continue to deploy, within its mandate, its special units, with the aim of effectively implementing the mandate;

10. *Also notes* the abolishment of a large number of national posts in South Kivu due to the Mission's withdrawal, and requests the Secretary-General to assist national staff in their transition to future professional careers, including through employment in vacant positions in the Mission and by collaborating with the United Nations country team, as well as with other international agencies present in the country;

11. *Further notes* the complex environment in which the Mission operates, and encourages the Secretary-General, to continue to strengthen his engagement and liaison with relevant regional and subregional organizations, and to ensure coherence and coordination with the Mission in compliance with the Mission's mandate;

12. *Requests* the Secretary-General to ensure the full implementation of the relevant provisions of its resolutions 59/296, 60/266, 61/276, 64/269, 65/289, 66/264, 69/307, 70/286 and 76/274;

13. *Also requests* the Secretary-General to take all action necessary to ensure that the Mission is administered with a maximum of efficiency and economy;

Budget performance report for the period from 1 July 2022 to 30 June 2023

14. *Takes note* of the report of the Secretary-General on the budget performance of the Mission for the period from 1 July 2022 to 30 June 2023;[55]

Budget estimates for the period from 1 July 2024 to 30 June 2025

15. *Decides* to appropriate to the special account for the United Nations Organization Stabilization Mission in the Democratic Republic of the Congo the amount of 994,544,400 dollars for the period from 1 July 2024 to 30 June 2025, inclusive of 907,983,500 dollars for the maintenance of the Mission, 65,980,100 dollars for the support account for peacekeeping operations, 11,516,600 dollars for the United Nations Logistics Base at Brindisi, Italy, and 9,064,200 dollars for the Regional Service Centre in Entebbe, Uganda;

Financing of the appropriation for the period from 1 July 2024 to 30 June 2025

16. *Decides* to apportion among Member States the amount of 467,544,000 dollars for the period from 1 July to 20 December 2024, in accordance with the levels updated in its resolution 76/239 of 24 December 2021, taking into account the scale of assessments for 2024, as set out in its resolution 76/238 of 24 December 2021;

17. *Also decides* that, in accordance with the provisions of its resolution 973 (X) of 15 December 1955, there shall be set off against the apportionment among Member States, as provided for in paragraph 16 above, their respective share in the Tax Equalization Fund of 14,836,800 dollars, comprising the estimated staff assessment income of 11,310,700 dollars approved for the Mission, the prorated share of 2,528,400 dollars of the estimated staff assessment income approved for the support account, the prorated share of 493,700 dollars of the estimated staff assessment income approved for the United Nations Logistics Base and the prorated share of 504,000 dollars of the estimated staff assessment income approved for the Regional Service Centre;

18. *Further decides* to apportion among Member States the amount of 29,728,200 dollars for the period from 21 to 31 December 2024, at a monthly rate of 82,878,700 dollars, in accordance with the levels updated in its resolution 76/239, taking into account the scale of assessments for 2024, as set out in its resolution 76/238, subject to a decision of the Security Council to extend the mandate of the Mission;

19. *Decides* that, in accordance with the provisions of its resolution 973 (X), there shall be set off against the apportionment among Member States, as provided for in paragraph 18 above, their respective share in the Tax Equalization Fund of 943,400 dollars, comprising the estimated staff assessment income of 719,200 dollars approved for the Mission, the prorated share of 160,800 dollars of the estimated staff assessment income approved for the support account, the prorated share of 31,400 dollars of the estimated staff assessment income approved for the United Nations Logistics Base and the prorated share of 32,000 dollars of the estimated staff assessment income approved for the Regional Service Centre;

20. *Also decides* to apportion among Member States the amount of 497,272,200 dollars for the period from 1 January to 30 June 2025, at a monthly rate of 82,878,700 dollars, in accordance with the scale of assessments for 2025 and the updated levels,[56] subject to a decision of the Security Council to extend the mandate of the Mission;

21. *Further decides* that, in accordance with the provisions of its resolution 973 (X), there shall be set off against the apportionment among Member States, as provided for in paragraph 20 above, their respective share in the Tax Equalization Fund of 15,780,100 dollars, comprising the estimated staff assessment income of 12,029,900 dollars approved for the Mission, the prorated share of 2,689,100 dollars of the estimated staff assessment income approved for the support account, the prorated share of 525,100 dollars of the estimated staff assessment income approved for

[55] A/78/640.

[56] To be adopted by the General Assembly.

the United Nations Logistics Base and the prorated share of 536,000 dollars of the estimated staff assessment income approved for the Regional Service Centre;

22. *Decides* that, for Member States that have fulfilled their financial obligations to the Mission, there shall be set off against their apportionment, as provided for in paragraphs 16, 18 and 20 above, their respective share of the unencumbered balance and other revenue in the amount of 55,662,100 dollars in respect of the financial period ended 30 June 2023, in accordance with the levels updated in its resolution 76/239, taking into account the scale of assessments for 2023, as set out in its resolution 76/238;

23. *Also decides* that, for Member States that have not fulfilled their financial obligations to the Mission, there shall be set off against their outstanding obligations their respective share of the unencumbered balance and other revenue in the amount of 55,662,100 dollars in respect of the financial period ended 30 June 2023, in accordance with the scheme set out in paragraph 22 above;

24. *Further decides* that the decrease of 560,100 dollars in the estimated staff assessment income in respect of the financial period ended 30 June 2023 shall be set off against the credits in the amount of 55,662,100 dollars referred to in paragraphs 22 and 23 above;

25. *Encourages* the Secretary-General to continue to take additional measures to ensure the safety and security of all personnel participating in the Mission under the auspices of the United Nations, bearing in mind paragraphs 5 and 6 of Security Council resolution 1502 (2003) of 26 August 2003;

26. *Invites* voluntary contributions to the Mission in cash and in the form of services and supplies acceptable to the Secretary-General, to be administered, as appropriate, in accordance with the procedure and practices established by the General Assembly;

27. *Decides* to include in the provisional agenda of its seventy-ninth session the item entitled "Financing of the United Nations Organization Stabilization Mission in the Democratic Republic of the Congo".

RESOLUTION 78/302

Adopted at the 95th plenary meeting, on 28 June 2024, without a vote, on the recommendation of the Committee (A/78/926, para. 6)

78/302. Financing of the United Nations Interim Administration Mission in Kosovo

The General Assembly,

Having considered the reports of the Secretary-General on the financing of the United Nations Interim Administration Mission in Kosovo[57] and the related report of the Advisory Committee on Administrative and Budgetary Questions,[58]

Recalling Security Council resolution 1244 (1999) of 10 June 1999 regarding the establishment of the United Nations Interim Administration Mission in Kosovo,

Recalling also its resolution 53/241 of 28 July 1999 on the financing of the Mission and its subsequent resolutions thereon, the latest of which was resolution 77/311 of 30 June 2023,

Acknowledging the complexity of the Mission,

Reaffirming the general principles underlying the financing of United Nations peacekeeping operations, as stated in its resolutions 1874 (S-IV) of 27 June 1963, 3101 (XXVIII) of 11 December 1973 and 55/235 of 23 December 2000,

Mindful of the fact that it is essential to provide the Mission with the financial resources necessary to enable it to fulfil its responsibilities under the relevant resolutions of the Security Council,

---

[57] A/78/581 and A/78/721.

[58] A/78/744/Add.7.

Mindful also of the need to ensure coordination and cooperation with the European Union Rule of Law Mission in Kosovo,

1. *Requests* the Secretary-General to entrust the Head of Mission with the task of formulating future budget proposals in full accordance with the provisions of its resolutions 59/296 of 22 June 2005, 60/266 of 30 June 2006, 61/276 of 29 June 2007, 64/269 of 24 June 2010, 65/289 of 30 June 2011, 66/264 of 21 June 2012, 69/307 of 25 June 2015, 70/286 of 17 June 2016 and 76/274 of 29 June 2022, as well as other relevant resolutions;

2. *Takes note* of the status of contributions to the United Nations Interim Administration Mission in Kosovo as at 30 April 2024, including the contributions outstanding in the amount of 36.1 million United States dollars, representing some 1 per cent of the total assessed contributions, notes with concern that only 118 Member States have paid their assessed contributions in full, and urges all other Member States, in particular those in arrears, to ensure payment of their outstanding assessed contributions;

3. *Expresses its appreciation* to those Member States that have paid their assessed contributions in full, and urges all other Member States to make every possible effort to ensure payment of their assessed contributions to the Mission in full;

4. *Expresses concern* at the financial situation with regard to peacekeeping activities, in particular as regards the reimbursements to troop contributors that bear additional burdens owing to overdue payments by Member States of their assessments;

5. *Emphasizes* that all future and existing peacekeeping missions shall be given equal and non-discriminatory treatment in respect of financial and administrative arrangements;

6. *Also emphasizes* that all peacekeeping missions shall be provided with adequate resources for the effective and efficient discharge of their respective mandates;

7. *Requests* the Secretary-General to ensure that proposed peacekeeping budgets are based on the relevant legislative mandates;

8. *Endorses* the conclusions and recommendations contained in the report of the Advisory Committee on Administrative and Budgetary Questions, subject to the provisions of the present resolution, and requests the Secretary-General to ensure their full implementation;

9. *Decides* to reclassify the post of Civil Affairs Officer in the Office of Community Support and Facilitation in Pristina from the P-4 to the P-5 level;

10. *Requests* the Secretary-General to ensure the full implementation of the relevant provisions of its resolutions 59/296, 60/266, 61/276, 64/269, 65/289, 66/264, 69/307, 70/286 and 76/274;

11. *Also requests* the Secretary-General to take all action necessary to ensure that the Mission is administered with a maximum of efficiency and economy;

Budget performance report for the period from 1 July 2022 to 30 June 2023

12. *Takes note* of the report of the Secretary-General on the budget performance of the Mission for the period from 1 July 2022 to 30 June 2023;[59]

Budget estimates for the period from 1 July 2024 to 30 June 2025

13. *Decides* to appropriate to the special account for the United Nations Interim Administration Mission in Kosovo the amount of 47,413,200 dollars for the period from 1 July 2024 to 30 June 2025, inclusive of 43,684,700 dollars for the maintenance of the Mission, 3,174,400 dollars for the support account for peacekeeping operations and 554,100 dollars for the United Nations Logistics Base at Brindisi, Italy;

[59] A/78/581.

Financing of the appropriation for the period from 1 July 2024 to 30 June 2025

14. *Decides* to apportion among Member States the amount of 23,706,600 dollars for the period from 1 July to 31 December 2024, in accordance with the levels updated in its resolution 76/239 of 24 December 2021, taking into account the scale of assessments for 2024, as set out in its resolution 76/238 of 24 December 2021;

15. *Also decides* that, in accordance with the provisions of its resolution 973 (X) of 15 December 1955, there shall be set off against the apportionment among Member States, as provided for in paragraph 14 above, their respective share in the Tax Equalization Fund of 2,307,600 dollars, comprising the estimated staff assessment income of 2,152,900 dollars approved for the Mission, the prorated share of 129,400 dollars of the estimated staff assessment income approved for the support account and the prorated share of 25,300 dollars of the estimated staff assessment income approved for the United Nations Logistics Base;

16. *Further decides* to apportion among Member States the amount of 23,706,600 dollars for the period from 1 January to 30 June 2025, in accordance with the scale of assessments for 2025 and the updated levels;[60]

17. *Decides* that, in accordance with the provisions of its resolution 973 (X), there shall be set off against the apportionment among Member States, as provided for in paragraph 16 above, their respective share in the Tax Equalization Fund of 2,307,500 dollars, comprising the estimated staff assessment income of 2,152,900 dollars approved for the Mission, the prorated share of 129,400 dollars of the estimated staff assessment income approved for the support account and the prorated share of 25,200 dollars of the estimated staff assessment income approved for the United Nations Logistics Base;

18. *Also decides* that, for Member States that have fulfilled their financial obligations to the Mission, there shall be set off against the apportionment, as provided for in paragraphs 14 and 16 above, their respective share of the unencumbered balance and other revenue in the amount of 1,446,900 dollars in respect of the financial period ended 30 June 2023, in accordance with the levels updated in its resolution 76/239, taking into account the scale of assessments for 2023, as set out in its resolution 76/238;

19. *Further decides* that, for Member States that have not fulfilled their financial obligations to the Mission, there shall be set off against their outstanding obligations their respective share of the unencumbered balance and other revenue in the amount of 1,446,900 dollars in respect of the financial period ended 30 June 2023, in accordance with the scheme set out in paragraph 18 above;

20. *Decides* that the decrease of 86,400 dollars in the estimated staff assessment income in respect of the financial period ended 30 June 2023 shall be set off against the credits in the amount of 1,446,900 dollars referred to in paragraphs 18 and 19 above;

21. *Encourages* the Secretary-General to continue to take additional measures to ensure the safety and security of all personnel participating in the Mission under the auspices of the United Nations, bearing in mind paragraphs 5 and 6 of Security Council resolution 1502 (2003) of 26 August 2003;

22. *Invites* voluntary contributions to the Mission in cash and in the form of services and supplies acceptable to the Secretary-General, to be administered, as appropriate, in accordance with the procedure and practices established by the General Assembly;

23. *Decides* to include in the provisional agenda of its seventy-ninth session the item entitled "Financing of the United Nations Interim Administration Mission in Kosovo".

RESOLUTION 78/303

Adopted at the 95th plenary meeting, on 28 June 2024, without a vote, on the recommendation of the Committee (A/78/927, para. 6)

[60] To be adopted by the General Assembly.

78/303. Financing of the United Nations Mission in Liberia

The General Assembly,

Having considered the report of the Secretary-General on the final performance of the United Nations Mission in Liberia[61] and the related report of the Advisory Committee on Administrative and Budgetary Questions,[62]

1. *Takes note* of the status of contributions to the United Nations Mission in Liberia as at 30 April 2024, including the contributions outstanding in the amount of 4.5 million United States dollars, representing some 0.05 per cent of the total assessed contributions, notes with concern that only 183 Member States have paid their assessed contributions in full, and urges all other Member States, in particular those in arrears, to ensure payment of their outstanding assessed contributions;

2. *Endorses* the conclusions and recommendations contained in the report of the Advisory Committee on Administrative and Budgetary Questions, and requests the Secretary-General to ensure their full implementation;

3. *Takes note* of the report of the Secretary-General on the final performance of the United Nations Mission in Liberia;

4. *Decides* that Member States that have fulfilled their financial obligations to the Mission shall be credited with their respective share of the net cash available in the special account for the United Nations Mission in Liberia in the amount of 12,337,000 dollars as at 30 April 2024, in accordance with the levels updated in its resolution 70/246 of 23 December 2015, taking into account the scale of assessments for 2018, as set out in its resolution 70/245 of 23 December 2015;

5. *Encourages* Member States that are owed credits referred to in paragraph 4 above to apply those credits to any accounts where they have outstanding assessed contributions;

6. *Urges* all Member States to make every possible effort to ensure payment of their assessed contributions in full;

7. *Decides* that, for Member States that have not fulfilled their financial obligations to the Mission, their respective share of the net cash available in the special account for the Mission in the amount of 12,337,000 dollars as at 30 April 2024 shall be set off against their outstanding obligations, in accordance with the scheme set out in paragraph 4 above;

8. *Also decides* that updated information on the financial position of the Mission shall be included in the report on the updated position of closed peacekeeping missions, to be considered by the General Assembly at its seventy-ninth session under the agenda item entitled "Administrative and budgetary aspects of the financing of the United Nations peacekeeping operations";

9. *Further decides* to delete from its agenda the item entitled "Financing of the United Nations Mission in Liberia".

RESOLUTION 78/304

Adopted at the 95th plenary meeting, on 28 June 2024, without a vote, on the recommendation of the Committee (A/78/928, para. 6)

[61] A/75/684.

[62] A/75/823.

78/304. Financing of the United Nations Disengagement Observer Force

The General Assembly,

Having considered the reports of the Secretary-General on the financing of the United Nations Disengagement Observer Force[63] and the related report of the Advisory Committee on Administrative and Budgetary Questions,[64]

Recalling Security Council resolution 350 (1974) of 31 May 1974 regarding the establishment of the United Nations Disengagement Observer Force and the subsequent resolutions by which the Council extended the mandate of the Force, the latest of which was resolution 2718 (2023) of 21 December 2023, by which the Council extended the mandate of the Force until 30 June 2024,

Recalling also its resolution 3211 B (XXIX) of 29 November 1974 on the financing of the United Nations Emergency Force and of the United Nations Disengagement Observer Force and its subsequent resolutions thereon, the latest of which was resolution 77/291 B of 30 June 2023,

Reaffirming the general principles underlying the financing of United Nations peacekeeping operations, as stated in its resolutions 1874 (S-IV) of 27 June 1963, 3101 (XXVIII) of 11 December 1973 and 55/235 of 23 December 2000,

Mindful of the fact that it is essential to provide the United Nations Disengagement Observer Force with the financial resources necessary to enable it to fulfil its responsibilities under the relevant resolutions of the Security Council,

1. *Requests* the Secretary-General to entrust the Head of Mission with the task of formulating future budget proposals in full accordance with the provisions of its resolutions 59/296 of 22 June 2005, 60/266 of 30 June 2006, 61/276 of 29 June 2007, 64/269 of 24 June 2010, 65/289 of 30 June 2011, 66/264 of 21 June 2012, 69/307 of 25 June 2015, 70/286 of 17 June 2016 and 76/274 of 29 June 2022, as well as other relevant resolutions;

2. *Takes note* of the status of contributions to the United Nations Disengagement Observer Force as at 30 April 2024, including the contributions outstanding in the amount of 27.6 million United States dollars, representing some 1.1 per cent of the total assessed contributions, notes with concern that only 104 Member States have paid their assessed contributions in full, and urges all other Member States, in particular those in arrears, to ensure payment of their outstanding assessed contributions;

3. *Expresses its appreciation* to those Member States that have paid their assessed contributions in full, and urges all other Member States to make every possible effort to ensure payment of their assessed contributions to the Force in full;

4. *Expresses concern* at the financial situation with regard to peacekeeping activities, in particular as regards the reimbursements to troop contributors that bear additional burdens owing to overdue payments by Member States of their assessments;

5. *Emphasizes* that all future and existing peacekeeping missions shall be given equal and non-discriminatory treatment in respect of financial and administrative arrangements;

6. *Also emphasizes* that all peacekeeping missions shall be provided with adequate resources for the effective and efficient discharge of their respective mandates;

7. *Requests* the Secretary-General to ensure that proposed peacekeeping budgets are based on the relevant legislative mandates;

8. *Endorses* the conclusions and recommendations contained in the report of the Advisory Committee on Administrative and Budgetary Questions, and requests the Secretary-General to ensure their full implementation;

9. *Requests* the Secretary-General to ensure the full implementation of the relevant provisions of its resolutions 59/296, 60/266, 61/276, 64/269, 65/289, 66/264, 69/307, 70/286 and 76/274;

[63] A/78/582 and A/78/720.

[64] A/78/744/Add.1.

10. *Also requests* the Secretary-General to take all action necessary to ensure that the Force is administered with a maximum of efficiency and economy;

Budget performance report for the period from 1 July 2022 to 30 June 2023

11. *Takes note* of the report of the Secretary-General on the budget performance of the Force for the period from 1 July 2022 to 30 June 2023;[65]

Budget estimates for the period from 1 July 2024 to 30 June 2025

12. *Decides* to appropriate to the special account for the United Nations Disengagement Observer Force the amount of 74,611,100 dollars for the period from 1 July 2024 to 30 June 2025, inclusive of 68,743,800 dollars for the maintenance of the Force, 4,995,400 dollars for the support account for peacekeeping operations and 871,900 dollars for the United Nations Logistics Base at Brindisi, Italy;

Financing of the appropriation for the period from 1 July 2024 to 30 June 2025

13. *Decides* to apportion among Member States the amount of 37,305,500 dollars for the period from 1 July to 31 December 2024, in accordance with the levels updated in its resolution 76/239 of 24 December 2021, taking into account the scale of assessments for 2024, as set out in its resolution 76/238 of 24 December 2021, subject to a decision of the Security Council to extend the mandate of the Force;

14. *Also decides* that, in accordance with the provisions of its resolution 973 (X) of 15 December 1955, there shall be set off against the apportionment among Member States, as provided for in paragraph 13 above, their respective share in the Tax Equalization Fund of 1,062,400 dollars, comprising the estimated staff assessment income of 819,100 dollars approved for the Force, the prorated share of 203,600 dollars of the estimated staff assessment income approved for the support account and the prorated share of 39,700 dollars of the estimated staff assessment income approved for the United Nations Logistics Base;

15. *Further decides* to apportion among Member States the amount of 37,305,600 dollars for the period from 1 January to 30 June 2025, at a monthly rate of 6,217,592 dollars, in accordance with the scale of assessments for 2025 and the updated levels,[66] subject to a decision of the Security Council to extend the mandate of the Force;

16. *Decides* that, in accordance with the provisions of its resolution 973 (X), there shall be set off against the apportionment among Member States, as provided for in paragraph 15 above, their respective share in the Tax Equalization Fund of 1,062,500 dollars, comprising the estimated staff assessment income of 819,100 dollars approved for the Force, the prorated share of 203,600 dollars of the estimated staff assessment income approved for the support account and the prorated share of 39,800 dollars of the estimated staff assessment income approved for the United Nations Logistics Base;

17. *Also decides* that, for Member States that have fulfilled their financial obligations to the Force, there shall be set off against the apportionment, as provided for in paragraphs 13 and 15 above, their respective share of the unencumbered balance and other revenue in the amount of 2,374,100 dollars in respect of the financial period ended 30 June 2023, in accordance with the levels updated in its resolution 76/239, taking into account the scale of assessments for 2023, as set out in its resolution 76/238;

18. *Further decides* that, for Member States that have not fulfilled their financial obligations to the Force, there shall be set off against their outstanding obligations their respective share of the unencumbered balance and other revenue in the total amount of 2,374,100 dollars in respect of the financial period ended 30 June 2023, in accordance with the scheme set out in paragraph 17 above;

19. *Decides* that the increase of 147,200 dollars in the estimated staff assessment income in respect of the financial period ended 30 June 2023 shall be added to the credits in the amount of 2,374,100 dollars referred to in paragraphs 17 and 18 above;

---

[65] A/78/582.

[66] To be adopted by the General Assembly.

20. *Encourages* the Secretary-General to continue to take additional measures to ensure the safety and security of all personnel participating in the Force under the auspices of the United Nations, bearing in mind paragraphs 5 and 6 of Security Council resolution 1502 (2003) of 26 August 2003;

21. *Invites* voluntary contributions to the Force in cash and in the form of services and supplies acceptable to the Secretary-General, to be administered, as appropriate, in accordance with the procedure and practices established by the General Assembly;

22. *Decides* to include in the provisional agenda of its seventy-ninth session, under the item entitled "Financing of the United Nations peacekeeping forces in the Middle East", the sub-item entitled "United Nations Disengagement Observer Force".

RESOLUTION 78/305

Adopted at the 95th plenary meeting, on 28 June 2024, by a recorded vote of 129 to 2, with 1 abstention,* on the recommendation of the Committee (A/78/929, para. 12)[67]

* *In favour:* Albania, Algeria, Andorra, Angola, Argentina, Armenia, Australia, Austria, Azerbaijan, Bahrain, Bangladesh, Barbados, Belarus, Belgium, Bhutan, Bolivia (Plurinational State of), Bosnia and Herzegovina, Brazil, Brunei Darussalam, Bulgaria, Cambodia, Cameroon, Canada, Chile, China, Colombia, Comoros, Costa Rica, Côte d'Ivoire, Croatia, Cuba, Cyprus, Czechia, Democratic People's Republic of Korea, Denmark, Djibouti, Dominican Republic, Ecuador, Egypt, El Salvador, Equatorial Guinea, Eritrea, Estonia, Ethiopia, Finland, France, Georgia, Germany, Ghana, Greece, Guatemala, Guyana, Honduras, Hungary, India, Indonesia, Iran (Islamic Republic of), Iraq, Ireland, Italy, Jamaica, Japan, Jordan, Kenya, Lao People's Democratic Republic, Latvia, Lebanon, Lesotho, Libya, Liechtenstein, Lithuania, Luxembourg, Malaysia, Maldives, Mali, Malta, Monaco, Mongolia, Montenegro, Morocco, Nepal, Netherlands (Kingdom of the), New Zealand, Nicaragua, Niger, Nigeria, Norway, Oman, Pakistan, Peru, Philippines, Poland, Portugal, Qatar, Republic of Korea, Republic of Moldova, Romania, Russian Federation, Rwanda, Saint Kitts and Nevis, Saint Lucia, San Marino, Saudi Arabia, Senegal, Serbia, Sierra Leone, Singapore, Slovakia, Slovenia, South Africa, Spain, Sri Lanka, Sudan, Suriname, Sweden, Switzerland, Syrian Arab Republic, Thailand, Trinidad and Tobago, Tunisia, Türkiye, Uganda, Ukraine, United Arab Emirates, United Kingdom of Great Britain and Northern Ireland, United Republic of Tanzania, Uruguay, Viet Nam, Yemen
Against: Israel, United States of America
Abstaining: Paraguay

78/305. Financing of the United Nations Interim Force in Lebanon

The General Assembly,

Having considered the reports of the Secretary-General on the financing of the United Nations Interim Force in Lebanon[68] and the related report of the Advisory Committee on Administrative and Budgetary Questions,[69]

Recalling Security Council resolution 425 (1978) of 19 March 1978 regarding the establishment of the United Nations Interim Force in Lebanon and the subsequent resolutions by which the Council extended the mandate of the Force, the latest of which was resolution 2695 (2023) of 31 August 2023, by which the Council extended the mandate of the Force until 31 August 2024,

Recalling also its resolution S-8/2 of 21 April 1978 on the financing of the Force and its subsequent resolutions thereon, the latest of which was resolution 77/313 of 30 June 2023,

Reaffirming its resolutions 51/233 of 13 June 1997, 52/237 of 26 June 1998, 53/227 of 8 June 1999, 54/267 of 15 June 2000, 55/180 A of 19 December 2000, 55/180 B of 14 June 2001, 56/214 A of 21 December 2001, 56/214 B of 27 June 2002, 57/325 of 18 June 2003, 58/307 of 18 June 2004, 59/307 of 22 June 2005, 60/278 of 30 June 2006, 61/250 A of 22 December 2006, 61/250 B of 2 April 2007, 61/250 C of 29 June 2007, 62/265 of 20 June 2008, 63/298 of 30 June 2009, 64/282 of 24 June 2010, 65/303 of 30 June 2011, 66/277 of 21 June 2012, 67/279 of 28 June 2013, 68/292 of 30 June 2014, 69/302 of 25 June 2015, 70/280 of 15 July 2016, 71/307 of 30 June 2017, 72/299 of 5 July

[67] The draft resolution recommended in the report was sponsored in the Committee by Uganda (on behalf of the States that are members of the Group of 77 and China).

[68] A/78/596 and A/78/725.

[69] A/78/744/Add.3.

2018, 73/322 of 3 July 2019, 75/250 A of 31 December 2020, 75/250 B of 30 June 2021,76/290 of 19 June 2022 and 77/313,

Reaffirming also the general principles underlying the financing of United Nations peacekeeping operations, as stated in its resolutions 1874 (S-IV) of 27 June 1963, 3101 (XXVIII) of 11 December 1973 and 55/235 of 23 December 2000,

Noting with appreciation that voluntary contributions have been made to the Force,

Mindful of the fact that it is essential to provide the Force with the financial resources necessary to enable it to fulfil its responsibilities under the relevant resolutions of the Security Council,

1. *Requests* the Secretary-General to entrust the Head of Mission with the task of formulating future budget proposals in full accordance with the provisions of its resolutions 59/296 of 22 June 2005, 60/266 of 30 June 2006, 61/276 of 29 June 2007, 64/269 of 24 June 2010, 65/289 of 30 June 2011, 66/264 of 21 June 2012, 69/307 of 25 June 2015, 70/286 of 17 June 2016 and 76/274 of 29 June 2022, as well as other relevant resolutions;

2. *Takes note* of the status of contributions to the United Nations Interim Force in Lebanon as at 30 April 2024, including the contributions outstanding in the amount of 134 million United States dollars, representing some 1.1 per cent of the total assessed contributions, notes with concern that only 109 Member States have paid their assessed contributions in full, and urges all other Member States, in particular those in arrears, to ensure payment of their outstanding assessed contributions;

3. *Expresses its appreciation* to those Member States that have paid their assessed contributions in full, and urges all other Member States to make every possible effort to ensure payment of their assessed contributions to the Force in full;

4. *Expresses deep concern* that Israel did not comply with resolutions 51/233, 52/237, 53/227, 54/267, 55/180 A, 55/180 B, 56/214 A, 56/214 B, 57/325, 58/307, 59/307, 60/278, 61/250 A, 61/250 B, 61/250 C, 62/265, 63/298, 64/282, 65/303, 66/277, 67/279, 68/292, 69/302, 70/280, 71/307, 72/299, 73/322, 75/250 A, 75/250 B, 76/290 and 77/313;

5. *Stresses once again* that Israel should strictly abide by resolutions 51/233, 52/237, 53/227, 54/267, 55/180 A, 55/180 B, 56/214 A, 56/214 B, 57/325, 58/307, 59/307, 60/278, 61/250 A, 61/250 B, 61/250 C, 62/265, 63/298, 64/282, 65/303, 66/277, 67/279, 68/292, 69/302, 70/280, 71/307, 72/299, 73/322, 75/250 A, 75/250 B, 76/290 and 77/313;

6. *Expresses concern* at the financial situation with regard to peacekeeping activities, in particular as regards the reimbursements to troop contributors that bear additional burdens owing to overdue payments by Member States of their assessments;

7. *Emphasizes* that all future and existing peacekeeping missions shall be given equal and non-discriminatory treatment in respect of financial and administrative arrangements;

8. *Also emphasizes* that all peacekeeping missions shall be provided with adequate resources for the effective and efficient discharge of their respective mandates;

9. *Requests* the Secretary-General to ensure that proposed peacekeeping budgets are based on the relevant legislative mandates;

10. *Endorses* the conclusions and recommendations contained in the report of the Advisory Committee on Administrative and Budgetary Questions, subject to the provisions of the present resolution, and requests the Secretary-General to ensure their full implementation;

11. *Requests* the Secretary-General to ensure the full implementation of the relevant provisions of its resolutions 59/296, 60/266, 61/276, 64/269, 65/289, 66/264, 69/307, 70/286 and 76/274;

12. *Also requests* the Secretary-General to take all action necessary to ensure that the Force is administered with a maximum of efficiency and economy;

13. *Reiterates its request* to the Secretary-General to take the measures necessary to ensure the full implementation of paragraph 8 of resolution 51/233, paragraph 5 of resolution 52/237, paragraph 11 of resolution 53/227, paragraph 14 of resolution 54/267, paragraph 14 of resolution 55/180 A, paragraph 15 of resolution 55/180 B,

paragraph 13 of resolution 56/214 A, paragraph 13 of resolution 56/214 B, paragraph 14 of resolution 57/325, paragraph 13 of resolution 58/307, paragraph 13 of resolution 59/307, paragraph 17 of resolution 60/278, paragraph 21 of resolution 61/250 A, paragraph 20 of resolution 61/250 B, paragraph 20 of resolution 61/250 C, paragraph 21 of resolution 62/265, paragraph 19 of resolution 63/298, paragraph 18 of resolution 64/282, paragraph 15 of resolution 65/303, paragraph 13 of resolution 66/277, paragraph 13 of resolution 67/279, paragraph 13 of resolution 68/292, paragraph 14 of resolution 69/302, paragraph 13 of resolution 70/280, paragraph 14 of resolution 71/307, paragraph 14 of resolution 72/299, paragraph 16 of resolution 73/322, paragraph 3 of resolution 75/250 A, paragraph 39 of resolution 75/250 B, paragraph 15 of resolution 76/290 and paragraph 14 of resolution 77/313, stresses once again that Israel shall pay the amount of 1,117,005 dollars resulting from the incident at Qana on 18 April 1996, and requests the Secretary-General to report on this matter to the General Assembly at its seventy-ninth session;

Budget performance report for the period from 1 July 2022 to 30 June 2023

14. *Takes note* of the report of the Secretary-General on the budget performance of the Force for the period from 1 July 2022 to 30 June 2023;[70]

Budget estimates for the period from 1 July 2024 to 30 June 2025

15. *Decides* to appropriate to the special account for the United Nations Interim Force in Lebanon the amount of 582,625,000 dollars for the period from 1 July 2024 to 30 June 2025, inclusive of 536,808,200 dollars for the maintenance of the Force, 39,008,100 dollars for the support account for peacekeeping operations and 6,808,700 dollars for the United Nations Logistics Base at Brindisi, Italy;

Financing of the appropriation for the period from 1 July 2024 to 30 June 2025

16. *Decides* to apportion among Member States the amount of 97,104,200 dollars for the period from 1 July to 31 August 2024 in accordance with the levels updated in its resolution 76/239 of 24 December 2021, taking into account the scale of assessments for 2024, as set out in its resolution 76/238 of 24 December 2021;

17. *Also decides* that, in accordance with the provisions of its resolution 973 (X) of 15 December 1955, there shall be set off against the apportionment among Member States, as provided for in paragraph 16 above, their respective share in the Tax Equalization Fund of 3,653,000 dollars, comprising the estimated staff assessment income of 3,019,500 dollars approved for the Force, the prorated share of 529,900 dollars of the estimated staff assessment income approved for the support account and the prorated share of 103,600 dollars of the estimated staff assessment income approved for the United Nations Logistics Base;

18. *Further decides* to apportion among Member States the amount of 194,208,300 dollars for the period from 1 September to 31 December 2024, at a monthly rate of 48,552,083 dollars, in accordance with the levels updated in its resolution 76/239, taking into account the scale of assessments for 2024, as set out in its resolution 76/238, subject to a decision of the Security Council to extend the mandate of the Force;

19. *Decides* that, in accordance with the provisions of its resolution 973 (X), there shall be set off against the apportionment among Member States, as provided for in paragraph 18 above, their respective share in the Tax Equalization Fund of 7,305,800 dollars, comprising the estimated staff assessment income of 6,039,000 dollars approved for the Force, the prorated share of 1,059,900 dollars of the estimated staff assessment income approved for the support account and the prorated share of 206,900 dollars of the estimated staff assessment income approved for the United Nations Logistics Base;

20. *Also decides* to apportion among Member States the amount of 291,312,500 dollars for the period from 1 January to 30 June 2025, at a monthly rate of 48,552,083 dollars, in accordance with the scale of assessments for 2025 and the updated levels,[71] subject to a decision of the Security Council to extend the mandate of the Force;

21. *Further decides* that, in accordance with the provisions of its resolution 973 (X), there shall be set off against the apportionment among Member States, as provided for in paragraph 20 above, their respective share in the

---

[70] A/78/596.

[71] To be adopted by the General Assembly.

Tax Equalization Fund of 10,958,700 dollars, comprising the estimated staff assessment income of 9,058,400 dollars approved for the Force, the prorated share of 1,589,900 dollars of the estimated staff assessment income approved for the support account, and the prorated share of 310,400 dollars of the estimated staff assessment income approved for the United Nations Logistics Base;

22. *Decides* that, for Member States that have fulfilled their financial obligations to the Force, there shall be set off against the apportionment, as provided for in paragraphs 16, 18 and 20 above, their respective share of the unencumbered balance and other revenue in the amount of 9,368,800 dollars in respect of the financial period ended 30 June 2023, in accordance with the levels updated in its resolution 76/239, taking into account the scale of assessments for 2023, as set out in its resolution 76/238;

23. *Also decides* that, for Member States that have not fulfilled their financial obligations to the Force, there shall be set off against their outstanding obligations their respective share of the unencumbered balance and other revenue in the amount of 9,368,800 dollars in respect of the financial period ended 30 June 2023, in accordance with the scheme set out in paragraph 22 above;

24. *Further decides* that the increase of 1,623,000 dollars in the estimated staff assessment income in respect of the financial period ended 30 June 2023 shall be added to the credits in the amount of 9,368,800 dollars referred to in paragraphs 22 and 23 above;

25. *Encourages* the Secretary-General to continue to take additional measures to ensure the safety and security of all personnel participating in the Force under the auspices of the United Nations, bearing in mind paragraphs 5 and 6 of Security Council resolution 1502 (2003) of 26 August 2003;

26. *Invites* voluntary contributions to the Force in cash and in the form of services and supplies acceptable to the Secretary-General, to be administered, as appropriate, in accordance with the procedure and practices established by the General Assembly;

27. *Decides* to include in the provisional agenda of its seventy-ninth session, under the item entitled "Financing of the United Nations peacekeeping forces in the Middle East", the sub-item entitled "United Nations Interim Force in Lebanon".

RESOLUTION 78/306

Adopted at the 95th plenary meeting, on 28 June 2024, without a vote, on the recommendation of the Committee (A/78/930, para. 6)

78/306. Financing of the United Nations Mission in South Sudan

The General Assembly,

Having considered the reports of the Secretary-General on the financing of the United Nations Mission in South Sudan[72] and the related report of the Advisory Committee on Administrative and Budgetary Questions,[73]

Having also considered the report of the Office of Internal Oversight Services on the evaluation of the contribution of the United Nations Mission in South Sudan to strengthening the rule of law and accountability in South Sudan,[74]

Recalling Security Council resolution 1996 (2011) of 8 July 2011, by which the Council established, as from 9 July 2011, the United Nations Mission in South Sudan, and the subsequent resolutions by which the Council extended the mandate of the Mission, the latest of which was resolution 2729 (2024) of 29 April 2024, by which the Council extended the mandate of the Mission until 30 April 2025,

Recalling also its resolution 66/243 A of 24 December 2011 on the financing of the Mission and its subsequent resolutions thereon, the latest of which was resolution 77/292 B of 30 June 2023,

[72] A/78/629 and A/78/754.

[73] A/78/744/Add.13.

[74] A/78/742.

Reaffirming the general principles underlying the financing of United Nations peacekeeping operations, as stated in its resolutions 1874 (S-IV) of 27 June 1963, 3101 (XXVIII) of 11 December 1973 and 55/235 of 23 December 2000,

Mindful of the fact that it is essential to provide the Mission with the financial resources necessary to enable it to fulfil its responsibilities under the relevant resolutions of the Security Council,

1. *Requests* the Secretary-General to entrust the Head of Mission with the task of formulating future budget proposals in full accordance with the provisions of its resolutions 59/296 of 22 June 2005, 60/266 of 30 June 2006, 61/276 of 29 June 2007, 64/269 of 24 June 2010, 65/289 of 30 June 2011, 66/264 of 21 June 2012, 69/307 of 25 June 2015, 70/286 of 17 June 2016 and 76/274 of 29 June 2022, as well as other relevant resolutions;

2. *Takes note* of the status of contributions to the United Nations Mission in South Sudan as at 30 April 2024, including the contributions outstanding in the amount of 332.7 million United States dollars, representing some 2.4 per cent of the total assessed contributions, notes with concern that only 81 Member States have paid their assessed contributions in full, and urges all other Member States, in particular those in arrears, to ensure payment of their outstanding assessed contributions;

3. *Expresses its appreciation* to those Member States that have paid their assessed contributions in full, and urges all other Member States to make every possible effort to ensure payment of their assessed contributions to the Mission in full;

4. *Expresses concern* at the financial situation with regard to peacekeeping activities, in particular as regards the reimbursements to troop contributors that bear additional burdens owing to overdue payments by Member States of their assessments;

5. *Emphasizes* that all future and existing peacekeeping missions shall be given equal and non-discriminatory treatment in respect of financial and administrative arrangements;

6. *Also emphasizes* that all peacekeeping missions shall be provided with adequate resources for the effective and efficient discharge of their respective mandates;

7. *Requests* the Secretary-General to ensure that proposed peacekeeping budgets are based on the relevant legislative mandates;

8. *Endorses* the conclusions and recommendations contained in the report of the Advisory Committee on Administrative and Budgetary Questions, subject to the provisions of the present resolution, and requests the Secretary-General to ensure their full implementation;

9. *Decides* to allocate 1 million dollars for the deployment of the new military contingents and formed police units;

10. *Takes note* of paragraph 41 of the report of the Advisory Committee;

11. *Requests* the Secretary-General to ensure the full implementation of the relevant provisions of its resolutions 59/296, 60/266, 61/276, 64/269, 65/289, 66/264, 69/307, 70/286 and 76/274;

12. *Also requests* the Secretary-General to take all action necessary to ensure that the Mission is administered with a maximum of efficiency and economy;

Budget performance report for the period from 1 July 2022 to 30 June 2023

13. *Takes note* of the report of the Secretary-General on the budget performance of the Mission for the period from 1 July 2022 to 30 June 2023;[75]

Budget estimates for the period from 1 July 2024 to 30 June 2025

14. *Decides* to appropriate to the special account for the United Nations Mission in South Sudan the amount of 1,355,899,200 dollars for the period from 1 July 2024 to 30 June 2025, inclusive of 1,237,887,300 dollars for the

[75] A/78/629.

maintenance of the Mission, 89,953,100 dollars for the support account for peacekeeping operations, 15,701,200 dollars for the United Nations Logistics Base at Brindisi, Italy, and 12,357,600 dollars for the Regional Service Centre in Entebbe, Uganda;

Financing of the appropriation for the period from 1 July 2024 to 30 June 2025

15. *Decides* to apportion among Member States the amount of 677,949,600 dollars for the period from 1 July to 31 December 2024, in accordance with the levels updated in its resolution 76/239 of 24 December 2021, taking into account the scale of assessments for 2024, as set out in its resolution 76/238 of 24 December 2021;

16. *Also decides* that, in accordance with the provisions of its resolution 973 (X) of 15 December 1955, there shall be set off against the apportionment among Member States, as provided for in paragraph 15 above, their respective share in the Tax Equalization Fund of 21,053,500 dollars, comprising the estimated staff assessment income of 15,940,600 dollars approved for the Mission, the prorated share of 3,666,200 dollars of the estimated staff assessment income approved for the support account, the prorated share of 715,900 dollars of the estimated staff assessment income approved for the United Nations Logistics Base and the prorated share of 730,800 dollars of the estimated staff assessment income approved for the Regional Service Centre;

17. *Further decides* to apportion among Member States the amount of 451,966,400 dollars for the period from 1 January to 30 April 2025, in accordance with the scale of assessments for 2025 and the updated levels;[76]

18. *Decides* that, in accordance with the provisions of its resolution 973 (X), there shall be set off against the apportionment among Member States, as provided for in paragraph 17 above, their respective share in the Tax Equalization Fund of 14,035,600 dollars, comprising the estimated staff assessment income of 10,627,100 dollars approved for the Mission, the prorated share of 2,444,100 dollars of the estimated staff assessment income approved for the support account, the prorated share of 477,200 dollars of the estimated staff assessment income approved for the United Nations Logistics Base and the prorated share of 487,200 dollars of the estimated staff assessment income approved for the Regional Service Centre;

19. *Also decides* to apportion among Member States the amount of 225,983,200 dollars for the period from 1 May to 30 June 2025, at a monthly rate of 112,991,600 dollars, in accordance with the scale of assessments for 2025 and the updated levels, subject to a decision of the Security Council to extend the mandate of the Mission;

20. *Further decides* that, in accordance with the provisions of its resolution 973 (X), there shall be set off against the apportionment among Member States, as provided for in paragraph 19 above, their respective share in the Tax Equalization Fund of 7,017,600 dollars, comprising the estimated staff assessment income of 5,313,500 dollars approved for the Mission, the prorated share of 1,222,000 dollars of the estimated staff assessment income approved for the support account, the prorated share of 238,600 dollars of the estimated staff assessment income approved for the United Nations Logistics Base and the prorated share of 243,500 dollars of the estimated staff assessment income approved for the Regional Service Centre;

21. *Decides* that, for Member States that have fulfilled their financial obligations to the Mission, there shall be set off against their apportionment, as provided for in paragraphs 15, 17 and 19 above, their respective share of the unencumbered balance and other revenue in the amount of 23,487,900 dollars in respect of the financial period ended 30 June 2023, in accordance with the levels updated in its resolution 76/239, taking into account the scale of assessments for 2023, as set out in its resolution 76/238;

22. *Also decides* that, for Member States that have not fulfilled their financial obligations to the Mission, there shall be set off against their outstanding obligations their respective share of the unencumbered balance and other revenue in the amount of 23,487,900 dollars in respect of the financial period ended 30 June 2023, in accordance with the scheme set out in paragraph 21 above;

23. *Further decides* that the increase of 2,327,800 dollars in the estimated staff assessment income in respect of the financial period ended 30 June 2023 shall be added to the credits in the amount of 23,487,900 dollars referred to in paragraphs 21 and 22 above;

[76] To be adopted by the General Assembly.

24. *Encourages* the Secretary-General to continue to take additional measures to ensure the safety and security of all personnel participating in the Mission under the auspices of the United Nations, bearing in mind paragraphs 5 and 6 of Security Council resolution 1502 (2003) of 26 August 2003;

25. *Invites* voluntary contributions to the Mission in cash and in the form of services and supplies acceptable to the Secretary-General, to be administered, as appropriate, in accordance with the procedure and practices established by the General Assembly;

26. *Decides* to include in the provisional agenda of its seventy-ninth session the item entitled "Financing of the United Nations Mission in South Sudan".

RESOLUTION 78/307

Adopted at the 95th plenary meeting, on 28 June 2024, without a vote, on the recommendation of the Committee (A/78/931, para. 6)

78/307. Financing of the United Nations Mission for the Referendum in Western Sahara

The General Assembly,

Having considered the reports of the Secretary-General on the financing of the United Nations Mission for the Referendum in Western Sahara[77] and the related report of the Advisory Committee on Administrative and Budgetary Questions,[78]

Recalling Security Council resolution 690 (1991) of 29 April 1991, by which the Council established the United Nations Mission for the Referendum in Western Sahara, and the subsequent resolutions by which the Council extended the mandate of the Mission, the latest of which was resolution 2703 (2023) of 30 October 2023, by which the Council extended the mandate of the Mission until 31 October 2024,

Recalling also its resolution 45/266 of 17 May 1991 on the financing of the Mission and its subsequent resolutions thereon, the latest of which was resolution 77/314 of 30 June 2023,

Reaffirming the general principles underlying the financing of United Nations peacekeeping operations, as stated in its resolutions 1874 (S-IV) of 27 June 1963, 3101 (XXVIII) of 11 December 1973 and 55/235 of 23 December 2000,

Noting with appreciation that voluntary contributions have been made to the Mission,

Mindful of the fact that it is essential to provide the Mission with the financial resources necessary to enable it to fulfil its responsibilities under the relevant resolutions of the Security Council,

1. *Requests* the Secretary-General to entrust the Head of Mission with the task of formulating future budget proposals in full accordance with the provisions of its resolutions 59/296 of 22 June 2005, 60/266 of 30 June 2006, 61/276 of 29 June 2007, 64/269 of 24 June 2010, 65/289 of 30 June 2011, 66/264 of 21 June 2012, 69/307 of 25 June 2015, 70/286 of 17 June 2016 and 76/274 of 29 June 2022, as well as other relevant resolutions;

2. *Takes note* of the status of contributions to the United Nations Mission for the Referendum in Western Sahara as at 30 April 2024, including the contributions outstanding in the amount of 49.8 million United States dollars, representing some 3.1 per cent of the total assessed contributions, notes with concern that only 116 Member States have paid their assessed contributions in full, and urges all other Member States, in particular those in arrears, to ensure payment of their outstanding assessed contributions;

3. *Expresses its appreciation* to those Member States that have paid their assessed contributions in full, and urges all other Member States to make every possible effort to ensure payment of their assessed contributions to the Mission in full;

---

[77] A/78/590 and A/78/723.

[78] A/78/744/Add.12.

4. *Expresses concern* at the financial situation with regard to peacekeeping activities, in particular as regards the reimbursements to troop contributors that bear additional burdens owing to overdue payments by Member States of their assessments;

5. *Emphasizes* that all future and existing peacekeeping missions shall be given equal and non-discriminatory treatment in respect of financial and administrative arrangements;

6. *Also emphasizes* that all peacekeeping missions shall be provided with adequate resources for the effective and efficient discharge of their respective mandates;

7. *Requests* the Secretary-General to ensure that proposed peacekeeping budgets are based on the relevant legislative mandates;

8. *Endorses* the conclusions and recommendations contained in the report of the Advisory Committee on Administrative and Budgetary Questions, and requests the Secretary-General to ensure their full implementation;

9. *Requests* the Secretary-General to ensure the full implementation of the relevant provisions of its resolutions 59/296, 60/266, 61/276, 64/269, 65/289, 66/264, 69/307, 70/286 and 76/274;

10. *Also requests* the Secretary-General to take all action necessary to ensure that the Mission is administered with a maximum of efficiency and economy;

Budget performance report for the period from 1 July 2022 to 30 June 2023

11. *Takes note* of the report of the Secretary-General on the budget performance of the Mission for the period from 1 July 2022 to 30 June 2023;[79]

Budget estimates for the period from 1 July 2024 to 30 June 2025

12. *Decides* to appropriate to the special account for the United Nations Mission for the Referendum in Western Sahara the amount of 75,349,100 dollars for the period from 1 July 2024 to 30 June 2025, inclusive of 68,791,100 dollars for the maintenance of the Mission, 4,998,800 dollars for the support account for peacekeeping operations, 872,500 dollars for the United Nations Logistics Base at Brindisi, Italy, and 686,700 dollars for the Regional Service Centre in Entebbe, Uganda;

Financing of the appropriation for the period from 1 July 2024 to 30 June 2025

13. *Decides* to apportion among Member States the amount of 25,116,400 dollars for the period from 1 July to 31 October 2024 in accordance with the levels updated in its resolution 76/239 of 24 December 2021, taking into account the scale of assessments for 2024, as set out in its resolution 76/238 of 24 December 2021;

14. *Also decides* that, in accordance with the provisions of its resolution 973 (X) of 15 December 1955, there shall be set off against the apportionment among Member States, as provided for in paragraph 13 above, their respective share in the Tax Equalization Fund of 1,139,100 dollars, comprising the estimated staff assessment income of 949,700 dollars approved for the Mission, the prorated share of 135,800 dollars of the estimated staff assessment income approved for the support account, the prorated share of 26,500 dollars of the estimated staff assessment income approved for the United Nations Logistics Base and the prorated share of 27,100 dollars of the estimated staff assessment income approved for the Regional Service Centre;

15. *Further decides* to apportion among Member States the amount of 12,558,200 dollars for the period from 1 November to 31 December 2024, at a monthly rate of 6,279,100 dollars, in accordance with the levels updated in its resolution 76/239, taking into account the scale of assessments for 2024, as set out in its resolution 76/238, subject to a decision of the Security Council to extend the mandate of the Mission;

16. *Decides* that, in accordance with the provisions of its resolution 973 (X), there shall be set off against the apportionment among Member States, as provided for in paragraph 15 above, their respective share in the Tax Equalization Fund of 569,500 dollars, comprising the estimated staff assessment income of 474,800 dollars approved for the Mission, the prorated share of 67,900 dollars of the estimated staff assessment income approved for the support

[79] A/78/590.

account, the prorated share of 13,300 dollars of the estimated staff assessment income approved for the United Nations Logistics Base and the prorated share of 13,500 dollars of the estimated staff assessment income approved for the Regional Service Centre;

17. *Also decides* to apportion among Member States the amount of 37,674,500 dollars for the period from 1 January to 30 June 2025, at a monthly rate of 6,279,100 dollars, in accordance with the scale of assessments for 2025 and the updated levels,[80] subject to a decision of the Security Council to extend the mandate of the Mission;

18. *Further decides* that, in accordance with the provisions of its resolution 973 (X), there shall be set off against the apportionment among Member States, as provided for in paragraph 17 above, their respective share in the Tax Equalization Fund of 1,708,700 dollars, comprising the estimated staff assessment income of 1,424,500 dollars approved for the Mission, the prorated share of 203,800 dollars of the estimated staff assessment income approved for the support account, the prorated share of 39,800 dollars of the estimated staff assessment income approved for the United Nations Logistics Base and the prorated share of 40,600 dollars of the estimated staff assessment income approved for the Regional Service Centre;

19. *Decides* that, for Member States that have fulfilled their financial obligations to the Mission, there shall be set off against their apportionment, as provided for in paragraphs 13, 15 and 17 above, their respective share of the unencumbered balance and other revenue in the amount of 3,657,200 dollars in respect of the financial period ended 30 June 2023, in accordance with the levels updated in its resolution 76/239, taking into account the scale of assessments for 2023, as set out in its resolution 76/238;

20. *Also decides* that, for Member States that have not fulfilled their financial obligations to the Mission, there shall be set off against their outstanding obligations their respective share of the unencumbered balance and other revenue in the amount of 3,657,200 dollars in respect of the financial period ended 30 June 2023, in accordance with the scheme set out in paragraph 19 above;

21. *Further decides* that the decrease of 150,700 dollars in the estimated staff assessment income in respect of the financial period ended 30 June 2023 shall be set off against the credits in the amount of 3,657,200 dollars referred to in paragraphs 19 and 20 above;

22. *Encourages* the Secretary-General to continue to take additional measures to ensure the safety and security of all personnel participating in the Mission under the auspices of the United Nations, bearing in mind paragraphs 5 and 6 of Security Council resolution 1502 (2003) of 26 August 2003;

23. *Invites* voluntary contributions to the Mission in cash and in the form of services and supplies acceptable to the Secretary-General, to be administered, as appropriate, in accordance with the procedure and practices established by the General Assembly;

24. *Decides* to include in the provisional agenda of its seventy-ninth session the item entitled "Financing of the United Nations Mission for the Referendum in Western Sahara".

RESOLUTION 78/308

Adopted at the 95th plenary meeting, on 28 June 2024, without a vote, on the recommendation of the Committee (A/78/932, para. 6)

78/308. Financing of the African Union-United Nations Hybrid Operation in Darfur

The General Assembly,

Having considered the reports of the Secretary-General on the financing of the African Union-United Nations Hybrid Operation in Darfur[81] and the related reports of the Advisory Committee on Administrative and Budgetary Questions,[82]

[80] To be adopted by the General Assembly.

[81] A/77/638 and A/78/702.

[82] A/77/780 and A/78/803.

Recalling Security Council resolution 1769 (2007) of 31 July 2007, by which the Council established the African Union-United Nations Hybrid Operation in Darfur for an initial period of 12 months from 31 July 2007, and the subsequent resolutions by which the Council extended the mandate of the Operation, the latest of which was resolution 2559 (2020) of 22 December 2020, by which the Council decided to terminate the mandate of the Operation as of 31 December 2020,

Recalling also its resolution 62/232 A of 22 December 2007 on the financing of the Operation and its subsequent resolutions thereon, the latest of which was resolution 76/244 B of 29 June 2022,

Reaffirming the general principles underlying the financing of United Nations peacekeeping operations, as stated in its resolutions 1874 (S-IV) of 27 June 1963, 3101 (XXVIII) of 11 December 1973 and 55/235 of 23 December 2000,

Mindful of the fact that it is essential to provide the Operation with the financial resources necessary to enable it to fulfil its responsibilities under the relevant resolutions of the Security Council,

1. *Takes note* of the status of contributions to the African Union-United Nations Hybrid Operation in Darfur as at 30 April 2024, including the contributions outstanding in the amount of 106.5 million United States dollars, representing some 0.6 per cent of the total assessed contributions, notes with concern that only 149 Member States have paid their assessed contributions in full, and urges all other Member States, in particular those in arrears, to ensure payment of their outstanding assessed contributions;

2. *Expresses its appreciation* to those Member States that have paid their assessed contributions in full, and urges all other Member States to make every possible effort to ensure payment of their assessed contributions to the Operation in full;

3. *Expresses concern* at the financial situation with regard to peacekeeping activities, in particular as regards the reimbursements to troop contributors that bear additional burdens owing to overdue payments by Member States of their assessments;

4. *Endorses* the conclusions and recommendations contained in the reports of the Advisory Committee on Administrative and Budgetary Questions, and requests the Secretary-General to ensure their full implementation;

5. *Notes* that the in-field liquidation activities of the mission have been completed;

6. *Authorizes* the Secretary-General, on an exceptional basis, with the prior concurrence of the Advisory Committee and subject to relevant rules and regulations, to enter into commitments in respect of expenditures related to the mandated operation and liquidation of the Operation that are identified after the closure of the Operation, and to use the Peacekeeping Reserve Fund for cash flow purposes if necessary, and to report thereon in the context of the final performance report;

7. *Requests* the Secretary-General to submit the final performance report during the seventy-ninth session of the General Assembly;

Budget performance report for the period from 1 July 2021 to 30 June 2022

8. *Takes note* of the report of the Secretary-General on the budget performance of the Operation for the period from 1 July 2021 to 30 June 2022;

9. *Also takes note* of the amount of 54,105,800 dollars comprising the unencumbered balance of 13,974,200 dollars in respect of the financial period ended 30 June 2022 and other revenue in the amount of 40,131,600 dollars in respect of the same period, and decides to defer action thereon until it considers the final performance report of the Operation;

10. *Further takes note* of the amount of 2,900,800 dollars representing the decrease in estimated staff assessment income in respect of the financial period ended 30 June 2022, and decides to defer action thereon until it considers the final performance report of the Operation;

Final disposition of the assets of the African Union-United Nations Hybrid Operation in Darfur

11. *Takes note* of the report of the Secretary-General on the final disposition of the assets of the African Union-United Nations Hybrid Operation in Darfur;

12. *Decides* to include in the provisional agenda of its seventy-ninth session the item entitled "Financing of the African Union-United Nations Hybrid Operation in Darfur".

RESOLUTION 78/309

Adopted at the 95th plenary meeting, on 28 June 2024, without a vote, on the recommendation of the Committee (A/78/933, para. 6)

78/309. Financing of the activities arising from Security Council resolution 1863 (2009)

The General Assembly,

Having considered the reports of the Secretary-General on the financing of the United Nations Support Office in Somalia[83] and the related report of the Advisory Committee on Administrative and Budgetary Questions,[84]

Recalling Security Council resolution 1863 (2009) of 16 January 2009, in which the Council expressed its intent to establish a United Nations peacekeeping operation in Somalia as a follow-on force to the African Union Mission in Somalia, subject to a further decision of the Council by 1 June 2009, and requested the Secretary-General, in order for the forces of the Mission to be incorporated into a United Nations peacekeeping operation, to provide a United Nations logistical support package to the Mission, including equipment and services,

Recalling also the subsequent resolutions of the Security Council by which the logistical support package for the Mission was extended, the latest of which was resolution 2710 (2023) of 15 November 2023, by which the Council extended the logistical support package until 30 June 2024,

Recalling further its resolution 63/275 A of 7 April 2009 on the financing of the activities arising from Security Council resolution 1863 (2009) and its subsequent resolutions thereon, the latest of which was resolution 77/315 of 30 June 2023,

Reaffirming the general principles underlying the financing of United Nations peacekeeping operations, as stated in its resolutions 1874 (S-IV) of 27 June 1963, 3101 (XXVIII) of 11 December 1973 and 55/235 of 23 December 2000,

Noting with appreciation that voluntary contributions have been made to the United Nations trust fund established to support the African Union Mission in Somalia,

1. *Takes note* of the status of contributions to the United Nations Support Office in Somalia as at 30 April 2024, including the contributions outstanding in the amount of 282.3 million United States dollars, representing some 3.8 per cent of the total assessed contributions, notes with concern that only 104 Member States have paid their assessed contributions in full, and urges all other Member States, in particular those in arrears, to ensure payment of their outstanding assessed contributions;

2. *Endorses* the conclusions and recommendations contained in the report of the Advisory Committee on Administrative and Budgetary Questions, subject to the provisions of the present resolution, and requests the Secretary-General to ensure their full implementation;

3. *Recalls* paragraph 24 of the report of the Advisory Committee, requests the Secretary-General to continue to make efforts to enhance selections and internal advancement of national staff, and to increase the participation of national staff, including national United Nations Volunteers, as appropriate, and requests that this be reviewed in the upcoming civilian staffing review;

4. *Also recalls* paragraph 36 of the report of the Advisory Committee, and requests the Secretary-General to conduct the upcoming civilian staffing review taking into account the existing context of the Office;

5. *Requests* the Secretary-General to ensure the full implementation of the relevant provisions of its resolutions 59/296 of 22 June 2005, 60/266 of 30 June 2006, 61/276 of 29 June 2007, 64/269 of 24 June 2010, 65/289

[83] A/78/622 and A/78/734.

[84] A/78/744/Add.8.

of 30 June 2011, 66/264 of 21 June 2012, 69/307 of 25 June 2015, 70/286 of 17 June 2016 and 76/274 of 29 June 2022, as well as other relevant resolutions;

Budget performance report for the period from 1 July 2022 to 30 June 2023

6. *Takes note* of the report of the Secretary-General on the budget performance of the Support Office for the period from 1 July 2022 to 30 June 2023;[85]

Budget estimates for the period from 1 July 2024 to 30 June 2025

7. *Decides* to appropriate to the special account for the United Nations Support Office in Somalia the amount of 547,409,500 dollars for the period from 1 July 2024 to 30 June 2025, inclusive of 499,765,200 dollars for the maintenance of the Support Office, 36,316,300 dollars for the support account for peacekeeping operations, 6,338,900 dollars for the United Nations Logistics Base at Brindisi, Italy, and 4,989,100 dollars for the Regional Service Centre in Entebbe, Uganda;

Financing of the appropriation for the period from 1 July 2024 to 30 June 2025

8. *Decides* to apportion among Member States the amount of 273,704,800 dollars for the period from 1 July to 31 December 2024, at a monthly rate of 45,617,458 dollars, in accordance with the levels updated in its resolution 76/239 of 24 December 2021, taking into account the scale of assessments for 2024, as set out in its resolution 76/238 of 24 December 2021, subject to a decision of the Security Council to extend the logistical support package;

9. *Also decides* that, in accordance with the provisions of its resolution 973 (X) of 15 December 1955, there shall be set off against the apportionment among Member States, as provided for in paragraph 8 above, their respective share in the Tax Equalization Fund of 6,169,200 dollars, comprising the estimated staff assessment income of 4,104,800 dollars approved for the Support Office, the prorated share of 1,480,200 dollars of the estimated staff assessment income approved for the support account, the prorated share of 289,100 dollars of the estimated staff assessment income approved for the United Nations Logistics Base and the prorated share of 295,100 dollars of the estimated staff assessment income approved for the Regional Service Centre;

10. *Further decides* to apportion among Member States the amount of 273,704,700 dollars for the period from 1 January to 30 June 2025, at a monthly rate of 45,617,458 dollars, in accordance with the scale of assessments for 2025 and the updated levels,[86] subject to a decision of the Security Council to extend the logistical support package;

11. *Decides* that, in accordance with the provisions of its resolution 973 (X), there shall be set off against the apportionment among Member States, as provided for in paragraph 10 above, their respective share in the Tax Equalization Fund of 6,168,900 dollars, comprising the estimated staff assessment income of 4,104,800 dollars approved for the Support Office, the prorated share of 1,480,100 dollars of the estimated staff assessment income approved for the support account, the prorated share of 289,000 dollars of the estimated staff assessment income approved for the United Nations Logistics Base and the prorated share of 295,000 dollars of the estimated staff assessment income approved for the Regional Service Centre;

12. *Also decides* that, for Member States that have fulfilled their financial obligations to the Support Office, there shall be set off against their apportionment, as provided for in paragraphs 8 and 10 above, their respective share of the unencumbered balance and other revenue in the amount of 24,738,700 dollars in respect of the financial period ended 30 June 2023, in accordance with the levels updated in its resolution 76/239, taking into account the scale of assessments for 2023, as set out in its resolution 76/238;

13. *Further decides* that, for Member States that have not fulfilled their financial obligations to the Support Office, there shall be set off against their outstanding obligations their respective share of the unencumbered balance and other revenue in the amount of 24,738,700 dollars in respect of the financial period ended 30 June 2023, in accordance with the scheme set out in paragraph 12 above;

---

[85] A/78/622.

[86] To be adopted by the General Assembly.

14. *Decides* that the increase of 251,700 dollars in the estimated staff assessment income in respect of the financial period ended 30 June 2023 shall be added to the credits in the amount of 24,738,700 dollars referred to in paragraphs 12 and 13 above;

15. *Invites* voluntary contributions to the United Nations trust fund established to support the African Union Transition Mission in Somalia;

16. *Decides* to include in the provisional agenda of its seventy-ninth session the item entitled "Financing of the activities arising from Security Council resolution 1863 (2009)".

IV. Decisions

Contents

2. *Decisions adopted on the reports of the Fifth Committee*

A. Elections and appointments

78/409. Election of members of the Committee for Programme and Coordination

B[1]

At its 53rd plenary meeting, on 16 January 2024, the General Assembly, on the basis of the nomination by the Economic and Social Council[2] and in accordance with the annex to Council resolution 2008 (LX) of 14 May 1976 and Assembly decision 42/450 of 17 December 1987, elected BULGARIA as a member of the Committee for Programme and Coordination for a term of office beginning on the date of the election and expiring on 31 December 2026.

As a result, as of 16 January 2024, the Committee for Programme and Coordination is composed of the following 34 Member States: ARGENTINA,** ARMENIA,*** BELGIUM,* BOTSWANA,* BRAZIL,*** BULGARIA,*** CAMEROON,*** CHILE,* CHINA,** COSTA RICA,*** CÔTE D'IVOIRE,*** FRANCE,* GERMANY,*** INDIA,*** IRAN (ISLAMIC REPUBLIC OF),*** ISRAEL,*** ITALY,*** JAPAN,*** KENYA,* LIBERIA,** MEXICO,*** MOROCCO,** PAKISTAN,*** PARAGUAY,* PHILIPPINES,** POLAND,*** REPUBLIC OF KOREA,** RUSSIAN FEDERATION,* RWANDA,*** SOUTH AFRICA,*** TUNISIA,** UNITED KINGDOM OF GREAT BRITAIN AND NORTHERN IRELAND,*** UNITED STATES OF AMERICA*** and URUGUAY.***

---

* Term of office expires on 31 December 2024.

** Term of office expires on 31 December 2025.

*** Term of office expires on 31 December 2026.

78/412. Extension of the appointment of the Under-Secretary-General for Safety and Security

At its 63rd plenary meeting, on 21 March 2024, on the proposal of the Secretary-General,[3] the General Assembly approved, notwithstanding section XI, paragraph 22, of resolution 59/276 of 23 December 2004, the exceptional extension of the term of Gilles Michaud (Canada) as Under-Secretary-General for Safety and Security by two years, until 30 June 2026.

78/413. Appointment of members of the Board of the 10-Year Framework of Programmes on Sustainable Consumption and Production Patterns

A

At its 63rd plenary meeting, on 21 March 2024, the General Assembly decided that the two-year term of office of the members of the Board of the 10-Year Framework of Programmes on Sustainable Consumption and Production Patterns shall begin on 21 March 2024, the date of their appointment, taking into account resolution 69/214 of 19 December 2014.

B

At its 63rd plenary meeting, on 21 March 2024, the General Assembly, in accordance with resolutions 67/203 of 21 December 2012 and 69/214 of 19 December 2014 and decision 78/413 A of 21 March 2024, decided to appoint BRAZIL, FINLAND, the RUSSIAN FEDERATION, SENEGAL, SOUTH SUDAN and the UNITED STATES OF AMERICA as members of the Board of the 10-Year Framework of Programmes on Sustainable Consumption and Production Patterns for a term of office beginning on 21 March 2024 and expiring on 20 March 2026.

---

[1] Decision 78/409, in section A of the *Official Records of the General Assembly, Seventy-eighth Session, Supplement No. 49* (A/78/49), vol. II, becomes decision 78/409 A.

[2] See A/78/519/Add.1; see also Economic and Social Council decision 2024/204.

[3] A/78/785.

As a result, as of 21 March 2024, the Board of the 10-Year Framework of Programmes on Sustainable Consumption and Production Patterns is composed of the following six Member States:[4] BRAZIL,* FINLAND,* RUSSIAN FEDERATION,* SENEGAL,* SOUTH SUDAN* and UNITED STATES OF AMERICA.*

At its 65th plenary meeting, on 3 April 2024, the General Assembly, in accordance with resolutions 67/203 and 69/214 and decision 78/413 A, decided to appoint BARBADOS as a member of the Board of the 10-Year Framework of Programmes on Sustainable Consumption and Production Patterns for a term of office beginning on 3 April 2024 and expiring on 20 March 2026.

At its 103rd plenary meeting, on 13 August 2024, the General Assembly, in accordance with resolutions 67/203 and 69/214 and decision 78/413 A, decided to appoint INDIA as a member of the Board of the 10-Year Framework of Programmes on Sustainable Consumption and Production Patterns for a term of office beginning on 13 August 2024 and expiring on 20 March 2026.

As a result, as of 13 August 2024, the Board of the 10-Year Framework of Programmes on Sustainable Consumption and Production Patterns is composed of the following eight Member States:[5] BARBADOS,* BRAZIL,* FINLAND,* INDIA,* RUSSIAN FEDERATION,* SENEGAL,* SOUTH SUDAN* and UNITED STATES OF AMERICA.*

* Term of office expires on 20 March 2026.

78/414. Election of non-permanent members of the Security Council

At its 86th plenary meeting, on 6 June 2024, the General Assembly, in accordance with Article 23 of the Charter of the United Nations, rule 142 of the rules of procedure of the Assembly and paragraph 17 of Assembly resolution 68/307 of 10 September 2014, elected DENMARK, GREECE, PAKISTAN, PANAMA and SOMALIA as non-permanent members of the Security Council for a two-year term of office beginning on 1 January 2025 to fill the vacancies occurring on the expiration of the terms of office of ECUADOR, JAPAN, MALTA, MOZAMBIQUE and SWITZERLAND.

As a result, as of 1 January 2025, the Security Council is composed of the following 15 Member States: ALGERIA,* CHINA, DENMARK,** FRANCE, GREECE,** GUYANA,* PAKISTAN,** PANAMA,** REPUBLIC OF KOREA,* RUSSIAN FEDERATION, SIERRA LEONE,* SLOVENIA,* SOMALIA,** UNITED KINGDOM OF GREAT BRITAIN AND NORTHERN IRELAND and UNITED STATES OF AMERICA.

* Term of office expires on 31 December 2025.

** Term of office expires on 31 December 2026.

78/415. Election of the President of the General Assembly at its seventy-ninth session[6]

At its 87th plenary meeting, on 6 June 2024, the General Assembly, in accordance with Article 21 of the Charter of the United Nations, rule 30 of the rules of procedure of the Assembly and paragraph 1 of the annex to resolution 33/138 of 19 December 1978, elected Philemon YANG of Cameroon as President of the General Assembly at its seventy-ninth session.

78/416. Election of the Vice-Presidents of the General Assembly at its seventy-ninth session

At its 87th plenary meeting, on 6 June 2024, the General Assembly, in accordance with rule 30 of the rules of procedure of the Assembly and paragraphs 2 and 3 of the annex to resolution 33/138 of 19 December 1978, elected

[4] Brazil, Senegal and the United States of America are serving their second consecutive term. Two vacancies for members from Asia-Pacific States, one vacancy for a member from Eastern European States and one vacancy for a member from Latin American and Caribbean States remain to be filled for a term of office beginning on the date of appointment and expiring on 20 March 2026.

[5] Brazil, Senegal and the United States of America are serving their second consecutive term. One vacancy for a member from Asia-Pacific States and one vacancy for a member from Eastern European States remain to be filled for a term of office beginning on the date of appointment and expiring on 20 March 2026.

[6] In accordance with rule 38 of the rules of procedure of the General Assembly, the General Committee consists of the President of the Assembly, the 21 Vice-Presidents and the Chairs of the six Main Committees.

the following 21 Member States as Vice-Presidents of the General Assembly at its seventy-ninth session: ALGERIA, ANGOLA, AUSTRIA, BARBADOS, CHINA, FRANCE, GHANA, GUATEMALA, ITALY, KYRGYZSTAN, MADAGASCAR, MICRONESIA (FEDERATED STATES OF), REPUBLIC OF MOLDOVA, RUSSIAN FEDERATION, SENEGAL, THAILAND, TONGA, TURKMENISTAN, UNITED KINGDOM OF GREAT BRITAIN AND NORTHERN IRELAND, UNITED STATES OF AMERICA and VENEZUELA (BOLIVARIAN REPUBLIC OF).

78/417. Election of the Executive Director of the United Nations Human Settlements Programme

At its 88th plenary meeting, on 7 June 2024, the General Assembly, upon nomination by the Secretary-General,[7] elected Anacláudia Marinheiro Centeno ROSSBACH (Brazil) as Executive Director of the United Nations Human Settlements Programme (UN-Habitat) for a four-year term of office.

The effective date of her appointment would be communicated to the General Assembly at a later stage.

78/418. Election of members of the Economic and Social Council

At its 88th plenary meeting, on 7 June 2024, the General Assembly, in accordance with rule 140 of the rules of procedure of the Assembly, elected the following as members of the Economic and Social Council:

(a) AUSTRALIA and FINLAND for the remainder of the terms of office of NEW ZEALAND and DENMARK, beginning on 1 January 2025 and ending on 31 December 2025;

(b) AUSTRIA for the remainder of the term of office of GERMANY, beginning on 1 January 2025 and ending on 31 December 2026.[8]

At the same meeting, the General Assembly, in accordance with Article 61 of the Charter of the United Nations, rule 145 of the rules of procedure of the Assembly and paragraph 17 of Assembly resolution 68/307 of 10 September 2014, elected ALGERIA, ANTIGUA AND BARBUDA, ARMENIA, AZERBAIJAN, BANGLADESH, CANADA, CÔTE D'IVOIRE, DJIBOUTI, the DOMINICAN REPUBLIC, ITALY, MEXICO, NETHERLANDS (KINGDOM OF THE), SAUDI ARABIA, SOUTH AFRICA, SRI LANKA, SWITZERLAND, the UNITED REPUBLIC OF TANZANIA and UZBEKISTAN as members of the Economic and Social Council for a three-year term of office beginning on 1 January 2025 to fill the vacancies occurring on the expiration of the terms of office of AFGHANISTAN, BELGIUM, BELIZE, CANADA, CHILE, CÔTE D'IVOIRE, CROATIA, CZECHIA, ESWATINI, INDIA, ITALY, KAZAKHSTAN, MAURITIUS, OMAN, PERU, TUNISIA, the UNITED REPUBLIC OF TANZANIA and the UNITED STATES OF AMERICA.

As a result, as of 1 January 2025, the Economic and Social Council is composed of the following Member States:[9] ALGERIA,*** ANTIGUA AND BARBUDA,*** ARMENIA,*** AUSTRALIA,* AUSTRIA,** AZERBAIJAN,*** BANGLADESH,*** BOTSWANA,* BRAZIL,* CABO VERDE,* CAMEROON,* CANADA,*** CHINA,* COLOMBIA,* COSTA RICA,* CÔTE D'IVOIRE,*** DJIBOUTI,*** DOMINICAN REPUBLIC,*** EQUATORIAL GUINEA,* FINLAND,* FRANCE,** HAITI,** ITALY,*** JAPAN,** KENYA,** LAO PEOPLE'S DEMOCRATIC REPUBLIC,* LIECHTENSTEIN,** MAURITANIA,** MEXICO,*** NEPAL,** NETHERLANDS (KINGDOM OF THE),*** NIGERIA,** PAKISTAN,** PARAGUAY,** POLAND,** QATAR,* REPUBLIC OF KOREA,* SAUDI ARABIA,*** SENEGAL,** SLOVAKIA,* SLOVENIA,* SPAIN,** SOUTH AFRICA,*** SRI LANKA,*** SURINAME,** SWEDEN,* SWITZERLAND,*** TÜRKİYE,* UNITED KINGDOM OF GREAT BRITAIN AND NORTHERN IRELAND,** UNITED REPUBLIC OF TANZANIA,*** URUGUAY,** UZBEKISTAN*** and ZAMBIA.**

* Term of office expires on 31 December 2025.

** Term of office expires on 31 December 2026.

*** Term of office expires on 31 December 2027.

[7] A/78/890.

[8] See A/78/876.

[9] One vacancy for a member from Eastern European States remains to be filled for a term of office beginning on the date of election and expiring on 31 December 2025.

78/419. Election of the Chairs of the Main Committees of the General Assembly at its seventy-ninth session

On 6 June 2024, the First, Special Political and Decolonization (Fourth), Second, Third, Fifth and Sixth Committees of the General Assembly held meetings in accordance with rules 99 (a) and 103 of the rules of procedure of the Assembly for the purpose of electing their Chairs.

At its 88th plenary meeting, on 7 June 2024, the President of the General Assembly announced that the following persons had been elected as Chairs of the First, Special Political and Decolonization (Fourth), Second, Third, Fifth and Sixth Committees of the Assembly at its seventy-ninth session:

First Committee:	Maritza CHAN VALVERDE (Costa Rica)
Special Political and Decolonization Committee (Fourth Committee):	Sanita PAVĻUTA-DESLANDES (Latvia)
Second Committee:	Muhammad Abdul MUHITH (Bangladesh)
Third Committee:	Zéphyrin MANIRATANGA (Burundi)
Fifth Committee:	Egriselda LÓPEZ (El Salvador)
Sixth Committee:	Rui VINHAS (Portugal)

B. Other decisions

1. *Decisions adopted without reference to a Main Committee*

78/504. Adoption of the agenda and allocation of agenda items

B[10]

At its 55th plenary meeting, on 7 February 2024, the General Assembly decided to consider directly in plenary meeting sub-item (c) entitled "Disaster risk reduction" of agenda item 18 entitled "Sustainable development", under heading A (Promotion of sustained economic growth and sustainable development in accordance with the relevant resolutions of the General Assembly and recent United Nations conferences), and to proceed expeditiously with the consideration of a draft decision.[11]

At its 57th plenary meeting, on 26 February 2024, the General Assembly decided to reopen consideration of sub-item (b) entitled "Social development, including questions relating to the world social situation and to youth, ageing, persons with disabilities and the family" of agenda item 24 entitled "Social development", under heading A (Promotion of sustained economic growth and sustainable development in accordance with the relevant resolutions of the General Assembly and recent United Nations conferences), to consider it directly in plenary meeting and to proceed expeditiously with the consideration of a draft resolution.[12]

At its 63rd plenary meeting, on 21 March 2024, the General Assembly decided to reopen consideration of agenda item 107 entitled "Crime prevention and criminal justice", under heading H (Drug control, crime prevention and combating international terrorism in all its forms and manifestations), and to proceed expeditiously with the consideration of a draft resolution.[13]

At its 69th plenary meeting, on 11 April 2024, the General Assembly decided to reopen consideration of agenda item 17 entitled "Follow-up to and implementation of the outcomes of the International Conferences on Financing for Development", under heading A (Promotion of sustained economic growth and sustainable development in accordance with the relevant resolutions of the General Assembly and recent United Nations conferences), to consider it directly in plenary meeting and to proceed expeditiously with the consideration of a draft resolution.[14]

At its 73rd plenary meeting, on 24 April 2024, the General Assembly decided to consider directly in plenary meeting agenda item 108 entitled "Countering the use of information and communications technologies for criminal purposes", under heading H (Drug control, crime prevention and combating international terrorism in all its forms and manifestations), and to proceed expeditiously with the consideration of a draft decision.[15]

At its 77th plenary meeting, on 2 May 2024, the General Assembly decided to reopen consideration of sub-item (a) entitled "Agriculture development, food security and nutrition" of agenda item 23 entitled "Agriculture development, food security and nutrition", under heading A (Promotion of sustained economic growth and sustainable development in accordance with the relevant resolutions of the General Assembly and recent United Nations conferences), to consider it directly in plenary meeting and to proceed expeditiously with the consideration of a draft resolution.[16]

At its 88th plenary meeting, on 7 June 2024, the General Assembly decided to consider directly in plenary meeting agenda item 25 entitled "Advancement of women", under heading A (Promotion of sustained economic

---

[10] Decision 78/504, in section B.1 of the *Official Records of the General Assembly, Seventy-eighth Session, Supplement No. 49* (A/78/49), vol. II, becomes decision 78/504 A.

[11] A/78/L.36/Rev.1.

[12] A/78/L.39.

[13] A/78/L.45.

[14] A/78/L.58.

[15] A/78/L.46.

[16] A/78/L.59.

growth and sustainable development in accordance with the relevant resolutions of the General Assembly and recent United Nations conferences), and to proceed expeditiously with the consideration of a draft resolution.[17]

At its 98th plenary meeting, on 10 July 2024, the General Assembly decided to consider directly in plenary meeting sub-item (i) entitled "Combating sand and dust storms" of agenda item 18 entitled "Sustainable development", under heading A (Promotion of sustained economic growth and sustainable development in accordance with the relevant resolutions of the General Assembly and recent United Nations conferences), and to proceed expeditiously with the consideration of a draft resolution.[18]

At its 103rd plenary meeting, on 13 August 2024, the General Assembly decided to reopen consideration of sub-item (b) entitled "Follow-up to and implementation of the SIDS Accelerated Modalities of Action (SAMOA) Pathway and the Mauritius Strategy for the Further Implementation of the Programme of Action for the Sustainable Development of Small Island Developing States" of agenda item 18 entitled "Sustainable development", under heading A (Promotion of sustained economic growth and sustainable development in accordance with the relevant resolutions of the General Assembly and recent United Nations conferences), and to proceed expeditiously with the consideration of a draft resolution.[19]

At the same meeting, the General Assembly decided to reopen consideration of sub-item (c) entitled "Agreement under the United Nations Convention on the Law of the Sea on the Conservation and Sustainable Use of Marine Biological Diversity of Areas beyond National Jurisdiction" of agenda item 75 entitled "Oceans and the law of the sea", under heading F (Promotion of justice and international law), and to proceed expeditiously with the consideration of a draft decision.[20]

At its 107th plenary meeting, on 6 September 2024, the General Assembly decided to reopen consideration of agenda item 11 entitled "Sport for development and peace: building a peaceful and better world through sport and the Olympic ideal", under heading A (Promotion of sustained economic growth and sustainable development in accordance with the relevant resolutions of the General Assembly and recent United Nations conferences), and to proceed expeditiously with the consideration of a draft resolution.[21]

At the same meeting, the General Assembly decided to reopen consideration of agenda item 18 entitled "Sustainable development", under heading A (Promotion of sustained economic growth and sustainable development in accordance with the relevant resolutions of the General Assembly and recent United Nations conferences), and to proceed expeditiously with the consideration of a draft resolution.[22]

Also at the same meeting, the General Assembly decided to reopen consideration of agenda item 68 entitled "Rights of Indigenous Peoples", under heading D (Promotion of human rights), to consider it directly in plenary meeting and to proceed expeditiously with the consideration of a draft resolution.[23]

78/528. Participation of non-governmental organizations, civil society organizations, academic institutions and the private sector in the third United Nations Conference on Landlocked Developing Countries

B[24]

At its 55th plenary meeting, on 7 February 2024, the General Assembly, on the proposal of its President,[25] recalling paragraph 51 (c) of its resolution 77/246 of 30 December 2022 on follow-up to the second United Nations Conference on Landlocked Developing Countries, decided to approve the participation of the non-governmental

[17] A/78/L.69.

[18] A/78/L.88.

[19] A/78/L.98.

[20] A/78/L.102.

[21] A/78/L.107.

[22] A/78/L.110.

[23] A/78/L.106.

[24] Decision 78/528, in section B.1 of the *Official Records of the General Assembly, Seventy-eighth Session, Supplement No. 49* (A/78/49), vol. II, becomes decision 78/528 A.

[25] A/78/L.40.

organizations, civil society organizations, academic institutions and the private sector as listed in the annex to the present decision in the third United Nations Conference on Landlocked Developing Countries and its preparatory process, to be held pursuant to resolutions 77/246, and 77/329 of 25 August 2023.

Annex

Action Contre la Pauvreté (ACP)

Association des Femmes pour le Développement Durable (AFDD)

Association des Jeunes Humanitaires Panafricains (HUMANUS)

Association Harmonie pour l'assainissement et le développement (ONG-ASHAD)

Association of Collegiate Schools of Planning

ASSOCIATION POUR LE DEVELOPPEMENT DE MOURTCHA (ADM)

Boys and Girls Educational Foundation

Brain Builders Youth Development Initiative

Center for Peace Building and Democracy in Liberia (CEPEBUD-Liberia)

Centre International Actions Technologiques Economiques Energétiques et Environnementales (CIAT3E)

Chambre de Commerce, d'Industrie, d'Agriculture, des Mines et d'Artisanat

Christian Care Foundation

Community Development Aid

Conseil National du Patronat du Mali

Coopératif Agro Sylvo-Pastorale des Amis pour la Solidarité

DECENT WORK FOR ALL BURUNDI

Earth Regenerative Project Sierra Leone

Employers Consultative Association of Malawi

Gender and Development for Cambodia (GADC)

Ghana Russia Center for Commerce and Relations

Global Energy Interconnection Development and Cooperation Organization

Global Good Net Works Ltd.

Hazras Charity Foundation

Hope for Humanity International

Instituția Privată Keystone Moldova

KALKAL HUMAN RIGHTS DEVELOPMENT ORGANIZATION (KAHRDO)

Kikandwa Environmental Association

LADLAD CARAGA INC.

Manzil Pakistan

Nash Vek Public Foundation

National Civil Society Council of Liberia

National Women Empowerment and Rehabilitation Organization (NWERO)

New World Hope Organization (NWHO)

Organisation d'intégration et de promotion des personnes atteintes d'albinisme (OIPPA)

Plateforme de la Société Civile Rwandaise (Rwanda Civil Society Platform)

Private Sector Foundation of Lesotho

Réseau des Jeunes pour le Climat au Tchad (REJEC-T)

RESEAU POUR LA RECHERCHE INTERNATIONALE SUR LA DESERTIFICATION (DesertNET International)

Rwanda Women Community Development Network

S&I STEP FORWARD Ltd.

Sea Rail (Botswana) (Proprietary) Limited

SINA (SOCIAL INNOVATION ACADEMY)

SOCIAL FORUM – ZAMSOF

Somaliler İş Adamları Derneği (Somali Business Association in Turkey)

SUSTAINABLE DEVELOPMENT COUNCIL

TRUE PROPHECY INTEGRATED DEVELOPMENT ACTORS (TIDA)

UNIVERSITY FOR DEVELOPMENT STUDIES

WELFARE

Women and Modern World Social Charitable Center (CWMW)

WOMEN IN PRESBYTERIAN MINISTRY UGANDA

World Future Active

C

At its 77th plenary meeting, on 2 May 2024, the General Assembly, on the proposal of its President,[26] recalling paragraph 51 (c) of its resolution 77/246 of 30 December 2022 on follow-up to the second United Nations Conference on Landlocked Developing Countries, decided to approve the participation of the non-governmental organizations, civil society organizations, academic institutions and the private sector as listed in the annex to the present decision in the third United Nations Conference on Landlocked Developing Countries and its preparatory process, to be held pursuant to resolutions 77/246, and 77/329 of 25 August 2023.

Annex

Action pour la Protection de l'Environnement et la Promotion des Filières Agricoles (APEFA)

AeTrade Group PLC

Africa-Europe Foundation

Agrodealers Association

ASSOCIATION FOR COMPETITIVE TECHNOLOGY

Bank of Kigali PLC

BETTER EDUCATION FOR DEPRIVED KIDS

BK GROUP PLC

Botswana Council of Non-Governmental Organizations

BOTSWANA GENDER BASED VIOLENCE PREVENTION AND SUPPORT CENTRE

[26] A/78/L.61.

CAYO – Concerned African Youth Organization

Chambre de Commerce et d'Industrie du Mali – CCIM

Chengeto Zimbabwe Organization

Chyau Bio Technologies Private Limited

Daka Space Technologies Ltd.

David Mogoma Foundation

Development Bank of Rwanda PLC

East African Centre of Excellence for Renewable Energy and Energy Efficiency

Ecobank Rwanda PLC

Farmer's Pride international

FÉDÉRATION DES ASSOCIATIONS DES FEMMES ENTREPRENEURES DE LA RÉPUBLIQUE CENTRAFRICAINE

Global Impact, Co-Develop

gold Youth Development Agency

Hear Their Voice Initiative (HTVI)

House of Mediation & Law

IMPRESSION STUDIO Ltd.

InspireLearn Limited

J.M. G Construction & General Trading Co. Ltd.

LE PARLEMENT EUROPEEN POUR LE DEVELOPPEMENT ET LA PLANIFICATION

Maison des Organisations de la Société Civile (MOSC) Anjouan

Marie-Claire N.Kuja Foundation

MASIELA TRUST FUND

Moti-Talk Creative Communications

Mouvement pour la Promotion de la Citoyenneté Responsable (MPCR)

One Africa Trust

Organization for Social and Economic Development

PEACE WORLD INTERNATIONAL

Petrohyper (Pty) Ltd.

PRIVATE SECTOR FEDERATION – RWANDA

PRO-FEMMES/TWESE HAMWE

Relief and Development Support Organization

Rwandan Organisation of Women with Disabilities

SEWA-USA

Tanshi Multiconcept Consults

The National Forum of Human Rights

Tongzhou Club (Beijing) Information Technology Co., LTD.

TRANSPORT CONSULT

Uthando Pharmacy

Water Access Consulting

YOUTH AND WOMEN FOR OPPORTUNITIES UGANDA

D

At its 107th plenary meeting, on 6 September 2024, the General Assembly, on the proposal of its President,[27] recalling paragraph 51 (c) of its resolution 77/246 of 30 December 2022 on follow-up to the second United Nations Conference on Landlocked Developing Countries, decided to approve the participation of the non-governmental organizations, civil society organizations, academic institutions and the private sector as listed in the annex to the present decision in the third United Nations Conference on Landlocked Developing Countries and its preparatory process, to be held pursuant to resolutions 77/246, 77/329 of 25 August 2023 and 78/315 of 10 July 2024.

Annex

Abigail and Partners

ACHAP

Africa Place & Equity Cities Foundation

African Landlocked Countries Research Centre

African Sun Energy

ASPIRING VISION IN SUPPORTING ADVANCEMENT ASSOCIATION (AVISA)

Association au Secours des Filles Mères (ASFM)

Association des Personnes Patriotes du Burundi (APPBU)

Association pour le Développement Socio-Economique et Technologique de la Jeunesse (ADEJ-Mali)

BARWAQA RELIEF ORGANIZATION

BENJY POETRY AND MUSIC GLOBAL CONCEPTS

Borderless Alliance

BORN Like This P.A.G

Botho University

Botswana Centre for Public Integrity

Botswana Exporters And Manufactures Association

Botswana Network for Mental Health

Botswana Organization for Sisters Empowering Junior Associates

Botswana Society For Human Development

Botswana Stock Exchange

CELEBRONS LE COURAGE DE LA FEMME (CCF)

Centre For Community Initiatives Against Human Trafficking (CIAHT)

ChildSafeNet

Culture Centre for the Deaf

[27] A/78/L.111.

Cynthia's Counselling and Empowerment Trust

Dandemutande Investments Private Limited

Dawn of Right

Destiny Creek Pty Ltd

Differently Abled Entrepreneurs Village

DigiGaon Foundation

디문파운데이션 DMUN Foundation

East Africa Job Center

Empower Success Solutions

Farmers Pride International

Foresight Generation Club

Formal Education Network for Private Schools (FENPS)

Foundation for Educational Demonstrations Preservation and Human Services (EDPAHS)

FRIENDLY INTEGRATED DEVELOPMENT INITIATIVES IN POVERTY ALLEVIATION

GÉANT

Global Bank Ethiopia S.C

Global Water Partnership Organization Botswana

Good Samaritan Association

Green Arrow (Pty) Ltd

Guangxi The Belt And Road Health Industry Investment Co., Ltd.

Holistic Innovation

Horn of Africa Social & Development Centre

iFirsh (Pty) Ltd

International Association Of Disaster Management (IADM)

Internet Society Botswana

Jeunes Acteurs pour le Développement Durable au Burkina Faso

JEUNESSE DU MONDE EN ACTION

Jeunesse pour la paix et le développement du monde rural (JPDMR)

JS Planning & Design

Kalahari Floor Tiles (PTY) Ltd

Lefifi Investments

Letloa Trust

Mobilisation pour le Developpement Integral du Niger (MDIN)

Molao Matters

MTN Group Limited

Mulika Afrika

Organisation pour la lutte contre les Stupéfiants, Boissons Prohibées, Tabagisme et Alcoolisme

Powertel Communications

Provincial Council For People of African Descent of New Brunswick INC

PULA SPACE

Qingdao Sherlock Manning musical instrument Co., Ltd

Queen Esther

Refugee Talent Group

Rewaste Solutions

Rosana Empowerment Foundation (REF)

Royal Academy

Satcom Industry Association

Sentebale

Shenzhen GLAT Fund Investment Management Co., Ltd

SININATU Children Support Organisation Limited

Société de Coopération pour le Développement Rural d'Afrique (SOCOODERA)

Society of Gender Professionals

Society of Road Safety Ambassadors

Southern Africa Telecentre Network

Stand As One

Sustain267

TANZANIA WOMEN AND YOUTH ADVISORY ORGANISATION

Temo-Thuo Setho Society

The Art Residency Center

The British School of Beijing, Shunyi

The Clicking Generation

The National Senior Citizens Organization of Liberia

The Shipping and Forwarding Agents Association of Zimbabwe

The Society For Children Orphaned By AIDS Inc.

The Upcycle Project

UGANDA FREIGHT FORWARDERS ASSOCIATION

ULAP Networks

Vertex Special Technology Pvt. Ltd.

Volunteer Hub International Trust

Women Advancing Nations (WOMAN)

Women for Development

Wuhan Cabell Energy Technology Co., Ltd

Yes We Can Relief Organization

Young Minds Africa

Youth Care Network

Zhongtai Jiye Investment Group Co., Ltd

ZTE Corporation

78/544. High-level plenary meeting on addressing the existential threats posed by sea level rise

At its 53rd plenary meeting, on 16 January 2024, the General Assembly, on the proposal of its President:[28]

(a) Decided to convene a one-day high-level plenary meeting of the General Assembly, within existing resources, on addressing the existential threats posed by sea level rise, on 25 September 2024;

(b) Requested the President of the General Assembly to finalize the organizational arrangements, including on a possible outcome document, for the high-level meeting, through open, transparent and inclusive consultations with Member States.

78/545. Report of the Secretary-General on the work of the Organization

A

At its 54th plenary meeting, on 7 February 2024, the General Assembly decided that, after the departure of the Secretary-General, his seat at the podium might be occupied by his representative.

B

At its 55th plenary meeting, on 7 February 2024, the General Assembly took note of the report of the Secretary-General on the work of the Organization.[29]

78/546. Authorization for the United Nations Office for Disaster Risk Reduction regarding the hosting of the secretariat of the Santiago network for averting, minimizing and addressing loss and damage associated with the adverse effects of climate change

At its 55th plenary meeting, on 7 February 2024, the General Assembly, on the proposal of Austria, Bulgaria, Canada, Croatia, Cyprus, Czechia, Denmark, Estonia, Finland, France, Germany Greece, Italy, Japan, Kenya, Latvia, Luxembourg, Malta, Netherlands (Kingdom of the), Norway, Poland, Portugal, the Republic of Moldova, Romania, Slovenia, Spain, Suriname, Sweden, Switzerland, the United Arab Emirates, the United Kingdom of Great Britain and Northern Ireland and the United States of America,[30] recalling the relevant resolutions regarding the United Nations Office for Disaster Risk Reduction, including resolutions 54/219 of 22 December 1999 and 56/195 of 21 December 2001, authorized the United Nations Office for Disaster Risk Reduction to enter into a memorandum of understanding with the Conference of the Parties to the United Nations Framework Convention on Climate Change and the Conference of the Parties serving as the Meeting of the Parties to the Paris Agreement regarding the hosting of the secretariat of the Santiago network for averting, minimizing and addressing loss and damage associated with the adverse effects of climate change, in line with decisions 6/CMA.5 and 2/CP.28.

78/547. Commemorative meeting of the General Assembly on the occasion of the International Day for the Elimination of Racial Discrimination

At its 63rd plenary meeting, on 21 March 2024, the General Assembly, on the proposal of its President, decided, without setting a precedent, to invite the Assistant Secretary-General for Human Rights, Ilze Brand Kehris, the Chair

[28] A/78/L.35.

[29] *Official Records of the General Assembly, Seventy-eighth Session, Supplement No. 1* (A/78/1).

[30] A/78/L.36/Rev.1; see also A/78/PV.55.

of the Committee on the Elimination of Racial Discrimination, Verene Albertha Shepherd, the Chair-designate of the Permanent Forum on People of African Descent, June Soomer, and the founder and Chief Executive Officer of Advancing Health Equity, Uché Blackstock, to make statements at the commemorative meeting on the occasion of the International Day for the Elimination of Racial Discrimination.

78/548. Commemorative meeting of the General Assembly to mark the International Day of Remembrance of the Victims of Slavery and the Transatlantic Slave Trade

At its 64th plenary meeting, on 25 March 2024, the General Assembly, on the proposal of its President, decided, without setting a precedent, to invite the Vice-Chancellor of the University of the West Indies and Chairman of the Reparations Commission of the Caribbean Community, Hilary Beckles, and youth activist Yolanda Renee King to make statements at the commemorative meeting on the occasion of the International Day of Remembrance of the Victims of Slavery and the Transatlantic Slave Trade.

78/549. Ad Hoc Committee to Elaborate a Comprehensive International Convention on Countering the Use of Information and Communications Technologies for Criminal Purposes

At its 73rd plenary meeting, on 24 April 2024, the General Assembly, on the proposal of Mexico,[31] recalling its resolutions 74/247 of 27 December 2019 and 75/282 of 26 May 2021, and taking note of the decision of the Ad Hoc Committee to Elaborate a Comprehensive International Convention on Countering the Use of Information and Communications Technologies for Criminal Purposes to resume its work at a later date with a view to concluding its work and providing the draft convention to the General Assembly at its seventy-eighth session, decided that the Ad Hoc Committee shall hold a reconvened concluding session of up to 10 days in New York at the soonest possible dates to allow the Committee to fulfil its mandate, and requested the Secretary-General to provide the necessary support and services for that purpose.

78/550. Postponement of the third United Nations Conference on Landlocked Developing Countries and the second session of the Preparatory Committee for the third United Nations Conference on Landlocked Developing Countries

At its 80th meeting, on 7 May 2024, the General Assembly, on the proposal of Botswana,[32] recalling its resolutions 76/217 of 17 December 2021, and 77/246 of 30 December 2022, by which the Assembly had decided to convene the third United Nations Conference on Landlocked Developing Countries in the first half of 2024 in Kigali at the highest possible level, including Heads of State and Government, and recalling also its resolution 77/329 of 25 August 2023, by which it had decided to hold the Conference from 18 to 21 June 2024 in Kigali and had also decided that the first and second sessions of the Preparatory Committee for the third United Nations Conference on Landlocked Developing Countries should have been should be organized from 5 to 8 February 2024 and from 29 April to 1 May 2024 in New York, decided that the third United Nations Conference on Landlocked Developing Countries shall be postponed to a later date, and also decided that the second session of the Preparatory Committee for the Conference shall be postponed to 3 to 5 June 2024.

78/551. Participation of non-governmental organizations, civil society organizations, academic institutions and the private sector in the Fourth International Conference on Financing for Development

At its 90th plenary meeting, on 13 June 2024, the General Assembly, on the proposal of its President,[33] as amended by a recorded vote of 59 to 10, with 40 abstentions,[34] recalling paragraph 4 (b) of its resolution 78/271 of 11 April 2024, entitled "Further modalities of the Fourth International Conference on Financing for Development", decided to approve the participation of the non-governmental organizations, civil society organizations, academic institutions and the private sector as listed in the annex to the present decision in the Fourth International Conference

[31] A/78/L.46.

[32] A/78/L.63.

[33] A/78/L.76.

[34] See A/78/PV.90 and A/78/L.79, as orally revised.

on Financing for Development and its preparatory process, to be held pursuant to resolutions 78/231 of 22 December 2023 and 78/271.

Annex

AlphaZULU Advocates

Asian Indigenous International Network

Boston University Global Development Policy Center

Catalan Fund for Development Cooperation

Centro Mexicano de Responsabilidad Global

Cercle des Filles pour le Développement (CFD)

Changing-Lives Verein

CLIMCOM Berlin – Climate & Company gGmbH

Commission for Development and Rights (CDAR)

Consejo Argentino para las Relaciones Internacionales

Daayyaa Generation Network (DGN)

Development Education Network-Liberia (DEN-L)

DMUN Foundation

Earth Regenerative Project Sierra Leone

FACT Coalition/Fund For Constitutional Government

Fair Tax Foundation

Fons Català de Cooperació al Desenvolupament

German Institute of Development and Sustainability (IDOS)

Germanwatch

Global Infrastructure, Finance and Development Authority, Inc. (GIFDA)

Global Poverty Project/Global Citizen

IE University Center for the Governance of Change

Inclusive Education for Sustainable Development (IESD)

International Youth Alliance for Family Planning (IYAFP)

KND Advisors OPC Pvt. Ltd

L'Alphabétisation et la Formation des Adultes (ANAFA)

Nash Vek Public Foundation

NOVACT

Positive Peace for Ethiopia

Project Starling

Red Latinoamericana por Justicia Económica y Social (LATINDADD)

Rural Aid Pakistan

Smart Talk Café

SOAS Centre for Sustainable Finance

Success Hands Tanzania Initiative

Sustainable Development Council

The Bretton Woods Project

TRACE KENYA

University for SDGs

Women for Positive Actions

Youths Enterprise Development and Innovation Society.

78/552. Building a peaceful and better world through sport and the Olympic ideal

At its 93rd plenary meeting, on 25 June 2024, the General Assembly took note of the solemn appeal made by the President of the General Assembly in connection with the observance of the Olympic Truce.[35]

78/553. Notification by the Secretary-General under Article 12, paragraph 2, of the Charter of the United Nations

At its 93rd plenary meeting, on 25 June 2024, the General Assembly took note of the note by the Secretary-General.[36]

78/554. Report of the Security Council

At its 94th plenary meeting, on 25 June 2024, the General Assembly took note of the report of the Security Council.[37]

78/555. Establishment of the list of speakers for the Summit of the Future

At its 98th plenary meeting, on 10 July 2024, the General Assembly, on the proposal of its President,[38] recalling its resolution 76/307 of 8 September 2022, in particular paragraphs 6 to 9 and 12 thereof, concerning the plenary meetings:

(a) Decided that the plenary meetings of the Summit of the Future shall be held, on the basis of two meetings a day, as follows:

Sunday, 22 September 2024: from 9 a.m.[39] to 3 p.m. and from 3 to 9 p.m.;

Monday, 23 September 2024: from 9 a.m. to 3 p.m. and from 3 to 9 p.m.;[40]

(b) Also decided that the list of speakers for the Summit shall be established in accordance with the procedure set forth in the annex to the present decision.

Annex

1. The list of speakers for the plenary meetings of the Summit of the Future will be established on the basis of four meetings. Following the opening segment from 9 to 10 a.m. on 22 September 2024, the remainder of that plenary

[35] A/78/917.

[36] A/78/300.

[37] *Official Records of the General Assembly, Seventy-eighth Session, Supplement No. 2* (A/78/2).

[38] A/78/L.77.

[39] The plenary meeting in the morning of 22 September will begin at 9 a.m. with the opening segment from 9 to 10 a.m. The opening segment will include the adoption of the outcome document followed by statements from the President of the General Assembly, the Secretary-General and youth representatives to be selected by the President of the General Assembly in consultation with Member States, pursuant to resolution 76/307 (para. 6 (a)).

[40] Including a closing segment from 8.30 to 9.00 p.m., which will feature a statement from the President of the General Assembly, pursuant to resolution 76/307 (para. 6 (b)).

meeting, until 3 p.m., will comprise 300 minutes for statements. The afternoon meeting of 22 September 2024 and the morning meeting of 23 September 2024 will each comprise 360 minutes for statements. The afternoon meeting of 23 September 2024 will comprise 330 minutes for statements, to be followed by the closing segment from 8:30 to 9 p.m.

2. The list of speakers for the plenary meetings of the Summit will be established initially as follows:

(a) The representative of the Secretary-General will draw one name from a box containing the names of all Member States, the Cook Islands, the Holy See, Niue and the State of Palestine, as well as the European Union (if presenting positions of the European Union and its member States as agreed by them, pursuant to paragraph 1 (a) of the annex to resolution 65/276 of 3 May 2011). This procedure will be repeated until all names have been drawn from the box, thus establishing the order in which delegations will be invited to choose their meetings and select their speaking slots;

(b) Four boxes will be prepared, each one representing a plenary meeting and each one containing numbers corresponding to speaking slots at that meeting, as follows:[41] 60 speaking slots for the morning meeting of 22 September 2024; 72 speaking slots for the afternoon meeting of 22 September 2024; 72 speaking slots for the morning meeting of 23 September 2024; and 66 speaking slots for the afternoon meeting of 23 September 2024;

(c) Once the name of a participating State or the European Union has been drawn by the representative of the Secretary-General, that delegation will be invited first to choose a meeting and then to draw from the appropriate box the number indicating the speaking slot in the meeting. The delegation will indicate to the Secretariat at that time the level of representation of the speaker and advise if its statement will be on behalf of a group. If, at the time when the speaking slot is selected, a delegation cannot indicate the level of its speaker, the Secretariat will record it as the level of Chair of delegation;

(d) If a delegation is absent from the meeting room when the name of that delegation is called, it will be given the opportunity to select a speaking slot from the box representing the preferred meeting (as availability permits) following the conclusion of the procedure for the drawing of lots and again prior to the end of the special meeting stipulated in paragraph 3 below. This opportunity will be given in the same order in which the delegation's name was initially drawn;

(e) Delegations that are unable to attend the special meeting for the drawing of lots may inscribe their names on the list of speakers for seven calendar days after the drawing of lots by contacting the Secretariat. These delegations will be given the opportunity to select a speaking slot from those remaining at the time of their inscription. After that deadline, no further inscriptions by States or the European Union (if presenting positions of the European Union and its member States as agreed by them, pursuant to paragraph 1 (a) of the annex to resolution 65/276) will be possible.

3. The establishment of the initial list of speakers for the Summit as outlined in paragraph 2 above will take place at a special meeting to be scheduled within one month of the adoption of the present decision.

4. Subsequently, the list of speakers for each meeting will be rearranged in accordance with the established practice of the General Assembly when organizing each category of speakers, following the order resulting from the selection process outlined in paragraph 2 above. Accordingly, within each plenary meeting, Heads of State will be accorded priority, followed by Vice-Presidents and Crown Princes or Princesses, Heads of Government, Deputy Prime Ministers, Ministers and Vice-Ministers, with group statements given further priority within each level. These levels will be followed by that of Chairs of delegation. Member States will be placed first within a given level at a given meeting, subject to the provision in paragraph (k) of the annex to resolution ES-10/23 of 10 May 2024.

5. The first provisional list of speakers will be made available shortly after the completion of the drawing of lots. Subsequent changes will be made in the following manner:

(a) If the level of representation changes, the speaker will be moved to the last speaking slot in the appropriate category at the same meeting;

(b) Participating States and the European Union may arrange to exchange their speaking slots. In cases of equality in the level of representation, a delegation will be moved to the exact position of the other delegation. In cases of inequality in the level of representation, a delegation will be moved to the last position in the appropriate category

[41] Based on the five-minute time limit applicable to participating States, pursuant to resolution 76/307 (para. 7).

at the meeting to which it is changing. Exchanges will be considered as completed only when all the delegations concerned have provided the Secretariat with their written confirmation of the exchanges as set forth above. Completed exchanges will only be cancelled upon notification by all the delegations concerned to the Secretariat of their intention to cancel the exchanges.

6. The second provisional list of speakers will be made available shortly after the deadline mentioned in paragraph 2 (e) above.

7. Following the circulation of the second provisional list, the Secretariat will open the remaining speaking slots to inscription by entities having received a standing invitation to participate as observers in the work of the General Assembly[42] and by the United Nations system, including the funds, programmes, specialized agencies and regional commissions, as well as the Bretton Woods institutions,[43] which are invited, time permitting, to make statements of up to three minutes, on a first-come, first served basis.

8. On the day of the plenary meetings, the list of speakers for each meeting shall be completed and no speakers will be rolled over to the next meeting. Speakers who are not present when their speaking turn comes will be automatically moved to the next available speaking slot within their category at the same meeting.

9. In order to accommodate all speakers at the Summit, statements by the participating States should be limited to five minutes, pursuant to paragraph 7 of resolution 76/307, on the understanding that this will not preclude the distribution of more extensive texts. Pursuant to rule 72 of the rules of procedure of the General Assembly, when a representative exceeds her or his allotted time, the President shall call the speaker to order without delay, which will be done by means of automatic microphone cut-off. In order to ensure that the statements from the list of speakers will begin on time at 10 a.m. at the morning meeting of 22 September 2024, any explanation of vote on the outcome document shall be incorporated into national statements instead of being made at the opening segment.

78/556. Participation of non-governmental organizations, civil society organizations, academic institutions and the private sector in the high-level Summit of the Future

At its 99th plenary meeting, on 11 July 2024, the General Assembly, on the proposal of its President,[44] as amended,[45] recalling paragraph 11 of its resolution 76/307 of 8 September 2022, entitled "Modalities for the Summit of the Future", decided to approve the participation of the non-governmental organizations, civil society organizations, academic institutions and the private sector as listed in the annex to the present decision in the high-level Summit of the Future, to be held pursuant to resolution 76/307.

Annex

100 Million Campaign

3 ideas

89up

Accountable Impact, Corp

ACD – Agency for Cultural Diplomacy (Agentur für Kulturdiplomatie)

ACTING FOR LIFE

Action 237-Suisse

ACTION DE DEVELOPPEMENT INTEGRAL POUR LA FEMME VEUVE, L'ENFANTA ABANDONNE ET LE JEUNE – ADIFEVEA World

Action des Jeunes pour l'epanouissement Global

[42] Resolution 76/307, para. 8.

[43] Ibid., para. 9.

[44] A/78/L.89.

[45] See A/78/PV.99 and A/78/L.91.

Action for Youth Development Uganda (ACOYDE)

Actions du Sud pour l'Environnement et le Développement Durable (ASE2D)

Action Solidaire pour la Paix et le Développement Intégré "ASPADI"

Active Help Organization

ACTS For Sustainable Development

Addictions Prevention and Rehabilitation Association of Kenya

Aden network for humanitarian works

A Diamond in the Dirt Foundation

Adjaristsqali Georgia LLC

Adoptees With Guatemalan Roots

Advocacy For Climate Change Education

Advocacy Network Against Irregular Migration

Advocates for Health and Rights of Women and Youths Initiative

AEFA (Agribusiness and Environmental Focus for Africa)

afflican company

Afghanistan Relief & Sustainable Development Organization (ARSDO)

AfICTA – Africa ICT Alliance

Aflatoun International

Africa2World Foundation

Africa Biodiversity Alliance

Africa Center for Health Systems and Gender Justice

Africa Communications Events France

Africa Diaspora Network Japan (ADNJ)

AFRICA DISASTER MANAGEMENT FOUNDATION

Africa Europe Foundation

Africa is Ready To Lead Foundation (ReadyToLeadAfrica)

Africa Law Students' Association (ALSA)

Africa Matters Initiative

African American Future Society

AFRICAN COALITION FOR DEVELOPMENT

African Diaspora Collective North and South America, Inc

AFRICAN DIPLOMATIC-ORGANIZATION – ADO

Africa Network Campaign on Education For All (ANCEFA)

AFRICAN FILM INSTITUTE

African Indigenous Governance Council

African Leaders Factory Initiative (ALFI)

African Liberators Economic Institute

African Network of Youth Policy Experts (AFRINYPE)

African Renaissance Trust

AFRICAN SCHOLARS CARE INITIATIVE

African Woman Global Network

AFRICAN WOMEN SOLIDARITY OF NEVADA INC

African Young Leaders Foundation – AYLF

African Youth Architects

Africa Place & Equity Cities Foundation

Africa Sustainable Climate and Environment Foundation (ASCEF)

Africa Unite

Afrivoices for Climate Change

AGAPE EARTH COALITION

Agbara Fund

Agency for Community Empowerment against Poverty

AgeWatch Africa Foundation

Ahadi Achievers Empowerment CBO

AIP-Kenya

AIS LLC

AKO Foundation

AKOFF Organization for Sustainable Development

ALBENA'A Development & Relief Organization (ADRO)

ALLIANCE CONTRE LA PAUVRETE AU MALI

Alliance for Accountability Advocates Zambia (AAAZ)

Alliance for Vietnam's Democracy

All In Foundation (AIF)

All Nations Arise and Manifest Initiative (ANAM Initiative)

AlMortaqa Foundation for Development

Alpha Development Model Foundation

Alsaid Foundation

Ambivium

Amedine International Citizens Center

AMERICAN AYUSH CORPORATION

AMERICAN FOOTBALL FOR AFRICAN MISSION

American Medical Women's Association

AMPLIFY GIRLS AFRICA

AMREF Health Africa

ANIJIE GLOBAL FOUNDATION

Anjiro Initiative

A PACK A MONTH

Arab Center for Cyberspace Research – ACCR

Arab Watch Coalition

Arab Youth Climate Movement Qatar

Arab Youth Sustainable Development Network

Area Power (Alliance for Rural Energy and Agriculture) Inc

Art Affair for Development Goals

ARTYC STUDIO SPA

ASFDH ONGDH/Action pour la Solidarité, la Formation et le développement de l'humain

Asian Development Bank Institute

Asian Indigenous International Network

Asia Pacific Mission for Migrants

ASOCIACION CIUDADANA POR LOS DERECHOS HUMANOS

ASOCIACION CIVIL POR DERECHOS DE NIÑOS, NIÑAS, ADOLESCENTES Y JOVENES DONCEL.

Asociación Cooperativa de Investigación Estadística [ACIES-Venezuela]

Asociación de Capacitación e Investigación para la Salud Mental

ASOCIACION DE DESORDENES DEL CICLO UREA Y ENFERMEDADES METABOLICAS PERU – ADCU METABOLICAS DEL PERU

Asociación Grupo de Pensamiento Afrodescendiente (GPA)

Asociación Instituto ipades para la Promoción de la Paz y el Desarrollo

Asociación Latinoamericana Ímpetu

ASOCIATION OF WOMEN IN ECONOMIC AND ENVIRONMENTAL DEVELOPMENT (AWEED)

Aspiration

Associação Casa Comum da Humanidade (Common Home of Humanity Association)

ASSOCIACAO INSTITUTO IUNGO

Associação InternetLab de Pesquisa em Direito e Tecnologia

Associação para Integridade de Crianças e Jovens em Angola (AICJA)

Association Club Amis de la Planète

ASSOCIATION CONGOLAISE POUR LE BIEN ETRE FAMILIAL

Association des Acteurs de Développement

ASSOCIATION DES FEMMES ARCHITECTES DU CONGO (AFARC)

Association des humanistes pour l'encadrement des filles mères et des personnes des œuvres

ASSOCIATION DES JEUNES COURAGEUX DU CONGO

Association des Personnes Patriotes du Burundi (APPBU)

Association for Generational Equity (operating publicly as Generation Squeeze)

Association for Long Term Existence and Resilience (ALTER)

Association for Promotion of the Ideas and Values of the United Nations MUNA – United Nations Assoc.

Association for Socially Applicable Research (ASAR)

Association For Voluntary Action

Association Global Humaniste

Association Jeunesse Verte Mali

Association Katawara

ASSOCIATION KIRIKOU Maroc

Association Maonah for Human Rights and immigration

Association of Private Nature Reserves of Minas Gerais

Association of Rwandan Female Journalists

Association of Uganda Professional Women in Agriculture and Environment (AUPWAE)

Association of Young Leaders United for Sustainable Development, AJLUDD

Association of Young People for Environmental Protection in Guinea-Bissau

ASSOCIATION PARLEMENT AFRICAIN DES JEUNES POUR L'EAU

Association pour la Justice Climatique, l'Environnement et la Nature pour le Développement Durable

Association pour le bien-etre familial Naissance desirable (ABEF-ND)

Association pour le Développement Socio-Economique et Technologique de la Jeunesse

Association SIRABA SCHOOL

Association Women for the Contemporary Society, Moldova

Astrea Media, Inc.

Atlantic College, a United World College

Atlantic State Legal Foundation Inc.

.au Domain Administration Limited

Authentic Caribbean Foundation Inc.

Autonomisation des Femmes et des Jeunes filles par le Tricotage (AAFJ/Trico BF)

Avandis Consulting

Aviva Investors

Awakening Africa Foundation Inc

AYGF (AFRICA YOUTH GROWTH FOUNDATION)

AYLF-AFRICAN YOUNG LEADERS FOUNDATION LBG

Aysplash Connect Limited

BAGMATI UNESCO CLUB

B AGRO CROP GH

Bajeti Hub (formerly International Budget Partnership Kenya)

Bangladesh Internet Governance Forum (BIGF)

Bangladesh Youth Leadership Center

Barguna nari Jagoran kormochuchi JAGO NARI

Barranquilla+20 Foundation

BARWAQA RELIEF ORGANIZATION

Bays Planet Foundation

BELEON HOLDINGS

Benadir University

Benevolence Coalition for Humanitarian Relief

Berkeley Existential Risk Initiative

BESMARK COFFEE COMPANY LIMITED

Beyond Poverty Africa Network

Bharatiya Stree Shakti

Biodiesel Georgia LLC

Biodiversity Hub International (BHI)

BIOSPHERE FOUNDATION UGANDA

Blavatnik School of Government, University of Oxford

BLESSED TO TRANSFORM

Blind Youth Association Nepal

Bloodman

Blue Heart International Org

Blue Planet Alliance

BMG3 Enterprises, Inc.

Bootblack

BORN Like This P.A.G

Bouygues Sa

boypro-ject consulting Inc.

Brain Builders Youth Development Initiative

Bridge 47

Bridges of Peace Initiatives (BPI)

Bridge That Gap Hope for Africa Initiative

Brigada 12

Bring Back Green Foundation

BRING LIGHT SAVE LIFE

Build Peace and Development

Bunchful, Inc.

Bureau de renforcement des capacités des femmes – training

BurnBright International

Butterfly Network – Global Health

Cadrell Advocacy Center

Campaign for Social Justice and Human Rights (CSJHR)

CANADA 2030

CANEUS International

Captain Planet Foundation

Care About Climate

Caregivers Asha Society

Caring Hands Foundation INC

Catálise Design e Inovação Social

CATMO ENTERPRISES

CAYO-Concerned African Youth Organization

CELEBRONS LE COURAGE DE LA FEMME

Cellfie Mobile LLC

Center Countering Digital Hate

Center For African Policy

Center for Fiscal Transparency

Center for Health Human Rights and Development (CEHURD)

Center for Indonesia's Strategic Development Initiatives

Center for School Leadership

Center for United Nations Constitutional Research

Center for Young Leaders in Africa (CYLA – Zambia)

Centre de Recherche sur l'Anti-Corruption

Centre for Education Policy and Climate Justice

Centre for Nonviolence and Gender Advocacy in Nigeria (CENGAIN)

CENTRE FOR SOCIAL DEVELOPMENT

Centre for Sport and Human Rights

Centre for Strategy and Cultural Diplomacy

Centre for Sustainable Development

Centre for Synchronous Leadership

Centro de Estudios en Libertad de Expresión (CELE)

Centro de Estudios y Capacitación con Prospectiva CECAPRO

Cercle des Filles pour le Développement (CFD)

CFW – Culture Funding Watch

Champions for Sustainable Development Goals

Change For Planet

Changing_Lives Verein

Check My Ads Institute

Chemichemi Foundation

Cherish A Child

Children Believe Fund

CHILD RIGHT AND DEVELOPMENT IMPLEMENTATION FOUNDATION INC

Child Rights International Network (CRIN)

CHINA-EUROPE TECHNOLOGY AND INNOVATION CONSULTING LIMITED

China Green Carbon Foundation

Christian Aid

Christian Care Foundation Pakistan

Christian Education and Development Organization (CEDO)

Christian Fellowship and Care Foundation

Chulaportraits-Multi Chula SL

CIRA, the Canadian Internet Registration Authority

Citizen Commons Advocacy International

CITY OF KISUMU URBAN AREAS ASSOCIATION

Civic Commission for Africa (CCfA)

Civics Unplugged

Civil Society Network on Climate Change in Nigeria

Civil Society on Sustainable Development Goals

Civil Society Organization

Civil Society SDGs Campaign/GCAP Zambia

Clean Air Fund

Clean Climate And Environment Campaign Initiative

Climate Action Network Canada

Climate Action Network – CAN AFRICA

Climate Governance Commission

Climate Resolve

Climate Science

ClimateWorks Foundation

Cloud Creative d.b.a The Convergence

Cloud Security Alliance Greater China Region

Club of Rome

Coalición Nacional de Mujeres Rurales, A. C.

Coalition Climat pour la Biodiversité et le Développement (CCBD-Congo)

Cochrane Collaboration (Cochrane)

Coding Rights

Columbia University

Comite de América Latina y el Caribe para la Defensa de los Derechos de las Mujeres CLADEM

Common awareness for future generations "FUTURE"

Community Action Against Plastic Waste (CAPws)

COMMUNITY ACTION FOR HEALTH & DEVELOPMENT (CAHED)

Community Advocacy and Awareness Trust

Community-Based Organization

Community Development and empowerment Initiative Programme (CDEIP)

COMMUNITY EDUCATION AND EMPOWERMENT CENTRE

Community Empowerment for Northern Development (CENOD)

Community Hands Foundation

Community Healing Network

CommUnity of the Deaf, Inc

Community Organization Training Programma

Community Restoration Initiative Project

Community Safety Project

Community United for Rural Development – CURD

Comunitatea Internet

Confederación de Nacionalidades Indígenas del Ecuador-CONAIE

CONGO CONNEXION

Congolese Young Leaders

Connected Advocacy for Empowerment and Youth Development Initiative

Connecticut Institute for Social Entrepreneurship

CONSEIL PROVINCIAL DE LA JEUNESSE DE KINSHASA (CPJ-kin)

Conservation Alliance of Kenya

Conservation Biology Institute

Consorcio para el Dialogo Parlamentario y la Equidad Oaxaca

Converse International Travel Agency LTD

Cooperation Canada

Coordenação das Associações das Comunidades Remanescentes de Quilombos do Pará (MALUNGU)

Coordination des Organisations des Peuples Autochtones de Guyane

Copenhagen Institute for Futures Studies

Corporación de Estudios y Desarrollo Norte Grande

Corporacion Movilizatorio

CorpsAfrica/Senegal

Corps des Jeunes Volontaires de la RDC

CORRE PRODUCOES SOCIOCULTURAIS LTDA

Lisa Russell Films, LLC

Creating Opportunities of Disadvantaged Persons (CODaP)

Creats International

CRISP

Culture All Nippon

Culture Centre for the Deaf

Customs Officers' Wives Association

Cysec Consulting Pvt Ltd

DAAYYAA GENERATION NETWORK (DGN)

Dalberg Catalyst

Dalit lives Matter Global Alliance

DAlpha, Inc.

Darfur Youth Center for Peace and development

Dark Matter Labs

DASTAK Women Rights and Awareness Foundation

Data Privacy Brasil

DATA -X- Tanzania

Datta Infotech Consultants

Daystar University

DDX

Democracy Without Borders

Destination Zero

Development Education Network-Liberia (DEN-L)

Development Impact Pathfinders Initiative

Development Reimagined

Dhanshiri Communication Limited

Dharma Alliance

Dholakia Foundation

Dhrubotara Youth Development Foundation

Dialogue intergénérationnel Platform DR Congo

DIAMS MultiCom International SARL

Diaspora organization

Digital Agenda for Tanzania Initiative

Digital Citizen Fund

Digital Empowerment Foundation

DigitalSENSE Africa

Digo Bikas Institute

Diplomacy for World Peace

DMS Academy

디문파운데이션 DMUN Foundation

Droits Humains Sans Frontières

Duke University

DUSHTHA SHASTHYA KENDRA (DSK)

DW Akademie

Dynamique des Femmes pour la Réforme de l'administration Publique

eArtH Projects

Earth Regenerative Project Sierra Leone

East Africa Job Center

Eastern Caribbean-Southeast Asia Chamber

e-CAB

ECB Sustainable Youth Foundation

ECO CLEAN ACTIVE INITIATIVE

EcoHarmony Eswatini

ECOHUMANITA

Economic and Trade Cooperation of African Youth – ETCAY

Eco Rafiki LLC

Eco-Social Development Organization (ESDO)

Ecosystem and Social Economic Development Organisation

ECO-UNION

ECUADORIAN RIVERS INSTITUTE

Education Development Trust

Education for All Coalition

Effective Altruism Hong Kong

EIA FEWA LTD (Effortless Insight Africa)

Eko Fondation

Elevate Young Minds

Eliberare Association

Emirates Human Rights Association

Empathy for Life Integrated Development Association (ELiDA)

EMPOWER AND SERVE KENYA

Empowered Women and Youth Globally

Enact Earth Foundation

Eniware, LLC

Enroot Innovation Foundation

Entreprise Forward

Environmental Protection and Development Association (EPDA)

ENVIRONMENT AND JUSTICE SOCIETY (ENJUS)

Enyuatta EcoJustice Centre

Espace Information Jeunesse Congo

Eureka soutien le bonheur

Euro-Med Youth Federation e. V

European Center for Not-for-Profit Law Stichting

European Climate Foundation

European Network of Medical Residents in Public Health (EuroNet MRPH)

European Partnership for Democracy

Eurovisioni AC

Evergreen Initiative for Empowerment and Constructive Development

Every Woman Treaty

Evidence Action

EY Georgia (EY LLC)

FAADEV – African women for development

Familiyaa Makers Services

FAMILLE ASSOCIEE DES JEUNES POUR LA PROMOTION DE L'AUTOCREATION D'EMPLOI AU BURUNDI « FAJPACEBU »

FAMILY GROWTH FOUNDATION

FAWAN ACTION NETWORK

FEDERACION DE COMUNIDADES NATIVAS FRONTERIZAS DEL PUTUMAYO

Federated Commodities LTD

Fédération Nationale des Jeunes Entrepreneurs du Congo

Federation of African Medical Students' Associations (FAMSA)

Federation of Community Forestry Users, Nepal (FECOFUN)

FEEDAR & HR COOPERATIVE AND MICROCREDIT UNIT WITH BOARD OF DIRECTORS

Feminist Dalit Organization

Feminists for Peace, Rights and Justice Center

FMC Corporation

FOGGS – Foundation for Global Governance and Sustainability

FONDATION AGAPE POUR L'ENFANT AFRICAIN (FAEA)

Fondation Culturelle Islamique de Geneve

Fondation Kalipa pour le Développement

Fondazione Think Tank ECCO ETS (ECCO)

Fonden World Climate Foundation

Footbridge Media Ltd

Fora: Network For Change

foraus

FOREIGN INVESTMENT NETWORK FIN

For The Fundamentals Limited

Forum for African Women Educationalists

Forum on Information and Democracy

FOUNDATION FOR CIVIL SOCIETY

Foundation for Community Development

Foyer de l'humanite pour un futur meilleur

Francis Koroma Foundation

Free Press Unlimited

French Solid Waste Partnership

FRIENDLY INTEGRATED DEVELOPMENT INITIATIVES IN POVERTY ALLEVIATION (FIIDIPA)

Fundación Centro de Implementación de Políticas Públicas para la Equidad y el Crecimiento (CIPPEC)

Fundacion Cultural Baur

Fundación Fuerza Del Presente

Humanidad Tecnológica

Fundación Karisma

Fundación Labradoras de San Isidro

Fundación Nueva Generación Argentina

Fundación para la Promoción del Conocimiento Indígena (FPCI)

FUNDACION SUSTENTABILIDAD SIN FRONTERAS

Fundacion Unimedicos

FUTURE ADVENTURE

Future International Foundation, Inc.

Gabidezin House of Fashion

Gargaar Organization

GEADIRR

Gender-Centru

Gender in Geopolitics Institute

Gender Media Connect

General federation of NGOs in Egypt

Generations Without Qat Organization

Geoscience Society of Somalia GSS

GEPHERRINI EXPORT LLC

Germanwatch

GESA – GROWING ECONOMIES AND SUSTANIBILITY ASSOCIATION

Getlit Creative LTD/GTE

GHANA HIV AND AIDS NETWORK

Ghana Russia Center for Commerce and Relations

GIBICTS CENTER FOR COMMUNITY AND YOUTH DEVELOPMENT

Gingando pela Paz

Girls Aid Movement

Girls Health Ed

GIRLS OUTLOUD LUWEERO-UGANDA

GIRON INFRA

Global Alliance for a Healthy Society

Global Alliance for Behavioral Health and Social Justice

Global Alliance for Surgical, Obstetric, Trauma, and Anaesthesia Care – G4 Alliance

GLOBAL CENTRE FOR CLIMATE & SECURITY GOVERNANCE (GCSG)

Global Challenges Foundation

Global Citizen Capital

Global Commission on Responsible Artificial Intelligence in the Military Domain

Global Community Engagement and Resilience Fund (GCERF)

Global Development Solutions

Global Education Futures

Global Energy Alliance for People and Planet (GEAPP), LLC

Global Environmental and Climate Conservation Initiative

Globale Studerende Danmark

Global Fund for Children

Global Governance Institute (GGI)

Global Greens (Verts Mondiaux)

Global Infrastructure, Finance and Development Authority, Inc.

Global Initiative for Digital Rights

Global Justice Now

Global Lighthouse Studios Foundation

Global Optimism Impact

Global Partners Digital

Global Partnerships Forum

Global Peace Initiative for the Poor

Global Shield (a project of Social and Environmental Entrepreneurs)

GLOBAL SURGERY UMBRELLA

Global Young Scientists π Community

Global Youth Forum

G N & Co Solicitors

GOAL Global

GobernArte

Gorgia

G P Y Recreational Services

GrandHedge International

GRAND SQUARED Corporation

Great African Arts Banner

Green Act for Fact Initiative

Green Congress of Kenya

Green Dimensions Network

Green Economy Coalition

Green Energy Mission Africa

Green Future Foundation – Section 8 Company Act

Green Growth Africa Sustainability Network (Green Growth Africa)

GREENING MUA ENVIRONMENTAL INITIATIVE (GMEI)

Greening the Islands Foundation

Green Landscape Association (GrEEN)

GreenLight Development Centre (GreenLight Initiative)

Green Loop Foundation

GREENREV GR

Greenspring Development Initiative

Grupo de Financiamiento Climático para Latinoamérica y el Caribe

GSS THINK

Gulf Research Center Foundation

Habitat Defenders Africa

Hablemos CO

Hack for Earth Foundation

Hainrichs Institut für Frieden und Nachhaltigkeitslösungen gUG

HAMI IMANI AFRICA

Hands of Help Children's Organization

Haraka Enterprise Development Initiative (HEDI) Trust

HARD WORKING FARMERS COMMON INITIATIVE GROUP

Hargeisa National Travel And Tourism Agency

Harvard Forest

Hawaii Local2030 Hub

Hazras Charity Foundation

Heads and Hands Initiative

HEAL Africa

Health and Water Foundation

Health & Help

HELP

Helping Africa Foundation

Henry L. Stimson Center

Her Dream Initiative

Higher Education for Good Foundation

HIGH LEVEL PROTOCOL SERVICES LIMITED

HIPERDERECHO

HIRED Consult

HOLU-NIKKA HUMANITARIAN FOUNDATION

Horizon 2045 Foundation

Hubei Shengze Carbon Technology Co., Ltd.

Huesofthemind Mental Wellbeing Foundation

Humana People to People

Human Concern USA

Humanitarian Enhancement Aid for Resilient Transformation-HEART

Humanitarian Journalism and Media Interventions, Methodist University of São Paul

Humanity For The World (HFTW)

Human Rights and Democratic Forum (FOHRID)

Human Rights and Development Services (HURDS)

Human Touch Foundation

Idec – Institute for Consumers Protection

IFEX

iLab

iLEAD AFRICA

illumine.earth

IMAL Initiative for Climate and Development

IMARISHA USAWA KENYA

Impact Compact, llc

Impactful Education

Impact Tank Analysis Foundation

Inclusive Society Institute

India Child Protection Fund

Indian National Trade Union Congress-INTUC

Indian Social Responsibility Network

India Youth For Society

INDIGENOUS FRIENDS OF THE MAU FOREST

Indigenous Women League Nepal – IWL Nepal

INITIATIVE DE PROMOTION DE L'EDUCATION DES BATWA POUR LE DEVELOPEMENT DURABLE, IPREBAD

INMATES EDUCATIONAL FOUNDATION

Innoignite

INSTITUT DE DIPLOMATIE PUBLIQUE / INSTITUTO DE DIPLOMACIA PUBLICA

Institut de la Culture Afro-Europeene a Paris (ICAEP)

Institute for Climate and Peace

Institute for Development and Leadership in Africa (IDEA)

Institute for future-fit economies

Institute for Justice and Reconciliation

Institute for Law & AI

Institute of Climate and Environment (ICE Institute), SIMAD University

Institute Of Neurodiversity (ION)

Instituto Alma Preta Jornalismo

Instituto BR Arte

Instituto de Referência Negra Peregum

INSTITUTO DE TECNOLOGIA E SOCIEDADE (ITS)

Instituto Haniel

Instituto Panamericano de derecho Y Tecnología (IPANDETEC)

Instituto VNDI

Integrated Rural Development Center (IRDC)

Intergenerational Center for Global Action

INTERNATIONAL CARBON NEUTRALITY INDUSTRY RESEARCH ORGANIZATION LIMITED

International Center for Future Generations (ICFG)

International Climate Change Development Initiative

international commission of culture and diplomatic relations

International Corporation ICR LLC

International Council of Traditional Sports and Games

International Federation of Coalitions for Cultural Diversity (IFCCD)

International Human Rights Consortium

International Institute for Environment and Development Europe

International Network for Governmental Science Advice (INGSA)

International Network of Human Rights Defenders

International social educational center "Barqaror Hayot"

International Society for Digital Earth (ISDE)

International Society of Diplomats

International Transport Workers Federation – ITF

International Treatment Preparedness Coalition Global NPC

International WeLoveU Foundation

International Youth Alliance for Family Planning

International Youth Council Yemen (IYCY)

International Youth Summit Sierra Leone

Internet New Zealand Incorporated (InternetNZ)

Intiative Bonne Gouvernance des Ressources Naturelles au Kivu

Irish Dairy Milk Nigeria Limited

ISA Sumak Kawsay

ISHAKA 2250

Istanbul Mineral and Metals Exporters' Association

Iswe Foundation

iVoting

iZone Hub Trust

Jafari Jata Solution

Jagaran Media Center (JMC)

Jaggarta Social Welfare Organization

Japan Youth Council

JEHOVAH ALIVE FOR OLD AGE (JAFOA)

Jesuit European Social Centre

Jeunesse du Monde en Action

Jeunesse pour la paix et le développement du monde rural (JPDMR)

Jeunes Verts Togo

Jhpiego

Joep Lange Institute

Journalists for Human Rights

Jóvenes Articulando Territorios A.C.

Joy for Children – Uganda

JSC TBC Bank

Jual Foundation Inc

JUHUDI COMMUNITY SUPPORT CENTER (JUHUDI CENTER)

Julie Ann Wrigley Global Futures Laboratory at Arizona State University

Juventud Poitica y Desarrollo JPD

Juventud Unida en Accion

kaalmo Community welfare

Kajiado Disability Inclusion Forum

Kamehameha Schools

KATETA PEOPLE LIVING WITH HIV/AIDS-KAPELA

Keeping Marriage Alive Initiative

Kelem Ethiopia

KEN G MORKA FOUNDATION

Kenya Institute of Puppet Theatre

Kenya Model United Nations

Kenya National Alliance of Street Vendors and Informal Traders (KENASVIT)

Kenyan Youth Biodiversity Network

Kenya Water and Sanitation Civil Society Network

Kerry Inc.

Kesharwani Shiksha Samiti

Keystone Academy 北京市鼎石学校

Kiiren AI Inc.

KILELE YOUTH ORGANIZATION

KOTHOWAIN (Vulnerable Peoples Development Organization) Bandarban Hill Tract, BANGLADESH

Kunashe Foundation

Kyoga Veritas Radio LTD

Lab for Future Generations

Labhya

LabJaca

L'AFRIKANA

Lake Region Womxn Health and Equal Rights (LARHWER) Kajulu Womens Health Rights Cbo

Land for Future

Land Rights Defenders Inc

Lanka Jathika Sarvodaya Shramadana Sangamaya

Laudato Si' Movement

LAWYERS TECH HUB FOUNDATION

LEADERS DE DEMAIN

Learning Planet Institute

Legal Aid Forum

Leonardo/ISAST

Les Amis du Bassin du Congo / Friends of the Congo Basin

LES FEMMES DE LA DIASPORA TCHADIENNE

LET US DREAM

Lex Consulting

L'humanité au cœur de nos actions (HU.CO.A.)

Life Makers Egypt

LIFT AFRICA FOUNDATION

Light Foundation for Development

LIMPS LTD

LiveWell Initiative LWI

Living Your Dream Initiative

Logictry & The Family Foundation (dba Keep Families Giving Foundation)

Lomisi JSC

London School of Hygiene & Tropical Medicine

Love To Help Organization

Machakos University

Magical Motors

Mahidol Public Health Association

Maltiti Foundation

MAMA AKUAVI AGBEMALE MEMORIAL FOUNDATION

MAPAS – Métodos de Apoio a Práticas Ambientais e Sociais

Marginalized Communities Advocacy Network

Marie-Claire N.Kuja Foundation

Masculinity Institute

Maseno University International Relations Scholars Association

MATERNAL CHILD HEALTH AND HIV AIDS FOUNDATION

Mengo Youth Development Link-Uganda

MENTAL RECOVERY INTERNATIONAL

Mesa por la Vida y la Salud de las Mujeres

METHADONE RECOVERY COMMUNITY EMPOWERMENT TANZANIA(MRCE-TZ)

Mexican Center for Philanthropy (Cemefi)

Microsoft Corporation

Migrant Help

Migration Action and Advocacy Foundation (MAF)

Migration Youth and Children Platform

milliongenerations foundation

Minderoo Foundation

Mission Exeko

MIssion Foundation Movement

Mizizi Afriqa

Monash University

Montagnards Indigenous Peoples

Morningstar Sustainalytics

Morobe Development Foundation

Moroccan Association of Green Economy for Environment and Climate Justice.

Most Influential People of African Descent (MIPAD)

Mother Earth Network

MOTION YOUTH HUB

Mouvement de la jeunesse Une et Indivisible de Djibouti

Movement for Community-led Development

Mtree Inc

MuemAction Post

MUHAMMAD AKRAM & SONS TRADING & INVESTMENT

Muhammad Akram Sons Trading Investment

Munansi Green Initiative

Munich Security Conference

MushinToTheWorld Foundation

Mutual Productions

My Empowerment Platform

MY GOALS FOUNDATION; AFRICA FOR SDGS

MY World Mexico: Hub of Action for Sustainable Development

NACIONALINE NEVYRIAUSYBINIU VYSTOMOJO BENDRADARBIAVIMO ORGANIZACIJU PLATFORMA

NAFAS

Nahugombe CBO

NairoBits Trust

NAJIMUDU EMPOWERMENT INITIATIVE

Nasco Foundation

Nash Vek Public Foundation

National Association of Reentry Professionals Inc.

National Democratic Institute

NATIONAL FORUM FOR ADVOCACY NEPAL (NAFAN)

National Human Rights Commission of Nepal (NHRC)

National Senior Citizens Organization of Liberia

National Youth Service Action and Social Development Research Institute

Natural Capitalism Solutions

Natural Resource Governance Institute

Nawiri Foresight

Neeman Global Capital

NELIG GROUP LTD

Nepal Peacebuilding Initiative

Network of Young Key Populations

Network of Youth for Sustainable Initiative

NEURO KIDS WARRIORS

New Lines Institute

Next Gene

NEXTGEN SCIENCE LTD

Nicklaus Children's Health System

Nicole Ilunga Foundation

Nile Girls Forum

Nile Humanitarian Development Agency

Nirwan University Jaipur, Rajasthan, India

Nkunzi Foundation Limited

Noble Citizen Foundation

Nominet UK

NOORNGESA

northerrn aid development agency

Novact Institute for Nonviolence

NOW! Aisbl

Oando Foundation

OBA Global Citizens Limited

Ohana One International Surgical Aid & Education

O'KANATA

OLABODE YOUTH AND WOMEN INITIATIVES (OYAWIN)

Olympes de la Parole Canada / Voices of Olympia Canada

One Africa Trust

ONE Campaign

One Future Collective

One World Trust

ONG ASDEMIN

ONG-ASHAD

ONG FUTURE FOR FUTURE

ONG Mutualité des Volontaires Africains pour le Développement

ONG SOLIDARITÉ AUX ENFANTS DEMUNIS Fond

ONG WOIYO KONDEYE

Onyeisi Care Foundation

Open Government Partnership

Open Knowledge Foundation

Ordre des Jeunes Leaders Africains (OJLA) / African Youth Leaders Order

Organisation Humanitaire pour le Développement Lcal (OHDEL)

ORGANISATION NATIONAL POUR LA DEFENSE DES DROITS DE L'HOMME ET DES LIBERTES PUBLIQUES

Organisation of Islamic Youth

Organisation Paysanne Pour le Développement Durable (OPDD)

Organisation Pour la Promotion Agro-Pastorale et le Développement au Congo (OPADEC)

Organisme à but non lucratif

Organization for prevention rehabilitation and integration of female street children (OPRIFS)

ORION Expertise Consulting

Our Kids' Climate

O-YES Global Foundation

Pak Mission Society

PALACE OF BREAKTHROUGH MINISTRIES

Pan Africa ILGA

Pan-African Council

PAN AFRICAN LAWYERS UNION

Pan African Womens Association (PAWA)

Panel d'Experts de la Résolution 2250

PANIER D'ASSISTANCE HUMANITAIRE AUX VULNERABLES EN SIGLE PAHV-ASBL

Panorama Global

Paradigm Initiative for Information Technology Development

Parakerja

Parents for Future UK

Parity

Parkers Mobile Clinic

Parlement des Jeunes Leaders de la Société Civile Guinéenne

Partnerships For Change

Partners in Population and Development

Pathfinders Global

Pathways for Women's Empowerment and Development (PaWED)

Pay-W Clinic

PCU-Nagasaki Council for Nuclear Weapons Abolition

Peace For Sustainable Development East and Horn of Africa

PEACE WORLD INTERNATIONAL

Pearlstone Associates

PELSE CONSULTING

Peoples Development Community (PDC)

Peoples Trust Jaipur India

Peregrine Ventures

Perkins School For The Blind India Foundation

Poverty Eradication and Sustainable Action Aid (PESAID)

Piraporiando

Planet Aid

PLANT-FOR-THE-PLANET FOUNDATION

Plataforma CIPÓ

Ploughshares Fund

POJAFCI

Powerful Management Leadership & Technology Center

Power House Youth Club

Powering Young Initiatives

Prakramika Vocational Institute

Prime Demand Solution

Professionals For Humanity (PROFOH)

PROGRESPECT

PROJECT 100

Project Starling

Promad Infotech Foundation

Prometheus Institute for Democracy and Human Rights

Promocao do Ensino de Qualidade S/A

Promotion Of Sustainable Development in Donga-Mantung Association

PROSPEKTIKER – European Institute for Futures Studies and Strategy

Psychology Of Winning

Public Fund Fund for Support of Labor Initiatives

QATAR CENTRE FOR PEACE AND DEMOCRACY LTD

Qhala Ltd

QS ImpACT

Quincy Institute for Responsible Statecraft

RadicalxChange Foundation

Rahmatullah Children's Support and Advocacy Foundation (RACAS Foundation)

Rainbow Refuge Africa

Raising Star Africa Foundation

Rangeen Khidki Foundation

REACHOUT SALONE

Recherches et Documentation Juridiques Africaines asbl

Red de Mujeres Afrolatinoamericanas, Afrocaribeñas y de la Diáspora

Red en Defensa de los Derechos Digitales (R3D)

Red Mexicana de Estudios en Cooperación Internacional y Desarrollo (REMECID)

Red Mundial de Jóvenes Políticos

ReformWorks

Refugee Consortium of Kenya

Re-Imagining New Communities

RELANCE ET RESTAURATION DE LA VIE SOCIALE "RESVISO"

RENEW Advisory

Reproductive Advocate Health Education Ghana

Rescue Mission International (ReMI)

Rescue Women Cameroon (REWOCAM)

Research Institute for Humanity and Nature

Reseau Burkinabe Pour une Economie Circulaire

RESEAU DE COMMUNICATION ET DE DEVELOPPEMENT DE LA FEMME SENEGALAISERECODEFSenegal

Réseau des Hommes Engagés pour l'Egalité de Genre en République Démocratique du Congo RHEEG-RDC PECS

RESEAU DES JEUNES POUR LE CLIMAT AU TCHAD

ReseaudesOrganisations des Jeunes Leaders Africains Des Nations Unies Section Cote D'IvoireROJALNUCI

Réseau des organisations de solidarité internationale France-Essonne

Resilient40

Resilient Communities Building Initiative

Res Non Verba – Civic House

Resources Legacy Fund

REVILA

RIDING-UP

ROLDÁN MILLÁN JOSÉ JOAQUÍN 2017 S.L.

Role Model Maker

ROOMS ART THERAPY LIMITED

Rooms Hotels Lab LLC

Rovira i Virgili University/Universitat Rovira i Virgili

Royal African Society

RUA PERU UCSM

Rural Aid Pakistan

Rural Area Development Programme (RADP)

SaciWATERs

Sadar Development Institute

Saddle River Day School

Safe Dada Foundation Kenya

SAHRiNGON TANZANIA CHAPTER

Saidika Organization

Saint Louis University, Madrid

salama women's institute

SAM Empowerment Foundation

Samprity Aid Foundation

Sarauniya International Development Organization

Scar Of Life Youth Organization

School of Democracy Nepal

School of International Futures

Science Undergraduate Society (SUS) of McGill University

SOAS University of London, SCRAP Weapons

S.D.TALENTOS MÚLTIPLUS – COMÉRCIO E PRESTAÇÃO DE SERVIÇOS (SU), LDA

SECURE LIVELIHOODS FOR WOMEN FORUM

Security NextGen

Senti Community Based Organisation

SEPP Kenya International

Set Free to Thrive

Sex & Samfund / Danish Family Planning Association (DFPA)

Shallom Love and Care Foundation

Sharjah Social Empowerment Foundation

She Forum Africa Initiative

SHIELDTHEM SUPPORT ORGANIZATION

Signals from the Grassroots

SilverLining

Simon Institute for Longterm Governance

Smart Talk Cafe

Social Good Fund Inc.

Social Linkages for Youth Development and Child Link

Social Welfare Development Programme – ACES – Africa Center

SOCIETE SOMMAC

Society of Gender Professionals

Solidaris – Union Nationale des Mutualités Socialistes – Solidaris (Solidaris)

Solidarity and Action Against the HIV Infection in India

Solutions for Our Climate

Somali Vulnerable Actors (SOVA)

Somali Youth Horizon

SOON Future Studies

Sortedlife Husika Afrika Group

Soulbeegood

South African Parenting Programme Implementers Network

Southern African AIDS Trust

SOUTH WEST MULTIPURPOSE FARMERS COMMON INTIATIVE GROUP

Soutien social

Space Era Germany

SPARK Foundation

Speculative Futures Aotearoa New Zealand

Stand As One

Starlight Foundation

STAR UP KOBIKA NA NDAKU SARL

STAWISHA AFRICA INITIATIVE

Stellenbosch University

Steve Global Adventures

St. Gallen Foundation for International Studies / St. Gallen Symposium

Stop TB Partnership-Kenya

Strategic Communications Lab

Student Energy

Student Partnership Worldwide India Project Trust (Restless Development India)

Student Platform for Engineering Education Development (SPEED)

Success Hands Tanzania Initiative

Sudanese Development Initiative

Sunshinengirls USA

Sustainability Week Pakistan

Sustainable Development And Response (STAR) Foundation

SUSTAINABLE DEVELOPMENT COUNCIL

Sustainable Energy and Enterprise Development for Communities

SUSTAINABLE ENVIRONMENT FOOD AND AGRICULTURE INITIATIVE

SUSTAINABLE FUTURES INITIATIVE

Sustainable Green Future Foundation

Sustainable Impact Capital & Holding

Sustainera Consulting Services

Swarovski Foundation

SYNERGIE DES FEMMES DE LA SOCIETE CIVILE

Tadamun Social Society (TASS)

Tag a Life International

Taha Enterprise

Talento Incluir

Talento Senior 45

tandemLEAP

TANGO

Tanyak

Tanzania Community Health Information and Support (TaCHIS)

Tanzania Human Rights Defenders Coalition (THRDC)

TANZANIA WOMEN AND YOUTH ADVISORY ORGANISATION

Tanzania Youths Behavioral Change Organization (TAYOBECO)

TaYA

Teaching Artist Institute

Teach the Future

Tears of the Earth Foundation

TEDIC – TECNOLOGIA, EDUCACION, DESARROLLO, INVESTIGACION Y ASOCIACION TEDIC COMUNICACION

Tegla Loroupe Peace Foundation

Terra Marine Research Institute India

Texas Women's Alliance

The African Youth Cafe

The Amina Agbo Foundation

The Assembly Innovation Hub Ltd

The Association of Professional Futurists

The B Team

The Children of Ukraine Foundation

The Club of Rome

The Confederation of Micro and Small Enterprises – Kenya Chapter (CMSEOK)

The Eagles for Life Kenya

The Earth

The Egyptian Food Bank

The Engineering Organization For Development

The Foundation for Post Conflict Development

The Futures Forum

The Global Listening Project

The Grace Foundation Hope For The Hopeless

The Green Economics Institute

The Gulmit Educational and Social Welfare Society

The Hack Foundation

The Harbor House

The Human Security Institute

The Indegenous

The Independent Commission for Human Rights in North Africa (CIDH AFRICA)

The Intelligent Indian

The Interfaith Alliance for Safer Communities

The Iraqi Institution for Development

The IREDE Foundation

The Jakaya Mrisho Kikwete Foundation

The Kenya Pro-Ageing Organization

The Light Millennium Inc

The Middle East Institute

The Milken Institute

The Millennials Movement

The Millennium Project

The National Forum of Human Rights

The New Global Order ETS

Theodora Anavhe Adamu Foundation (TAAF)

The Open-Led Company

The REACH Programme

The Resiliency Initiative

The Society For Children Orphaned By AIDS Inc.

The Soil Solution

The South Australian Youth Forum Inc.

The special physically challenged care foundation

The Strategic Priorities Hub

The Sustainable Development Response Organization

The Undivide Project

Refugee Congress

The Viden Fate Foundation

The Winford Centre for Children and Women

The Working Group on Girls

The Young and Woman Initiative YAWI

THE YOUNG CHANGEMAKERS

The Youth Agenda

The YP Foundation

Think Tank

Thriving Up Initiative

Tiger Kim's Academy (KIMHOSUL, Inc.)

Tiriig Technology

TITI FOUNDATION

Together

TonyWild Foundation Limited

TQH Consulting Private Limited

TRACE KENYA

Trailblazer For This Generation

Trans*Alliance Kenya (TAK)

Transcultural Psychosocial Organization Nepal (TPO Nepal)

Transformative Leaders Network- Africa (TRANET-Africa)

Transparency International UK

TRIUNE FOUNDATION

Trust for Indigenous Culture and Health (TICAH)

Tuboreshe Pamoja CBO

Turkish Academy of Sciences

Twaweza Community Development Agenda

UDGOON SUSTAINABLE DEVELOPMENT INITIATIVE

Ujana Youth Sustainable Development Network

Último Recurso

UNDER PRIVIEGED EDUCATIONAL WELFARE SOCIETY

Under Privileged Advancement by Youth (UPAY)

UN Global Compact Network Georgia

UNGP for SDGs

UNICEF Sweden

UNION DES JEUNES CONGOLAIS POUR LE CHNAGEMENT

Union des Jeunes pour le Développement Durable

UNITED INSTITUTIONS FOUNDATION

United Nations Association Indonesia

United Nations Association of Chad

United Nations Association of Ethiopia (UNA-ET)

United Nations Association of South Sudan

United Nations Association of Tanzania

United Nations Association of the USA Bronx Chapter

United Nations Association of the USA – Capital Area Division

United Nations Association of Uganda

United Nations Association (Z) UNA

United Voices For Global Impact Corporation

United Youth Initiative for Africa

UNITY AND SENDING PEACE TO ALL TRIBES

Universal Farmers Association (UFA), Inc.

Universal Greening Organistion

Universidad del País Vasco/Euskal Herriko Unibertsitatea

Universidad Externado de Colombia

Universidad Nacional Autónoma de México

Université Laval

University for SDGs

University of California, Davis

University of Cambridge

University of Castilla-La Mancha

University of Connecticut

University of Notre Dame / Keough School of Global Affairs

University of Wales, Trinity Saint David

Unlocking Communities

Unlock Young Leaders Summit

UN Youth Australia

Urdd Gobaith Cymru

URGENCE CONTRE LA FAIM (UCF)

Usawa Agenda

Ustawi Analytica Limited

US Women's Caucus

UWEZO YOUTH GROUP

VALUE FE-MALE NETWORK

Vibrant Voices Villages Community Based Organization.

Victim Advocates International

Vijana Amani Pamoja (VAP)

Vijana Think Tank

Village Farmers Initiative (VFI)

Virgin Foundation, trading as Virgin Unite

VIVA ART e.V.

VIVA HUMAN INC.

Voces de Mujeres Afrodescendientes en Panamá

Voice Life Health Organization

VolCare Foundation (VCF)

VOLUNTARY ACTION NETWORK INDIA

Voluntary Association for Peoples Service (VAPS)

VOW Social Work Service Centre

Vyaelea Organization (Vyaelea)

Wa3i Foundation

Wama Organization for Development and Human Rights

Wangoh Dynamics Technologies, Inc-USA

WANWOD DEVELOPMENT ORGANIZATION

Waso Trustland

Water Witness International

Wazi Community Based Organization

Wellbeing Economy Alliance

Welsh Centre for International Affairs

Wemos

Western States Legal Foundation

We The World Botswana Chapter Proprietary Limited

Wetlands Conservation Organisation

We Yone Child Foundation

Winston-Salem Permaculture Collective

Wissol Group

Women and Children's Legal Aid Organization

Women and Girls Initiative Salone

Women and Youth Environmental Safety and Empowerment Organisation

Women EdTech

WOMEN EMPOWERING WOMEN INITIAITVE (WEWIN)

Women Empowerment Against Poverty of Nepal (WEAPoN)

Women for Human Rights Single Women Group (WHR)

Women for Peace and Gender Equality Initiative

Women For Positive Actions (WOPA)

Women In Crisis Movement (WICM)

Women In Democracy And Governance (WIDAG)

Women in Distress Organisation

Women In Monitoring & Auditing Global Elections

Women Inspiration Development Center (WIDC)

Women's Coalition of Zimbabwe (WCoZ)

Women's Counsil Denmark

World Council on Intercultural and Global Competence

World Digital Technology Academy

WORLD FDEDERALST MOVEMENT – INSTITUTE OF GLOBAL POLICY

World Humanitarian Forum

World Institute on Disability

World Mission Society Church of God

Worldreader

World Youth Forum

World Youth Summit NPC

Wote Youth Development Projects CBO

XUFANCHENG CULTURE STUDY CENTER

Yanabia Al-Khair Charity Foundation

Yayasan Kesehatan Perempuan (YKP)

Yemenland for humanitarian development foundation

Ylva

YOD-International

York University

Young African Policy Research Hub

Young ChangeMakers Initiative (YALI RLC EA, Kenya)

Young Diplomats of Canada

Young Jewels Foundation

Young Women Growing Initiative

Young Women in Sustainable Development

Youth4Nature

Youth and cultural development foundation

YOUTH AND WOMEN FOR OPPORTUNITIES UGANDA (YWOU)

Youth Bridge Kenya

Youth Building the Future Global

Youth Center for Research and Development

Youth Empowerment and Artivism

Youth Empowerment and Leadership Initiative (YELI)

Youth for Darfur Organization

Youth for Human Rights International Foundation and Research

Youth for Sustainable Travel

Youth For Transparency International

YOUTH INITIATIVE FOR LAND IN AFRICA (YILAA) / INITIATIVE DE LA JEUNESSE POUR LE FONCIER EN AFRIQUE

Youth International Leadership Institute (YIL-Network) Inc.

Youth Leaders Foundation (YLF)

Youth Parliament Pakistan

Youth Peace & Leadership Organization

Youth Peer Education Association (YPEER Nepal)

Youths Enterprise Development and Innovation Society

Youths for Transparency International

Youth Vision the Gambia

YPEER Pakistan

Yuvsatta

Zaina Foundation

Zango Foundation

Zanzibar Maisha Bora Foundation

ZhongGuanCun Smarter City Information Industry Alliance

Zimbabwe National Network of PLHIV

ZuluLegacy Youth Leadership 8 Uganda

78/557. Accreditation and participation of an intergovernmental organization in the Fourth International Conference on Financing for Development

At its 101st plenary meeting, on 16 July 2024, the General Assembly, on the proposal of its President,[46] taking note of the note by the Secretariat,[47] decided to accredit the organization identified in the note by the Secretariat and invite it to participate as an intergovernmental organization in the work of the Fourth International Conference on Financing for Development and its preparatory process, as an observer, in accordance with paragraph 3 (b) of its resolution 78/271 of 11 April 2024.

78/558. Enhancing action on sea level rise

At its 102nd plenary meeting, on 1 August 2024, the General Assembly, on the proposal of its President,[48] recalling its decision 78/544 of 16 January 2024, in which it had decided to hold a high-level plenary meeting of the General Assembly on addressing the existential threats posed by sea level rise, in New York on 25 September 2024, during the high-level week of the seventy-ninth session of the Assembly, recalling also its resolution 78/319 of 1 August 2024 on the scope, modalities, format and organization of the high-level plenary meeting on addressing the existential threats posed by sea level rise, recognizing the importance of enhanced international cooperation and collective action to address sea level rise, and determined to strengthen the global response and support to developing countries, especially those that are particularly vulnerable to the adverse effects of climate change, and coastal communities, to build resilience and adapt to its consequences, decided:

(a) To commit to strengthening international cooperation and partnerships to enhance comprehensive and effective responses to sea level rise;

(b) To request the Secretary-General to prepare a report, including by inviting contributions from Member States, to be submitted near the conclusion of the seventy-ninth session or early in the eightieth session of the General Assembly, to provide information on challenges related to sea level rise and on ways and approaches to address sea level rise;

(c) To request the President of the General Assembly to organize a one-day high-level plenary meeting of the General Assembly, no later than the last day of the general debate of the Assembly at its eighty-first session, to further

[46] A/78/L.94.

[47] A/78/958.

[48] A/78/L.101, as orally revised.

consider sea level rise, which would result, without setting a precedent for similar meetings, in a concise, action-oriented and intergovernmentally negotiated declaration agreed by consensus.

78/559. Participation of non-governmental organizations, civil society organizations, academic institutions and the private sector in the high-level meeting on antimicrobial resistance

At its 102nd plenary meeting, on 1 August 2024, on the proposal of its President,[49] as amended,[50] the General Assembly, recalling paragraph 11 of its resolution 78/269 of 25 March 2024, entitled "Scope, modalities, format and organization of the high-level meeting on antimicrobial resistance convened by the President of the General Assembly", decided to approve the participation of the non-governmental organizations, civil society organizations, academic institutions and the private sector as listed in the annex to the present decision in the high-level meeting on antimicrobial resistance to be held pursuant to resolution 78/269.

Annex

Access to Medicine Foundation

Action Coalition On Tuberculosis

Action des Jeunes contre la Résistance aux Antimicrobiens

Action for Health Initiatives, Inc. (ACHIEVE)

Action on Antibiotic Resistance Africa

Africa Coalition on TB (ACT) Swazi Chapter

Africa Coalition on Tuberculosis

Africa Public Health Students Network Initiative

AFRICA SOCIETY FOR LABORATORY MEDICINE

Africa Sustainable Climate and Environment Foundation (ASCEF)

Afro Global Alliance

Alliance Myanmar

AMBA TB Charity Association

American Medical Women's Association

American Society for Microbiology

AMR Action Fund

Antibiotic Research UK

ARMoR (Alliance for Reducing Microbial Resistance)

Asian Indigenous International Network

Asociacion de Personas Afectadas por Tuberculosis del Peru ASPAT PERU

Associacao de Mineiros Mocambicanos – AMIMO

Association Health Innovation and Investment Exchange (HIEx)

Association of Persons with Disabilities living with HIV(ADPHA) Uganda

Aviva investors

BEAM Alliance

[49] A/78/L.97.

[50] See A/78/L.103.

bioMerieux
Branch of Caritas Internationalis in Tajikistan
Bridge Consultants Foundation
Brigada 12
BUGWORKS RESEARCH INC
Campaigns in Global Health
CARB-X (Boston University)
CaribVET
Center for Global Development
Center for New Democratic Processes
Centre for Public Health and Zoonoses
CHARITABLE ORGANIZATION "CHARITABLE FUND "TB EUROPE COALITION"
Charitable Organization TB PEOPLE UKRAINE
CHIMABA SANAA GROUP
Club des Amis Damien
Community Action Against Plastic Waste (CAPws)
Community And Family Aid Foundation – Ghana
Community Health and Inclusion Association
Cystic Fibrosis Foundation
DEBRICHE HEALTH DEVELOPMENT CENTRE
Disaster and Environmental Management Trust
디문파운데이션 DMUN Foundation
dsm-firmenich Animal Nutrition and Health
Ducit Blue Foundation
Ethiopian TB Association
European Federation of Pharmaceutical Industries and Associations (EFPIA)
European Network of Medical Residents in Public Health – EuroNet MRPH
European Public Health Alliance (EPHA)
F. Hoffmann-La Roche
Family Welfare Foundation
FIND
Focus Droits et Accès ONG
FOR IMPACTS IN SOCIAL HEALTH
Forum Ong Aids RS
Foundation for Environmental Watch
Friends of the Global Fight Against AIDS, Tuberculosis and Malaria

GARDP Foundation

Gavi, the Vaccine Alliance

German Center for Infection Research – DZIF

Ghana National TB Voice Network

Global AMR Media Alliance (GAMA) and CNS (Citizen News Service)

Global Environment & Technology Foundation

Global Health Strategies (India)

Global Health Strategies (US)

Global Health Technologies Coalition

Global Institute for Disease Elimination (GLIDE)

Global Strategy Lab at York University

Good Samaritan University Hospital

Great Lakes Peace Centre Organization Uganda

Green Landscape Association

GSK plc

Gyals

Health and Global Policy Institute

Health Care Without Harm Europe

Health Diplomacy Alliance

HealthforAnimals

Humanity For The World (HFTW)

INDIGENOUS FRIENDS OF THE MAU FOREST

Infectious Diseases Society of America

INSTITUTE FOR GLOBAL HEALTH AND DEVELOPMENT

Integrita Healthcare Foundation

inter-governmental not for profit

International Centre for Antimicrobial Resistance Solutions (ICARS)

International Livestock Research Institute

International Society of Antimicrobial Chemotherapy (ISAC)

International Vaccine Institute

International Veterinary Students' Association

International WeLoveU Foundation

IRD – Institut de Recherche pour le Développement (the French National Research Institute for Sustainable Development)

Janna Health Foundation

Japan Center for International Exchange

Japan Pharmaceutical Manufacturers Association

Johnson & Johnson

Khmer HIV/AIDS NGO Alliance

Khulna Mukti Seba Sangstha (KMSS)

Life Bliss Foundation Singapore

Life Bliss Of New Zealand

Mask Ethiopia

Medical Impact

Microbiology Society

Migrant Clinicians Network

MOLBIO DIAGNOSTICS PRIVATE LIMITED

Most at Risk Young Mothers and Teenage Girls Living with HIV Initiative (MOYOTE)

Mott MacDonald

Mouvement Universel pour la Survie de l'Humanité (MUSUHUM)

MOVEMENT OF MEN AGAINST AIDS IN KENYA (MMAAK)

Mwitikio wa Kudhibiti Kifua Kikuu na Ukimwi Tanzania (MKUTA)

NARI MAITREE

National Ex-Miners and Allied Workers Association

Nithyananda Dhyanapeetam of Houston

NITHYANANDA DHYANAPEETAM OF SAN JOSE

Nithyananda Dhyanapeetam of Seattle

Nithyananda Dhyanapeetam Temple & Cultural Center

Nithyananda Meditation Academy

NOORNGESA

Norwegian Cancer Society

Nostics

Novo Nordisk Fonden

Nucleo de Advocacy em Saude

One Health Society

One Health Trust

ONG-ASHAD

Pak One Health Alline

Pan-African Treatment Access Movement

Panorama Global

Paris Peace Forum

Partners in Health

PAY-W Clinic

Philomera Hope Center Foundation

PhRMA

Positive Women Together in Action

Professionals For Humanity (PROFOH)

Public Citizen

Rabin Martin

REACH Ethiopia

reach52

Reaching Sky Foundation

REACHOUT SALONE

Results Education

Roll Back Antimicrobial resistance Initiative (RBA Initiative)

Salma Attah foundation for women and girls support

Samprity Aid Foundation

Sepsis Alliance

Service, Health and Development for People Living Positively with HIV/AIDs (SHDEPHA+)

Shionogi & Co., Ltd.

Sir Howard Dalton Centre University of Warwick

Society for Family Health

Sovereign Sustainability and Development Ltd.

Stichting TB Europe Coalition

STOP TB PARTNERSHIP – KENYA

STOP TB PARTNERSHIP GHANA

Support to Health Public Union

Sustainable Communication Response for Tuberculosis

Tanzania TB Community Network

TBpeople Global

The AMR Narrative

The Milken Institute

The Swedish Cancer Society (Cancerfonden)

Uganda Stop TB Partnership

UNITE Parliamentarians Network for Global Health

University of KwaZulu – Natal

Uppsala Universistet (ReAct Europe)

USK Foundation

Usmanu Danfodiyo University Young Antimicrobial Resistance Stewards (UDUYARS)

Volunteer Health Services

WORLD FUTURE ACTIVE

World Small Animal Veterinary Association

Wote Youth Development Projects Community Based Organization (CBO)

Zihi Institute

Zimbabwe National Network of PLHIV

78/560. Agreement under the United Nations Convention on the Law of the Sea on the Conservation and Sustainable Use of Marine Biological Diversity of Areas beyond National Jurisdiction

At its 103rd plenary meeting, on 13 August 2024, on the proposal of Australia and Belize,[51] the General Assembly, by a recorded vote of 146 to 2, with 1 abstention,[52] recalling its resolution 78/272 of 24 April 2024, noting that the organizational meeting of the Preparatory Commission for the Entry into Force of the Agreement under the United Nations Convention on the Law of the Sea on the Conservation and Sustainable Use of Marine Biological Diversity of Areas beyond National Jurisdiction and the Convening of the First Meeting of the Conference of the Parties to the Agreement was held from 24 to 26 June 2024, requested the Secretary-General to convene the first and second sessions of the Preparatory Commission from 14 to 25 April and from 18 to 29 August 2025, respectively, and to convene at least one session of 10 working days in 2026, on dates to be determined in consultation with the Co-Chairs, with full conference services, including documentation, provision for parallel meetings and overtime, webcast and press and meeting coverage, for the duration of the substantive sessions, and also requested the Secretary-General to make proposals in the context of the proposed programme budget for 2025 in order to strengthen the capacity of the Division for Ocean Affairs and the Law of the Sea of the Office of Legal Affairs of the Secretariat to continue to provide the Preparatory Commission, including any intersessional work that might be convened by the Co-Chairs, with the assistance necessary for the performance of its work, including meeting and secretariat services and the provision of essential background information and relevant documents.

78/561. Question of equitable representation on and increase in the membership of the Security Council and other matters related to the Security Council

At its 104th plenary meeting, on 27 August 2024, the General Assembly, on the proposal of its President:

(a) Decided to reaffirm the central role of the General Assembly concerning the question of equitable representation on and increase in the membership of the Security Council and other matters related to the Security Council and the commitment of Heads of State and Government representing the peoples of the world to instil new life in the discussions on the reform of the Security Council;

(b) Decided to immediately continue intergovernmental negotiations on Security Council reform in informal plenary of the General Assembly at its seventy-ninth session, as mandated by Assembly decisions 62/557 of 15 September 2008, 63/565 B of 14 September 2009, 64/568 of 13 September 2010, 65/554 of 12 September 2011, 66/566 of 13 September 2012, 67/561 of 29 August 2013, 68/557 of 8 September 2014, 69/560 of 14 September 2015, 70/559 of 27 July 2016, 71/553 of 19 July 2017, 72/557 of 29 June 2018, 73/554 of 25 June 2019, 74/569 of 31 August 2020, 75/569 of 22 June 2021, 76/572 of 12 July 2022 and 77/559 of 29 June 2023, building on the informal meetings held during its seventy-eighth session, as reflected in the letter dated 29 April 2024 from the Co-Chairs, and on the document entitled "Co-Chairs' Revised Elements Paper on Convergences and Divergences on the question of equitable representation on and increase in the membership of the Security Council and related matters", circulated on 2 August 2024, as well as the positions of and proposals made by Member States, reflected in the text and its annex circulated on 31 July 2015, to help to inform its future work;

[51] A/78/L.102.

[52] See A/78/PV.103.

(c) Welcomed the active engagement, initiatives and intensive efforts of the President of the General Assembly, and noted with appreciation the active role and concrete efforts of the Co-Chairs undertaken in a consultative manner with a view to an early comprehensive reform of the Security Council;

(d) Welcomed the holding of structured dialogues on models presented by Member States and Groups of States, appreciated the active participation of the Member States, and noted their usefulness to increasing the overall convergences and better understanding of individual proposals;

(e) Noted the contribution on Security Council reform from the intergovernmental negotiations to the Pact for the Future;

(f) Decided to convene the Open-ended Working Group on the Question of Equitable Representation on and Increase in the Membership of the Security Council and Other Matters related to the Security Council during the seventy-ninth session of the General Assembly, if Member States so decide;

(g) Also decided to include in the agenda of the seventy-ninth session of the General Assembly the item entitled "Question of equitable representation on and increase in the membership of the Security Council and other matters related to the Security Council".

78/562. High-level meeting to commemorate and promote the International Day against Nuclear Tests

At its 105th plenary meeting, on 4 September 2024, the General Assembly, on the proposal of its President, decided, without setting a precedent, to invite the Executive Secretary of the Preparatory Commission for the Comprehensive Nuclear-Test-Ban Treaty Organization, Robert Floyd, the Director of the International Atomic Energy Agency Liaison Office in New York, Vivian Okeke, on behalf of the Director General of the Agency, Rafael Mariano Grossi, research assistant at the Arms Control Association and former Office for Disarmament Affairs Youth Champion, Shizuka Kuramitsu, and Professor at the Elliott School of International Affairs of George Washington University, Sharon Squassoni, to make statements at the high-level meeting to commemorate and promote the International Day against Nuclear Tests.

78/563. Participation of non-governmental organizations, civil society organizations, academic institutions and the private sector in the high-level plenary meeting on addressing the existential threats posed by sea level rise

At its 107th plenary meeting, on 6 September 2024, the General Assembly, on the proposal of its President,[53] recalling paragraph 9 of its resolution 78/319 of 1 August 2024, entitled "Scope, modalities, format and organization of the high-level plenary meeting on addressing the existential threats posed by sea level rise", decided to approve the participation of the non-governmental organizations, civil society organizations, academic institutions and the private sector as listed in the annex to the present decision in the high-level plenary meeting under the theme "Addressing the threats posed by sea level rise", to be held pursuant to resolution 78/319.

Annex

ACCOUNTABLE IMPACT CORP

ADIFEVEA World

Africa Youth Forum International

African Health Innovation Centre

Asian Indigenous International Network

Association Congolaise pour le Bien-Etre Familial

CELEBRONS LE COURAGE DE LA FEMME (CCF)

Center for Migration, Gender, and Justice

[53] A/78/L.112.

Creats International

Earth Regenerative Project Sierra Leone

EarthEcho International

Global Youth Parliament Botswana

Hawaii Local2030 Hub

REACHOUT SALONE

Rosana Empowerment Foundation (REF)

Society of Gender Professionals

Sustainable Energy and Enterprise Development for Communities, Inc. (Seed4com)

The Alliance for Just Deliberation on Solar Geoengineering

The National Senior Citizens Organization of Liberia

We Are Forces of Nature

78/564. Speakers for the opening segment of the Summit of the Future

A

At its 107th plenary meeting, on 6 September 2024, the General Assembly, under rule 81 of its rules of procedure, decided to reconsider the provision contained in the first footnote in paragraph (a) of decision 78/555 of 10 July 2024.

B

At its 107th plenary meeting, on 6 September 2024, the General Assembly, on the proposal of its President, decided that, in addition to those listed in resolution 76/307 of 8 September 2022 and decision 78/555 of 10 July 2024, the opening segment of the Summit of the Future would also feature statements by the President of the Republic of Namibia and the Chancellor of the Federal Republic of Germany in lieu of their national statements from the plenary list of speakers.

78/565. Strengthening the role of mediation in the peaceful settlement of disputes, conflict prevention and resolution

At its 108th plenary meeting, on 6 September 2024, the General Assembly decided to include the sub-item entitled "Strengthening the role of mediation in the peaceful settlement of disputes, conflict prevention and resolution" of the item entitled "Prevention of armed conflict" in the draft agenda of its seventy-ninth session.

78/566. Question of the Comorian island of Mayotte

At its 108th plenary meeting, on 6 September 2024, the General Assembly decided to include the item entitled "Question of the Comorian island of Mayotte" in the draft agenda of its seventy-ninth session.

78/567. Zone of peace, trust and cooperation of Central Asia

At its 108th plenary meeting, on 6 September 2024, the General Assembly decided to include the item entitled "Zone of peace, trust and cooperation of Central Asia" in the draft agenda of its seventy-ninth session.

78/568. Request for an advisory opinion of the International Court of Justice on the legal consequences of the separation of the Chagos Archipelago from Mauritius in 1965

At its 108th plenary meeting, on 6 September 2024, the General Assembly decided to include the item entitled "Request for an advisory opinion of the International Court of Justice on the legal consequences of the separation of the Chagos Archipelago from Mauritius in 1965" in the draft agenda of its seventy-ninth session.

78/569. Implementation of the resolutions of the United Nations

At its 108th plenary meeting, on 6 September 2024, the General Assembly decided to include the item entitled "Implementation of the resolutions of the United Nations" in the draft agenda of its seventy-ninth session.

78/570. Financing of the United Nations Mission in East Timor

At its 108th plenary meeting, on 6 September 2024, the General Assembly decided to include the item entitled "Financing of the United Nations Mission in East Timor" in the draft agenda of its seventy-ninth session.

2. *Decisions adopted on the reports of the Fifth Committee*

78/542. Questions deferred for future consideration

B[54]

At its 53rd plenary meeting, on 16 January 2024, the General Assembly, on the recommendation of the Fifth Committee,[55] decided to defer until the first part of its resumed seventy-eighth session consideration of the following documents:

Item 139

Human resources management

Amendments to the Staff Regulations and Rules

Report of the Secretary-General on the amendments to the Staff Regulations and Rules[56]

Related report of the Advisory Committee on Administrative and Budgetary Questions[57]

C

At its 73rd plenary meeting, on 24 April 2024, the General Assembly, on the recommendation of the Fifth Committee,[58]

Section A

Decided to defer until the second part of its resumed seventy-eighth session consideration of the following documents:

Item 134

Programme budget for 2024

---

[54] Decision 78/542, in section B.6 of the *Official Records of the General Assembly, Seventy-eighth Session, Supplement No. 49* (A/78/49), vol. II, becomes decision 78/542 A.

[55] A/78/664, para. 13.

[56] A/78/177.

[57] A/78/671.

[58] A/78/664/Add.1, para. 6.

Revised estimates relating to the programme budget for 2024 under section 1, Overall policymaking, direction and coordination, and section 29B, Department of Operational Support

Report of the Secretary-General on the revised estimates relating to the proposed programme budget for 2024 under section 1, Overall policymaking, direction and coordination, and section 29B, Department of Operational Support[59]

Related report of the Advisory Committee on Administrative and Budgetary Questions[60]

Item 139

Human resources management

Seconded active-duty military and police personnel

Report of the Secretary-General on seconded active-duty military and police personnel[61]

Related report of the Advisory Committee on Administrative and Budgetary Questions[62]

Section B

Decided to defer until the first part of its resumed seventy-ninth session consideration of the following documents:

Item 132

Review of the efficiency of the administrative and financial functioning of the United Nations

Supply chain activities in the United Nations Secretariat

Report of the Secretary-General on supply chain activities in the United Nations Secretariat[63]

Related report of the Advisory Committee on Administrative and Budgetary Questions[64]

Report of the Office of Internal Oversight Services on audit of acquisition of aviation services in United Nations peace operations[65]

Item 139

Human resources management

Report of the Secretary-General on the composition of the Secretariat: staff demographics[66]

Related report of the Advisory Committee on Administrative and Budgetary Questions[67]

Report of the Secretary-General on the proposal on the movement of Secretariat staff from the General Service category to the Professional category[68]

Related report of the Advisory Committee on Administrative and Budgetary Questions[69]

---

[59] A/78/753.

[60] A/78/7/Add.46.

[61] A/78/602.

[62] A/78/762.

[63] A/78/679.

[64] A/78/805.

[65] A/78/767.

[66] A/78/569.

[67] A/78/745.

[68] A/78/569/Add.1.

[69] A/78/745/Add.1.

Report of the Secretary-General on his practice in disciplinary matters and cases of possible criminal behaviour, 1 January 2022 to 31 December 2022[70]

Related report of the Advisory Committee on Administrative and Budgetary Questions[71]

Note by the Secretary-General on monitoring of staff attendance[72]

Related report of the Advisory Committee on Administrative and Budgetary Questions[73]

Item 141

Joint Inspection Unit

Note by the Secretary-General drawing attention to the report of the Joint Inspection Unit entitled "Review of mental health and well-being policies and practices in United Nations system organizations" (JIU/REP/2023/4)[74]

Note by the Secretary-General transmitting his comments and those of the United Nations System Chief Executives Board for Coordination on the report of the Joint Inspection Unit entitled "Review of mental health and well-being policies and practices in United Nations system organizations"[75]

D

At its 95th plenary meeting, on 28 June 2024, the General Assembly, on the recommendation of the Fifth Committee,[76] decided to defer until the main part of its seventy-ninth session consideration of the following documents:

Item 134

Programme budget for 2024

Revised estimates relating to the programme budget for 2024 under section 1, Overall policymaking, direction and coordination, and section 29B, Department of Operational Support

Report of the Secretary-General on the revised estimates relating to the proposed programme budget for 2024 under section 1, Overall policymaking, direction and coordination, and section 29B, Department of Operational Support[77]

Related report of the Advisory Committee on Administrative and Budgetary Questions[78]

[70] A/78/603 and A/78/603/Corr.1.

[71] A/78/756.

[72] A/78/604.

[73] A/78/759.

[74] A/78/695.

[75] A/78/695/Add.1.

[76] A/78/664/Add.2, para. 5.

[77] A/78/753.

[78] A/78/7/Add.46.

Annex I

Allocation of agenda items[a]

1. The following items and sub-items, which had been allocated to the Second Committee, were also considered directly in plenary meeting during the resumed seventy-eighth session, under heading A (Promotion of sustained economic growth and sustainable development in accordance with the relevant resolutions of the General Assembly and recent United Nations conferences):[b]

17. Follow-up to and implementation of the outcomes of the International Conferences on Financing for Development.

18. Sustainable development:

(b) Follow-up to and implementation of the SIDS Accelerated Modalities of Action (SAMOA) Pathway and the Mauritius Strategy for the Further Implementation of the Programme of Action for the Sustainable Development of Small Island Developing States;

(c) Disaster risk reduction;

(i) Combating sand and dust storms.

23. Agriculture development, food security and nutrition:

(a) Agriculture development, food security and nutrition.

2. The following item and sub-item, which had been allocated to the Third Committee, were also considered directly in plenary meeting during the resumed seventy-eighth session, under heading A (Promotion of sustained economic growth and sustainable development in accordance with the relevant resolutions of the General Assembly and recent United Nations conferences):[b]

24. Social development:

(b) Social development, including questions relating to the world social situation and to youth, ageing, persons with disabilities and the family.

25. Advancement of women.

3. The following item, which had been allocated to the Third Committee, was also considered directly in plenary meeting during the resumed seventy-eighth session, under heading D (Promotion of human rights):[b]

68. Rights of Indigenous Peoples.

4. The following items, which had been allocated to the Third Committee, were also considered directly in plenary meeting during the resumed seventy-eighth session, under heading H (Drug control, crime prevention and combating international terrorism in all its forms and manifestations):[b]

107. Crime prevention and criminal justice.

108. Countering the use of information and communications technologies for criminal purposes.

---

[a] Organized under headings corresponding to the priorities of the Organization.

[b] See decision 78/504 B in section IV.B of the present volume.

Annex II

Checklist of resolutions and decisions

Resolutions

Resolution number	*Title*	*Item*	*Plenary meeting*	*Date of adoption*	*Page*
78/242.	Financial reports and audited financial statements, and reports of the Board of Auditors				
	Resolution B	131	95th	28 June 2024	172
78/250.	Financing of the United Nations Multidimensional Integrated Stabilization Mission in Mali				
	Resolution B	155	95th	28 June 2024	173
78/259.	International Day of Science, Technology and Innovation for the South	13	52nd	9 January 2024	3
78/260.	International Year of Sustainable and Resilient Tourism, 2027	18	57th	26 February 2024	4
78/261.	"World Social Summit" under the title "Second World Summit for Social Development"	24 (b)	57th	26 February 2024	5
78/262.	New Partnership for Africa's Development: progress in implementation and international support	65 (a)	57th	26 February 2024	7
78/263.	Promotion of durable peace through sustainable development in Africa	65 (b)	57th	26 February 2024	16
78/264.	Measures to combat Islamophobia	14	62nd	15 March 2024	24
78/265.	Seizing the opportunities of safe, secure and trustworthy artificial intelligence systems for sustainable development	13	63rd	21 March 2024	26
78/266.	International Year of Peace and Trust, 2025	14	63rd	21 March 2024	32
78/267.	International Day for the Prevention of and Fight against All Forms of Transnational Organized Crime	107	63rd	21 March 2024	34
78/268.	International Day of Play	14	64th	25 March 2024	36
78/269.	Scope, modalities, format and organization of the high-level meeting on antimicrobial resistance convened by the President of the General Assembly	125	64th	25 March 2024	37
78/270.	The role of diamonds in fuelling conflict: breaking the link between the illicit transaction of rough diamonds and armed conflict as a contribution to prevention and settlement of conflicts	30	65th	3 April 2024	41
78/271.	Further modalities of the Fourth International Conference on Financing for Development	17	69th	11 April 2024	44
78/272.	Agreement under the United Nations Convention on the Law of the Sea on the Conservation and Sustainable Use of Marine Biological Diversity of Areas beyond National Jurisdiction	75 (c)	73rd	24 April 2024	46
78/273.	Revised estimates relating to the Independent Institution on Missing Persons in the Syrian Arab Republic	134	73rd	24 April 2024	175

78/274.	Revised estimates relating to the programme budget for 2024 under section 3, Political affairs, and section 36, Staff assessment: special political missions – thematic cluster III: regional offices, offices in support of political processes and other missions – United Nations Integrated Transition Assistance Mission in the Sudan	134	73rd	24 April 2024	176
78/275.	Amendments to the Staff Regulations and Rules	139	73rd	24 April 2024	177
78/276.	Joint Inspection Unit	141	73rd	24 April 2024	178
78/277.	Follow-up to the Declaration and Programme of Action on a Culture of Peace	14	77th	2 May 2024	48
78/278.	International Day of the Markhor	13	77th	2 May 2024	54
78/279.	International Year of the Woman Farmer, 2026	23 (a)	77th	2 May 2024	55
78/280.	Global health and foreign policy: addressing global health challenges in the foreign policy space	125	77th	2 May 2024	57
78/281.	World Football Day	11	80th	7 May 2024	66
78/282.	International Day of Reflection and Commemoration of the 1995 Genocide in Srebrenica	14	82nd	23 May 2024	68
78/283.	Status of internally displaced persons and refugees from Abkhazia, Georgia, and the Tskhinvali region/South Ossetia, Georgia	32	85th	4 June 2024	70
78/284.	Central Asia's unified resolve and cooperation to effectively address and counter drug-related challenges	64	85th	4 June 2024	72
78/285.	Review of the implementation of General Assembly resolution 75/290 A on the strengthening of the Economic and Social Council and resolution 75/290 B on the high-level political forum on sustainable development and the follow-up and review of the 2030 Agenda for Sustainable Development at the global level	13 and 117	88th	7 June 2024	76
78/286.	International Day for Dialogue among Civilizations	14	88th	7 June 2024	77
78/287.	International Year of Quantum Science and Technology, 2025	18	88th	7 June 2024	79
78/288.	Twenty-fifth anniversary of the International Day for the Elimination of Violence against Women	25	88th	7 June 2024	80
78/289.	International Year of Cooperatives 2025	13	91st	19 June 2024	82
78/290.	Improving global road safety	12	92nd	24 June 2024	83
78/291.	Comprehensive review of the whole question of peacekeeping operations in all their aspects	51	95th	28 June 2024	170
78/292.	Seconded active-duty military and police personnel	139	95th	28 June 2024	179
78/293.	Support account for peacekeeping operations	146	95th	28 June 2024	180
78/294.	Financing of the Regional Service Centre in Entebbe, Uganda	146	95th	28 June 2024	182
78/295.	Financing of the United Nations Logistics Base at Brindisi, Italy	146	95th	28 June 2024	183
78/296.	Closed peacekeeping missions	146	95th	28 June 2024	185
78/297.	Financing of the United Nations Interim Security Force for Abyei	147	95th	28 June 2024	185

78/298.	Financing of the United Nations Multidimensional Integrated Stabilization Mission in the Central African Republic	148	95th	28 June 2024	188
78/299.	Financing of the United Nations Operation in Côte d'Ivoire	149	95th	28 June 2024	191
78/300.	Financing of the United Nations Peacekeeping Force in Cyprus	150	95th	28 June 2024	191
78/301.	Financing of the United Nations Organization Stabilization Mission in the Democratic Republic of the Congo	151	95th	28 June 2024	194
78/302.	Financing of the United Nations Interim Administration Mission in Kosovo	153	95th	28 June 2024	197
78/303.	Financing of the United Nations Mission in Liberia	154	95th	28 June 2024	199
78/304.	Financing of the United Nations Disengagement Observer Force	156 (a)	95th	28 June 2024	200
78/305.	Financing of the United Nations Interim Force in Lebanon	156 (b)	95th	28 June 2024	203
78/306.	Financing of the United Nations Mission in South Sudan	157	95th	28 June 2024	206
78/307.	Financing of the United Nations Mission for the Referendum in Western Sahara	158	95th	28 June 2024	209
78/308.	Financing of the African Union-United Nations Hybrid Operation in Darfur	159	95th	28 June 2024	211
78/309.	Financing of the activities arising from Security Council resolution 1863 (2009)	160	95th	28 June 2024	213
78/310.	World Fair Play Day	11	97th	1 July 2024	87
78/311.	Enhancing international cooperation on capacity-building of artificial intelligence	13	97th	1 July 2024	88
78/312.	World Kiswahili Language Day	124	97th	1 July 2024	91
78/313.	World Conjoined Twins Day	125	97th	1 July 2024	93
78/314.	United Nations Decade on Combating Sand and Dust Storms (2025–2034)	18 (i)	98th	10 July 2024	94
78/315.	Further modalities of the third United Nations Conference on Landlocked Developing Countries	20 (b)	98th	10 July 2024	96
78/316.	Safety and security of nuclear facilities of Ukraine, including the Zaporizhzhia nuclear power plant	62	99th	11 July 2024	96
78/317.	The Antigua and Barbuda Agenda for Small Island Developing States: A Renewed Declaration for Resilient Prosperity	18 (b)	100th	16 July 2024	99
78/318.	Modalities of the "World Social Summit" under the title "the Second World Summit for Social Development"	24 (b)	101st	16 July 2024	115
78/319.	Scope, modalities, format and organization of the high-level plenary meeting on addressing the existential threats posed by sea level rise	13 and 117	102nd	1 August 2024	117
78/320.	Fostering sustainable forest management, including afforestation and reforestation, in degraded lands, including drylands, as an effective solution to environmental challenges	18	103rd	13 August 2024	120
78/321.	Decade of Action for Cryospheric Sciences, 2025–2034	18	103rd	13 August 2024	123
78/322.	Multidimensional vulnerability index	18 (b)	103rd	13 August 2024	125
78/323.	International Day of Women and Girls of African Descent	69	103rd	13 August 2024	129

78/324.	Consideration of decision 14/1 of the Open-ended Working Group on Ageing, entitled "Recommendations regarding the identification of possible gaps in the protection of the human rights of older persons and how best to address them"	119	103rd	13 August 2024	130
78/325.	United Nations Games	11	107th	6 September 2024	131
78/326.	World Rural Development Day	13	107th	6 September 2024	133
78/327.	Modalities of the 2026 United Nations Water Conference to Accelerate the Implementation of Sustainable Development Goal 6: Ensure availability and sustainable management of water and sanitation for all	18	107th	6 September 2024	134
78/328.	Enhancing the participation of Indigenous Peoples' representatives and institutions in meetings of relevant United Nations bodies on issues affecting them	68	107th	6 September 2024	153
78/329.	Biennialization of the agenda item entitled "Elimination of unilateral extraterritorial coercive economic measures as a means of political and economic compulsion"	122	107th	6 September 2024	154
78/330.	Multilingualism	124	107th	6 September 2024	155
78/331.	United Nations action on sexual exploitation and abuse	128	108th	6 September 2024	164

Decisions

Decision number	*Title*	*Item*	*Plenary meeting*	*Date of adoption*	*Page*
78/409.	Election of members of the Committee for Programme and Coordination				
	Decision B	114 (a)	53rd	16 January 2024	220
78/412.	Extension of the appointment of the Under-Secretary-General for Safety and Security	115	63rd	21 March 2024	220
78/413.	Appointment of members of the Board of the 10-Year Framework of Programmes on Sustainable Consumption and Production Patterns				
	Decision A	115 (g)	63rd	21 March 2024	220
	Decision B	115 (g)	63rd 65th 103rd	21 March 2024 3 April 2024 13 August 2024	220
78/414.	Election of non-permanent members of the Security Council	113 (a)	86th	6 June 2024	221
78/415.	Election of the President of the General Assembly at its seventy-ninth session	4	87th	6 June 2024	221
78/416.	Election of the Vice-Presidents of the General Assembly at its seventy-ninth session	6	87th	6 June 2024	221
78/417.	Election of the Executive Director of the United Nations Human Settlements Programme	114 (d)	88th	7 June 2024	222
78/418.	Election of members of the Economic and Social Council	113 (b)	88th	7 June 2024	222
78/419.	Election of the Chairs of the Main Committees of the General Assembly at its seventy-ninth session	5	88th	7 June 2024	223

78/504.	Adoption of the agenda and allocation of agenda items				
	Decision B	7	55th 57th 63rd 69th 73rd 77th 88th 98th 103rd 107th	7 February 2024 26 February 2024 21 March 2024 11 April 2024 24 April 2024 2 May 2024 7 June 2024 10 July 2024 13 August 2024 6 September 2024	224
78/528.	Participation of non-governmental organizations, civil society organizations, academic institutions and the private sector in the third United Nations Conference on Landlocked Developing Countries				
	Decision B	20 (b)	55th	7 February 2024	225
	Decision C	20 (b)	77th	2 May 2024	227
	Decision D	20 (b)	107th	6 September 2024	229
78/542.	Questions deferred for future consideration				
	Decision B	132	53rd	16 January 2024	280
	Decision C	132	73rd	24 April 2024	280
	Decision D	132	95th	28 June 2024	282
78/544.	High-level plenary meeting on addressing the existential threats posed by sea level rise	13 and 117	53rd	16 January 2024	232
78/545.	Report of the Secretary-General on the work of the Organization				
	Decision A	110	54th	7 February 2024	232
	Decision B	110	55th	7 February 2024	232
78/546.	Authorization for the United Nations Office for Disaster Risk Reduction regarding the hosting of the secretariat of the Santiago network for averting, minimizing and addressing loss and damage associated with the adverse effects of climate change	18 (c)	55th	7 February 2024	232
78/547.	Commemorative meeting of the General Assembly on the occasion of the International Day for the Elimination of Racial Discrimination	69	63rd	21 March 2024	232
78/548.	Commemorative meeting of the General Assembly to mark the International Day of Remembrance of the Victims of Slavery and the Transatlantic Slave Trade	118	64th	25 March 2024	233
78/549.	Ad Hoc Committee to Elaborate a Comprehensive International Convention on Countering the Use of Information and Communications Technologies for Criminal Purposes	108	73rd	24 April 2024	233
78/550.	Postponement of the third United Nations Conference on Landlocked Developing Countries and the second session of the Preparatory Committee for the third United Nations Conference on Landlocked Developing Countries	20 (b)	80th	7 May 2024	233

78/551.	Participation of non-governmental organizations, civil society organizations, academic institutions and the private sector in the Fourth International Conference on Financing for Development	17	90th	13 June 2024	233
78/552.	Building a peaceful and better world through sport and the Olympic ideal	11	93rd	25 June 2024	235
78/553.	Notification by the Secretary-General under Article 12, paragraph 2, of the Charter of the United Nations	112	93rd	25 June 2024	235
78/554.	Report of the Security Council	26	94th	25 June 2024	235
78/555.	Establishment of the list of speakers for the Summit of the Future	122	98th	10 July 2024	235
78/556.	Participation of non-governmental organizations, civil society organizations, academic institutions and the private sector in the high-level Summit of the Future	122	99th	11 July 2024	237
78/557.	Accreditation and participation of an intergovernmental organization in the Fourth International Conference on Financing for Development	17	101st	16 July 2024	271
78/558.	Enhancing action on sea level rise	13 and 117	102nd	1 August 2024	271
78/559.	Participation of non-governmental organizations, civil society organizations, academic institutions and the private sector in the high-level meeting on antimicrobial resistance	125	102nd	1 August 2024	272
78/560.	Agreement under the United Nations Convention on the Law of the Sea on the Conservation and Sustainable Use of Marine Biological Diversity of Areas beyond National Jurisdiction	75 (c)	103rd	13 August 2024	277
78/561.	Question of equitable representation on and increase in the membership of the Security Council and other matters related to the Security Council	121	104th	27 August 2024	277
78/562.	High-level meeting to commemorate and promote the International Day against Nuclear Tests	99	105th	4 September 2024	278
78/563.	Participation of non-governmental organizations, civil society organizations, academic institutions and the private sector in the high-level plenary meeting on addressing the existential threats posed by sea level rise	13 and 117	107th	6 September 2024	278
78/564.	Speakers for the opening segment of the Summit of the Future				
	Decision A	122	107th	6 September 2024	279
	Decision B	122	107th	6 September 2024	279
78/565.	Strengthening the role of mediation in the peaceful settlement of disputes, conflict prevention and resolution	31 (b)	108th	6 September 2024	279
78/566.	Question of the Comorian island of Mayotte	37	108th	6 September 2024	279
78/567.	Zone of peace, trust and cooperation of Central Asia	64	108th	6 September 2024	279
78/568.	Request for an advisory opinion of the International Court of Justice on the legal consequences of the separation of the Chagos Archipelago from Mauritius in 1965	88	108th	6 September 2024	280
78/569.	Implementation of the resolutions of the United Nations	119	108th	6 September 2024	280
78/570.	Financing of the United Nations Mission in East Timor	152	108th	6 September 2024	280